WHAT THE
BIBLE SAYS
ABOUT

THE
KINGDOM
OF GOD

WHAT THE
BIBLE SAYS
ABOUT
THE
KINGDOM
OF GOD

Given Blakely

College Press Publishing Company, Joplin, Missouri

Copyright © 1988
College Press Publishing Company

Printed and Bound in the
United States of America
All Rights Reserved

Library of Congress Catalog Card Number: 88-71154
International Standard Book Number: 0-89900-260-9

Dedication

In heartfelt appreciation to my father and mother, Fred O. and Rubye W. (Burnham) Blakely, my first teachers in things pertaining to God, and present yokefellows in the journey to Glory.

This volume is also gratefully dedicated to the brethren meeting at 78th Avenue and Independence Street, Merrillville, Indiana, who, for over 27 years, have walked with me in trials and triumphs, sorrows and joys — a fellowship where I have enjoyed the unity of the faith with many saints, including my parents, my good wife, and my ten children.

Table of Contents

ACKNOWLEDGMENTS

No work of this magnitude is accomplished independently. The human spirit is sensitive, and often requires the support of kindred spirits in its labors. Such has been my experience in the preparation of this volume.

A special tribute is here given to my wife, June Ellen. Her unwavering support in this work, as well as her personal sacrifice, has contributed immeasurably to my labors. She is to be commended for her tireless efforts and consistent devotion to the cause of Christ and the expansion of His Kingdom.

My children have also been a source of encouragement in these labors. I here acknowledge the heritage given me of my Father in heaven: Pamela Lynn, Rochelle Faith, Michelle Hope, Michael Paul, Leah Ann, Mark Phillip, Adah Lael, Jonathan David, Benjamin Seth, and Eva Christine. May the Kingdom of God profit from their lives and ministries.

ACKNOWLEDGMENTS

INTRODUCTION

Adherents of the Campbell/Stone Restoration Movement historically have done a good job of rediscovering and bringing to light some of the foundations of the faith, and the way of salvation for men proffered by God. However, there has not always been equal effectiveness in building upon the premises thus unearthed, by pursuing their scriptural and logical implications.

Here is a book that, to a notable extent, points the way to that end. This is done by drawing out and elaborating upon the things "most surely believed among us," as we are exhorted to do (Heb. 6:1-3). Everything in this volume is in complete accord with historic Restoration doctrine and principles. Yet it presents its subject matter in a fresh, invigorating, and challenging way that can well serve the reader.

It will be recalled that God's requirement of the Israelites in the wilderness was they must subsist on fresh, not stale, manna. So it is with the church of His dear Son. It is not enough to continually thresh the old straw, or canvass the well-known ground. A living, vibrant people must be ministered new insights into old truths.

11

It will be noted that *The Kingdom of God* makes a strong appeal for, as well as itself being a good demonstration of, exact thinking and reasoning in contemplation of the things of God. As such demonstration, it contrasts sharply with the generally superficial and comparatively loose mode of thought and logic characteristic of much contemporary religious writing.

It was Alexander Campbell, more than any other man, who amplified the Restoration principles which began to be proclaimed by his father Thomas, among others. Brother Given has done something of that kind in this book, with reference to the things for which historic Restorationism stands. We think that his labors in that connection are in the high tradition of Bethany's sage, and those other noble stalwarts that wrought with and followed him.

The genius of the present volume, from this viewpoint, lies also in its peculiar adaptedness to the times. Although the confusion and issues in religion continue to be essentially those of a century and a half ago, they have assumed new guises and different modes of expression. The author here comes squarely to grips with the situation as it now is. That makes the work especially appropriate to and needful for today. It is able to instruct the reader in Christ's heavenly reign, build him up in the most holy faith, and equip him to cope with the religious error and confusion that confront him. By reading and digesting the book's contents, one will be more discerning of Divine things, and better furnished as a "good soldier of Jesus Christ."

Fred O. Blakely

PREFACE

The Objective of the Book

The objective that dictated both the subject and the content of this volume is the glory of God. His Kingdom, like Himself, is great, and thus is apt to be perceived less clearly than is possible. Because the Kingdom of God involves His deliberate dealings with men, it is of particular importance to them. To neglect the Kingdom is to neglect God Himself, while to "seek first the Kingdom of God," is to seek Him first.

We cannot think properly about God in separation from His Kingdom. It is related to His objectives, His will, and His Person. The law of God, the grace of God, the salvation of God — all are resident in, and associated with, the Kingdom of God.

Any concept of God or His Kingdom that introduces contradictory thoughts or that mystifies God's person and work, contributes to man's basic spiritual ignorance. Such concepts obscure Deity, and thus constitute alienating influences.

My purpose is to elaborate upon that most worthy objective of the

Restoration Movement: to glorify God, and to advantage men by clarifying the nature of God's Kingdom, and establishing the priority of an intelligently revealed religion as evidenced in the Holy Scriptures.

In the early days of the Restoration Movement, the fire of spiritual fervor was ignited across the land. It was not the result of a dynamic personality, Divine coercion, or carnal spontaneity. It was the progressive result of the apprehension of the truth — truth that had been covered by the rubble of tradition. Now, over 150 years later, there is a call for that same fervor once again — a discerned requirement for insight into the implications of the truth.

Righteous movements are not destined to stagnation. They can live again when the truth is believed and embraced. This can occur in our generation — now! It only takes a discerning proclamation and its hearty embrace by faith.

It is to that end that this volume is sent forth. The power of truth has been evidenced throughout history, and we are determined to see it demonstrated in our time. This will come when the implications, trends, and purposes of the Gospel are perceived — in other words, when we build upon the foundation that has already been laid.

PART ONE:
IDENTIFYING GOD'S KINGDOM

1

THE KINGDOM OF GOD DEFINED

Introduction

The Kingdom of God! There is something awesome about the term! Something that captivates the inquiring mind. The Kingdom is a reign of authority, of submission, of purpose, and of Divine objective. It is a rule and reign that is deliberate, and that is maintained with specific objectives in mind. The Kingdom of God postulates confrontation . . . a rule exists in the midst of potential adversaries. Because it is the Kingdom of God, it shall ultimately overcome — obviously overcome — all contrary Kingdoms, all opposition, all rebellion! That is what was prophesied by Daniel (Dan. 2:44b), and is repeatedly foretold in the new covenant writings (Phil. 2:10-11; Heb. 10:13; Rev. 11:15).

Because the Kingdom deals with the unseen, men tend to ignore it, or to distort its reality to suit their own objectives. But God's Kingdom is real, and it is my aim to unveil something of its magnitude, that men may seek it "first," together with God's righteousness (Matt. 6:33). What is the Kingdom of God? How may I perceive it? What is its

15

relevance to me as a believer in Christ . . . or as an unbeliever living in God's world?

God's Specific Objectives

The Kingdom of God, in its simplest implication, means the reign of the Almighty; the exercise of His authority. This is a rule maintained with specific objectives in mind. It is an intelligent reign, being characterized by perceptible reason. God does nothing "without a cause" (Ezek. 14:23). He always works with "purpose" in mind (Eph. 1:11). When the power or authority of God is devoted to a specific objective, that is a revelation of His Kingdom!

Objectives Illustrated in Israel

This is graphically illustrated in God's dealings with the ancient people Israel. They were chosen by Him to be the Divinely appointed custodians of "the oracles of God" (Rom. 3:2). In this procedure He had in mind the schooling of the world. That is to say, to bring men to the knowledge of God! God's purpose involved the preparation of men for the redemption that is in Christ Jesus. Thus, He focused His attention upon the vessels to be used for that purpose, and concentrated His Divine power on that objective. Israel, the chief means of implementing this purpose in those early times, was called "a Kingdom of priests" unto God (Exod. 19:6). Certainly this was not due to any exceptional submission to Him on their part. They were noted throughout their history for being a "disobedient and gainsaying people" (Rom. 10:21). They were not a "Kingdom" because of their personal superiority, but only because they were identified with Divine objective!

The Objective Revelation

When the prophet Daniel spoke of God's setting up a "Kingdom" in the days of world empires and the show of external power and force (Dan. 2:44), he was not proclaiming that God was not working, or that He was not ruling — absolutely ruling — prior to the time when He would "set up a Kingdom" that would "never be destroyed"! God forbid that such a notion should be entertained! What Daniel was saying is this: that God was going to implement a specific objective during a most unlikely time. That would be a time of competition and pride; a time of arrogance and the vaunting of vanity! In spite of its apparent un-

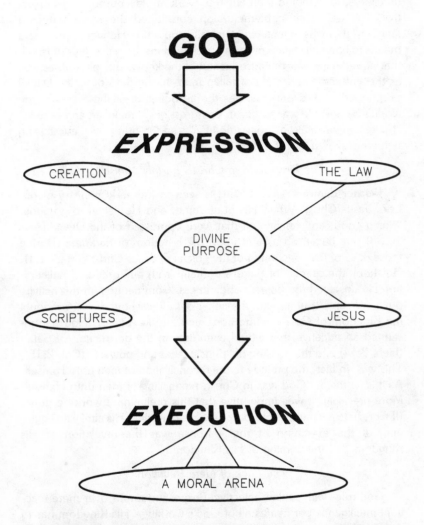

timeliness, God would then begin to work out His purpose, His objective, His will! That implementation constituted the revelation of a kingdom that was essentially restorative in nature! He would provide a means to bring His fallen offspring back to Himself. In the days of Israel, that undertaking was the introduction of the knowledge of God, as well as the sinfulness and need of fallen man. In the days of which Daniel prophesied, God's purpose was the introduction of the Messiah, the world's Savior. He was to "finish transgression," "make an end of sins," "make reconciliation for iniquity," and "bring in everlasting righteousness" (Dan. 9:24).

The Illustration in Christ's Earthly Ministry

Further demonstration of this is seen in the early ministry of our Lord Jesus Christ. When His hour came, and He began to go about "doing good, and healing all that were oppressed of the Devil" (Acts 10:38), He began an assault upon the Kingdom of darkness. During those days of the "beginning of the gospel of Jesus Christ" (Mark 1:1), He shook the citadels of Satan's domain! With authority and deliberation He unseated the powers of darkness. Commenting on this activity our Lord said; "But if I with the finger of God cast out devils, no doubt the Kingdom of God is come upon you" (Luke 11:20). God had instituted an initiative that would eventuate in the destruction of Satan (Heb. 2:14) and the spoiling of "principalities and powers" (Col. 2:15). This was, in fact, the prelude to the reconciliation of men unto Himself. As it is writteen, "God was in Christ, reconciling of men unto Himself. More precisely, it was imperative that this preliminary work be done. (II Cor. 5:19). That was His purpose, His objective, His aim! The beginning of the execution of that purpose was the revelation of His Kingdom . . . the coming of His Kingdom.

The Lack of Mere Reaction

God rules with settled objective! Purpose triumphs over mere reaction! Intelligence permeates all of God's workings! His Kingdom has to do with the outworking of His purpose. It involves the devotion of His authority and character to the fulfillment of that purpose. The Kingdom of God does not involve mere demonstration, but the implementation of previously determined purpose.

The accomplishment of Divine objective, which end is that sought by the Kingdom, is always associated with the working of God. When our Lord Jesus said, "My Father works hitherto, and I work" (John 5:17), He was bearing witness to the Kingdom's current function. God's purposes do not forever remain upon the trestleboard of His desire or intent. They are brought to fruition by the execution of His energy. That is the involvement of Ephesians 1:11; ". . . Him who works all things after the counsel of His own will." God implements what He purposes, and that implementation constitutes "the Kingdom of God," or His rule.

God's Purpose in Our Time

In our day, God's revealed objective is the redemption of man; the reconciliation of His fallen "offspring" to Himself. His operation is repeatedly so represented. "It is God which works" in us "both to will and to do of His good pleasure" (Phil. 2:13). It is "His working which works in us" (Col. 1:29). We read of "the working" (Eph. 1:19; Phil. 3:21), and of God's working "in you" (Heb. 13:21). This "working" is actually the revelation of the Kingdom of God; the implementation of Divine objective. That is precisely as Jesus represented the situation in Luke 11:20.

A Summary of Objective Rule

The Kingdom of God functions by Divine objective, and objective is implemented by work — effectual work! "Work" speaks of productivity, but in this case of more; of purposeful productivity — work with a purpose, an objective, an aim! "Work" denotes Divine initiative — the thrust of God's influence and His power. The Divine Kingdom is technically "over all." The inhabitants of the earth and the armies of heaven together are governed by God — but with objective in mind! The discernible boundaries of God's Kingdom extend no further than His immediate purpose, and in no instance fail to encompass that purpose. That is, God's power and influence appear inactive where His objectives are not being implemented. Thus evil often pervades the society of men without apparent restraint. Such is only apparent, however. The situations are still fully controlled and held in check by Divine power; but in a manner evident only to faith!

Since the revelation to men of God's purpose, His Kingdom has become increasingly more apparent. Think of Israel's deliverance from Egyptian bondage, the giving of the Law at Mount Sinai, the earthly ministry of the Lord Jesus, and the foundational ministry of the "Apostles of the Lamb." These revelatory periods of time were not mere novelties! They involved the progressive implementation of Divine objective, and were actually a revelation of the Kingdom of God. They drew attention to the area of Divine activity, and underscored the activity of God among men. The Kingdom of God, then, is the power and influence of God devoted to the achievement of His objective, which objective is accomplished by the working of God.

The Focus of God's Attention

While God's authority unquestionably extends to the impersonal creation, His primary purpose does not concern that realm. That is to say, the Kingdom of God does not basically have to do with the sun, moon, and stars; with nature and biological functions. An intelligent purpose can be properly implemented only in a moral arena. In other words, where there is right and wrong, acceptance and rejection, submission and rebellion. Choice, decision, evaluation, participation, and conscious involvement: they are what constitutes a moral arena.

Not a Rule of Force

God does not govern His Kingdom by coercion. He does not implement His primary purpose by irresistible power, but by inscrutable wisdom. Where, among free moral beings, there is force, there can never be profit; never blessing; never Divine fellowship! There have been significant demonstrations of this throughout God's dealings with men. Adam and Eve were forced to leave that Edenic paradise (Gen. 3:22-24). God "set a mark" upon that first murderer, Cain, leaving him no alternative but to go "out from the presence of the Lord" (Gen. 4:15-16). The diabolical unity that surfaced at Babel in "a plain in the land of Shinar," when men conspired to build a tower "whose top may reach into heaven," was interrupted by Divine intrusion! God confounded their language, and "scattered them abroad from thence" (Gen. 11:1-8). He brought an abrupt end to the rebellion of men when He sent the flood of Noah's day, "and all flesh died that lived upon the earth" (Gen. 7:21-23).

Other examples of Divine force or coercion are the driving out of the inhabitants of Canaan, the land given to Israel (Josh. 17:12), the subjugation of Pharaoh in the deliverance of Israel (Exod. 12-13), the over-

20

throw of Sodom and Gomorrah (Gen. 18-19), and the removal of that wicked king Herod (Acts 12:20-23). But not a one of these occurrences was associated with benefit for those that were fully acted upon. They were invariably curses for the ungodly! Technically, they did not constitute an implementation of Divine objective, but the removal of things that inhibited that implementation.

In the case of Saul of Tarsus, however, there was no Divine coercion! When "suddenly there shined about him a light from heaven," and "he fell to the earth," the Lord Jesus did not pound him into subjection! Instead, there was a moral appeal. Saul of Tarsus was thrust into the arena of responsibility, not forced response. "Saul, Saul, why persecutest thou me?", was our Lord's question! Saul had to think; he had to review his actions; he had to determine a renewed course of action. His answer shows that he arrived at an acceptable resolution: "Who art thou, Lord . . . what wilt thou have me to do?" (Acts 9:3-6).

Here is an example of how God controls His Kingdom! He does so within a moral environment; a realm of responsibility: a moral arena, if you please. The Kingdom of God is not a rule of force, but is an inscrutably wise way of implementing Divine objective.

Implementation by Revelation

The implications of this situation have eluded many. In fact, they have actually been obscured by diverse false dogmas, perpetrated by "demons" (I Tim. 4:1). Men, under the influence of these demonic doctrines, have prayed for God to overpower people and thrust them into a state of salvation. This is a procedure of ignorance! It is not the way that the Kingdom of God "comes" (Matt. 6:10).

The Kingdom of God is implemented primarily by revelation, and secondarily by the intrusion of Divine authority. Revelation is the exposure of man's mind to fixed reality and "eternal purpose," and it creates a moral arena! It brings with it the responsibility of choice, decision, and involvement! God's purpose in Christ Jesus is the salvation of men, and that purpose is achieved when men that are exposed to the truth choose life, buy the truth, and obey that form of the doctrine delivered to them (Deut. 30:29; Prov. 23:23; Rom. 6:17). All of the Divine resources have been made available for the accomplishment of these ends! Where there is a willing heart, a submissive spirit, and a tender conscience, the power of God is operable in man. That is how God rules; that is how He reigns; that is how His kingdom is manifested! That is how He ruled in Noah's day, Abraham's day, and Moses' day! He has always executed His purpose in an arena of responsibility . . . a moral realm! It is how he has chosen to reveal Himself! This is how he has chosen to execute His purpose!

God Has Used the Direct Method

I must press this point! There have been great physical phenomena wrought by the hand of Almighty God. An earth-cleansing flood (Gen. 6-7). Fire and brimstone falling from heaven (Gen. 19). The parting of great bodies of water (Exod. 14; Josh. 4). The temporary cessation of night following day (Josh. 10). Earthquakes and mighty winds of devastation! They are all in the repertoire of God! He can "call for a famine" (Psa. 105:16), "send wild beasts" (Lev. 26:22), and "swarms of flies" and "plagues" (Exod. 8:21; 9:14). He can make fish swallow prophets (Jonah 1), gourds die on the vine (Jonah 4), fig trees wither (Matt. 21), and mountains shake (Exod. 19:16-18). But when it comes to the sons of men, God does not move them like mountains, send them like flies, or constrain them like fish!

God Working with Man

God has made man in His own image, and consequently motivates him in a unique way! Even in instances where heathen kings were constrained by God to fulfill aspects of His purpose, it was not a constraint of force. When God, for example, "rules in the kingdom of men, and gives it to whomsoever He will" (Dan. 4:17), He does not do it by force, or unintelligible coercion! He does it by means of His authority. He alters circumstances, surroundings, and situations. He produces an environment that constrains the hearts of those involved to of themselves choose to do what God has determined to occur in history. When Nebuchadnezzar came on "Tyrus" and the "land of Egypt," according to God's determination (Ezek. 26:7; 29:19), he did so because he wanted to, not because he was forced to do so.

It is written of Joseph, that young man with a determination for purity, "the Lord was with Joseph, and he was a prosperous man" . . . "and the Lord made all that he did to prosper in his hand" . . . "because the Lord was with him, and that which he did, the Lord made it to prosper" (Gen. 39:2,3,23). But let none suppose that

22

this was accomplished by direct power, as in the shaking of Sinai. This was accomplished by the Divine use of means; by God surrounding men with situations that provoked deliberation and choice. In the case of Potiphar, for example, he gave everything into Joseph's hand because he wanted to, not because he had to! The keeper of the prison was actually inclined to make Joseph a steward in the prison, and did so because that was his preference. To be sure, God was in all of this, but He was ruling in a moral arena, using moral means! That is one of the chief differences between direct power and moral authority!

The Employment of Wisdom

In the case of the Kingdom of God, the use of authority requires wisdom, discretion, purpose, and objective. The Kingdom of God — God's implementation of redemption in Christ — is not accomplished by the manipulation of men! God does not force men into Christ! He does not manipulate them into a state demanding condemnation! Men are not pawns! They are not robots! They have been created in the image of Almighty God — and He is neither pawn nor robot! God may command impersonal ravens to feed Elijah the prophet (I Kgs. 17:4-6), but when He "commanded a widow woman" to feed the fiery prophet, it was quite different! The ravens brought bread and flesh to Elijah, but Elijah went to the widow! The widow had to confront Elijah, evaluate his condition within the context of her impossible situation (I Kgs. 17:10-12). She had to willingly obey the word of the prophet: "make me thereof a little cake first." Her choosing to obey (I Kgs. 17:12-13) the commandment of the Lord for her to feed the prophet was brought about by authority, not coercion! Although it seemed that she and her son would die if they gave all of their meager substance to the prophet, God's authority mandated that death would not occur in her house as a result of this decision! In fact, it was quite the opposite: "The barrel of meal shall not waste, neither shall the cruse of oil fail, until the day that the Lord sendeth rain upon the earth," was the promise of the prophet (I Kgs. 17:14). But the blessing was based upon her response . . . God was governing in a moral arena! His authority was effectual within the context of obedience! Had she not fed the prophet, her oil would have run out, and the meal would have been consumed when she made the cakes for her son and herself!

Christ's Use of Authority

Government by authority instead of direct power, was evidenced throughout the earthly ministry of our Lord Jesus Christ, particularly in connection with His miracles. With few exceptions, His "mighty works" were prefaced by the involvement of men's volition; the response of moral beings to His word. Think of these words, uttered in connection with some of His miracles: "Launch out into the deep, and let down your nets for a draught" (Luke 5:4); "Rise, take up thy bed, and walk" (John 5:8); "Go wash in the pool of Siloam" (John 9:7); "Stretch forth thy hand" (Matt. 12:13)!

The point here is that an operation performed within a moral arena requires authority and freewill response to it, not constraint without involvement! Christ did not merely work upon people, they were consistently made participants when blessed by Him. Whether it was Lazarus coming out of the grave, ten lepers experiencing miraculous cleansing, or the restoration of one possessed of demons — there was a consistent and willing involvement by those being blessed! Lazarus was not forced to come out of the grave, the grave was forced to release him! Again, the distinction of authority is perceived!

God alters circumstances, but man must submit to the alteration! God makes fig trees die and the earth quake, never without a cause, but always apart from intelligent involvement on the part of nature! But when it comes to men — and His Kingdom is among men — He neither blesses nor curses without a cause! In God's kingdom, authority is identified with purpose, objective, and design! It is not reactive, but initiative!

The Tentative and Ultimate Revelation

The Kingdom of God speaks of God's authority and resources devoted to the implementation of His revealed objectives! His Kingdom, then, is as wide as His objectives, and as narrow as His purpose! So far as we are concerned, that "eternal purpose" (Eph. 3:11) is a perceivable one, and is being executed in the midst of intelligent beings capable of discerning it. The issues in His Kingdom involve right and wrong, righteousness and unrighteousness, good and evil. It requires man's attentiveness, deliberation, choice, and personal involvement. In His workings the stamp of His Person and purpose are found. Coupled with His written Word, they become a basis for personal involvement in that purpose. Profitable inquiry into the Kingdom of God without personal involvement is not possible! The entire structure of God's Kingdom is perceptible only from within. Thus did our Lord Jesus proclaim, "Except a man be born again, he cannot see the Kingdom of God. . . . Except a man be born of water and of the Spirit, he cannot enter into the Kingdom of God" (John 3:3,5).

This introductory word is provided to alert the reader to the ever-present temptation to merely be curious about the working of the Lord. This treatise is not a mere fact gathering mission, but an effort to so define the heavenly Kingdom as to constrain you to involvement and participation in it.

In a sense, not all of God's workings are meant to be permanent. Some of them are designed to be introductory and tentative. God has worked with a view of acquainting man with His ways, and thereby preparing man for His primary work or objective. This was the case when God worked with Israel of old. His objective, however, does not terminate with the tentative. Preparation is not an end of itself.

Israel — Preparation

"Israel" (Exod. 14:30; I Cor. 10:18), the "Jews" (Neh. 1:2; John 4:22), the "Hebrews" (Exod. 3:18; Phil. 3:5), the "Israelites" (Exod. 9:7; Rom. 9:4), the "children of Israel" (Num. 14:10; II Cor. 3:7). These are all terms describing a "peculiar people" (Deut. 14:2). Their peculiarity was not due to their geographical location! It was not the outcome of their fleshly lineage! It was traceable to, and only to, their involvement in the Divine objective! Apart from the purpose of God regarding redemption, there is no place for Israel, no position of significance! God determined to use them to introduce Himself and His purpose to the race of fallen men.

The Assignment of Responsibility

To Israel was committed the stewardship of fulfilling this objective. God brought them into a closer association with Himself than any society of men had ever known. While the relationship was not, nor was it designed to be, the ultimate in intimacy, it was superior to all previous involvements of men with the Living God. To Israel "pertained the adoption" (Rom. 9:4a). All revelations of Himself belonged to them! To Israel belonged "the glory" (Rom. 9:4b). Every proclaimed intention to benefit man was given to them; they alone entered into agreements with the God of heaven. Theirs were "the covenants" (Rom. 9:4c). Moreover, when the Lord unveiled to the world a moral code — a code which was a reflection of His own nature — He gave it to Israel! To them belonged "the giving of the Law" (Rom. 9:4d). Not only that, but they alone were given the honor of serving God in an intelligent manner; i.e., in a manner dictated by revelation. To them only belonged "the service of God" (Rom. 9:4e) and "the promises" of future blessings (Rom. 9:4f).

Likewise, the progenitors of an acceptable race all pertained to Israel. Abraham! Isaac! Jacob! They were not the fathers of the Egyptians, the Assyrians, or the Romans. They were appointed of God to be the fathers of the Israelites. Truly, to them belonged "the fathers" (Rom. 9:4g). And, the greatest external benefit of all belonged to them! It was their race that brought forth the Messiah, the Savior of the world! It was of them, "concerning the flesh," that "Christ came, who is over all, God blessed forever" (Rom. 9:4h).

The Development of Awareness

But this singular blessing was not an end of itself! It was intended to prepare the way for the superior blessing! Israel's adoption was external, but it introduced the world to the concept of men being related to God by divine preference.

The covenants of God with Israel were largely of an external nature: they spoke of prosperity, fruitful fields, and increased flocks (Deut. 28). Those covenants, however, brought to men an awareness of the interaction of men with the God of heaven. They spoke of a God that was desirous to bless and benefit man; a God that actually would enter into covenant with His offspring!

When God "gave the Law" to Israel, He did it in an outward manner, writing it on tables of stone. That law delivered a moral code to men that was actually a reflection of God's nature . . . an articulation of God's character. With the giving of the Law, the veil that hung over the Person of God began to be lifted. The "service of God" committed to Israel was also outward. It involved priests with priestly garments, sacrifices, vessels, lamps, and bread; but it injected into the society of men the concept of God being preeminent in men's actions: of men concentrating on pleasing and serving God in a conscientious manner

26

(Heb. 9:1-6).

Think of the promises of God to Israel! A coming "Prophet" to whom the people would "hearken" (Deut. 18:15), a time when sins would be remitted, and every person in covenant with God would know Him, "from the least of them unto the greatest of them" (Jer. 31:34). To that special people came promises that spoke of "salvation" and "righteousness" being joined together; a time when men would be saved without any compromise of the integrity or uprightness of God (Isa. 45:8-24; Rom 3:26). Here, in Israel, was a nation from whose womb would spring the "only begotten of the Father, full of grace and truth" (John 1:14).

The point to see here is that God focused His attention on Israel, and concentrated on executing a particular purpose through them. In that assocation He developed a spiritual vocabulary: a means of communicating Divine concepts to men. Pivotal concepts like "sacrifice," "cleansing," "forgiveness," "atonement," and "transgression" were developed, and became the means of communicating Divine objectives. When we want to learn about these things, we do not go to the philosophers or to the heathen religions: we go to Israel, and to God's dealings with her!

How may we speak more precisely concerning God working with Israel? This was the Kingdom of God! God was deliberately going about the development of His purpose. His power, His Person, His character: they were all devoted to the execution of His will through the nation of Israel.

That working was a tentative working; i.e., it was leading to something better, something more lofty! There was a day appointed on the horizon of Divine purpose when the Living God would take the foundation laid by Israel and build upon it. There is objective, purpose, deliberation: THE KINGDOM OF GOD!

The Church — Participation

The objective of God was to reconcile men unto Himself so they could participate in the Divine enterprises. When "the day of Pentecost was fully come" (Acts 2:1), a foretaste of that planned participation began. It was then that men actually became "laborers together with God" (I Cor. 3:9). Now, justified men became "the light of the world" and "the salt of the earth" (Matt. 5:13-14). Washing was no longer a

27

mere ceremony, but men were "baptized into Christ," and were made "partakers of the Divine nature" (Gal. 3:27; II Pet. 1:4). Now, with the dawn of "the day of salvation" (II Cor. 6:2), God did not merely work upon man, or only in the behalf of men: He was joined to man! Glorious reality! The Spirit witnesses through "holy men" that "he that is joined to the Lord is one spirit" (I Cor. 6:17) — that is participation!

A Conscious Participation

This is a conscious participation! In Christ Jesus, men are not just "used" of God; they become a part of His work! Their heart is in it; their abilities are employed in works of righteousness! In fact, those that have been "washed from their sins" (Rev. 1:5) are so involved in the work of God, that they are associated with the most lofty accomplishments. "For what knowest thou, O wife, whether thou shalt save thy husband? or how knowest thou, O man, whether thou shalt save thy wife" (I Cor. 7:16)! Speaking of his apostolic office, and of its identification with the purpose of God, Paul wrote; ". . . I magnify mine office: if by any means I may provoke to emulation them which are my flesh, and might save some" (Rom. 11:14). And what of that astounding announcement made to the former rebel of Tarsus concerning his role in the Kingdom of God: ". . . now I send thee to open their eyes, and to turn them from darkness unto light, and from the power of Satan unto God . . ." (Acts 26:17-18).

There is also the type of participation that calls upon men to grapple with the highest order of wicked personages. "For we wrestle not against flesh and blood, but against principalities, against powers, against the rulers of the darkness of this world, against spiritual wickedness in high places" (Eph. 6:12). If those that have been made "partakers of Christ" (Heb. 3:14) will "resist the devil," he will "flee" from them (James 4:7). Even though our adversary Satan "as a roaring lion walks about, seeking whom he may devour," the children of God can effectually "resist" him, "stedfast in the faith" (I Pet. 5:8-9). That is PARTICIPATION!

Kingdom Initiative

Kingdom citizens are brought into the role of "ambassadors for Christ" (II Cor. 5:20) and "the oracles of God" (I Pet. 4:11). Being called "unto the fellowship of His Son Jesus Christ our Lord" (I Cor.

1:9), the "man of God" is made to be "thoroughly furnished unto all good works" (II Tim. 3:16-17), "meet for the Master's use, and prepared unto every good work" (II Tim. 2:21). It is men that "take the sword of the Spirit" (Eph. 6:17) and effectually wield it against the powers of darkness! It is men that are commissioned to "cast down imaginations, and every high thing that exalts itself against the knowledge of God . . . bringing into captivity every thought to the obedience of Christ" (II Cor. 10:5).

But these things are not wrought in the energy of the flesh; they are not accomplished by the transmission of some sort of magic power! They are the immediate result of man's union with the Living God in Christ Jesus! Man has become a participant in the Kingdom of God! Jesus promised, "If a man love me, he will keep my words: and my Father will love him, and we will come unto him, and make our abode with him" (John 14:23). PARTICIPATION! In Christ's great High Priestly prayer, uttered amidst groanings on the eve of His betrayal, He spoke of this participation in these words: "That they all may be one; as thou, Father, art in me, and I in Thee, that they also may be one in us: I in them, and Thou in me, that they may be made perfect in one . . ." (John 17:21,23). Speaking of the grand objective of salvation, the Spirit witnessed of the church; ". . . for ye are the temple of the living God; as God hath said, "I will dwell in them and walk in them; and I will be their God, and they shall be my people" (II Cor. 6:16). It is "Christ in" us that constitutes "the hope of glory" (Col. 1:27).

We are in the Kingdom as participants, not uninvolved beneficiaries!

The World to Come

It is "the world to come" that is the object of apostolic emphasis (Heb. 2:5). The "ages to come" is the period of ultimate demonstration as regards the redemption of Christ and its effects (Eph. 2:7). Think of the promises made by Christ Himself to the "churches." They spoke of His objective for them, and of Divine purpose. They speak, without question, of participation and personal involvement! "And he that overcomes, and keeps my works unto the end, to him will I give power over the nations: and he shall rule them with a rod of iron; as the vessels of a potter shall they be broken to shivers: even as I received of my Father" (Rev. 2:26-27); "Him that overcomes will I make a pillar in the temple of my God . . ." (Rev. 3:12); "To him that overcomes will I

29

grant to sit with me in my throne, even as I also overcame, and am set down with my father in His throne" (Rev. 3:21). These promises reflect the same objectives taught by the "apostles of the Lamb" (Rev. 21:14). What a grand purpose they proclaimed when they said; "If we suffer with Him, we shall also reign with Him . . ." (II Tim. 2:12); "And if children, then heirs; heirs of God, and joint-heirs with Christ; if so be that we suffer with Him, that we may be also glorified together" (Rom. 8:17). In a stirring challenge to the believers at Corinth to become involved in the kingly activity of "righteous judgement," Paul wrote, "Do ye not know that the saints shall judge the world? . . . Know ye not that we shall judge angels?" (I Cor. 6:2-3). A high destiny, indeed!

An Actual Rule

In His parables, Jesus spoke of faithful servants being given "authority over ten cities," and being placed over "five cities" (Luke 19:17,19). In a clear prophetic note, Daniel spoke of a time when "the saints of the most High shall take the kingdom, and possess the kingdom forever and ever" (Dan. 7:18); a time when "the saints possessed the kingdom," and it shall be "given to the people of the saints of the most High" (Dan. 7:22, 27). That is speaking of the kingdom into which we enter "through much tribulation" (Acts 14:22). That is the kingdom which we shall "inherit" and the ungodly shall "not inherit" (I Cor. 6:9). It is the full revelation of the Kingdom introduced by the Law, and in which initial participation is enjoyed in Christ Jesus!

Conclusion

The Kingdom of God is not houses and lands, meat and drink, or military exploits! It is the fulfillment of Divine objective, accomplished in a moral arena in an intelligent manner. Are you a part of it?

PART TWO:
WORKING PRINCIPLES OF THE KINGDOM

2

THE KINGDOM OF GOD — OTHERWORLDLY

While the Kingdom of the living God deals with things beyond the comprehension of men, it speaks more of the execution of revealed purpose than of the ultimate extent of divine influence and rule. It is that intelligent and perceptible aspect of God's objective that is the focus of our attention. Unprofitable ventures into the realm of philosophical probings are by no means either lawful or attractive for those that "know the Lord." Moses, that "servant faithful in all his house" (Heb. 3:2,5), spoke a truth transcendent to the covenant which he mediated when he said, "The secret things belong unto the Lord, but the things which are revealed belong unto us and to our children forever . . ." (Deut. 29:29). Revealed things "belong" to those to whom they have been made known. They are theirs to probe, to discern, to comprehend, and to lastingly benefit from! Thus it is with the Kingdom of God — the revealed objective of the Lord! It belongs to us! "We have received a kingdom which cannot be moved" (Heb. 12:28). That reception carries with it a responsibility to arrive at some intelligent apprehension concerning the Kingdom's nature and benefits!

What Is "Otherworldly"?

Here I want to underscore the otherworldiness of God's kingdom. By this, I mean that God's kingdom never has, nor does it now, center in this world. God's objectives do not have as their focal point a realm that has been cursed — a realm that is rife with rebellion and insurrection! While God is most certainly active in the affairs of men, being the "Governor among the nations" (Psa. 22:28), His purposes are centered in higher realms, in loftier spheres, where the curse has not penetrated and rebellion is unknown!

The Heavenly Domain's Superiority

"God is in the heavens" (Psa. 115:3). That reality alone makes earth inferior and heaven superior! Our Lord Jesus "speaks from heaven" (Heb. 12:25), from which He shall ultimately "descend" to conclude the activities of the earth as we know it (I Thess. 4:16).

Now think of the realm to which we have come in Christ Jesus! ". . . mount Zion, the city of the Living God, the heavenly Jerusalem . . . and innumerable company of angels . . . the general assembly and church of the Firstborn, which are written in heaven . . . to God the Judge of all . . . the spirits of just men made perfect . . . to Jesus the Mediator of the New Covenant . . . to the blood of sprinkling that speaks better things than that of Abel" (Heb. 12:22-24). There is something that all of these things have in common — they are not of this world; not centered in flesh and blood; not an integral part of the temporal order!

There is not a thoughtful person among us that would deny that all of these realities are superior! The heavenly assembly is superior to the earthly one! The "heavenly Jersualem" is to be preferred over the earthly one! The "innumerable company of angels" far transcend the worth of mere political or military powers! Think how the presence of "the spirits of just men made perfect" in the heavenly safety zone graphically demonstrates the superiority of that realm.

There the "tempter" (Matt. 4:3; I Thess. 3:5) no longer allures, "flesh and blood" (I Cor. 15:50) no longer hinders, and the confession of sin (I John 1:9) is not longer required. Even prior to "the resurrection

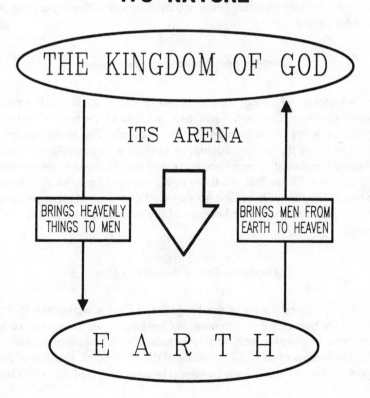

of the just" (Luke 14:14), those identified with the heavenly realm are associated with perfection — "the spirit of just men made perfect." The view is provided in order to encourage men to engage in an earnest quest for that sphere of tranquility and flawlessness.

And, it needs to be considered that the presence of "the blood of sprinkling" in the heavenly sphere has made it effectual for the remission of sins! Christ's blood in this world did not accomplish the objectives of God. It was when Jesus entered into that transcendent "holy place" "by His own blood" that He "obtained eternal redemption for us" (Heb. 9:11-12). In this case, it was "the altar that sanctifieth the gift" (Matt. 23:19); the superior realm that made the presentation of the redemptive blood acceptable. Christ's blood, offered only in this world, had no more effectuality than the blood of those brute beasts that were slain under a typical economy. But once "entered into heaven," the "blood of Christ" became effectual in the accomplishment of God's purpose. A superior realm!

Entrance into Heaven Increases Value

Whenever anything enters heaven, great value and higher significance is attached to it. "Just men" are termed "perfect" when their spirits leave this realm to enter into the heavenly! The blood of Christ "speaks better things" — redemptive testimony, accomplished reconciliation! Consistently, anywhere and everywhere heaven is mentioned, it is superior! Those that are there never appear inferior as compared to earth! The Kingdom of God is otherwordly because of the superiority of the "other world," and because of the inferiority of this "present" world!

Heavenly Things Brought to Men

The otherworldliness of the Kingdom of God is again seen in the bringing of heavenly things to men. In Christ Jesus, we are not primarily recipients of tangible and earthly benefits, but of heavenly realities. The forgiveness of sins, the presence of the Holy Spirit, the fruit of the Spirit — they all come from heaven! They are provided to us by God

34

the Father through the "one Mediator between God and man" (I Tim. 2:5); and both the Father and the Mediator are in heaven! True wisdom comes from "above," together with "every good and perfect gift" (James 1:17). The "glorious Gospel," which has been the source of our blessing, the means of transmitting the awareness of an accomplished reconciliation, was ministered at the first "with the Holy Ghost sent down from heaven" (I Pet. 1:12). The things of heaven were brought to men!

A Heavenly Message

From the very inception of the Gospel, heaven has been the source of information, of blessing, of benefit! The announcement of Jesus' birth came from "an angel of the Lord" (Matt. 1:20), and the affirmation of His Sonship following His baptism was made by "a voice from heaven" (Matt. 3:17). Jesus Himself said that he "came down from heaven" (John 3:13), and so far as His life-giving ministry was concerned, He was that "bread from heaven" (John 6:31-32). If it is true that the Kingdom of God involves the transmission of the realities of heaven to men in the earth, then the climax of that transmission was the Person of Christ Jesus. The things of heaven were brought to men!

Heavenly Benefits

Think of the current and superior benefits of redemption! They are all from heaven! The "love of God" is "shed abroad in our hearts" by a heavenly minister (Rom. 5:5). "Grace and peace" are declared to come "from God," who is in heaven (Col. 1:2; I Thess. 1:1). That glorious hope which enlivens the soul is caused to "abound though the power of the Holy Ghost," who is from heaven (Rom. 15:13). We are "strengthened with might by His Spirit in the inner man" (Eph. 3:16), and "Christ in us" constitutes the "hope of glory" (Col. 1:27).

Heavenly realities are those things not tainted by the curse, not associated with the world, not destined to "pass away." "The world passes away, and the lust thereof" (I John 2:15-17), but the things which are provided to men in the Kingdom of God are eternal in nature; they cannot pass away! If you do not ultimately profit from kingdom benefits, it is not because of any inferiority or temporality in them! It is only because you, failing to perceive their transcendent value, have not met the requirements for receiving and retaining them, which is to give them the absolute priority in your life!

Men from Earth Are Brought to Heaven

Perhaps this seems like an elementary point; but I bid you to examine it closely. The objective of God's kingdom is not to establish your position upon earth! It is not to correct injustices that have occurred within the society of men! God's objective is to save men "From this untoward generation" (Acts 2:40), not to help them feel at home in it! He draws our eyes upward to heaven, not downward to earth! "Set your affection on things above, not on things on the earth," admonished the apostle (Col. 3:2).

In a challenging exhortation of the church, the Spirit says, "If ye then be risen with Christ, seek those things which are above, where Christ sits on the right hand of God" (Col. 3:1)! The objective of God's rule in Christ is to bring you "up" in your thoughts, in your desires, in your personal aim! His entire kingdom — the enterprise of redemption — is centered in heaven! Take heaven away — remove the thought of God, Christ, and His atoning blood — and nothing of worth is left! It makes little difference how ideal the home, the government, the world: all is vanity if there is no heaven, no eternal realm! God is bringing men from earth to heaven!

The term "sanctification" speaks of this upward thrust; it is a word that speaks of the process of getting men from earth to heaven. Think of that apostolic prayer: "And the very God of peace sanctify you wholly; and I pray God your whole spirit and soul and body be preserved blameless unto the coming of our Lord Jesus Christ" (I Thess. 5:23). The coming of the Lord Jesus Christ will occasion our full induction into the eternal world . . . the "ages to come" (Eph. 2:7). Take that "coming" away, and life is futile! Bring this view of things into focus and scriptural "santification" assumes its proper value! Our Lord Jesus died that He might "sanctify and cleanse" the church (Eph. 5:26) . . . i.e., to bring it from earth to heaven; from labor to rest; from battle to victory; from death unto life! If God's objective is to bring me from earth to heaven, I am out of synch with heaven if my objectives are otherwise!

The Divine Emphasis

The revelation that God's kingdom is otherworldly mandates a proper emphasis! Divine resources are not adapted for the accomplishments of purely earthly enterprises, and matters that are fundamentally of this world do not require Divine resources. Thus, those that emphasize this world thereby de-emphasize the world to come; and those that emphasize the world to come minimize this world. These are circumstances that cannot be avoided! The only way to benefit from the redemption in Christ Jesus is to assume a position of spiritual aloofness from the world. By "aloofness" I do not mean indifference, or a refusal to address our responsibilities. I do mean that we refuse to become absorbed into the world order, to adopt its priorities, or permit its mode of reasoning to captivate our heart. ". . . the fashion of this world passeth away" (I Cor. 7:31).

The Conflict with This World

A fact that has willingly escaped many a soul is this: the Kingdom of God is in conflict with the kingdom of this world! Heaven and earth are at variance! To become absorbed in "the world to come" causes this world to become offensive and inhibitive! The reader ought not to perceive this as going "too far." It is the Lord by James that tells us in His Word, ". . . know ye not that friendship with the world is enmity with God? Whosoever therefore would be a friend of the world is the enemy of God" (James 4:4). John affirms this truth with equal pungency; "Love not the world, neither the things that are in the world. If any man love the world, the love of the Father is not in him" (I John 2:15). He adds, "For all that is in the world, the lust of the flesh, and the lust of the eyes, and the pride of life, is not of the Father, but is of the world" (I John 2:16).

Any heart that believes these penetrating assertions can perceive that an obvious conflict exists between this world and the one to come; between the kingdoms of this world and the Kingdom of God! Little wonder that we are admonished with fervency, "I beseech you therefore, brethren, by the mercies of God that ye . . . be not conformed to this world . . ." (Rom. 12:1-2). There is a corrosion of the soul that attends an emphasis of this world.

The Requirement of Reason

This emphasis is not a mandate of law! It is not something that you do simply because you have to! There is sound reason behind it. Remember, God's kingdom is characterized by intelligence, purpose, and revealed objective. Because the things that are revealed "belong unto us," it is our responsibility to uncover the reasons behind the mandate; else we will not be able to fulfill it acceptably.

We are told that "the whole world lies in wickedness" (I John 5:19); i.e., the entire world has been influenced by the arch-rebel, Satan himself. His thoughts, his values, his insurrection have permeated the whole of society. There is not a continent, a country, a city, a province, a family, or an individual that has not been infected by sin as a result of the fall (Rom. 3:23).

The Mandate of Proper Emphasis

But we must further delineate this truth. I am not promoting a morose spirit, or a spirit of negativism. The world is "evil" in the context of God's purpose. The whole world "lies in wickedness" from the perspective of salvation. The impotence of the world to provide us with profitable access to eternity is what promotes a godly revulsion to it.

Sinful desires that are associated with this world are to be denied, and God's grace instructs us in that activity, "The grace of God that brings salvation hath appeared to all men, teaching us that, denying ungodliness and worldly lusts, we should live soberly, righteously, and godly, in this present world" (Titus 2:10-11). I might add that this persuasion comes by the exposure of the mind to the superior things of God rather than by an in-depth analysis of the evils of this world.

There is a twofold reason for denying "wordly lusts." First, because they are corrupt and relate us to a cursed realm: "The world passeth away, and the lust thereof" (I John 2:17). Secondly, they are inhibitive of spiritual-mindedness, creating a competitive influence. This is graphically taught in our Lord's explanation of His parable of the sower. Evidencing an intense desire for men to comprehend the truth, He explained that He had been addressing matters concerning "the Kingdom of God" (Mark 4:11), and that the distribution of "the word" was the particular consideration being developed. Luke identifies it as "the word of God" (Luke 8:9), and Matthew refers to it as "the word of the kingdom" (Matt. 13:19). This is the means God uses to implement His kingdom among men — "the word of God." The parable of the sower speaks of men's reaction to the proclamation of God's purpose and the means by which they become profitably involved in it!

These words of our Lord are explicit, and they clearly point up a jeopardy to which every hearer of the word is subjected. "And these are they which are sown among thorns; such as hear the word, and the cares of this world, and the deceitfulness of riches, and the lusts of other things entering in, choke the word, and it becomes unfruitful." (Mark 4:18-19). This world, then, is an arena of competitive influence! The "cares of this world" conflict with the concerns of God's Kingdom. When the word is "received" in the context of an emphasis on earth, it is destined to futility; it will yield no fruit. It cannot be received "among the thorns" without being ultimately unfruitful! The realm of the seen militates against that of the unseen; it is not neutral! This world's emphases and principles are to be abandoned for a higher order! The reason? They conflict with the world to come "whereof we speak" (Heb. 2:5).

Eternal Issues at Stake

The point to be grasped here is that an emphasis must be placed upon "the things of the Spirit of God" (I Cor. 2:14)! To make the things of this world primary is to betray our trust! At this point we enter into an extremely sensitive area; but someone must enter into it in the Name of the Lord!

When men focus our attention upon this world — upon the seen, upon the things "of this life" — they thereby neutralize the word of God! They may mean well, they may be engaged in an attempt to help men; but they have ineffectualized the "word of the kingdom." They have handicapped their hearers, deprived their hands of strength, and weakened their knees (Heb. 12:12).

Let us not be ambiguous on this point, it is a critical one. For the word to be "choked" and become "unfruitful," and for the individual to "bring no fruit to perfection," cannot but result in condemnation! Our Lord Jesus Christ has declared that unfruitfulness will bring removal from the source of life: "Every branch in me that bears not fruit He [God] takes away . . . if a man abide not in me, he is cast forth as a branch, and is withered; and men gather them, and cast them into the fire, and they are burned" (John 15:2,6).

When we, therefore, speak of the "cares of the world," or the "cares and riches and pleasures of this life," we are not referring to a tolerable situation. Through ensnarement by these things, we have entered into real jeopardy — a jeopardy for which no provision has been made in salvation. The "salvation in Christ" (II Tim. 2:10), which is brought to us by the "grace of God" (Titus 2:11), has no provision for security while engulfed by the cares of this world. Grace will not strengthen or fortify the soul that maintains an inordinate attentiveness to this life. To be sure, "there is forgiveness" with the Lord (Psa. 130:4); but that forgiveness postulates an abandonment of this world's priorities. To "approve the things that are excellent" (Phil. 1:10) requires an awareness of their superiority, and the consequent inferiority of the things of this world.

The entire thrust of salvation is heavenward — otherworldly! It involves the forgiveness of sin — sin that is the result of responding to the lower order! It involves "hope" that draws away from this world toward a "world to come." All of the Divine resources are calculated to neutralize the effects of the world, to wean us from its delusions, and to strengthen us for direct conflict with it.

In view of that circumstance, an emphasis on this world is tantamount to rebellion and a rejection of the Gospel. Does that seem strong? It is as strong as the "choking" of the word! The concerns that center in this life, if they are allowed to become dominant, will drive out and overcome the concerns of the next life! Imperceptibly the love of the world will stifle spiritual life, and render men unfruitful in the knowledge of Christ.

Conclusion

The Kingdom of God has to do with God's objective in due focus, particularly as regards men and their reconciliation to Him (I Cor. 5:18-20). It involves heavenly designs, and therefore cannot be fully developed without separation from this world. "Love not the world, neither the things that are in the world," and "be not conformed to this world," are not mere suggestions (I John 2:15; Rom. 12:2). They are an attitude and relation necessary for the saints' spiritual survival!

This world is under the curse of God: "Heaven and earth shall pass away" (Matt. 24:35). With the destined passing of the world order will come an abrupt end to the gratification of the appetites and fulfillment of the desires which it creates. "The world passes away and the lust thereof" (I John 2:17). Until these lusts "pass," they interfere with the realization of heavenly pursuits, detract from the Divinely appointed goal, and "choke the word."

Let no man, therefore, emphasize this world and its associations! Look beyond the seen to the things "unseen" (II Cor. 4:18). Concentrate on things that do not fail, that are eternal, and that pass not away. The kingdom to which you have been called is otherworldly, and shall never pass away!

3

THE KINGDOM AND MAN'S INITIATIVE

Man is an integral consideration in the Kingdom of God. In Christ Jesus, the current Administrator of the Kingdom (Matt. 28:20; I Pet. 3:22), the primary objective of God is to benefit mankind. The essence of that benefit is set forth in the assertion, "God was in Christ reconciling the world unto Himself" (II Cor. 5:19). Benefits disassociated from reconciliation are only temporal at best, and incidental to God's "eternal purpose" (Eph. 3:11). The entire ministry of Christ revolves around reconciliation, redemption, salvation, etc. — all varying views of the same reality. Remove man from the picture and there is no need for Jesus of Nazareth, His incarnation, ministry, humiliation, resurrection, or current rule.

The Inconsistency of Temporal Blessings

The benefits of blessings of God fall into two general categories: temporal and eternal, carnal and spiritual, seen and unseen. Conferment of the former category — the temporal, carnal, or seen — is not characterized by consistency, nor is it necessarily associated with Divine requirements. A few examples of such benefits are "rain" (Matt. 5:45), longevity of days (Psa. 91:16; 90:10), prosperity (Psa. 128:1-2), health (Psa. 103:2), the earth made serviceable for man (Psa. 104:14-15), and children (Psa. 127: 5). For these and other kindred benefits an acceptable moral state is not necessarily required. Both the godly and the ungodly, the righteous and the unrighteous, the saint and the sinner, may experience them.

Furthermore, the underlying cause for temporal blessings is not always clear. The morally decadent may have sufficient rain on his crops, live a long life, be healthy, and have a "quiver" full of children. Contariwise, the "godly man" may experience drought, die young, be ill, and be childless.

Discernible logic may on occasion be perceivable in connection with temporal benefits and afflictions. But not necessarily so. Joseph prospered (Gen. 39:3), some Corinthians were sick (I Cor. 11:30), and Israel received rain (Lev. 26:4) for obvious reasons. On the other hand, Timothy was sick (I Tim. 5:23), early saints were "poor" (Rom. 15:26), and the life of the Apostle James was cut short (Acts 12:2), where the reasons are not apparent.

The Reason for the Inconsistency

There is, of course, a reason for temporal benefits being conferred after this manner. They are not central to God's objective in Christ; they are incidental! They are not consistently initiated by God in response to acceptable behavior and demeanor of life. There is an area of life — the temporal area — where benefits are not necessarily associated with moral discipline and godly conduct. The "ungodly" may "prosper in this world" and "increase in riches" (Psa. 73:12), while the godly man may be a "beggar . . . full of sores" (Luke 16:20).

A Possible Source of Confusion

This condition has been the cause of confusion in many minds. That "sweet psalmist of Israel" (II Sam. 23:1), once stumbled at confrontation with this apparently unjust situation. Perceiving how the "ungodly" prospered and increased — especially in view of his own difficulties — he cried, "Verily I have cleansed my hands in innocency. For all the day long have I been plagued, and chastened ever morning" (Psa. 73:12-14). The contemplation of this apparent incongruity was actually

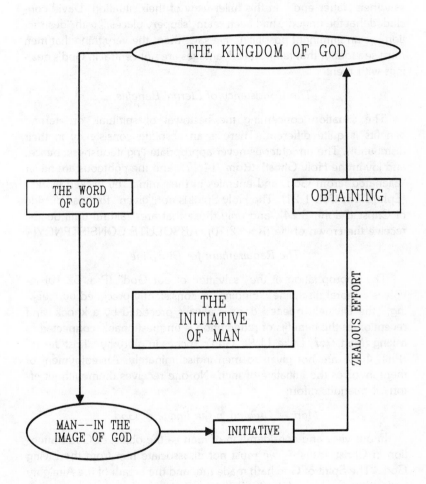

"too painful" for him UNTIL he "went into the sanctuary of God."

There, in the presence of the Almighty, his perspective was enlarged. Rather than viewing the current experience of the ungodly, he saw their "latter end." In this fuller view of their situation, David concluded that the ungodly had been set in "slippery places," with "destruction" as an imminent possibility. He saw, then, the very thing that men must see today, that temporal advantages are not central in God's dealings with men!

The Consistency of Eternal Benefits

The situation concerning the bestowal of spiritual, or eternal, benefits is quite different. There is an absolute consistency in their distribution. The unrighteous never appropriate "righteousness, peace, and joy in the Holy Ghost" (Rom. 14:17), and the righteous are never "alienated" from God, and enemies in their mind "by wicked works" (Eph. 4:18; Col. 1:21). The Holy Spirit is not "given" to those outside of Christ (I John 3:24), and only those that are "faithful until death" receive the crown of life (Rev. 2:10). ABSOLUTE CONSISTENCY!

The Requirement for Discipline

The appropriation of the "salvation of our God" (Psa. 52:10) involves a moral discipline. "Finding" is consistently preceded by "seeking," the Divinely opened door is always preceded by a knock, and reception of the benefits of redemption is unquestionably connected to asking (Matt. 7:7; Luke 11:9). God's "riches in glory by Christ Jesus" (Phil. 4:19) are not given to men indiscriminately. An enjoyment of them involves the initiative of men. No one receives them without effort . . . serious effort!

Man — Created in the Image of God

In our view and consideration of man — the object of God's attention in Christ Jesus — we must not disassociate him from the Living God. "The Spirit of God hath made me, and the breath of the Almighty hath given me life" (Job. 33:4). "And God said, Let us make man in our image, after our likeness. . . . So God created man in His own image, in the image of God created He him: male and female created he them. . . . And the Lord God formed man of the dust of the ground, and breathed into his nostrils the breath of life; and man became a living soul" (Gen. 1:26,27; 2:7). What a glorious beginning! In the image of God!

Man's Image a Focal Point

Throughout the Word of God, reference is made to the fact that man is in the "image of God." That "image" was not destroyed by sin; it was only marred. Because man is in the image of god, capital punishment was instituted by God Himself in the days following the flood; "Whoso sheddeth man's blood, by man shall his blood be shed: for in the image of God made He man" (Gen. 9:6). To the church at Corinth Paul wrote ". . . man . . . is the image and glory of God" (I Cor. 11:7), and James decried the practice of cursing men "which are made after the similitude of God" (James 3:9).

That image was not physical, for the Living God is "invisible" (Col. 1:15; I Tim. 1:17; Heb. 11:27). He is "a Spirit" (John 4:24), imperceptible to the eye or sense of flesh and blood! When Israel stood trembling at the foot of Sinai, they "saw no manner of similitude" because He has "no manner of similitude" (Deut. 4:15). The body with which man is clothed is not in the image of God. It is the "inner man" (Eph. 3:16), the essential part of man, that bears the Divine image of God.

A Moral Image

That image is a moral image; a reflection of God's Person, in distinction from a "shape" (John 5:37). God is primarily known by means of His intelligent and objective works; the things that He has done and said. They have all been with purpose, and have been characterized by objective and deliberate design.

The heavens and the earth, together with man himself, can be objectively studied and analyzed. They are the handiwork of our God! Take, too, the proclaimed and accomplished purposes of God: the Noahic flood (Gen. 6-7), the scattering of the rebels at Babel (Gen. 11), the calling of Abraham (Gen. 12 and 15), the raising up of the nation of Israel (Rom. 11), the deliverance of Israel from Egyptian bondage (Exod. 12-15), the giving of the Law (Exod. 20), the salvation that is in Christ Jesus with eternal glory (II Cor. 5:18-20).

All of these workings have the strong thread of intelligence and purpose woven throughout their fabric. They all show the character and Person of our God! He is known by what He has done! He is known by what He has said! And He is seen to be determinate, a God of choice, possessed of will and purpose.

This is the image in which man was made: a moral image! It is an image that brought with it the ability to choose, to determine, to purpose, to plan, to be intelligently involved! Man possesses inherent capabilities like his Maker! Truly, a staggering thought! No swarm of insects or herd of beasts is capable of that kind of function, because they are not in the image of God.

Let us not cloud the point! Man is a moral being with the ability to reason and judge. He has a spirit to be enlightened, and a will to make determinations and choices. He is "in the image of God"!

Taking the Kingdom of God by Initiative

The Kingdom of God does not "come" to the individual with overpowering force. It is proclaimed by the Gospel (Mark 1:14-15; Acts 28:32; Rom. 14:17), and appropriated through personal initiative (Matt. 6:33). "Initiative" speaks of the employment of God-given abilities (the "image of God") toward a central and focused objective. What God gives must be appropriated! It is not bestowed by overpowering man, but by appealing to him!

In fact, the kingdom of God when preached, urges men to involvement, to participation, to do something! Energy and aptitude are challenged into action by the proclamation of God's purpose in Christ Jesus! The truth of this is perceived in the various responses produced when men were confronted with kingdom realities. "What must we DO?" (Acts 2:37); "What must I DO to be saved?" (Acts 16:30; "What shall I DO Lord?" (Acts 22:10); "Here is water; what doth hinder me to be baptized?" (Acts 8:36).

It is true that in the Kingdom of God, you obtain what you seek, and that only. You grow in the areas where you apply effort, you possess what you have appropriated by faith. That is the manner of God's Kingdom.

The Element of Spiritual Violence

Our Lord made an intriguing observation following His commendation of John the Baptist (Matt. 11:7-11). "And from the days of John the Baptist until now the Kingdom of heaven suffereth violence, and the violent take it by force" (Matt. 11:12). The expression ". . . the kingdom of God suffereth violence, and the violent take it by force" is also translated as follows: "ardent multitudes have been crowding into the Kingdom of Heaven" (Living Bible); "the Kingdom of heaven has been subjected to violence and the violent are taking it by storm" (Jerusalem Bible); "now men have been taking the Kingdom of Heaven by storm and impetuously crowding into it" (Goodspeed); "the Kingdom of God has endured violent assault, and violent men seize it by force (as a precious prize) — a share in His Kingdom is sought with most ardent zeal and intense exertion" (Amplified New Testament).

The Newness of the Phenomenon

Prior to the days of John the Baptist, neither prophets nor priests were followed by multitudes. There had not been an intense effort on the part of men to appropriate the message of the Almighty. The prophets went to the people; the priests interceded for the people. The involvement of the people themselves was generally passive.

But with John the Baptist and his climatic time, a dramatic change took place. It is said of that rough and isolated prophet that "there went out unto him all the land of Judaea, and they of Jerusalem" (Mark 1:5). These multitudes were not prompted by mere curiosity. They were "baptized of him in Jordan, confessing their sins" (Matt. 3:6). Men were taking the kingdom by violence!

The Continuance in Christ's Ministry

This response continued in the ministry of Christ Jesus, even accelerating in its manifestation. The multitudes would follow Jesus (Matt. 4:25; 8:1), sailed in ships to find Him (John 6:22-25), thronged places where He taught (Mark 3:7-9), and crowded into houses to hear Him (Mark 2:1-2). On one occasion, they followed Him for three days without eating (Matt. 15:32). They crowded into synagogues (Matt. 13:54), went into the desert (Matt. 14:13), and stood in a plain to hear His gracious words (Luke 6:17ff). This is something that neither Moses nor the prophets experienced! Men were taking the Kingdom by violence.

This condition fulfilled the once mysterious prophecy of Moses, the servant of God; "The Lord thy God will raise up unto thee a Prophet . . . unto Him shall ye hearken" (Deut. 18:15). The people had not hearkened unto Moses, and they did not hearken unto the prophets that followed him (Matt. 5:12; 23:31). Under the Old Covenant there was not a general eagerness to obtain the knowledge of God. The Law and the prophets were not perceived as a treasure, except by very few. Men did not take the kingdom by violence!

The unusual response of which Jesus spoke was the result of an unprecedented exposure to men of the mind of the Lord. John the Baptist announced that "the Kingdom of Heaven" was "at hand," and called upon men to "repent" (Matt. 3:1-3). He doubtless brought the anticipation of men to unequaled heights when he said, "There comes one mightier than I after me, the latchet of whose shoes I am not worthy to stoop down and unloose" (Mark 1:7). Once he startled the multitudes with the perceptive announcement, "Behold the Lamb of God that taketh away the sin of the world" (John 1:29).

Our Lord Jesus Himself accelerated the demand for moral initiative when He "began to preach and to say, Repent, for the Kingdom of Heaven is at hand" (Matt. 4:17). Even in the selection of his disciples, He appealed to decision and choice; "Follow me, and I will make you fishers of men" (Matt. 4:19). Inherent in the message of Christ was a demand for choice, decision, and determination! He announced a kingdom that directly involved the initiative and determined devotion of men!

Energetic Effort Urged

When our Lord Jesus confronted men with their own proclivities to sin, He insisted that they deal with those sinful inclinations themselves. "If thy right eye offend thee, pluck it out . . . if thy right hand offend thee, cut it off . . . " (Matt. 5:29-30). The point of that proclamation was not self-mutilation, but the exercise of God-given willpower in personal discipline.

The Kingdom of God assumes the involvement of man prior to the conferment of benefit or advancement! Those that would enjoy establishment in the faith are expected to, not only hear the "sayings" of Christ, but to also do them (Matt. 7:24-27). Those that would enjoy the rest and fruit of faith are required to "come" to Christ, and to "learn" from Him (Matt. 11: 28-30).

That is initiative! Our Lord challenged men, and urged them to take the initiative in things pertaining to God: "Who hath ears to hear, let him hear" (Matt. 13:9); "If any man will come after Me, let him deny himself, and take up his cross, and follow me" (Matt. 16:24). The "first and great commandment" involves the initiative of man; "Thou shalt love the Lord thy God with all thy heart, and with all thy soul, and with all thy mind" (Matt. 22:37). The very induction of an individual into the Kingdom of God's "dear Son" (Col. 1:12-13) requires the resolute exercise of his initiative: "He that believeth and is baptized, shall be saved" (Mark 16:16).

To take the kingdom "by violence," however, requires our best interest and response. The Kingdom is perceived as a prize of paramount value, worthy of the loss of all else, if necessary (Matt. 13:44-46). Unusual effort, unparalleled energy, unwavering preferences: those are the qualities required to become profitably involved in the Kingdom of God!

When it comes to being "saved," the demand is to "strive to enter the strait gate" (Luke 13:23-24). In the matter of overcoming the opposition of satanic forces, we must "wrestle" against them (Eph. 6:12). The moral course that leads to glory is appropriately referred to as "the race" that is "set before us," and it is to be traversed on the "run" (Heb. 12:2). We must "fight the good fight of faith, lay hold on eternal life" (I Tim. 6:12). With the goal of eternal life in our eye, we are to "press toward the mark" (Phil. 3:14) with a firm resolve to "endure to the end" (Matt. 24:13).

All of these terms depict unusual involvement! All of our resources are required to achieve the stated objectives. A casual spirit cannot reach the goal. If you want to receive those benefits that are "in Christ Jesus," you must "look" unto Him (Heb. 12:2)! If Satan is to be thwarted in his desire to "devour" you (I Pet. 5:8), you must "resist" him (James 4:7). If you are to continue to experience union with the Lord Jesus, you must cleave unto Him "with purpose of heart" (Acts 11:23). That is but to say, if you will "take" the kingdom, you must take it with "violence"; with intense and unrelenting effort!

This is not, however, to say that we are under a system of "works," one whereby the salvation of God is obtained solely by man's effort. God forbid! Salvation, in all of its provisionary aspects, is "of the Lord" (Jonah 2:9), and will ultimately be ascribed in all of its fullness to Him (Rev. 7:10).

Every provided element of our redemption is by our God. A Savior (I John 4:14), a Mediator (Heb. 12:24), a New Covenant (Heb. 8:13),

51

the Holy Spirit (I Thess. 4:8): all have been provided by our God, without and independently of the efforts of sinful men! Further, the forgiveness of sins (Eph. 1:7), "righteousness, peace, and joy in the Holy Ghost" (Rom. 14:17), strength in the "inner man" (Eph. 3:16), etc., are benefits made available equally apart from the efforts of men.

But the initiative of man, as the term is here used, does not involve the provision of these salvational components, but of their appropriation. It refers not to their availability, but to their experience by the individual. Apart from the exercise of such initiative, it is impossible to benefit from God's provisions in Christ Jesus! The gospel calls men to act, demands the exercise of their will, and requires the enlistment of all their resources. God has determined that the appropriation of spiritual blessings shall be only by means: through appointed channels. He has made man with a moral constitution, and has endowed him with certain aptitudes. Man must employ these enduements energetically if he is to actually participate in the Kingdom of God! They must not lie dormant!

Candidly, it is my prayer that this generation will be challenged to action by the preaching of the "everlasting Gospel" (Rev. 14:6). When the church of the Lord Jesus Christ preaches discerningly and with power, moral force will be exerted upon men that they will not be able to ignore. That preaching will appeal to the initiative of men, and constrain the submissive to take the Kingdom "by violence"! Those that believe the Gospel will "strive to enter the strait gate" (Luke 13:24), and those that have made the commitment of faith will "press toward the mark for the prize of the high calling in Christ Jesus" (Phil. 3:14).

Seeking First the Kingdom

The Kingdom of God involves the initiative of man to personally appropriate what God has provided in Christ for men, and it is man's responsibility to appropriate it! The effort expended to obtain these saving benefits, however, cannot be casual, nor can it be secondary to a prior concern. Our Lord Jesus Christ Himself underscored this requirement for priority when He said, "Seek ye first the Kingdom of God and His righteousness" (Matt. 6:33). The preeminent objective is to obtain the Kingdom of God and His righteousness! Our primary effort is to be in this direction!

Seeking the Kingdom of God necessarily involves the consistent selection of good, as well as the complementary rejection of evil. An upright Kingdom cannot be obtained by unrighteous means. That is why Jesus commanded us to "seek" first the Kingdom of God "and His righteousness." Participation in God's righteousness . . . that is to be our quest!

Actually, this requirement for quest of the Kingdom is not unlike that for other pursuits by men of great values. The Kingdom of God emphasizes God's purpose, and that purpose is sought by fervent desire to become favorably connected with it. If you view the Kingdom of God from the standpoint of its components, the admonition is, "Seek those things which are above, where Christ sits on the right hand of God" (Col. 3:1). The things which we are admonished to seek are separate from this world; not an integral part of it! They are in fact, completely isolated from "the lust of the flesh, the lust of the eyes, and the pride of life" (I John 2:16). The natural senses cannot appropriate these things! It is obvious, then, that men cannot seek "first the kingdom of God" if they are inordinately enamored with the "fashion of this world" (I Cor. 7:31).

Synonyms for Seeking "First"

Seeking "first the Kingdom of God and His righteousness" does not refer to intensive library research, or a probing into the mystical. It speaks of a diligent and perceptive involvement in the will of God as revealed in the Scriptures. Seeking "first" also postulates zealous effort; effort that is characterized by intensity and sincerity! This is laboring "for that food which endures unto everlasting life" (John 6:27); being "fervent in spirit, serving the Lord" (Rom. 12:11). In a day of overwhelming casualness and outright detachment, God's people must realize the imperative of zealous effort in matters pertaining to the Kingdom of God. A great God cannot be found by small effort! A superior Kingdom cannot be appropriated by inferior quests! A Savior that declared with Divine determination that He "must work the works of Him that sent" Him, cannot be found by casual and half-hearted effort! The labors by which we seek for glory and honor and immorality are to be "stedfast and unmovable," as we are "always abounding in the work of the Lord" (I Cor. 15:58).

This zeal, when confronted with the apathy of the world, the sinful proclivities of the flesh, and the animosity of the wicked, refuses to be "weary in well doing," knowing that "in due season we shall reap, if we faint not" (Gal. 6:9). This seeking is a pressing "toward the mark for the prize of the high calling of God in Christ Jesus" (Phil. 3:14) — pressing through hindrances, making progress in spite of obstacles. It is being "zealous of good works," in accordance with God's objective in Christ (Titus 2:14). This is what Jude called "earnestly contending for the faith which was once delivered unto the saints" (Jude 3). It is an objective effort, an earnest quest, characterized by concentrated and unrelenting energy! This is what is involved in seeking "first the Kingdom of God and His righteousness."

The Futility of Casual Effort

The Kingdom of God cannot be sought or obtained by casual effort. To be casual and passive about the Kingdom of God is to deprive oneself of it. The Living God was zealous about our redemption, smiting and afflicting His only begotten Son, laying upon Him "the iniquity of us all" (Isa. 53:4-7). This was something that required the "zeal of the Lord of hosts" (Isa. 37:32), else it would never have been accomplished.

Prophetically, our Lord Jesus Christ was depicted as being "clad with zeal as a cloak" (Isa. 59:17). During His earthly ministry, His disciples associated His conduct with the words of the Psalmist, "The zeal of Thy house hath eaten me up" (Psa. 69:9; John 2:17). With unrelenting zeal, He "laid down His life for us" (I John 3:16).

Everything about the revelation of God's Kingdom in Christ Jesus is characterized by zeal! To think that the blessings of that Kingdom could be appropriated by efforts that were not hearty is an incongruity of the greatest sort; a contradiction unparalleled in magnitude!

Other synonymous expressions for seeking first the Kingdom of God are numerous ". . . .work out your own salvation with fear and trembling" (Phil. 2:12); "Stand, therefore . . ." (Eph. 6:14ff); "Let us go forth therefore unto Him without the camp, bearing His reproach" (Heb. 13:13); "As newborn babes, desire the sincere milk of the word, that ye may grow thereby" (I Pet. 2:2); ". . . be diligent, that ye may be found of Him in peace, without spot, and blameless" (II Pet. 3:14); ". . . let us lay aside every weight, and the sin which doth so easily beset us, and let us run with patience the race set before us . . ." (Heb. 12:1).

Every exhortation is saturated with a sense of urgency that requires zeal, commitment, and unwavering resolve. The Kingdom of God simply cannot be sought any other way!

The Initiative Is Man's

This entire initiative required above pertains to man; it is his responsibility to respond. God will not do it for him! God created man for this activity; He has endowed him with capacities that are adapted to it — seeking "first the Kingdom of God and His righteousness." In fact, this is the ordained and preeminent occupation of man. As it is written; "He hath made of one blood all nations of men to dwell on all the face of the earth, and hath determined the times before appointed, and the bounds of their habitation; that they should seek the Lord . . ." (Acts 17:26,27). God's creation of man reflected this revealed objective. Man has been made to seek God!

Even under the dim illumination of the First Covenant, this activity was clearly imposed. "Seek the Lord and His strength, seek His face continually" (I Chron. 16:11); ". . . if ye seek Him, He will be found of you . . ." (II Chron. 15:2). The Psalmist, out of a preredemptive intimacy with the Living God, proclaimed, "Seek ye the Lord, and His strength . . ." (Psa. 105:4), while Isaiah admonished, "Seek ye the Lord while He may be found . . ." (Isa. 55:6).

The Lord, His strength, His face: they are to be the objects of earnest inquiry! The "Lord" speaks of His Person, "His strength" is the exertion of His authority in the behalf of man, while "His face" proclaims God's focused beneficence and favor upon a individual. An acquaintance with God's Person, the experience of His strength, and the realization of His favor are obtained only by those that "seek" Him!

The fact that God has made himself accessible to men in Christ evidences His intense desire for fellowship with His "offspring" (Acts 17:28-29). The appointed occupation of man to seek the Lord, and the specific requirement to seek "first the Kingdom of God and His righteousness" is a reflection of the love of God; an expression of our Father's great and unquestionable affection for man. The conscientious effort to fulfill this Divine requirement will surely result in the obtaining of God's favor and the realization of His blessing. It will, in summary, bring you into the Kingdom of God!

Seeking God Is Not Vain

In the pursuit of the things of God, our energies are not spent in vain. It is as true with the time of Christ's government as it was during the dominance of Israel: "I said not unto the seed of Jacob, Seek ye me in vain: I the Lord speak righteousness, I declare things that are right" (Isa. 45:19). In matters pertaining to God, lawful effort is consistently rewarded.

Our Lord Jesus proclaimed this with refreshing clarity when He said, "Ask, and it shall be given unto you; seek, and ye shall find; knock, and it shall be opened to you: for every one that asks receives; and he that seeks finds, and to him that knocks it shall be opened" (Matt. 7:7-8). The due rewarding of effort! Think of that impelling promise: ". . . for in due season we shall reap, if we faint not" (Gal. 6:9). Let no man doubt it: "whatsoever good any man doeth, the same shall he receive of the Lord" (Eph. 6:8).

Our very induction into the Kingdom of God is the result of our efforts: "Repent and be baptized, every one of you in the name of Jesus Christ, for the remission of sins, and ye shall receive the gift of the Holy Spirit" (Acts 2:38); "Believe on the Lord Jesus Christ, and thou shalt be saved . . ." (Acts 16:31). The experience of remission is always and consistently preceded by the efforts of men. These are efforts determined by Divine directives, to be sure, but they are efforts!

Promises Held Out

Under the administraiton of Christ Jesus, the "Mediator of the New Covenant" (Heb. 12:24), we are taught to associate the realization of the promises with the expenditure of effort. "To them who by patient continuance in well doing seek for glory and honor and immortality, eternal life" (Rom. 2:27); "For ye have need of patience, that, after ye have done the will of God, ye might receive the promise" (Heb. 10:36); "Let us labor therefore to enter into that rest . . ." (Heb. 4:11). "Draw nigh unto God, and He will draw nigh unto you" (James 4:8). ". . . be thou faithful unto death, and I will give thee a crown of life" (Rev. 2:17).

This is a consistent emphasis throughout Scripture. God continually summons men to involvement in His kingdom: involvement that requires intense effort. Particularly since the exaltation of Christ, an appeal has been made for men to "awake to righteousness, and sin not" (I Cor. 15:34). With singleness of heart, men are to "put off" those things that displease God, and "put on" those things provided by the redemption that is in Christ Jesus (Eph. 4:22,24; Col. 3:9-12). There is no possibility for these things to be done independently of man's initiative. He must respond to the King of heaven if he is to be blessed by Him.

Demonstrations of This Principle

How often this principle is illustrated in Scripture! Abraham had to leave Ur before he could get into Canaan (Gen. 12:1). Israel had to depart Egypt before they could begin the journey to the promised land (Exod. 12). Peter, Andrew, James, and John had to forsake their boats and nets in order to follow Christ (Mark 1:16-20). Even our Lord Jesus Christ, in the accomplishment of His death (Luke 9:31), had to "set His face stedfastly to go to Jerusalem" (Luke 9:51) — a term denoting the marshalling of His personal resources for the work at hand.

Even though all of these examples involved the unquestionable will of God, yet He did not accomplish that "will" independently of the initiative of man. That is how our God rules! That is the manner of His kingdom!

Conclusion

When it comes to the matter of "eternal salvation" (Heb. 5:9), man is summoned to the most comprehensive use of his abilities. He is not primarily acted upon in redemption, but is challenged by the message of God's love in Christ Jesus to profitable initiative. In fact, "the love of Christ constrains us" (II Cor. 5:14)! The perception of God's sacrificial preference for fallen man awakens within men the very capabilities that have been blighted and numbed by sin!

How wonderfully becoming of our God to have innaugurated such a plan of reconciliation! In the grandest and fullest manifestation of God's kingdom, man is not overwhelmed, nor is he brought into God's favor by a secret and irresistible appointment. Rather, he experiences Divine provision as a result of the exercise of his initiative in response to the Gospel of Christ (Rom. 1:16).

In the entire matter the sovereign rule of God is not diminished, nor is His authority inactive. This is God's chosen manner of ruling. It is what dictated how man was created, as well as the image he bears. This manner of the Kingdom is at the very heart of redemption, whether in its dim and preparatory state under the "first covenant" (Heb. 9:1-10), or in its full administration by Christ Jesus (Heb. 8:6; 9:15). Wherever

God has had dealings with men, He has always required initiative. His promised benefits were never conferred independently of man's personal involvement.

It ought to be clear to every reader that the lack of hearty initiative in things pertaining to God is completely unacceptable! It is out of harmony with everything we know about our Lord. May you personally be a member of that company of individuals that are laboring to enter the rest that has been provided in Christ Jesus.

4

THE KINGDOM OF GOD, PERCEPTIONS AND VALUES

The Kingdom of God, to be properly understood, must be viewed in all of its varied aspects. Perceived from the viewpoint of its revelation, for example, it is the manifestation of God's rule. Thus, when Christ began shaking the kingdom of darkness, He said, "But if I with the finger of God cast out devils, no doubt the Kingdom of God is come upon you" (Luke 11:20); i.e., God openly demonstrated His reign by an overt assertion of His authority. Viewing that Kingdom from the vantage point of its Administrator, it is called "the Kingdom His Dear Son" (Col. 1:13).

Observe this same Kingdom from the standpoint of man's experience, and it is "righteousness, peace, and joy in the Holy Ghost" (Rom. 14:17). The contemplation of God's Kingdom from the standpoint of ultimate involvement in His "eternal purpose," prompted the Apostle to write of inheriting "the Kingdom of God" (I Cor. 6:9). See the Kingdom of God in contrast to this "present evil world" (Gal. 1:4), and you read of entering it, "through much tribulation (Acts 14:22). All of these representations deal with the Kingdom of our God — a single

59

Kingdom perceived from many different angles.

The Reality of Kingdom Worth

There is objective reality in the Kingdom of God — a whole body of interrelated truths. That reality is of supreme value to men. The grace of God, is the vehicle through which the Kingdom is administered. It is called a "treasure," and is possessed in our "earthern vessels" (II Cor. 4:7), the framework of our souls. This "Kingdom," positioned in heaven, is "like unto treasure hid in a field" (Matt. 13:44). Those that have, by faith an inheritance in that Kingdom have "treasure in heaven" (Mark 10:22).

The means of participation in this kingdom are the "treasures of wisdom and knowledge" (Col. 2:3). The realities that comprise the Kingdom are appropriately called the "true riches" (Luke 16:11).

The communication of God's purpose in Christ is called the "riches of His grace" (Eph. 1:7). All the benefits within the compass of the New Covenant are truly the "unsearchable riches of Christ" (Eph. 3:8). This Kingdom is actually the revelation of God in its highest and most detailed form. The Apostle referred to this marvelous revelation as "His riches in glory by Christ Jesus" (Phil. 4:19).

Valuable, But Not Scarce

The Kingdom of God is characterized by absolute and incontestable worth! It is not a figment of the imagination to which we are summoned by the Gospel; not an empty and vain "tradition" (I Pet. 1:18). Unlike the riches of this world, however, the worth of Kingdom treasures is not due to their scarcity. Heavenly realities are in abundance, as is depicted by the frequently used terms "freely" and "abundantly" (Rom. 8:32; I Cor. 2:12; Rev. 21:6; 22:17; Titus 3:6; II Pet. 1:11). Their value is determined by their eternality — by their inherent ability to outlast the present heavens and earth.

Completely independent of man's evaluation, everything about God's Kingdom is valuable, and has intrinsic worth! Whether it is perceived or not, the Kingdom of God is like a treasure. That is its nature!

The Priority of Perception

Perception is required in order to participate in the Kingdom of

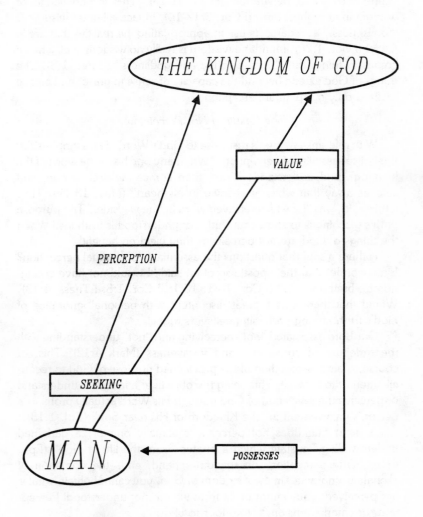

God. Perception speaks of "understanding" (Col. 2:2), comprehension (Eph. 3:18), and persuasion (Heb. 11:13). This is knowledge or wisdom in its highest form (I Cor. 2:12-14). In fact, all other wisdom is "foolishness," as regards its use in appropriating the realities that are in Christ (I Cor. 1:20). Mundane wisdom is really no wisdom at all when it comes to things that "pertain to life and godliness" (II Pet. 1:3). The things of God extend beyond the capacity of sense to grasp, and can be realized only by spiritual perception.

The Result of Not Perceiving

With reference to men's response to God's Word, Jesus emphasized the indispensability of perception. "When any one hears the word of the kingdom, and understands it not, then comes the wicked one, and catches away that which was sown in his heart" (Matt. 13:19). This, Christ said, was "he which received word by the wayside." The purpose of this teaching is to show that truth not understood is truth lost! When the things of God are not perceived, they yield no benefit!

Is there a soul that questions the essentiality of spiritual perception? Little wonder that the Apostle so often said "I would not have you ignorant, brethren . . ." (I Cor. 10:1; 12:1; II Cor. 1:8; I Thess. 4:13). Would that there was a great discontent with personal ignorance of God's truth among professing believers today!

Our Lord associated "not" perceiving and "not" understanding with the forfeiture of conversion and forgiveness (Mark 4:12). This, of course, is but a recognition of the proclaimed purpose of God to reconcile men unto Himself. This being the objective, a failure to understand or perceive the revelation of God through His Word actually prohibits a person's involvement in "the Kingdom of His dear Son" (Col. 1:13).

A heart that does not perceive is actually one of "a darkened understanding," a state which alienates "from the life of God" (Eph. 4:18). True perception, on the other hand, ends the dominion of alienating ignorance. In the Kingdom of God, you cannot obtain what is not perceived; you cannot profit from what is not understood! Perception, or comprehension, is the door to blessing.

The Exaltation of Understanding

Permit me to emphasize this point; it can easily be missed. God's objective in Christ is not merely to rule over men! Such an objective would not have required the vicarious sacrifice of God's "only begotten Son" (John 3:16). Men, further, cannot content themselves with merely conforming to religious ritual or outward form. Such things do not necessarily require the discernment and participation of the heart, nor do they essentially result from understanding! Literally myriads are attempting to serve the Living God in a state of spiritual ignorance. Such an effort is a contradiction, and it is impossible for it to succeed.

In God's Kingdom, what the eyes do not see, the heart must perceive. What the senses do not apprehend, faith must grasp! Everything about the full revelation of God and His "eternal purpose" in Christ summons us to perception, understanding, and comprehension. Unapprehended truth yields no blessing. A Savior that is not beheld is spiritually unavailing. A revelation that is not discerned cannot possibly confer benefit.

A basic truth of Scripture is that God Himself and His Kingdom can be discerned. If it were otherwise, the Scriptures are really irrelevant, if not completely useless. In that case the Bible would constitute the revelation of imperceivable realities, the awareness of which it yet represents as necessary to our salvation. Such a presentation would be unbecoming of the God of the Bible.

Our Heavenly Father asserted His desire for "understanding" in "his offspring." He said, "Let not the wise man glory in his wisdom, neither let the mighty man glory in his might, let not the rich man glory in his riches: but let him that glories glory in this, that he understands and knows Me . . . for in these things I delight . . ." (Jer. 9:23-24). God's Kingdom is never more in evidence than when men, to some measurable extent, comprehend God and His purpose!

Kingdom Perception Must Be Valued

One of the great ironies associated with the Kingdom of God is that although it is valuable — nay, of inestimable worth — yet it may be contemplated with indifference, or even rejection. That "certain ruler" who came "running" to Jesus, asking, "Good master, what shall I do to inherit eternal life?" (Luke 18:18; Mark 10:17) demonstrated the possibility.

The Savior pulled back the curtain that had veiled the Kingdom of God, and proclaimed both the the uniqueness of "God," and the possibility of securing treasure in His Kingdom. He also indicated something of the cost entailed when we "follow" Him (Mark 10:18-21; Matt. 19:21). While that revelation to the ruler was not the ultimate, yet it unquestionably exposed his heart and mind to the realities of God's Kingdom and the fact that there were exacting conditions for its obtainment. The young man heard the pronouncement, thought upon it, and perceived somewhat of its significance. He then decided to refuse that Kingdom . . . to reject the opportunity of having "treasure in heaven"! He valued the temporal things of this life above the eternal ones of heaven. It is written that "he went away sorrowful: for he had great possessions" (Matt. 19:22). He thus judged himself "unworthy" of the very "everlasting life" he had sought to "inherit" (Acts 13:46).

It is also possible for those that once embraced the Kingdom to make "shipwreck of the faith" (I Tim. 1:19), to "fall away" (Luke 8:13; Heb. 6:6)), and to have their preference for heavenly things "choked" with the "cares of this world" (Mark 4:19). In other words, it is possible to lose a proper sense of values once they are possessed. Not only must the Kingdom of God be duly esteemed initially, that evaluation must be maintained by fighting the "good fight of faith" (I Tim. 6:12) and by "patient continuance in well doing" (Rom. 2:7).

It is not enough, therefore, to be introduced to the Kingdom of God! To come into the threshold of reality is not sufficient. One must personally value what is perceived and respond accordingly.

The Truth in Parables

In two parables of immediate relevance, our Lord emphasized the need for recognition of the Kingdom's worth.

"The Kingdom of heaven," He proclaimed, "is like unto a treasure hid in the field." That "treasure" was "found" by "a man"! Engaged in the foreordained pursuit of the Living God (Acts 17:26-27), he discovered eternal realities. So wonderful were they that the man, persuaded of its value, "goes, and sells all that he has, and buys that field" (Matt. 13:44). He refused to permit the seen to obscure the unseen, the temporal to conceal the eternal. He valued what he saw!

Again, Jesus said that "the Kingdom of heaven is like unto a merchant man seeking goodly pearls: who, when he had found one pearl of great price, went and sold all that he had, and bought it" (Matt. 13:46). The emphasis of this parable is different from that of the preceding one. The first stressed the inherent worth of the Kingdom, independent of man's awareness of it. It is like a hidden treasure. God has provided a great and valuable Kingdom for men, though they know not of it.

This second parable emphasizes man's awareness of the Kingdom's genuine worth: a lively recognition, as it were, of its preeminent value. This cognizance is due to the reality of the Kingdom of God rather than man's quest for it.

Man, made in the image of God, is inclined Godward for at least three reasons. 1. There is a Kingdom for which man is adapted by creation. 2. Man has been created in the image of the Ruler of that Kingdom. 3. God has "determined" man's principal activity, which is to seek the Kingdom; and has created him with disposition toward that end. The "man seeking goodly pearls" speaks of the individual that engaged in his appointed pursuit with more than a casual effort.

Perceived by Contrast

Actually, the value of the Kingdom of God is perceived by contrast. When it is compared with "the things that are seen," it is unquestionably superior. In reference to this very experience, the Apostle wrote, "But what things were gain to me, those I counted loss for Christ" (Phil. 3:7). Elaborating, he continued: "Yea, doubtless, and I count all things but loss for the excellency of the knowledge of Christ Jesus my Lord: for whom I have suffered the loss of all things, and do count them but dung" (Phil. 3:8-9). The "knowledge of Christ" is nothing more than the experience of the Kingdom of God; the interplay of man's essential person with the objectives of God Himself, as they are revealed in Christ Jesus.

A determined preference for the Kingdom of God is absolutely essential! The reason for the abandonment of purely earthly pursuits by Paul was "that I may win Christ, and be found in Him . . . having . . . the righteousness which is of God by faith" (Phil. 3:8b-9). Without the proper and resolute evaluation of the perceived Kingdom of God, there will be no fellowship with Christ and no acceptable righteousness before God. That is simply another way of saying that there is no salvation or promise of eternal life unless men abandon earthly priorities for the Kingdom's demands of them.

A Price Must Be Paid

The Divine requirement for participation in the Kingdom is proclaimed in a fundamental requirement of Christ. "So likewise, whosoever he be of you that forsakes not all that he has, he cannot be my disciple" (Luke 14:33). A "disciple" is a learner, a student, one that is "taught of God" (John 6:45).

Think of the implications of this pronouncement! Unless a person, of his own volition, seeks first the Kingdom of God, considering everything in this world unworthy of preeminence, he cannot be taught by Christ. The Lord Jesus will not instruct such a one in things pertaining to God! He will not be a "Counsellor" to those that do not pay the price required to "buy the truth" (Prov. 23:23). It is a sad reality that literally multitudes of casual inquirers have been excluded from Divine instruction simply because they were not willing to "leave all."

Jesus' recognition of this necessity — to sanctify Him and the Kingdom in the heart — is unmistakable. "And every one that hath forsaken houses, or brethren, or sisters, or father, or mother, or wife, or children or lands, for my name's sake, shall receive an hundredfold, and shall inherit eternal life" (Matt. 19:29).

This must not be construed as a mandate to withdraw from all social and domestic responsibilities! It is, instead, an announcement that competitive interests must be subordinated to the things of God. At the point where temporal relationships interfere with spiritual progress, a decision must be made! Heaven or earth! God or man! The Kingdom of God or the kingdoms of men! That choice cannot be ignored! Confrontation with the truth will bring inevitable conflict. The degree of that conflict may vary, but when it comes — whatever the degree — men either prefer the things of God or lose them; they either desire the personal tutelage of Christ, or forfeit it! There are no alternatives.

The blessed recompense of such sacrifice, as proclaimed by the Lord in the cited text, or course, must be kept in mind. It yields "an hundredfold," and produces "eternal life" for those who make it. God, of a truth, "is able," and unfailingly will, give "much more than this" to those who put Him and His Kingdom first in their hearts and lives (II Chron. 25:9). Thus Paul's assertion, "I reckon that the sufferings of this present time are not worthy to be compared with the glory which shall be revealed in us" (Rom. 8:18).

Once an individual perceives the Kingdom of God and, duly evaluating it, embraces the Kingdom, direct confrontation with the world and its system begins. This world competes with "the world to come" (Heb. 2:5), and the lusts that are part and parcel of this world (I John 2:15-17) war against one's interest in and devotion to the coming world.

A Decision Must Be Made

There are at least two possible responses to this inevitable conflict. Either men will "confess" Christ "before men," acknowledging their preference for the truth, or they will "deny" Him before men, permitting the pressures of earth's kingdoms to neutralize their affection for God. Speaking of this very conflict, Jesus proclaimed, "Whosoever shall confess me before men, him will I confess also before my Father which is in heaven. But whosoever shall deny me before men, him will I also deny before my father which is in heaven" (Matt. 10:32-33).

Not only, therefore, is the Kingdom of God preeminent; there cannot be participation in it without an open acknowledgement of that superiority and determined committment to it. The confession or acknowledgement of Christ is not merely verbal, although that is involved. That confession is the embracing of the things He reveals, and a refocusing of our attention and energies upon the unworldly kingdom He administers. Various expressions in Scripture proclaim the superior value of the Kingdom of God. The Head of the Kingdom Himself is "precious." He is identified as a "precious corner stone," determining the direction and boundaries of the Kingdom (Isa. 28:16; I Pet. 2:6). Peter, elaborating upon this reality, states, "To whom coming, as unto a living stone, disallowed indeed of men, but chosen of God, and precious" (I Pet. 2:4).

Because Christ Himself is precious, our faith which connects us with Him is also precious. Thus we read of "like precious faith" (II Pet. 1:1). That very faith transmits to our consciousness the inestimable value of Christ. Therefore we read, "Unto you therefore that believe, He is precious . . ." (I Pet. 2:7). VALUE! The blood of Christ, which is the foundation of the New Covenant, is appropriately called "the precious blood of Christ" (I Pet. 1:19). All of the promises of God in Christ, further, are truly "great and precious promises" (II Pet. 1:4), and the faith that embraces them is a "like precious faith" (II Pet. 1:1).

Everything about the Kingdom of God, therefore, is of inherent and exceeding great worth! Its Administrator — Christ Jesus, the basis for its administration — Christ's blood, the commitments of God — His prom-

67

ises, and the means of embracement — faith: all are exceeding precious!

Conclusion

Divine benefits have been made accessible to men by the plain words of Scripture. The means through which they are embraced is faith. It is "the substance of things hoped for, the evidence of things not seen" (Heb. 11:1). If there are not things "hoped for," there can be no faith, for faith is the "substance" of preferred and sought for heavenly realities. When "the testimony of God" (I Cor. 2:1) is received, and the favorable persuasion of that reality settles upon the soul, we have the "evidence of things not seen" — faith! Everything associated with that process is "precious"!

But these things must be preferred because of their value. They must be wholeheartedly embraced, not merely acknowledged. In Christ Jesus, God's Kingdom is administered through this means. God will not use His omnipotence to compensate for a refusal to embrace the truth. He will not ignore the requirement for faith, nor will He intrude faith into a rebellious heart. But for those that hear the truth, perceive its reality, and consider it of greater value than "the whole world" (Matt. 16:26), God's Kingdom is said to be effectually "received" (Heb. 12:28).

No word on this subject is complete without a hearty exhortation to embrace "the word of the Kingdom" (Matt. 13:19) at all cost! When you perceive it, you are perceiving reality, not a figmentary concept. When you see it as "precious," you are perceiving it as it is. When you confess its reality in the face of settled opposition, you are conforming to Divine rule.

The converse is, of course, equally true. When you hear the announcement of God's beneficent rule in Christ, and do not inquire into it, desiring to appropriate its fullness, you have denied the truth and excluded yourself from eternal life. What God proclaims must be believed! What He provides must be embraced! What He gives must be received! That is the way He rules — that is the way He administers His Kingdom.

5

THE KINGDOM OF GOD, INCENTIVES
AND REWARDS

The Kingdom of God — the inscrutibly wise implementation of Divine purpose — involves a sincere appeal to man. The intention of God is to "bless" man in "turning away every one . . . from his iniquities" (Acts 3:26). Because of the unique constitution of man, God has chosen to involve both Himself and man in His plan of redemption. God's desire and man's desire intermingle in the Divine undertaking: to turn away every one "from his iniquities."

Salvation, which is the ultimate objective of the Kingdom of God's "dear Son" (Col. 1:13), involves the highest known expressions of both God and man! God appears in His most lofty capacity in the provision of redemption, and man is found at his apex in the appropriation of that redemption by faith.

God's Intent to Benefit Man

While this point has already been made, it requires further elaboration because of its current obscurement. In the consideration of God's Kingdom, it must be remembered that the purpose is to benefit man.

God is not represented as being pleased merely because He does whatever He wills.

The term "the good pleasure of His will" (Eph. 1:5,9) does not imply that God is pleased merely because He executes His preference. It is the nature of that will in Christ that makes it particularly pleasing to God.

Think of the frequent references to what pleased God, and how they are immediately associated with the reconciliation of man. "Having predestinated us unto the adoption of children by Christ Jesus to Himself, according to the good pleasure of His will" (Eph. 1:5); "Having made known unto us the mystery of His will, according to His good pleasure which He hath purposed in Himself: that in the dispensation of the fullness of times He might gather into one all things in Christ . . ." (Eph. 1:9-10). In these texts, God is represented as determining the ultimate good of all that are in Christ. That good is conferred "by" and "in" Christ.

God's Good Pleasure

Concerning the actual accomplishment of reconciliation it is written, ". . . when it pleased God to reveal His Son . . ." (Gal. 1:15); ". . . it pleased the Father that in Him [Christ] should all fulness dwell . . . " (Col. 1:19). In the proclamation of His unqualified pleasure in Christ Jesus, He proclaimed at His baptism and at His transfiguration, ". . . this is my beloved Son, in Whom I am well pleased . . ." (Matt. 3:17; 17:5).

The point to be seen in all of this is that what pleased God involved His provision for man's salvation. His satisfaction and good pleasure, then, involves the extension of His love to His intelligent "offspring." This is why He has "no pleasure in the death of the wicked" (Ezek. 18:32; 33:11). The very thought of their death in their rebellion and sin contravenes His desire for men — the salvation revealed for them.

This is why God "will have all men to be saved, and to come unto the knowledge of the truth" (I Tim. 2:4). Again it is declared, "For God so loved the world . . ." (John 3:16). The revealed fact is that He "is not willing that any should perish, but that all should come to repentance" (I Pet. 3:9). There can be no doubt; God wants to bless us! He desires that every one be saved and come into a personal awareness of the truth! He does not desire or prefer the damnation of anyone.

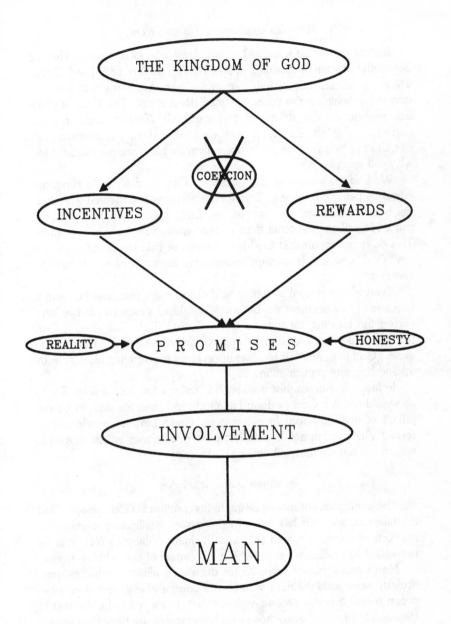

Why Do Unpleasing Things Occur?

But the fact is that some will perish, some will not be saved. "He that believeth not shall be damned" (Mark 16:16), declared our Lord. There will be those that have "their part in the lake that burns with fire and brimstone: which is the second death" (Rev. 21:8). The Lord of glory will pronounce the doom of the damned: "Depart from me, ye cursed . . ." (Matt. 25:41). If God wants all men saved, then why will not all men be saved? If He is not willing that any should perish, then why will any perish?

We find the answer to this question in the facet of God's Kingdom currently being considered: Divine coercion is not connected with eternal benefit. God will not, in this life, force men to acknowledge the truth. He will not use other than earnest appeals in order to save men. This does not mean that God is not King, or that His Kingdom is not real! God is no less Sovereign because He does not bestow benefit by coercion!

Everywhere eternal benefit is held out to men, response by them is required. No response, no blessing! The Lord Jesus Christ has procurred the blessing for man; it is "in Christ" (Eph. 1:3; 3:6; II Cor. 5:17); and it is there to be had by all who will receive it. But no man can expect God to confer His blessing upon him by overriding his will, or by forcing him into participation.

In fact, blessing cannot possibly be conferred in such a way. To do so would require God to deny His Godhood, and for man to be deprived of his manhood. In either case, God's purpose would not be served! Once this principle is understood, sincere men will be moved to activity — activity that will obtain the blessing.

Intelligence and Incentives

The intelligence of man is owing to his creation in God's image. God is intelligent, and thus His "offspring" are also. Intelligence refers to the ability to discern, comprehend, and evaluate. Objective facts can be presented to intelligent beings with the prospect of favorable response.

Man's moral power refers to his decision-making capabilities, particularly as regards the determination of good and evil, and choice between them. It is this unique aptitude that is referred to by the text in Hebrews 5:14: ". . . even those who by reason of use have their senses

exercised to discern both good and evil."
"The Man Christ Jesus" (I Tim. 2:5) fully demonstrated this ability
and practice. It was prophesied of Him that He would be able to "know
to refuse the evil, and choose the good" (Isa. 7:15). Here ability was
augmented by knowledge, for it is not enough to merely be cognizant of
good and evil. There must be an ability and inclination to "refuse the
evil and choose the good"; else the ability is but a source of condemnation.

The Kingdom Presented Intelligently

The Kingdom of God is represented to us by verbal expression —
"the word of the Kingdom" (Matt. 13:19,20,22,23), or the "gospel of
the Kingdom" (Matt. 24:14). God, in His Word, freely declares His purpose in Christ Jesus, together with the requirements for participation in
that purpose.

Included in that proclamation are certain incentives designed to at-
tract our spirits to reality. Incentives are a requirement for intelligent
moral beings. A change of heart and a reestablishment of goals cannot
be accomplished by a mere mandate. The truth of this was
demonstrated by "the law" which "made nothing perfect" (Heb. 7:19).

An intelligent presentation promotes thought, and thought enables
men to participate. The primary responsibility of man is to love the Lord
his God with all his "Mind" (Mark 12:30; Luke 10:27). The Apostle
recognized that serving God involved the mind when he said, ". . . with
my mind I myself serve the law of God" (Rom. 7:25). The position of
man's mind in the fellowship of the truth is repeatedly proclaimed. We
read of "readiness of mind" (Acts 17:11), "humility of mind" (Acts
20:19), and "a willing mind" (II Cor. 8:12). Our minds are employed in
the glorification of God (Rom. 15:6), and we are exhorted, "Gird up
the loins of your mind" (I Pet. 1:13).

These expressions complement the Scriptural presentation of God's
Kingdom. Its very proclamation summons the most noble use of man's
mind. The mind finds its greatest challenge in the embracement of God's
Kingdom. God's aim, in Christ, is to reconcile those that are "alienated
and enemies" in their mind "by wicked works" (Col. 1:21). This condition is remedied when the mind is employed in the apprehension of "all
things that pertain unto life and godliness" (II Pet. 1:3).

The heavenly Kingdom cannot be embraced unless it is perceived.

73

That condition necessitates an intelligent acquaintance with it. Preaching what is mysterious brings no spiritual benfit. Kingdom incentives constitute an intelligent appeal to men. They are necessary because of the reflection of the Divine image in man. Incentives, further, enable men to have a rational view of God's Kingdom. The compatibility of truth with reason is essential if it is to be embraced.

The Offer of Reward Is Trustworthy

The promise of a reward constitutes an incentive. With men, promises are sometimes untrustworthy, but not so with the Living God. His promises are a reflection of His Person, and may be relied upon with all confidence. They are a legitimate appeal to man, and are without guile in their nature.

God's promises are perfectly harmonious with His purpose. At no point are they at variance with His redemptive undertaking. It is "by these" that men become "partakers of the Divine nature" (II Pet. 1:4) and experience participation in the Kingdom.

Two distinct periods are referenced by the promises of God. "Today" is a Scriptural term describing the time allotted to mankind in this present world (Psa. 95:7; Heb. 3:7,13,17; 4:7). This period of time is also referred to as "now" (II Cor. 6:2; Eph. 3:10; I Pet. 1:8). "The ages to come" (Eph. 2:7), on the other hand, allude to the future, when there will be "new heavens and a new earth" (II Pet. 3:13). Then the "first," or current, heaven and earth shall have "passed away" (Rev. 21:1).

Ultimately, there are only two times: "now" (I John 3:2) and "then" (I Cor. 13:12). Also, there are, in the final analysis, only two places: "here" (Heb. 13:14) and "there" (Rev. 21:25; 22:5). God's promises, or commitments, apply to both times and both places.

Rewards Are Promised

The offer of Divine reward provides a motive for faithfulness. In order to accomplish this objective, the offer must be understandable. It must also be perceived as honest and straightforward. When God made the promises in His Word, He underscored their absolute reliability. His Kingdom and its realization revolve around His Word — the "word of the Kingdom."

There are rewards that may be realized "here" and "now." To those who are "careful for nothing," but rather make known their requests to God, it is promised, "and the peace of God, which passes all understanding, shall keep your hearts and minds through Christ Jesus" (Phil. 4:6-7). Men that "seek first the Kingdom of God and His righteousness" are promised the temporal necessities of this life (Matt. 6:31-33). The promise of Divine companionship is held out to men that separate from "coveteousness" and are "content with such things" as they have (Heb. 13:5). These promises are absolute truth!

There are also incentives given to men regarding the "ages to come" — the "then" and "there." "Whosoever therefore shall confess me before men," declared our Lord Jesus, "him will I also confess before my Father which is in heaven" (Matt. 10:32). Responsive souls that "give diligence" to make their "calling and election sure" are promised, "For so an entrance shall be ministered unto you abundantly into the everlasting Kingdom of our Lord and Savior Jesus Christ" (II Pet. 1:10-11). To those who subdue fleshly inclinations, it is promised, "When Christ, who is our life, shall appear, then shall ye also appear with Him in glory" (Col. 3:1-4). These are very real and definite commitments!

God Cannot Lie

The truth is that the Living God simply does not lie, He cannot lie! That is a matter of revelation. "In hope of eternal life, which God, that cannot lie, promised before the world began" (Titus 1:2). God's inability to lie is not due to His restraint by certain laws or established guidelines external to Himself. Lying is contrary to His very nature, and He "cannot deny Himself" (II Tim. 2:13). For God to lie would involve an abandonment of His Godhood — an impossibility! If our God has declared it, men can implicitly rest in that declaration.

The fact that God Himself has made the promises — and has given the incentives — removes any question concerning their reliability. He "is not slack concerning His promise" (II Pet. 3:9), and is "faithful and just" (I John 1:9) to do exactly what He has promised. His commitments are not hyperbole, or exaggerations. If they seem too good to be true, unbelief has made them so appear.

No Variableness With Him

It is truly refreshing to contemplate the absolute faithfulness of God.

He does not make commitments only to break them. "God is not a man, that He should lie; neither the son of man, that He should repent," declared an unwitting prophet (Num. 23:19). That the assertion is true, Samuel confirmed (I Sam. 15:29).

David, taking up the theme of God's lack of variableness, declared, "The counsel of the Lord standeth forever" (Psa. 33:11). Again, clearly identifying God's commitments with His Word, he said, "Forever, O Lord, thy word is settled in heaven" (Psa. 119:89). In Personal confirmation of this truth, God Himself said, "I am the Lord, I change not . . . " (Mal. 3:6). His "counsel" is, indeed, "immutable" (Heb. 6:18).

James proclaimed that the "Father of lights" is He "with whom is no variableness, neither shadow of turning" (James 1:17). That is language for faith, but apart from faith it holds no blessing! God has made His commitments in view of Christ, and all that "cleave" unto Him "with purpose of heart" (Acts 11:23) are assured of their realization. Those that elect to play with God forfeit all promises of good — and with God, there is "no variableness neither shadow of turning."

Real Effort, Real Reward

In an alarmingly successful effort, Satan has deceived many concerning the reign of Almighty God. Myriads live in the persuasion that God will bring the blessing independently of their personal efforts. God's Kingdom, to them, involves the powerful overthrow of their sinful inclinations, and the personal establishment of them in glory in spite of their waywardness. Nothing could be further from the truth! Rewards are promised to the laborers, not to the slothful. Incentives are held out to the workers, not to the indolent.

If we are to receive the promise of "the rest" (Heb. 4:9), we must "labor" to enter it (Heb. 4:11). The reaping of eternal benefits is conditional: ". . . we shall reap in due season, if we faint not" (Gal. 6:9). God has declared that "if we suffer, we shall also reign with Him" (II Tim. 2:12). The things that God has reserved are "for them that love Him" (I Cor. 2:9). The fact is our reward is only as secure as our effort to obtain it. Real effort, real reward!

The spiritual blessing of God is contingent upon obedience. This is the consistent representation throughout the Scriptures. "If thou wilt diligently hearken . . . " (Exod. 15:26); ". . . if ye will obey my voice indeed . . ." (Exod. 19:5); "Only if thou carefully hearken unto the voice of the Lord thy God . . ." (Deut. 15:4). It is "after we have done the will of God" that we are assured of receiving the promise (Heb. 10:36). Faithfulness "unto death" necessarily precedes the reception of "the crown of life" (Rev. 2:10). Godly individuals that have preceded us demonstrated that "through faith and patience" the promises are inherited (Heb. 6:12).

The incentives offered to us in the Gospel of Christ, when embraced by faith, enable us to be "stedfast and unmovable, always abounding in the work of the Lord" (I Cor. 15:58). Without those Gospel incentives, efforts are apt to eventually wane and cease.

Legitimate Self-Interest

Man, by nature, seeks his own interests. "No man ever yet hated his own flesh; but nourisheth and cherisheth it . . ." (Eph. 5:27), declares the Word of God. "Self-esteem," as it is often called, is an unavoidable part of the natural makeup of man. The above text does not mean there has never been an individual that was inconsiderate of his personal welfare. What it does mean is that any such attitude must be acquired — it is not natural.

God's Kingdom speaks of man in his natural condition, one which is characterized by unavoidable self-interest. The requirement for self-denial is given with this situation in mind (Matt. 16:24; Luke 14:26; John 12:25). The denial of self is not a requirement for a portion of our race, but for all it! Continued pursuit of earthly self-interests will eventuate in spiritual death. "For if ye live after the flesh, ye shall die," proclaims the Apostle (Rom. 8:13). A strong word like this would have no significance were it not for man's strong proclivity toward selfishness.

There are at least three ways to deal with the unavoidable presence of self-interest. One can cast all hope of glory aside, and pursue the gratification of fleshly appetites. This will, however, only bring eternal condemnation. One can also retreat into the practice of self-abuse, like the monks of bygone days. Starvation, self-flagellation, together with senseless and punishing disciplines, will not achieve merit or bring the commendation of God. The only acceptable approach to this situation is to engage in a quest for the highest personal benefit! It is to our ultimate advantage to seek first the Kingdom of God and His righteousness.

In the provision of salvation, there is an appeal made to personal benefit. It is "he that believeth and is baptized" that "shall be saved" (Mark 16:16). The individual that seeks is the individual that finds (Matt. 7:7). When we lay up treasures in heaven, it is for ourselves, and not for another (Matt. 6:19). The reason why men are encouraged to energetically "run" the appointed obstacle course to glory is that they might "obtain" the prize of eternal life (I Cor. 9:24).

In all of the promises, God appeals to our basic interest in self. However, rather than offering to us the temporal gratification of the flesh, He summons us upward to Himself. Fellowship with Him brings the highest and most lasting degree of satisfaction. Looking beyond the curse, David cried, "I shall be satisfied, when I awake, with Thy likeness" (Psa. 17:15).

In an expression depicting man's interest in personal advantage, David said, "My soul shall be satisfied as with marrow and fatness . . ." (Psa. 63:5). He was speaking of finding God, and of the experience of Divine fellowship. He had expressed his personal thirst for the Living God — his craving to behold and perceive His power, and to experience His lovingkindness (Psa. 63:1-3). Satisfaction would be his when this was realized. His attitude had been provoked by his submission to the Word of God!

Behold the appeal to personal interest in the promises of God. "But if any man love God, the same is known of him" (I Cor. 8:3). Personal intimacy with the living God — there is no higher form of gratification! "And let us not be weary in well doing," exhorts the Apostle, "for in due season we shall reap if we faint not" (Gal. 6:9). If there were no eternal reaping, one would be hard pressed to find a sound reason for energetically pursuing "well doing"!

The Lord provides us with good reason for willingly doing service unto the Lord instead of unto men: "Knowing that whatsoever good thing any man doeth, the same shall he receive of the Lord . . ." (Eph. 6:8). There it is — an appeal to self-interest. But it is a righteous appeal!

Moses was confronted with a choice that involved self-interest. He could choose temporal benefit or eternal benefit — the gratification of the lower nature, or an investment in the future. It is written that he "refused to be called the son of Pharaoh's daughter . . . esteeming the reproach of Christ as greater riches than the treasure in Egypt: for he had respect unto the recompense of the reward" (Heb. 11:24-26). The point here is that submission to God produced this attitude. The reason — God deliberately appeals to man's interest in himself!

The promise of "eternal life" (Titus 1:1) is God's principal appeal to you. Take personal advantage out of the Gospel, and there really is not much left! "There remains a rest to the people of God" (Heb. 4:9), ". . . a crown of righteousness . . ." (II Tim. 4:8), "Draw nigh unto God, and He will draw nigh unto you" (James 4:8). God does not demand our allegiance without the offer of rewards. It is not a matter of obligation — God owes us nothing. However, His salvation is precisely structured for His "offspring." It appeals to men by the presentation of advantages and rewards.

Saving Yourselves

"This is a faithful saying, and worthy of all acceptation, that Christ Jesus came into the world to save sinners . . ." (I Tim. 1:15). This is a "faithful" saying in that it cannot be contradicted or negated. It is "worthy of all acceptation" because there is not a son of Adam to whom it does not apply. This is why Jesus came into the world (Matt. 18:11; John 12:47). His incarnation was not to bring destruction, but salvation (Luke 9:56).

This great salvation, however, does not exclude man's initiative and involvement. The rule and will of God, particularly in man's reconciliation, is not accomplished without man's participation. The salvation of God requires the involvement of those being saved. Faith and obedience are the required responses. Without them, there can be no salvation.

There is no more legitimate form of self-interest than the desire to be saved! In fact, if a person is not seriously interested in being saved, he cannot be saved! The desire, will, and effort of man are some of the means through which salvation is implemented.

During the inauguration of the church, the "keys of the Kingdom" (Matt. 16:19) were used to give men access to heaven. With earnest appeal, Peter cried, "Save yourselves from this untoward generation" (Acts 2:40)! There is a crooked, a perverse, a contaminated generation that applies relentless pressure on everyone within its domain. Recognizing this situation, Peter said, "Save yourselves"! Place your illuminated interests above those of this wicked and unjust generation!

Taking Heed Unto Yourselves

There is a sense in which Divine blessings are administered because of personal interests. Both the old and new covenants require devotion to self. "Take heed unto yourself and unto the doctrine; continue in them: for in doing this you shalt both save yourself, and them that hear you" (I Tim. 4:16).

Taking heed to yourself involves pursuing your highest interests. It is seeking to gain the best and lawful advantage for yourself. Diligent effort is required in this matter. "Study to show thyself approved unto God, a workman that needeth not to be ashamed, rightly dividing [handling aright] the word of truth" (II Tim. 2:15). The "study" indicates that this effort requires the employment of the heart and mind. It is not to be casual, or performed with little interest.

The essentiality of taking heed to ourselves is often proclaimed in Scripture. In the work of reclaiming those overtaken with faults, we are admonished, "considering yourself, lest you also be tempted" (Gal. 6:1). It is ourself that is to be shown a "pattern of good works" (Titus 2:7). In addition, the maintenance of purity is a personal responsibility; "Keep yourself pure" (I Tim. 5:22).

Conclusion

There is good reason for these admonitions. The Kingdom of God involves an appeal to men; the offering of incentives and rewards. These are very real, and may be obtained by all that desire them. Everyone of them appeal to the individual, and the individual is clearly profited by them. Eternal life, peace, joy, righteousness, strength — they are all personalized in Christ. None of them is impersonal — all of them are fitted to the individual.

So far as you are concerned, there is no point to eternal life if you do not possess it! The covenantal blessings of God in Christ are for you. Your interest in them, however, must precede your realization of them. They will not be conferred upon you arbitrarily, but will come in Divine response to your preference of and desire for them.

The promises of God — the proclamation of His incentives and rewards — are the appointed means of kindling the interest of man. They all speak of personal advantage and individual benefit. They presume that those hearing them have an interest in their own welfare.

The Gospel of Christ sets the truth before the mind. It provides a Divine perspective of this world and the one to come. Then, within that vista, it offers promises of personal reward and benefit. "He that believeth and is baptized shall be saved" (Mark 16:16); "But he that shall endure to the end, the same shall be saved" (Matt. 24:13). Those that embrace "the truth in Christ" (I Tim. 2:7) obtain for themselves "in heaven a better and an enduring substance" (Heb. 10:34).

The nature of God, the nature of man, and the nature of the New Covenant, require that incentives be provided to alert and encourage man. He is in a hostile environment that is governed by his adversary, the "prince" and "god" of this world (John 14:30; II Cor. 4:4). Not only is man faced with the opposition of Satan himself, but "the flesh lusts against the Spirit, and the Spirit against the flesh," producing great inhibitions (Gal. 5:17). "Principalities," "powers," "the rulers of the darkness of this world," and "spiritual wickedness in high places" also maliciously war against man (Eph. 6:12).

Faced with these extremely adverse conditions, it is not enough to merely know one's obligation Godward. His spiritual makeup requires that incentives be provided. Man's heart and mind, his strength and aptitude are awakened by his response to Divine incentives. Thus believers are exhorted, "Having therefore these promises, dearly beloved, let us cleanse ourselves from all filthiness of the flesh and spirit, perfecting holiness in the fear of God" (II Cor. 7:1).

The revelation of God's many incentives does not simply indicate that there are a lot of benefits in Christ. It is also an indication of the heart of Jehovah God. He has offered many incentives because His great heart yearns for His offspring. God "so loved the world" — that is anything but an empty and heartless proclamation.

I would certainly be remiss in my responsibility, if I did not urge you to personally and seriously consider the promises of God. They are the Divine incentives. Take them seriously, for they are meant to be so taken. In settled persuasion of the absolute dependability of His "great and precious promises" (II Pet. 1:4), "labor" for "that meat which endures unto everlasting life" (John 6:27).

6

MAN'S ACCOUNTABILITY TO GOD

God does not bring salvation by acting upon men, but by working within those that "receive the love of the truth" (II Thess. 2:10). By means of the truth, God impregnates the spirit of man. There is a basic union wrought between God and man. "He that is joined to the Lord is one spirit," asserts the Apostle (I Cor. 6:17). The minuteness of this unity is proclaimed in Paul's description of the church: "For we are members of His body, of His flesh, and of His bones" (Eph. 5:30).

The obvious reference is to the original creation of Adam and Eve. "And the Lord God caused a deep sleep to fall upon Adam . . . and He took one of his ribs . . . and the rib . . . made He a woman, and brought her unto the man" (Gen. 2:21-22). Adam assessed the gift in these words: "This is now bone of my bones, and flesh of my flesh . . . therefore . . . they shall be one flesh" (Gen. 2:23-24).

We have here the representation of two aspects of unity: source and participation. As Adam was the source of Eve's life, so Christ is the source of the life of the church. Equally true, as Eve partook of the nature of Adam, so the church partakes of "Christ," or of the "Divine nature" (Heb. 3:14; II Pet. 1:4). This is what is comprehended in the saying, "members of His body, of His flesh, and of His bones."

The very possibility of union between God and man introduces the element of responsibility. Men are responsible to God for availing themselves of this provision, for God has prepared it specifically and exclusively for them. Those that experientially participate in this union are charged with the responsibility of maintaining it to God's glory.

The Necessity of Accountability

God has given account to man "of His matters," even though He was not obligated to do so (John 33:13). In fact, He has gone to great lengths to explain His great works. He has provided us with the reason for His creation of man (Gen. 1:26,28-29; Heb. 2:5-8). He has provided us with the history of and the reason for the destruction of the world by a flood (Gen. 6-7). God has explained why He chose Abraham to father the elect nation of Israel (Gen. 18:19).

The Living God, Who is under no obligation to provide us reasons for His judgments, has explained precisely why people will be condemned (Mark 16:16; John 3:19-20), and why they will be saved (Mark 16:16; Acts 4:12; 16:31). When certain members of the Corinthian church grew weak and sickly, and some even died, God told them why it occurred (I Cor. 11:29-32). He even revealed why Jerusalem fell into the hands of its enemies (Matt. 23:37-38).

A detailed explanation has been provided of why Christ died (I Cor. 15:3), why He arose (Rom. 4:25), and why He is coming again (Heb. 9:28). God has explained why the Holy Spirit has been sent into the world (John 16:7-11), and why He has inspired the Scriptures (I Tim. 3:16-17).

For God to give account of His matters mandates that His offspring do the same. This is a principle that is applicable to moral beings. The Heavenly Father gives account without obligation. Man, however, is under obligation to do so.

Man Is God's Offspring

Man is not an accident. He is not the result of a supposed evolutionary progression. He is the intelligent offspring of the Monarch of creation (Acts 17:28,29). It was the "breath of life," breathed into man's nostrils by God Himself that constituted him a "living soul," distinct from

84

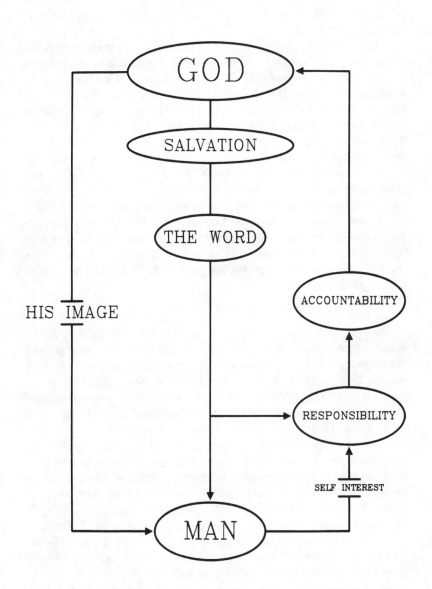

all other life. This is what made man God's "offspring"; he has a nature like that of his Maker.

Man is the result of Divine contemplation: "Let us make man in our image, after our likeness . . ." (Gen. 1:26). Here we have an index to the nature of the Godhead. Inherent in the Person of God is a desire for the extension of the "Divine nature." While God is supreme, He is not Self-centered, not Egocentric. It is true that He will not "give" His glory "to another," or share His praise with "graven images" (Isa. 42:8). That is, He will not permit those that are by nature "no gods" (Jer. 2:11) to be credited with Divine attributes.

Man was made, however, with the Divine image deliberately stamped upon him. This condition is the reflection of God's purpose for man, a purpose which involved man's participation in Divine rule. "Let them have dominion," said the Lord (Gen. 1:26). This did not constitute a reliquishment of rule by God, but a sharing of Divine rule with man. That is God's ultimate objective for man. That is why he was created. That is why he bears the image of God. That is why he is called God's "offspring."

Divine Reasoning

As the offspring of God, it is man's responsibility to be knowledgeable about His Creator. His thoughts of God must be proper. "Forasmuch then as we are the offspring of God, we ought not to think that the Godhead is like unto gold, or silver, or stone, graven by art and man's device" (Acts 17:29). We are obliged to formulate concepts of God that are independent of our own imagination. It is "the only true God" (John 17:3) that man must know.

It is therefore imperative that man turn away from ungodlike involvements. Such associations were formed because of the ignorance of God, and must be deliberately terminated. "And the times of this ignorance God winked at; but now commandeth all men everywhere to repent," says the Lord (Acts 17:30). In Christ, God has sufficiently revealed Himself. He will no longer tolerate ignorance of His Person.

God will call all men into accountability for their response to His appeal to reconciliation (II Cor. 5:18-20). The requirement for universal repentance is "because He hath appointed a day, in the which He will judge the world in righteousness by that man whom He hath ordained . . ." (Acts 17:31). Accountability, then, is not only

86

reasonable; it is a Divine appointment. A particular day has already been designated for it to occur.

The judgment of the world shall be accomplished by "that Man whom He hath ordained," the "man Christ Jesus" (II Tim. 2:5). No man can doubt the actuality of that appointed day. God has "given assurance unto all men, in that He hath raised Him from the dead" (Acts 17:31).

This judgment is required because man is God's offspring, because he has been created in the image of God. He has been made to participate in the rule of the Almighty, and has been endowed with Divine capabilities. This condition requires that man be accountable to God.

Created But Contaminated

Though created by God, man has become contaminated because of a preference for the cursed order. Apart from Christ, man is depicted as "dead in trespasses and sins" (Eph. 2:1), "without strength" (Rom. 5:6), and in the process of coming "short of the glory of God" (Rom. 3:23). Man cannot, of himself, achieve the purpose for which he was created. He has been, by personal transgression, plunged into spiritual degradation.

All of this has occurred in God's world. Man is responsible for having become corrupted in a world belonging to a holy and righteous God! Man's creation is credited to God. His contamination is his personal responsibility. He cannot take credit for his basic nature, and God is not responsible for the defilement of that nature. Even though man is in God's world, God did not stop him from committing sin. He had a freedom inherent in the Divine imagery that permitted him to select the wrong, prefer the cursed, and choose the evil.

Throughout the ages, men have stood in consternation when confronted with the fact of sin in God's world. Some have foolishly charged God with its existence, saying that it is here by His determination. Because man is God's offspring, he possesses moral powers which permit him to determine his own character and destiny. It is that way by design, and God has not abandoned any of His attributes in that arrangement. Made by God, defiled by personal choice. Those are the facts in the case.

The Requirement for Purpose

The accountability of man to God requires the existence of Divine purpose. Men will be measured by God's objective for them. In the broadest sense, that objective is for them to "seek the Lord, if haply they might feel after Him, and find Him . . . " (Acts 17:26). In the more precise sense, the objective is that they might be "reconciled to God" through the redemption that is in Christ Jesus (II Cor. 5:18-20). In the minute sense, it is that those availing themselves of "the atonement" (Rom 5:11) might minister "as of the ability God gives" (I Pet. 4:11).

Each of these views is permeated with purpose. In fact, without purpose, they would have no meaning. God's Kingdom is not the execution of mere legal requirements. It is not the implementation of a mere ethical moral objective. In "the end" (I Cor. 15:24), every man will be measured by His degree of involvement in God's revealed purpose.

The Reality of Stewardship

Stewardship is the allocation of responsibility. In the very beginning, God gave man responsibility. "And the Lord took man, and put him into the garden of Eden to dress it and to keep it" (Gen. 2:15). In a broader sense, the whole world was man's stewardship. "Be fruitful, and multiply, and replenish the earth, and subdue it . . ." (Gen. 1:28), declared the Lord amidst that ancient paradise. That pronouncement reflected the objective of God for man — discharge intelligent responsibility.

Those that are in Christ Jesus are to be "good stewards of the manifold grace of God" (I Pet. 4:10). God has dispensed to every regenerated man the "proper gift" (I Cor. 7:7). He has endowed each individual with the ability to administer righteous judgment in needful areas. The administration requires the employment of the Divine image in man: discretion, the will, determination, creativity, and dedication.

In the parable of the talents, Jesus developed the concept of stewardship. "For the Kingdom of heaven is as a man travelling into a far country, who called his own servants, and delivered unto them his goods" (Matt. 25:14). Here the Lord declares that His return to heaven, following the accomplishments of His death for sin (Luke 9:31), would involve the allocation of responsibility. In a very real sense, He was going to leave His work in the hands of others. "And I will give to you the keys of the kingdom," He announced to Peter (Matt. 16:19). Again, Paul, speaking for Christ's messengers, says, ". . . and has committed unto us the word of reconciliation. Now then we are ambassadors for Christ, as though God did beseech you by us: we pray you in Christ's stead, be ye reconciled to God" (II Cor. 5:20).

The existence of such awesome responsibility confirms the necessity of accountability. Every man shall be called to "give an account" of his stewardship (Luke 16:2). That covers everything from the responsibility to find God, to that of obeying God and the proper handling of His truth.

The Objective of God's Salvation

"All have sinned, and come short of the glory of God," declares the Apostle (Rom. 3:23). Men, by nature, have willingly acted in contrariety to the Living God. They have preferred their own interests above His, and are unable, in the natural state, to obtain Divine approval. Transgression is now associated with men, whereas it was before identified with Satan (Hosea 6:7; Isa. 14:12-14). The "law of sin" now resides in men (Rom. 7:23), and, apart from Christ, they have "no hope, and are without God in the world" (Eph. 2:12).

But God has not abandoned man; He has not left him in a hopeless state. He has determined to again provide access to Himself through a "living way" (Heb. 10:20). His power and His character have been devoted to the loftiest enterprise ever conceived by Deity — the reconciliation of man unto Himself. He has determined that conformity "to the Image of His Son" will ultimately supplant the image marred by sin (Rom. 8:29). All of His dealings upon earth have been, and continue to be, focused upon the objective of recovering man. His "mighty acts" (Psa. 145:4), the "giving of the Law" (Rom. 9:4), and the testimony of His prophets (Acts 3:21) have all had this central purpose. The recovery of man from the fall, the blessing of man, the reconciling of man — that is the design in all of these things.

Rather than abandoning man, God has, in redemption, intensified His activity toward him. If God is not perceived by men, it is not because He has hidden Himself, or because He does not desire to be seen.

Not Totally Depraved

Throughout church history, a battle has raged over the state of fallen

89

man. How far did he fall? How marred is the image of God in which he was made? How helpless is he? One segment of Christendom states that man is totally incapable of seeking or responding to God. It requires Divine stimulus to awaken him from his spiritual death. The term used to identify this supposed condition is "total hereditary depravity." Simply stated, it means that man's powers have been so corrupted by sin that he cannot seek God, desire God, or respond to God. He is insensitive concerning God, and completely incapable of being any other way.

The Scriptures do assert that man is "dead in trespasses and sins" (Eph. 2:1), and that he is "alienated" and an enemy of God in his mind by wicked works (Col. 1:21). It is true that "the natural man receives not the things of the Spirit of God" (I Cor. 2:14), and that "they that are in the flesh cannot please God" (Rom. 8:8). The indictment of the whole race is, "There is none righteous, no not one . . ." (Rom. 3:10-18). The question is not whether or not these things are true, but what they mean.

They mean that man cannot achieve fellowship with God apart from His revelation. He cannot, independently of revelation, comprehend the mind of the Lord with eternal profit. Man cannot rectify his situation by his own achievement, or erase the fact that he comes short of God's glory.

Man is described as "having no hope" (Eph. 2:12), but not as being hopeless. Confined to his own resources, he has no hope of obtaining heavenly approval or substance. God Himself has ordained that this fallen creature "seek the Lord" (Acts 17:27), and that "all men everywhere repent" (Acts 17:30). If this were not possible, God would be guilty of guile!

Unbelief and belief (John 3:18), rejection and acceptance (John 12:48) — they are all credited to men. The entire scheme of redemption is based upon response — upon the response of men! Further, the destiny of all men is ultimately based on their response to God's provisions. The Gospel, for instance, is "preached to every creature" to elicit a response (Mark 16:15-16). Divine messages were proclaimed within the context of responsibility, not inability! The proclamation of an intelligent message to intelligent creatures incapable of responses is a contradition of both reason and Divine purpose. If man, in the fall, lost all ability to respond to God, he ceased to be intelligent. Response is an essentiality of intelligence!

Man is accountable to God. "This is the condemnation," proclaimed the Lord, "that light is come into the world, and men loved darkness rather than light . . ." (John 3:19). The condemnation was not that they could not receive the light, but that they did not receive it. It is the preference of men that will determine their destiny, not their ability or inability.

Salvation Defined

In its most precise sense, the Kingdom of God is the administration of salvation from sin and its consequences. Salvation can be viewed from at least three perspectives. 1. Its foundation (I Cor. 3:11; Heb. 13:20). 2. The conditions for its appropriation (Mark 16:16; Acts 2:38; 16:31). 3. Man's personal participation in it (II Cor. 6:16-18). The foundation is required as a basis for conferring salvation. Conditions are presented as a means of appropriating the salvation. Participation addresses the matter of a conscious enjoyment of the benefits of salvation.

Both God and man are involved in all three of these aspects of salvation. God provides the foundation, while man is confronted with it. God presents the conditions, man conforms to them. God and man join together in man's participation in salvation. Each of these aspects is presented intelligently by God, and intelligently embraced by man.

The nature of salvation requires accountability. God, in His mercy, has provided a "propitiation" or covering, for man's sin (Rom. 3:25; I John 2:2; 4:10). He has revealed the details of this provision in the "Gospel of Christ," which is His "power unto salvation" (Rom. 1:16). He has set forth conditions that can be met by any individual desiring to meet them. Men will be held accountable for their response to this provision! The accountability is a just one, and when the day of its requirement occurs, there will not be a legitimate objection registered to it in all of God's intelligent creation.

The Purpose of the Day of Judgment

The day of judgment is sure because of its Divine appointment — "He hath appointed a day . . ." (Acts 17:31). It is also sure because it is required — "We must all appear before the judgment seat of Christ . . ." (II Cor. 5:10). Man's nature, together with the responsibilities that have been given to Him by God, demand a day of judgment — a time of accountability! Unlike the judgment of ancient Israel, this day cannot be averted or postponed (Num. 13:27-31).

Even the hosts of darkness have an acute awareness of this day of accountability. They know that torment awaits them as a result of that time. On one occasion, a united group of them cried out to Jesus, ". . . art Thou come to torment us before the time?" (Matt. 8:29). Alluding to that day in regard to those very personalities, Peter wrote, "God spared not the angels that sinned, but cast them down into hell, and delivered them into chains of darkness, to be reserved unto judgment." Elaborating on that day, Peter brought mankind into the picture — in particular those that have rejected the atonement. "The Lord knows how to . . . reserve the unjust unto the day of judgment . . ." (II Pet. 2:4,9).

The Inclusion of All Men

The day of judgment is not for a portion of our race, but for all of it! It is the "world" — the entirety of God's offspring — that shall be judged (Acts 17:31). Twice the Apostle proclaimed that "all" must "stand" or "appear before the judgment seat of Christ" (Rom. 14:10; II Cor. 5:10). The judgment shall include "the living and the dead" (Acts 10:42; II Tim. 4:1; I Pet. 4:5). These terms encompass "all men." In a graphic depiction of the day of judgment, John the Revelator proclaims its association with all men.

And I saw the dead, small and great, stand before God; and the books were opened: and another book was opened, which is the book of life: and the dead were judged out of those things which were written in the books, according to their works. And the sea gave up the dead which were in it; and death and hell [hades] delivered up the dead which were in them: and they were judged every man according to their works (Rev. 20:12-13).

Here, the use of the word "dead" reflects the passing of the natural order. No one will be "in the body" of flesh and blood at this time. Those that have died are raised, and those that were alive at the Lord's return have been changed (I Cor. 15:51-53). Thus "all men" are referred to as "the dead" — having been separated from the tabernacle of the flesh. They are viewed as having completed their tenure upon the earth.

The entirety of God's offspring are viewed in respect to their apparent achievement — "small and great." The unassuming and the assuming, the rich and the poor, the weak and the mighty, the servant and the ruler — they are all there! On earth both "small and great" were admonished to "fear Him" (Rev. 11:18; 19:5), and now they appear to give an account of their response!

Even the "sea gave up the dead which were in it" — an enormous number! At one time, the waters formed the grave for every living person on the face of the earth, only eight being excluded (Gen. 7:21-23). Since then, the seas have received inconceivable numbers of vacated bodies, ranging from infants sacrificed by idolators to victims of war and raging winds. They shall all be present at the judgment!

"Death and hell" delivered up the dead that were in them. "Death" refers to the grave, which shall have lost its "victory" at that time. Every grave in every place shall yield to the resurrection of the dead, as "Death is swallowed up in victory" (I Cor. 15:54-55). "Hell," or hades, is the abode of disembodied spirits. It is the residence of both "the rich man" and "Lazarus." It is where the souls of martyrs reside "under the altar" (Rev. 6:9), as well, as where Jesus preached when He was "put to death in the flesh" (I Pet. 3:18-19; 4:6). Both places will yield up their constituents, and, with spirit and resurrected bodies united, all men will stand before the judgment seat. They will all be there! They will all be aware of the hour! All of their deeds will then be examined with Divine scrutiny! They were made by God, and they are all accountable to God. There, before an assembled universe, the appointed day will come to pass!

Vindication, Not Determination

The glorification of God is at the heart of the purpose of the day of judgment. It is not to be a time of initial determination — a time when the eternal destiny of men is decided. In a very real sense men are determining their destiny now — in this world. "He that believes on Him is not condemned: but he that believes not is condemned already," proclaimed the Lord (John 3:18). Believing and not believing are responses to the gospel taking place in this world, not the world to come! It is here, amidst the "temporal" order, that men either believe or believe not. These are not terms identifying God's reaction to men, but men's reaction to Him!

Men do not have to wait until the day of judgment to know where they will spend eternity. ". . . behold now is the accepted time; behold now is the day of salvation" (II Cor. 6:2). Now, in this time, a proper response to the Gospel of Christ will enable one to have "boldness in the day of judgment" (I John 4:17). A confident assurance can be possessed when the appointed judgment is confronted. That is the doctrine of Scripture. This would be a foolish presumption if destinies were determined "then." "Now" is the time of determination, "then" is the time of evaluation and announcement and revelation.

In this world, men are judging God's Word. They are evaluating it, and consequently accepting or rejecting it. But when men "appear before the judgment seat of Christ," their evaluation and response to the Word will be judged. At that time God shall be vindicated. Before an assembled universe the unquestionable reality of His revelation to men will be established. Paul, taking a thought from Psalm 51:4, wrote of this vindication. ". . . yea, let God be true, but every man a liar; as it is written, That Thou mightest be justified in Thy sayings, and mightest overcome when Thou art judged" (Rom. 3:4). When all men "stand before God" and the "books" are opened, God will be "justified" in His sayings! The conflict between men and God will be exposed, and He will be seen as true, while all that are contrary to Him will be clearly perceived as "liars."

God governs the world in prospect of the day of judgment. He permits men to contradict Him, and to despise and reject His Word. But those that interpret this condition as one reflecting indifference by God have jeopardized their souls. God will be vindicated concerning everything He has revealed. Men will be saved or lost eternally because of their response to the announcement of His provision for their reconciliation. If one soul could enter into heaven while ignoring and contradicting God's Word, God would be proved a liar. Also, if a single personality were consigned to hell even though the truth were embraced and conformed to, God would be found a liar.

The day all men are openly accountable to God, He will be "found true"! He will be vindicated, His Word exonerated, and the truth confirmed. That is when the ultimate confrontation of man and God will take place. God will be found true, and every opposing man a liar. That is the time He will overcome, though he has been judged by men (Rom.

3:4b). That is vindication!

Preparing for That Day

The Kingdom of God is characterized by intelligent purpose. As regards man, that purpose involves more than the mere transmission of information from God to man. Integral to the reign of the Almighty is His desire for man's fellowship. When, for instance, He tells us of the appointed judgment day (Heb. 9:27), it is in order that we might prepare for it! It is His desire that our love be "made perfect, that we may have boldness in the day of judgment" (I John 4:17).

This "boldness" can be perceived from at least two perspectives. First, man obtains boldness by intimate fellowship with "God, the Judge of all" (Heb. 12:23). Knowing God is not only the objective of eternal life, it is eternal life (John 17:3). The "knowledge of God" is the means through which "grace and peace" are administered (II Pet. 1:2). "Grace" addresses the matter of standing favorably before God. "Peace" embraces that inward confidence and assurance that reigns while conscious of the true God.

Secondly, boldness is the result of a purged conscience — the experiential hallmark of the New Covenant. The Old Covenant could not bring a cleansed conscience. All of its bloody sacrifices could "never take away sin" (Heb. 10:4). Meticulous obedience to all of its requirements still left a "remembrance" of sin (Heb. 10:3). Therefore, there was no "boldness" or confidence before God.

The blood of Christ, however, is "able to purge your conscience from dead works to serve the living God" (Heb. 9:14). "Being now justified by His blood, we shall be saved from wrath through Him," declares the Apostle (Rom. 5:9). That will produce boldness in the day of judgment.

Man's preparation for the day of judgment consists of knowing God, and receiving "the atonement" or reconciliation (Rom. 5:11). Man must avail himself of the "great salvation" provided in Christ Jesus. One of the objectives of that salvation is to prepare men for their appointment with the Judge! The Gospel, the means and power of God unto salvation, must be embraced heartily in order to survive the day of accounting!

The knowledge of God and the appropriation of salvation both involve separation from the world. The "fashion of this world" (I Cor.

7:31) conflicts with that of the world to come. The absorption of an individual into the temporal order puts him out of synch with the world to come. Such a condition will make the day of judgment a day of condemnation. Incompatibility with "the world to come" (Heb. 2:5) will require one's exclusion from it. The exhortation to "cleanse ourselves from all filthiness of the flesh and spirit" (II Cor. 7:1) is not a call to mere regimentation. It is a summons to preparation; a challenge to rid ourselves of spiritual contaminants that render men unfit for heaven.

If men are to be judged by the Word of God — by the revelation of His mind — they must hear the Word, receive the Word, and obey the Word! Their minds must grasp it and their hearts must cherish it. As that Word is received, contradictory inclinations will become evident. It is then that we must "lay aside every weight, and the sin that doth so easily beset us," and "run with patience the race that is set before us" (Heb. 12:1). The "race that is set before us" consists of an identified way to God through Christ Jesus. It involves the laying aside of "all filthiness and superfluity of naughtiness" (James 1:21). The outgrowth of the Adamic nature is laid aside by spiritual discipline — by keeping under our body, and bringing it into subjection (I Cor. 9:27).

Conclusion

The Kingdom of God, because it involves the execution of intelligent purpose, imposes upon man the element of responsibility. By His very nature, God is responsible: He "cannot deny Himself" (II Tim. 2:13). Because the reconciliation of estranged man is the objective of God's rule through Christ, man is responsible; responsible to receive the atonement (Rom. 5:11), responsible to obey the Gospel (II Thess. 1:8), responsible to "be not conformed to this world" (Rom. 12:1-2). All men will be judged in accordance with the Word of God and the provisions of redemption. Their response to these things will be reflected in their works. Thus will they be judged "according to their works."

Life on earth is a preparation — a preparation for the day of judgment, as well as a preparation for eternity itself. This preparation is marked by intelligent involvement, not Divine coercion. The Lord proclaims, man hears (Rom. 10:17). Christ calls, man answers (John 7:37-38). The Spirit leads, man follows (Rom. 8:14). Salvation in the Kingdom demands our response!

PART THREE:
GOD HAS MAGNIFIED HIS WORD

7

THE KINGDOM IS COMMUNICATED THROUGH GOD'S WORD

God's Kingdom involves the implementation of His objectives in inscrutable wisdom. In the reconciliation of man, He has chosen to execute these purposes within an arena of intelligent personalities. His purpose in Christ is not fulfilled by manipulating men, but by appealing to them.

Divine appeals have a twofold characteristic. First, they are an exact reflection of the desire of the Living God. They are truthful, precise, and earnest. Second, if believed, they have a powerful, constraining influence. This is because they are perfectly adapted to man. Once embraced, the appeals enable him to experience a fullness of joy, and a liberty of expression that is not otherwise possible.

The foundation for all blessing from God is Divine objective — "eternal purpose" (Eph. 3:11), the "will of the Lord" (Eph. 5:17). Comprehension must undergird man's participation in the will of God. His purpose must be perceived; His objective must be understood! This is the reason for the fervent prayer of the Apostle Paul for the Ephesian believers. "For this cause I bow my knees unto the Father of our Lord

Jesus Christ, that He would grant you . . . to be strengthened with might by His Spirit in the inner man . . . that ye may be able . . . to comprehend . . . what is the breadth, and length, and depth, and height . . . that ye might be filled with all the fullness of God" (Eph. 3:14-19). This "inner" strength is required for spiritual discernment. It fortifies man's essential nature, and permits him to grasp the mind of the Lord.

God's purpose is wide in its expanse, liberal, and characterized by a large horizon. It has "breadth"! It stretches from "before the foundation of the world" (Matt. 25:34) into "the ages to come" (Eph. 2:7). It has "length"! It is characterized by profound wisdom, Divine perfection, and meticulous workings (Rom. 11:33). It has "depth"! This purpose has touched high and lofty realms! God Himself has permeated it with His love (Titus 3:4). The Son of God emptied Himself in order to become a part of it (Phil 2:6-7). The Spirit of God has become involved in it (John 16:8-11). The holy angels have become an unquestionable part of it (Heb. 1:113-14). It has "height"!

His Desire to Make Known His Purpose

Although the fullness of God's purpose in Christ was "kept secret from the foundation of the world" (Matt. 13:35; Rom. 16:25-26), it did not delight the Lord to do so. He does not take pleasure in secrecy! Since "the world began," God had determined to provide a way for man to recover from the fall. Its early secrecy was not mandated by God's nature, but by man's dullness. Due to man's sin, the Lord was not able to clearly articulate His objective to him. Man's understanding had become darkened because of his choice of sin (Eph. 4:18). However, God was so determined to unveil His will that He began preparing man for its reception. His varied dealings with men, together with the giving of the Law, were preparative measures. They readied men for the revelation of "the mystery."

The prophet Jeremiah received a revelation concerning the nature of God — a revelation that may now be perceived. "Thus saith the Lord, Let not the wise man glory in his wisdom, neither let the mighty man glory in his might, let not the rich man glory in his riches: but let him that glorieth glory in this, that he understands and knows Me, that I am the Lord who exercises lovingkindness, judgment, and righteousness, in the earth: for in these things I delight, saith the Lord"

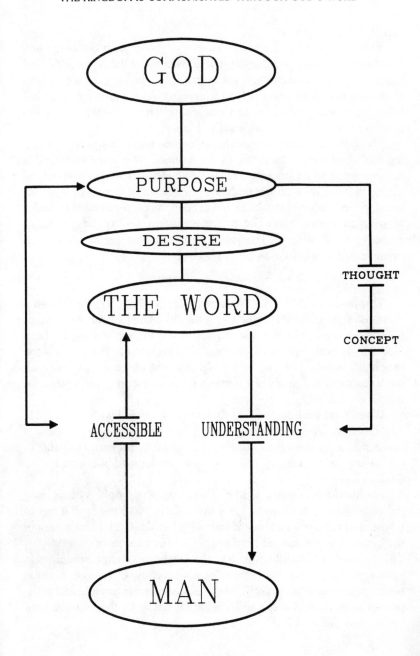

(Jer. 9:23-24).

You will observe that God takes delight in man knowing and understanding Him. It is, further, the knowledge of the purpose of God that reveals His character and manners. There, in the execution of His good pleasure, the Person of God is unveiled. And, mark this well, God takes joy when men know and understand Him — when they comprehend His Person and understand His will.

Those that proclaim a mysterious God and bring confusion concerning His Word are contradicting God's purpose. The worship of God is not promoted by an ignorance of Him! Men do not stand in awe of God simply because they cannot understand His ways. If that were the case, worship and adoration would have been more predominant under Moses than under Christ. The greater revelation of Christ has produced a clearer view of God. The result has been a realization of an unprecedented level of God's good pleasure.

Perceived in the Prophets

Throughout history, the "holy prophets" (II Pet. 3:2) have been a demonstration of God's desire to reveal His will. His heart so yearned for His fallen offspring that He inspired Amos to say, "Surely the Lord God will do nothing, but He revealeth His secret unto His servants the prophets" (Amos 3:8). It was not His desire to obscure, but to reveal; not to conceal, but to open! It is man's sin that obscures God's purpose, not God's nature!

When God had determined to destroy the world with a flood, He could not keep it quiet. He revealed it to Noah, and Noah became a "preacher of righteousness" (II Pet. 2:5) while he prepared the ark "to the saving his house; by the which he condemned the world . . ." (Heb. 11:7).

For hundreds of years, God spoke through the prophets concerning the coming of a Redeemer. They faithfully foretold the "sufferings of Christ, and the glory that should follow" (I Pet. 1:10-11). The nature of the Savior was proclaimed centuries before His incarnation (Isa. 9:6-7). The manner of His sufferings, and the Divine reasoning behind them were announced (Isa. 53:1-12). The effectiveness of His ministry was boldly prophesied by Malachi (Mal. 4:2). Jeremiah foretold His prosperous reign (Jer. 23:5), and Zechariah wrote of the provision for forgiveness (Zech. 13:1).

100

Why were these prophecies given? Because our God delights to reveal, to open up, and to illuminate His objective! That is His nature, and that is the manner of His Kingdom. The Kingdom of God is no more manifest than where God's will is known and loved! The Lord reigns, but not as a tyrant! He rules, but not in obscurity! He is a God of light. In fact, "God is light" (I John 1:5). How wonderfully this is seen in the writings of the prophets.

Witnessed in John the Baptist

From the beginning, God's intention was to save man by a man — the "Seed" of the woman (Gen. 3:15). Immediately after Eve had confessed to her voluntary submission to Satan, God announced His purpose — and He announced it the Deceiver himself. He could not keep it quiet; it would be against His nature to do so.

Four millennia of time passed before that promised "Seed" was dispatched to the contaminated planet! "But when the fullness of the time was come, God sent forth His Son, made of a woman, made under the law." His mission was "To redeem them that were under the law, that we might receive the adoption of sons" (Gal. 4:4-5). Since the fall, man had been lulled into sleep. There was a general indifference toward the promise of a Redeemer, and "gross darkness" blanketed the people (Isa. 60:2).

To awaken mankind to the coming of the Redeemer, we again witness the desire of the Lord to make His will known. He chose to alert men with a messenger — John the Baptist. This prophet came out of the wilderness with a thunderous message — an intelligent word addressed to the conscience of the people; "Repent ye: for the kindgom of heaven is at hand" (Matt. 3:2). He was the fulfillment of Isaiah's prophecy, "The voice of one crying in the wilderness, Prepare ye the way of the Lord, make His paths straight" (Matt. 3:3). He came publicly, with a public message. His words were the message, not merely his appearance!

When he came, "John did no miracle," but utilized the highest form of Divine witness — speaking! It is witnessed that "all things that John spake of this man [Jesus] were true" (John 10:41). The most intelligent form of communication between personalities consists of words — of speech, of the transmission of thought! This is precisely what John was known for — the communication of the purpose of God in words.

101

Who will ever forget his arresting words, "Behold, the Lamb of God, which takes away the sin of the world" (John 1:29). This was a precise expression of God's objective . . . an objective that could not possibly be discerned by merely looking on Jesus of Nazareth. A word was required, and that is what John gave!

Clarity in Christ

The revelation of God's design reaches its appex in Christ Jesus. It is written, "For in Him [Christ] dwelleth all the fullness of the Godhead bodily" (Col. 2:9). This was a deliberate arrangement, "For it pleased the Father that in Him should all fullness dwell" (Col. 1:19). The purpose of the incarnation was to illumine man, to expose our race to God's "eternal purpose." The "mystery of His will" has now been made know unto us, and the revelation has been dictated by God's "good pleasure" (Eph. 1:9).

The "fullness of the Godhead in Christ encompasses several things. First, the very character of God was put on display to man. Philosophers had groped in vain to understand the veiled God. Limited revelations of Him had been granted through the prophets. But now, in the Person of Christ, man actually was given a full manifestation of the Father; of His character, His ways, and His responses. Jesus is the "brightness of His glory, and the express image of His Person" (Heb. 1:3). His revelation of God was so complete that he declared, "he that hath seen Me, hath seen the Father" (John 14:9).

But there is another aspect to this "fullness." In Christ we see an intelligent communication of God's objective undertaking to save man. It is communicated in Christ's words. Often His speech pointed men away from the mundane to heavenly aims. "I am not come to call the righteous, but sinners to repentance" (Matt. 9:13). "Even as the Son of man came not to be ministered unto, but to minister, and to give His life a ransom for many" (Matt. 20:28). "The Son of man is not come to destroy men's lives, but to save them" (Luke 9:56). "For the Son of man is come to seek and to save that which was lost" (Luke 19:10). These words reflect objective — heavenly objective. They speak of purpose — Divine purpose. They are an interpretation of the mind and will of the Living God!

Christ's works also were a means of communicating the Divine objective. His compassion upon the multitudes, His gracious works, His mighty miracles — they were not ends of themselves. Jesus said, "I must work the works of Him that sent me . . . " (John 9:4). ". . . the works that I do in my Father's name, they bear witness of me" (John 10:25). They were not a mere performance, not a mode of entertainment! They were not meant to cause men to stand in awe. They were a communication — a communication of the will of God. In confirmation of this, Jesus said, ". . . though ye believe not me, believe the works: that ye may know, and believe, that the Father is in me, and I in Him" (John 10:38).

God was communicating His purpose to men in the enfleshed Christ! It was in this sense that Jesus was "the Word": the expression of God's plan. He was "in the beginning," was "with God," and "was God" (John 1:1). God has never been without a means of expression, because He is a God of expression, not a God of secrecy! He is a God of revelation, not a God of mystery! When "the Word became flesh, and dwelt among us," a heavenly message was being transmitted.

This revelation was intended for man's mind. God wanted His purpose to be discerned, understood, and comprehended! He had created man with the capacity to discern, and here, in Christ, was the highest and loftiest reality to be discerned: the Word enfleshed!

The Apostles' Doctrine

Christ's residency upon earth was brief, according to God's will. A prolonged tenure in this world would only have served to distract men from God. The physical presence of Jesus provided such a contrast with the temporal order and those within it, that curiosity often supplanted contemplation. Rather than perceiving the significance of Christ's words and works, the multitudes became enamored of the novelty of His deeds. In divine lament, Jesus once said to an apparently eager multitude, "Ye seek me not because ye saw the miracles, but because ye did eat of the loaves, and were filled" (John 6:26). They had been distracted by appearance. This condition was not owing to a lack of Divine clarity, but rather to human infirmity.

The existence of this condition was one of the reasons our Lord returned to heaven. Not only was His presence in glory necessary for the meditation of the New Covenant and the formal acceptance by God of His sacrifice; it was required for the successful transmission of Kingdom knowledge. While men remained in the flesh, their apprehension of heavenly provision and reality must be by faith. That faith required a word from God — an intelligent articulation of Divine purpose.

Jesus chose certain men to be His Apostles, twelve in number (Luke 6:13). He selected them "they they should be with Him, and that He might send them forth to preach" (Mark 3:14). These were to continue the work following His return to heaven. They were to make known the provisions of redemption and the mind of the Lord. He would send them the Holy Spirit to illuminate their understanding, and make their memories profitable (John 15:26-27; 16:7-15). Before leaving, He commissioned them to "preach the Gospel" (Mark 16:15), and to "teach all nations" (Matt. 28:19).

Their preaching was accompanied by signs and wonders. But those external demonstrations were not their mission. They served to confirm their mission. God was "bearing them witness, both with signs and wonders, and with divers miracles and gifts of the Holy Ghost . . ." (Heb. 2:4). Even as Jesus' works testified to the truth of His words, so the "signs of an apostle" (II Cor. 12:12) confirmed the truth of his doctrine. The rejection or the acceptance of their persons was not the point, but the rejection or acceptance of their message! "How shall we escape, if we neglect so great salvation; which at the first began to be spoken by the Lord, and was confirmed unto us by them [apostles] that heard Him" (Heb. 2:3).

The Apostles have no Kingdom value apart from their worlds! Their works have ceased. Their persons have been removed from the earth. The only thing we have from them now is their word, their doctrine, their message.

Note the absence of apostolic biographies in the Scripture. Most of the Apostles disappear from the narrative after Christ's ascension. Andrew, Philip, Bartholomew, Thomas, Matthew, James the son of Alphaeus, Lebbaeus, Simon the Canaanite, and Matthias — scarcely a word is said of them after the day of Pentecost had "fully come" (Acts 2:1). We know of the martyrdom of James (Acts 12:2), but little more. We know something of the travels of Paul through the writings of Luke the physician, but little is known of other dominant Apostles like Peter and John.

The message of the Apostles was consistent; they did not preach different gospels. For this reason, the emphasis is on the "Apostles' doctrine" instead of their persons or their travels (Acts 2:42). They were selected to preach, not to make a name for themselves. It is their message that is exalted, not their persons. The next world is the place for personal exaltation, not this one. It is then that "every man shall have praise of God" (I Cor. 4:5).

"Doctrine" is the means God has appointed for the communication of His will, His "eternal purpose," His mind! No doctrine, no communication! This involves an appeal to man's mind, and indicates that God's will can be comprehended. The Apostles admonished us, "Be not unwise, but understanding what the will of the Lord is" (Eph. 5:17).

In Christ, God governs His Kingdom by intelligent means, not direct power. He does so because He desires — fervently desires — that "all men be saved and come to the knowledge of the truth" (I Tim. 2:4).

The appointed interpreters of Divine purpose are the Apostles. The church is "built upon the foundation of the apostles and prophets, Jesus Christ Himself being the chief corner stone" (Eph. 2:20). Both apostles and prophets are known for what they say. In fact, neither office would exist if there were no message!

The Motivating Power of Words and Thought

The fact that God has chosen to employ "the word of reconciliation" (II Cor. 5:19) in the accomplishment of His objective is proof of the superiority of that means. Because of the nature of man, thought and concept are the highest means of motivation. Thinking men are the men most motivated!

Consideration of Jewish history will confirm this observation. This nation experienced the most dynamic external displays of Divine power ever witnessed. In all of earth's history, what can compare to the ten plagues of Egypt (Exod. 7-12)? The parting of the waters at the Red Sea is unparalleled for magnitude (Exod. 14-15). Rivers of water gushing from a desert "rock of flint" (Num. 20:11; Deut. 8:15; Psa. 78:16), and bread raining every morning from heaven for 40 years (Exod. 16:4-16).

Time would fail us to mention the Divine presence at Sinai (Exod. 19:16-25), the slaying of 185,000 Assyrian soldiers one night by a single angel (II Kgs. 19:35), and the sun and the moon standing still for a day (Josh. 10:12).

If "seeing is believing," and men are constrained primarily by sight, Israel should have been the most obedient body of people in history. But this was not the case at all. Moses' valedictory address to them provided an accurate appraisal of their response to God's mighty works. "Ye have been rebellious against the Lord from the day that I knew you" (Deut. 9:26). God Himself, reviewing all of His dealings with them, said, "All day long I have stretched forth my hands to a disobedient and gainsaying people" (Rom. 10:21). Their best responses were short-lived, and the witness of overt power never produced satisfactory reactions among them.

The superiority of the New Covenant — the most advanced revelation of the Kingdom of God — is evident. Central in the New Covenant are matters for thought and contemplation. It does not present men with tangible things, but "heavenly things" (Heb. 8:5). These are to be the subject of man's consideration. "Think on these things," admonished the Apostle in Philippians 4:8. This was not the proclamation of a legal requirement, but an indication of the way to a Kingdom benefit. Thinking on the things of God motivates man. David said, ". . . while I was musing the fire burned" (Psa. 39:3). The contemplation of revealed truth caused his spirit to assert itself Godward.

Building Blocks for Reason

God calls upon men to reason — to reason with Himself. "Come," He calls, "let us reason together" (Isa. 1:18). The result of that reasoning is declared: "though your sins be as scarlet, they shall be as white as snow; though they be red like crimson, they shall be as wool." How could such a benefit result from reasoning? Because man is never more like his Maker than when he reasons acceptably with Him and about Him! A close walk with God is described as being in a state of agreement (Amos 3:3) — a state resulting from reasoning!

The building blocks for reason are thoughts and concepts. A man's reasonings or views are as sound as his thoughts! His contemplations are the substance of his life philosophy.

Recognizing this situation, Paul often "reasoned" with those about him (Acts 17:2; 18:4,19; 24:25). His reasoning consisted of a perception and enunciation of the revealed mind of God — revealed initially in the Law, and ultimately in Christ. The implications of reality were articulated — expressed in words, and an appeal made to the minds of men. No sign or wonder could accomplish this, no physical phenomenon, no display of might or power! Words were presented, because words alone constitute the embodiment of thought! Thinking cannot be achieved without words, and reasoning cannot be accomplished without thought!

The point to be seen here is that God has revealed His will in words — words that foster sound and beneficial thinking. You cannot learn God's will by studying nature. Its voice is too subdued to form comprehensive concepts of the Almighty God.

Further, God has not achieved basic communication with man by means of wonders that transcend nature. While miracles have occurred, they have not been the primary basis for saving faith. Faith always has, and continues to, come "by hearing," not seeing (Rom. 10:17).

Thorough Employment of Man's Ability

Made in the image of God, man possesses powers required for dominion. Creativity, discretion, judgment, and analysis — they are all possible to man. Further, the Gospel of Christ appeals to these traits.

It is the genius of salvation that it has provided for the optimum utilization of these resources. The Gospel of Christ is a revelation that is "the power of God unto salvation" (Rom. 1:16). It constitutes a manifestation of the purpose of God, and it has been given in "words which the Holy Ghost teaches" (I Cor. 2:13).

Once grasped, these words completely activate man. For the first time, he is able to fulfill the first and great commandment. He now can love God with "all" of his heart, "all" of his soul, "all" of his mind, and "all" of his strength (Luke 10:17).

These terms encapsulate the entirety of man's personality. His "heart" speaks of the citadel of his being, the inmost part of him. This is the God-breathed part of man. The "soul" refers to the expressive part of him, and involves the intellect, emotion, and will. The "mind" of man concentrates particularly on his unique ability of thinking, judging, discerning, and comprehending. The "strength" of man refers to his ability to arise to the occasion. He can initiate an offensive (II Cor. 10:5), wax valiant in fight (Heb. 11:34), and recover himself from the snare of the devil (II Tim. 2:26).

God's Word — the communication of His purpose — calls for the total involvement of man. No miracle, no sign, no wonder can accomplish this! God's desire, therefore, is not primarily demonstrated in overt phenomenon, but in the proclamation of His Word.

Godlike Traits

God's objective for all men is for them to be like Himself. He is the Archetype of humanity. "Be ye perfect, even as your Father in heaven is perfect," demands Jesus (Matt. 5:48). Peter reminded us that we are to be "holy in all manner of conversation; because it is written, Be ye holy ; for I am holy" (I Pet. 1:15-16).

In this world, the primary way in which we become like God is in our thoughts. It is man's thinking that determines his manner of life. "For as he thinketh in his heart, so is he . . ." (Prove. 23:7). Once again, man is never more like God than when he thinks like God, and he is never more unlike God than when he does not think like Him. God's indictment of the people of Israel demonstrated this. "For my thoughts are not your thoughts . . . for as the heavens are higher than the earth, so are . . . my thoughts than your thoughts" (Isa. 55:8-9).

Impotence of Worldly Wisdom

We cannot conceive of God's purpose without God's Word. That is how He has revealed His purpose. Worldly wisdom is impotent when it comes to discovering God, His nature, or His objectives. Philosophy is a well too shallow to yield the water of life! In His inscrutable wisdom, God has circumscribed the wisdom of men. It cannot extend beyond this "present evil world" (Gal. 1:4). Man can arrive at understanding concerning earthly life, disease, and physical laws. But when it comes to heavenly realities, and to the God of salvation, his wisdom is vain.

God has destroyed "the wisdom of the wise" (I Cor. 1:19). He has done so by proclaiming a purpose that is anchored in another world — a world that is inaccessible to an unilluminated mind. "Hath not God made foolish the wisdom of this world" (I Cor. 1:20)? It is by "the foolishness of preaching" that God has chosen "to save them that believe" (I Cor. 1:21). The preaching, or proclamation, is "foolish" from earth's perspective. But for those that "are called" (I Cor. 1:24), it brings access to Christ, the power of God.

A Requirement for Fellowship

Jesus confirmed the nature of Divine fellowship when He said, "If a man love me, he will keep my words: and my Father will love him, and we will come unto him, and make our abode with him" (John 14:23).

Only an intelligent person can keep Christ's words, retain them in his memory, and deliberately conform his life to them. It cannot be accomplished any other way. The physical senses are of no value in this work. It takes place in the heart and mind, or it does not take place at all!

Christ is eager for this fellowship. He speaks to the church concerning His desire — a desire that is thwarted by indifference and lukewarmness. "Behold, I stand at the door and knock: If any man will hear my voice, and open the door, I will come in to him, and will sup with him, and he with me" (Rev. 3:20).

This "fellowship" reaches its fullness when God is in all of our thoughts (Psa. 10:4). It is then that one can confess, ". . . how precious are Thy thoughts . . . when I awake, I am still with Thee" (Psa. 139:17,18). In a statement that transcended the times in which he lived, David confessed, "In the multitude of my thoughts within me, Thy comforts delight my soul" (Psa. 94:19). Divine fellowship was experienced within the processes of legitimate thought. In fact, there can be no Divine fellowship apart from thought!

The Contradiction of Unintelligent Involvement

It is unfortunate that so much of the religion of our day is characterized by a marked absence of intelligence. Some are teaching that God overwhelms us in a mighty display of power. The Holy Spirit is said to "slay" people, knock them unconscious, and lead them in strange and unexplainable ways. God is perceived as mysterious, and His workings beyond comprehension. Salvation is viewed as a once-for-all transaction, initiated and guaranteed forever by a single response of man to the Gospel. It is thought to be strangely maintained by God in spite of man's waywardness. These views, however, are mythical, not truthful.

Man, made in God's image, is an intelligent creation. As a consequence, he is a personality, capable of intimacy with the ultimate Personality — the Living God. Actually, it is impossible for an intelligent God and an intelligent creation to have fellowship unintelligently. Where there is no comprehension, there is no involvement. Where there is no understanding, there is no fellowship. Where there is no discernment, there is no walk with God!

The "knowledge of God" is intelligence in its highest form. This

109

"knowledge" is the means through which man becomes identified with God. It is "through the knowledge of Him" that we receive "all things that pertain to life and godliness" (II Pet. 1:3). "Grace and peace are multipled unto us "through the knowledge of God" (II Pet. 1:2). Our escape from "the pollutions of the world" is accomplished through "the knowledge of the Lord and Savior Jesus Christ" (II Pet. 2:20).

The Weakness of Mere Experience

The Kingdom of God does not exclude experience. Experience is the affectation of our persons by heavenly influence. It extends beyond sensation, and is intensely personal. Moses went up into the mount, and there confronted God Almighty (Exod. 19:20). That was an experience. Naaman the leper experienced cleansing from leperosy (II Kgs. 5:1-27). That was an experience. Saul of Tarsus saw a great light from heaven, and was blinded by it (Acts 9:3-8). That was an experience. The two on the road to Emmaeus walked with Jesus, and heard Him open up the Scriptures to them (Luke 24:13-31). That was an experience.

There are people earnestly seeking for something to happen to them — a religious experience. They want to see an external display of Divine power, sense in their bodies a moving of the Spirit, and have personal pledges of heavenly support. But mere experience cannot sustain men for long. The impact is generally short-lived. If the effects of experience remain for a prolonged period, it is because the thought processes have become involved.

That is what happened to Peter when he saw a net let down from heaven. That was an extraordinary experience. God was teaching him concerning the acceptability of the Gentiles. A decade had passed since Pentecost, and the preaching of the Gospel was still confined to the Jewish community. Surely the vision of the net containing "all manner of four footed beasts of the earth and wild beasts, and creeping things, and fowls of the air" would get the point across. The vision was even attended by words: "Rise, Peter, kill and eat." Three times the net was lowered, three times the words were spoken. Three times an explanation was given; "What God hath cleansed, that call not thou common" (Acts 10:12-16).

The benefit, however, was not realized until "Peter thought on the vision" (Acts 10:19). There is where Peter became involved — not at the point of the experience, but at the point of the involvement of his mind. In this historical example, God has provided us with insight into the nature of Divine fellowship. It is not, nor has it ever been, based upon experience. It is, rather, based upon perception. Further, the highest form of perception is faith (Heb. 11:3), the means by which every Divine benefit is received, and Divine fellowship realized.

Conclusion

God has a purpose, and it has been revealed in Christ — both in His Person, and in His Word. That communication has been addressed to the mind of man, and requires the thoughtful involvement of man. To be averse to thought is to forfeit knowledge of the truth. To be ignorant of God is to be alienated from Him. There can be no comprehension of God's will apart from an understanding of His Word. That apprehension is not administered through intuition, mere experience, or philosophical probings.

8

GOD'S WORD — NECESSARY IN AN ECONOMY OF FAITH

The New Covenant is the most extensive provision for man's involvement with the living God that has ever been revealed to men. It transcends all that was before it! It is the ultimate demonstration thus far of God's love for fallen man, and has been executed in the grandest display of Divine wisdom ever witnessed by intelligent creatures (Eph. 1:8). Under the provisions of the New Covenant, men are purged from their sins, their hearts are purified, and they come into experiential involvement with the very God they have offended.

All of this has been accomplished without the Lord compromising His own character. In fact, rather than modifying His inherent nature, He has found a way to display it more fully. Through providing for the extrication of men from the dilemma of sin, God has remained both "just and the Justifier of him that believes in Jesus" (Rom. 3:26).

But what does all of this have to do with the Word of God?

The Essential Elements

Everything about this "great salvation" (Heb. 2:3) is beyond the pale of physical sense; outside the sphere of flesh and blood. The Lord Jesus, who has accomplished the reconciling death, is not apparent. The blood of Christ, which cleanses and reconciles, is not perceived with the senses. The "blessed God" (I Tim. 1:11), satisfied with the vicarious sacrifice of His dear Son (Isa. 53:11) is "invisible," "no man" having "seen Him at any time" (Heb. 11:27; John 1:18).

The great and abiding realities to which we have come in Christ are all unseen! That is the postulate of their untouchability occurring in Hebrews 12:18: "For ye are not come unto the mount that might be touched!" Instead of that mount of sensible discernment, "ye are come unto mount Zion, and unto the city of the living God, and to an innumerable company of angels, to the general assembly and church of the firstborn, which are written in heaven, and to God the Judge of all, and to the spirits of just men made perfect, and to Jesus the Mediator of the new covenant, and to the blood of sprinkling that speaks better things than that of Abel" (Heb. 12:22-24).

Looking at the Unseen

How can we fail to comprehend the elevated nature of the Kingdom of God as perceived from within the new covenant? Righteousness, peace, joy — they are intangible, but they constitute "the kingdom of God" (Rom. 14:17). God, Christ, the Spirit, the "holy angels" — access to none of them may be had by the senses. They are all unseen, unperceived by the natural eye, unsensed by our fallen natures! This is the reason for Paul's classic statement of the case: "We look not at the things which are seen, but at the things which are not seen: for the things which are seen are temporal; but the things which are not seen are eternal" (II Cor. 4:18).

There is an unseen world! It is called "the world to come," and it expressly has to do with men (Heb. 2:5-8). Real substance is found there, and men are urged to lay up for themselves treasures there, where moth and rust fail to corrode and corrupt (Matt. 6:19-20). God calls upon us, in the new covenant, to abandon earthly priorities, and seek "first the kingdom of God and His righteousness" (Matt. 6:33); both are unseen! Even our Lord Jesus has gone beyond our sight and touch; He is "passed into the heavens" (Heb. 4:14). Everything of genuine worth and substance is unseen, unsensed, and beyond carnal apprehension!

114

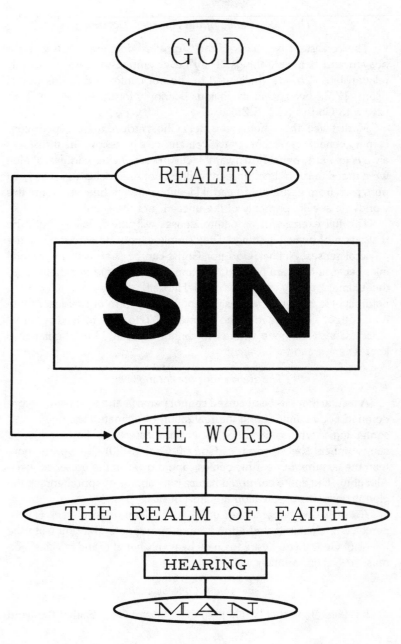

The Consistency of the Apostles' Doctrine

The consistent emphasis of the "Apostles' doctrine" (Acts 2:42) is heaven and heavenly things. They never emphasize earth or earthly relationships. We are challenged to "be not conformed to this world" (Rom. 12:2), because of its obvious inferiority for those that are "baptized into Christ" (Gal. 3:28).

Mark it well, that whether the Holy Ghost moved men to speak concerning benefit, experience, involvement, or expression, the thrust was always upward, never downward! Heavenward, never earthward! Men were urged to lay hold of unseen realities, not seen delusions! The Lord pulls men from earth, not to earth! He woos men to heaven, not to this world! He speaks primarily of the unseen, not the seen!

The full exercise of all natural senses will utterly fail to bring the realization of heavenly things! They simply cannot be perceived by the physical senses! Neither God nor Christ can be seen with the natural eye, because they are beyond the capacity of that eye to behold! Too, the ultimate reality, which is God Himself, simply cannot be seen naturally! He is a Spirit, and is not confined by form or physical restriction, both of which are required if something is to be perceived by carnal vision. Christ has gone where He cannot be seen! Our inheritance is kept where it cannot be seen!

The Reason for the Intangibility

A faculty that has been cursed cannot perceive the uncursed. A condemned body cannot bring the realization of ultimate blessing. That is something of what is meant by the inspired assertion; "flesh and blood cannot inherit the kingdom of God" (I Cor. 15:20). It involves more than the fact that our earthly bodies cannot dwell in the presence of the Almighty. The entire corrupted nature is incapable of apprehending the glorious benefits of salvation in Christ Jesus!

A disciplined body cannot do it! A scholarly mind of itself cannot perceive it! Unilluminated effort cannot appropriate it! If you want the things of God, if you desire to enjoy heavenly benefits and realities, you must seek them another way!

Discernment Only by Faith

It is faith alone that lays hold of the things of God. Faith is the hand

116

of the soul, the eye of the inner man. Faith turns unseen realities into substance, and Divine assertion into evidence. Is it not written, "Now faith is the substance of things hoped for, the evidence of things not seen" (Heb. 11:1)? In other words, faith obtains what sense cannot appropriate, and the results are very real. Sense is bypassed, and a persuasion of unseen reality settles upon the soul!

Faith is transcendent to sense; it is of a higher order, and is the Divinely appointed means of appropriating the truth. God and the things of God cannot be discerned or received through natural resources because they are beyond the sphere of nature.

God, for instance, is termed "invisible" (Col. 1:15; Heb. 11:27), and the "things of God," or the particular aspects of Himself that are manward, are also termed "invisible" (Rom. 1:20). Invisibility, in this case, is not the result of micro-size or physical geography, but rather of dimension. "God is a Spirit" (John 4:24), and the "things of God" are spiritual (I Cor. 2:13) — that is what makes them "invisible"; beyond the scope of the seeable.

Because the kingdom of God "is not meat and drink" (Rom. 14:17), the physical senses are rendered impotent in its realization. Although the situation is contradictory to much contemporary thought, a spiritual awareness of God and His Son, therefore, cannot be transmitted through the natural senses. That is to say, they cannot be seen, felt, or heard audibly with profit. Visual potential and fleshly sensation are completely powerless for the verification or realization of God or the things of God. This has never before been as true as now, since the exaltation of the Lord Jesus Christ, God's "express" Image (Heb. 1:3).

While it is true that there have been sensible representations of God in His dealings with men, they have not been attended by any degree of understanding or perception by men. Israel heard the voice of the Almighty, and He "came down in the sight of all the people upon Sinai" (Exod. 19:12-10; 20:19). But they really "neither heard His voice" nor saw "His shape" any more than those contemporaries of our Lord Jesus Christ (John 5:37). Their eyes could not penetrate the sphere of spirit; their ears could not perceive the intimate communications of the Lord; their hands could not touch the heavenly mount! Both God and they were limited by their cursed capacities! They could confess like Job, "Lo, He goeth by me, and I see Him not; he passeth on also, but I

117

perceive Him not" (Job. 9:11).

So far as nature is concerned, God dwells "in the light which no man can approach unto" (I Tim. 6:16). That is why "no man hath seen God at any time" (I John 4:12; John 1:18). Physical sense — how limited it is! Even if one were to break through into the presence of the Almighty, he could not sustain the confrontation! God Himself declared of those "in the body": "Thou canst not see my face: for there shall no man see me and live" (Exod. 33:20).

The Superiority of Faith

The situation I have described has mandated an economy of faith — a superior and Divinely-appointed means of profitable realization. In fact, "without faith it is impossible" to please God (Heb. 11:6). Faith speaks of persuasion, conviction, confident perception.

Faith is not a miracle; it is not an intrusion of the Divine will upon an impotent human spirit. Faith is the belief of testimony — Divine testimony or "record" (I John 5:10). From the perspective of the new covenant, faith is also the "testimony of Jesus" (Rev. 12:17); the witness of Deity concerning things alien to the blighted and corrupted capacities of nature. This testimony is provided in an intelligent format, and is addressed to the understanding. It conveys the awareness of otherwise imperceptible reality.

The things faith embraces are brought within the grasp of the human spirit by the Word of God. The means of appropriating that reality is "hearing." "So then faith comes by hearing . . ." (Rom. 10:17), declares the King's Word! This is an inward hearing — one within man's spirit, and is called "the hearing of faith" (Gal. 3:2,5). There is an inseparable link between true faith and the hearing of which we speak. This hearing involves more than a mere awareness of activity. It is joined to desire, willingness, and intention. Those that do not receive and act upon what they hear do not possess the "hearing of faith." The mere "hearing of the ear" (Job 42:5) is not enough!

Faith and Hearing

In the kingdom of God, one cannot believe until he has heard. ". . . how shall they believe on Him of whom they have not heard?" (Rom. 10:14). No word, no hearing! No hearing, no faith! The mere witness of God's overt working will not produce the required conviction of kingdom realities that is essential for salvation. Not even a Divine miracle will of itself create such an awareness. The personal witness of the events surrounding the resurrection of the Lord Jesus Christ from the dead, for example did not foster faith in the soldiers (Matt. 28:2-4).

Faith comes by hearing, not be seeing! Faith comes by hearing, not feeling! Faith comes by hearing, not intuitive inclinations! Faith comes by hearing, not mere intellectual probings!

Hearing is superior to seeing! Above it! Transcendent to it! "Hear and your soul shall live" cries the Father Himself (Isa. 55:3). The Lord Jesus confirmed that this promise spans both covenants (John 5:25). Little wonder that the apostolic doctrine demands that every man "be swift to hear" (James 1:19). Hearing is integral to life — spiritual life! Hearing is associated with faith — saving faith! While we are in the body, there is infinitely more to be heard than there is to be seen! The blessing is pronounced upon those that "hear," not those that "see" (Matt. 3:16; John 20:29; Rev. 1:3).

When it comes to doing the will of God — and that is certainly an essential element in God's Kingdom — it is hearing that profitably precedes doing. ". . . whosoever hears these sayings of mine, and does them . . ." (Matt. 7:24). Our Lord Jesus still admonishes, ". . . take heed how ye hear . . ." (Luke 8:18). "Take heed what ye hear . . ." (Mark 4:24). The clarion voice of King Jesus is still heard through His mighty Word: "He that has ears to hear, let him hear" (Matt. 11:15; 13:9,43; Luke 8:8). Why? Because "hearing" is the appointed means through which we obtain the salvation of God!

Living by the Word of God

Now we have come to the crux of the matter: the Word of God is absolutely necessary in an economy of faith — an economy where chief assets and benefits are unseen, unsensed, and inaccessible to the physical apparatus of man. God has "magnified His Word above all His name" (Psa. 138:2) because man has no other way of apprehending eternal things. If God does not speak, man will not know! If God does not articulate clear and authentic words concerning heavenly realities, man will have no bona fide concepts of those things.

There is life in God's kingdom, and that life is sustained by the Word of God. This is a higher life, and is maintained by a loftier resource. "Man shall not live by bread alone," our Lord proclaimed, "but by every

119

word that proceeds out of the mouth of God" (Matt. 4:4).

Man's life, therefore, consists of more than physical or external matters. Life sustained by mere "bread" actually is inferior, as well as "temporal" (II Cor. 4:18). The life that is supported by the word of God is that of spiritual knowledge of and in relation to Him. In Christ we are "alive unto God" (Rom. 6:11), and it is that life which requires "every word of God for" its sustenance.

Response Integral to Life

An individual is only alive to the degree of his responsiveness to his environment. When, for instance, our earthly bodies totally cease to respond to earth's environment, we are dead. If we are unable to appropriate natural resources through our bodily functions, we simply are no longer alive!

The same principle prevails in the kingdom of God. For life — eternal life — to be had, there must be reciprocity; proper response to Divine availabilities. God's love, mercy, grace, guidance, and Person, will yield no spiritual benefit unless they are "received," brought into our persons by faith. Faith is the faculty for appropriation, the Word of God is the vehicle through which Divine resources are made available. The order of progression here is this: 1. Reality, 2. Word, 3. Appropriation. There can be no Divine word unless there is reality, and there can be no appropriation without that word! "Man . . . shall live by every word of God."

Representation by the Word

The Word of God is not merely a legal code; it is the articulation of a whole body of reality. Our association with that reality determines whether or not we are alive unto God. Further our participation in that reality is determined by our perception and reception of the word of God. We are speaking of "the word of the kingdom" (Matt. 13:19-23); the "Scriptures" (Rom. 16:26); the "holy Scriptures" (Rom. 1:2), etc. The Word of God nourishes our faith, which is the "evidence of things not seen." It confirms to our hearts the presence of sustaining reality! Take away the Word of God, and faith has no food, no resource, no means of support.

120

The Word Works Effectually

Often the Scriptures are referred to in a personal sense, as though they had the attributes of an individual: "The comfort of the Scriptures" (Rom. 15:4); "the Scripture says" (Rom. 9:17; 10:11); "the Scripture foreseeing that God would justify the heathen through faith" (Gal. 3:8); "the Scripture has concluded all under sin" (Gal. 3:22), etc. It is also declared that "the word of God is living and powerful" (Heb. 4:12), and that the "engrafted word" is "able to save the soul" (James 1:21).

God has virtually equated Himself and His benefits with His Word. Certainly not because the Word and He are identical, or because the Word and eternal benefits are the same. God is personally and conceptually separate from His word, and His benefits exists in distinction to the Word. The word of God however, is an expression of His Person, and the intelligent transmission of the reality of His benefits.

When it comes to "finding God" (Acts 17:27), "obeying God" (Acts 5:29), or "believing God" (Acts 27:25), the word is absolutely necessary! None of these things can be accomplished without the word of God. In fact, these are all actually responses to God's word — and response is evidence of life!

By way of contrast, ignoring the things of God, and living for pleasure, is actually death. "She that lives in pleasure is dead while she lives" (I Tim. 5:6) — dead to God and the things of God! Impervious to heavenly stimuli! Unaware of heavenly realities! The means of getting saving persuasion into the heart — the word of God — has been ignored. Thus life in Christ is rendered impossible, and death dominates, for man does "live by every word of God."

The Priority of Hearing

In view of this situation — that "man lives by every word of God" — what a high priority should be placed upon the Word! Familiarity with it, a joyful reception of it, and a willing submission to it are imperative for spiritual life!

Let us be clear about this: without spiritual life there is no hope of heaven, and without the word of God, there is no possibility of that life. Ignorance of the Scriptures is an intolerable situation! It actually alienates from God, and renders heavenly reality inaccessible (Eph. 4:18). This simply means that man cannot have "eternal life" apart from the "knowledge of God" (I Cor. 15:34), and this saving knowledge is administered through the Word of God.

God's personality is in His Word. His purpose is clearly reflected there. When your mind is subjected to the "holy Scriptures," you are submitting yourself to the mind of the Lord! You are being ushered into the realm of life when you pick up your Bible and begin to take it seriously!

The Word of God is not mystical; it is not magical! Its purity (Prov. 30:5) and accessibility (Rom. 10:8) combine, when received, to convey to the mind of man the great and beneficent love of God toward His offspring! The power of the Word (Heb. 4:12) is not basically, however, in the message that it declares, but in the Person that has given it. It is as the message is associated with the Person of God, that His Word becomes effectual.

It is possible to read the Bible without realizing genuine profit; to submit our minds to the "scriptures" in vain. What a tragic possibility! Our Lord Jesus indicted the Pharisees: "Search the scriptures; for in them ye think ye have eternal life: and they are they which testify of me . . . and ye will not come to me that ye might have life" (John 5:39-40; 8:47). They had failed to make the connection between God and His Word, and thus had no faith or life!

The Necessity of Hearing

I must labor this point; it is a pivotal truth that must be apprehended by the heart! During the early days of the Restoration Movement, the Scriptures had lost their identity with God in the minds of myriads. Experience, philosophy, and independent views had supplanted the lofty revelation of the Almighty. One of the great contributions of those spiritual stalwarts was their exaltation of God's Word and their stress of our absolute dependence upon it. Faith cannot be had or maintained apart from the Word of God, and spiritual life is undeniably dependent upon it.

The pressing need of our day is to again exalt the Word of God making plain its indispensable role in the salvation of man. It was a noble work that was done by earlier Restorationists, but it must be done again. Men must be made aware that "man shall not live by bread alone, but by every word that proceedeth out of the mouth of God!"

The Word and Eternal Life

The Word of God is "able to build you up, and give you an inheritance among all them that are sanctified" (Acts 20:32). Peter recognized the inseparable unity between God's word and His purpose. "Whereby are given unto us exceeding great and precious promises, that BY THESE ye might be partakers of the Divine nature," he wrote (II Pet. 1:4). This sharing in the "Divine nature" is elsewhere referred to as being "joined to the Lord" (I Cor. 6:17), being "baptized into Christ" (Gal. 3:28), and being "in Christ" (II Cor. 5:17). Peter associates this blessed unity with the promises of God — the articulated promises of God.

God has no promises that are not spoken, that have not been couched in intelligent words! There are no hidden promises — they are all revealed; revealed in the Word of God! Were you to take all of the promises of God relative to redemption in Christ Jesus, and place them in a single statement, it would read like this; "This is the promise that He hath promised us, even eternal life" (I John 2:25).

Oh, what a glorious statement is that! "ETERNAL LIFE"! This is the intimate knowledge of God of which our Lord Jesus spoke, when He prayed to His Father; "And this is life eternal, that they might know Thee, the only true God, and Jesus Christ, whom Thou has sent" (John 17:3). John further elaborated on "eternal life" when he wrote: "And we know that the Son of God is come, and has given us an understanding, THAT WE MAY KNOW HIM that is true, and we are in Him that is true, even in His Son Jesus Christ. THIS IS THE TRUE GOD, AND ETERNAL LIFE" (I John 5:20). All of the promises are gathered together in the single phrase "eternal life"!

Peter has declared that we partake of the Divine nature — simply another view of eternal life — by means of the promises! They are the appointed means through which we "lay hold of eternal life" (I Tim. 6:12,19). Further, there are no promises that are not in the Word of God; that is the container into which every single promise has been deposited. There can be no awareness of the promises apart from the Word of God. There can be no enjoyment of the promises apart from that Word.

Conclusion

The Word of God is necessary in an economy of faith! The "faith"

123

deals with an unseen world, an unseen God, an unseen Mediator, and an unseen inheritance. The knowledge of all these things is brought to us exclusively through the Word of God — the Scriptures. The faith by which we are justified (Rom. 5:1) can only come by "hearing" — the hearing that involves submission to the Word of God. No Word, no faith! No faith, no salvation!

The involvement which is so sorely needed by us all is produced through faith. Hearts are "purified by faith" (Acts 15:9); the child of God "lives" by faith (Heb. 10:38); we "stand" in a state of acceptability "by faith" (Rom. 11:20); we have access to God "by faith" (Eph. 3:12); and Christ "dwells" in our hearts "by faith" (Eph. 3:17). It is thus true that "without faith it is impossible to please God" (Heb. 11:6); and it is equally true that where there is no word, there is no faith.

This Word of God has been invested with power to "convert the soul," "make wise the simple," "rejoice the heart," and "enlighten the eyes" (Psa. 19:7-8). It but remains for you to capitalize on this Divine and unique resource. It is for you!

9

KNOWING REALITY THROUGH WORDS

There are at least three ways of obtaining knowledge: experience, philosophy, and revelation. The first two are valid means of appropriating earthly knowledge, but are inferior, and sometimes invalid, in respect to obtaining heavenly reality. The Kingdom of God is a heavenly Kingdom, and has to do with the implementation of Divine objectives. It does not center in this world, nor can it be discerned by those enamored of it. The knowledge of the nature of the Kingdom is essential for fellowship with God, abiding in Christ, and the communion of the Holy Spirit. Oneness with Deity cannot be achieved in a state of ignorance!

Experience is the most rudimentary means of obtaining knowledge. The old aphorism, "Experience is the best teacher," does not hold true in God's Kingdom. On one occasion, Jesus fed a multitude of people with five loaves and two fishes. Over five thousand "did eat and were filled" (Matt. 14:15-21). It is difficult to conceive of an experience more wonderful. A miracle wrought before their very eyes, and their bellies filled with the evidence. But it did little for their spirits because its significance was not grasped. "Ye seek me not because ye saw the miracle," i.e. discerned its import, the Lord later said (John 6:26). They did not apply their hearts to the matter, and thus it did not profit them. They were so insensitive to the work that when the Son of God proclaimed the significance of it, "many of His disciples went back, and walked no more with Him" (John 6:65).

Philosophy as a Source of Knowledge

Philosophy has reason as its highest source, and earthly experience as its foundation. It can only probe into things unknown in terms of what is known or experienced in earthly life. When it comes to the things of God, philosophy is like a man groping in the dark. Presumption saturates all of its efforts, and certainty is virtually unknown. It is unassisted understanding. It tries to arrive at heavenly reality by starting with earth — the same type of error made by those at the tower of Babel (Gen. 11). This is the philosophy and "vain deceit" of which the Apostle warned (Col. 2:8).

Philosophy is limited to the realm of human experience, unless developed upon the foundation of revelation. Unassisted, it is valueless as touching eternal things. It makes no difference how keen the mind, or how disciplined the quest for knowledge, "the wisdom of men" cannot appropriate things "pertaining to life and godliness" (I Cor. 3:19; II Pet. 1:3).

Revelation

Revelation starts with God and ends with man. It requires an initial inclination on the part of God, and a capacity to receive on the part of man. Both exist by the will of God — God is willing and man is able. Not only, however, is God willing; He has articulated His will to men in "the Scriptures" (Rom. 16:26).

What God reveals must be discerned to be profitable. Truth is apprehended by the understanding of it. This is coming "unto the knowledge of the truth" (I Tim. 2:4). The "things of the Spirit of God" (I Cor. 2:14) are in heaven and cannot be apprehended with the senses. Further, they lie beyond the reach of man's curiosity. It is only through the comprehension of faith that they can be perceived. Revelation requires belief, not experience, to produce and maintain life toward God.

The proclamation of the purpose of God is declared to be the

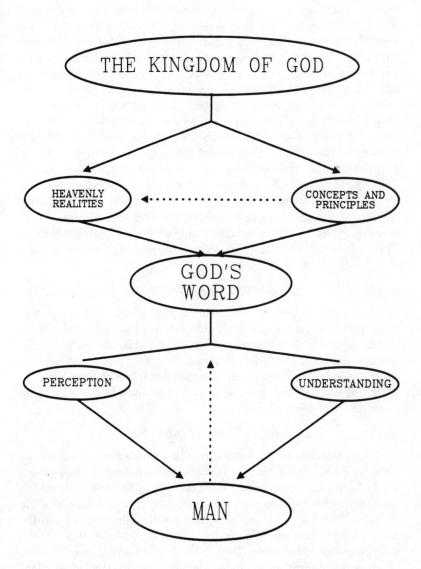

127

"revelation of the mystery which was kept secret since the world began" (Rom. 16:25). If God had not revealed it, it would still be secret — still obscured to men. The basic message was revealed "to His holy Apostles" (Eph. 3:5). That message is not the result of earnest inquiry, nor the product of mere human analysis. It is true with the Apostles, as with the prophets of old, that ". . . no prophecy of Scripture is of any private interpretation. For the prophecy came not in old time by the will of man, but holy men of God spake as they were moved by the Holy Ghost" (II Pet. 2:20-21). When it comes to the Word of God — the expression of His mind — God shared His purpose with men in words. Holy men did not merely convey to us what they thought God meant. The Scriptures are not a personal and private interpretation of God's mind. The intellectual ability of the Apostles was not their chief resource, but rather their faith. Faith dominated their reason as God revealed the truth to them, and then "moved them" to speak that truth. They did not speculate on the meaning of the revelation . . . they knew it!

Philosophy Versus Revelation

Philosophy gropes, revelation finds! Man is the chief resource in philosophy, God is the resource in revelation. Philosophy is characterized by neutrality — it does not carry with it logical demands. Revelation, on the other hand, is not neutral. It is the communication of a desirous God to needy man, and demands a response from man. To thrust the Word of God from us is to "judge" ourselves "unworthy of everlasting life" (Acts 13:46).

The Word Brings Truth to Man

Pilate, unaware of the Person standing before him, asked Christ, "What is truth?" (John 18:38). This was not an honest question, else it would have been answered by our Lord. Jesus had just declared His association with the truth, as well as man's obligation to hear what He declared. "To this end was I born, and for this cause came I into the world, that I should bear witness unto the truth. Everyone that is of the truth hears my voice" (John 18:37). Truth is not ambiguous; it can be clearly asserted. Further, everyone identified with the truth gives attention to what Jesus declared. His "witness" consists of His words, His teaching, His proclamation. He came to declare in speech what could not otherwise be known!

Christ was the embodiment of truth. "I am the . . . truth," He proclaimed (John 14:6). He was a tangible demonstration of God's Person and will. When He was correctly perceived, an acquaintance with the Lord was achieved: "He that hath seen me hath seen the Father" (John 14:9), Christ declared. Viewed from the standpoint of the Illuminator of truth, we read, "the Spirit is truth" (I John 5:6). He takes the things of God and shows them to men; i.e., unveils them to their understanding (John 16:13-15). The Scriptures are the expression of reality in words. Thus did Jesus confess, "Thy word is truth" (John 17:17). Whether we speak of Christ, the Spirit, or the Word of God, it is the reality being communicated that is the point. It is what Jesus said and what Jesus did that constituted the revelation. It is what the Spirit illuminates that is the point, and what the Word proclaims that is to be embraced.

The Value of Persuasion

The Word of God makes truth accessible to men; it brings reality within their grasp. Laying hold of truth, however, is not an accomplishment of the senses. It is not something that is "felt" or transmitted to the spirit of man by sight or touch. It is the belief of the testimony that brings the possession of the truth. From the standpoint of the result of faith, this reception is called "persuasion" — when one is convinced of the truth, he possesses it. When he is persuaded in his heart that what God's Word said precisely represents reality, the truth has been apprehended. When Abraham was "fully persuaded that what He [God] had promised, He was able also to perform" (Rom. 4:21), the fulfillment of the promise was on the way! Those that "doubt" the testimony, however, shall not receive the benefit. The testimony is the means of participation, and persuasion is the way men lay hold of the testimony.

The faithful Hebrews of old were given promises that were beyond the realm of contemporary experience. But they received the testimony of those good things, and being "persuaded of them," embraced them conforming their manner of life to those unseen realities (Heb. 11:13). On the other hand, Agrippa deprived himself of the blessing of eternal life, being only "almost" persuaded of the things of which the Apostle spoke (Acts 26:28). Persuasion is the overcoming of doubt and unbelief. Where it is absent, the Word has not been received, and thus the truth has not been appropriated. There has been, in such a case, no blessing, no benefit, no participation in the Kingdom of God.

The Exclusiveness of the Word

The impression of the things of God upon the spirit of man is essential for their enjoyment. But this cannot be accomplished without the Word of God. Men cannot ascend up into heaven to bring the truth down. As it is written,

> But the righteousness which is of faith speaketh on this wise, Say not in thine heart, Who shall ascend into heaven? (that is, to bring Christ down from above;) or, Who shall descend into the deep? (that is, to bring Christ up again from the dead). But what saith it? THE WORD IS NIGH THEE, even in thy mouth and in they heart: that is, THE WORD OF FAITH, which we preach (Rom. 10:6-8).

The Word of God is the exclusive means of bringing Christ and His work to men. It is called "the word of faith" because it is the vehicle through which faith comes. The Word of God does not, however, produce faith of itself. If it is not believed, it is powerless. It must be believed, accepted, embraced! No dream, no fleshly experience, no physical sensation is equivalent to the Word. It is the Word that is nigh, or near, unto us. That is, the Word of God is in our language, adapted to our minds, and suited to our needs. It gives substance to the things of God, exposes us to His mind, and brings to us the good news of His provisions for man. "Good is the word of the Lord"! (II Kgs. 20:19).

Right Thinking Is Essential

A conception is an understanding, true or false. While men are free to develop their own concepts, they are not free to establish their validity. Concepts, or views, of truth are ultimately subject to the scrutiny of God. He will "make manifest the counsels of the hearts" (I Cor. 4:5). It may be true, in a temporal sense, that "every man has a right to his own opinion," but the results of that opinion are not optional, and are critical. It is imperative that sound conceptions and proper thoughts be had concerning things pertaining to God.

The thoughts of a man reflect his person and determine his character. Solomon spoke the truth when he said, "For as he thinks in his heart, so is he . . ." (Prov. 23:7). Elaborating upon that reality,

Jesus said, "A good man out of the treasure of his heart brings forth that which is good; and an evil man out of the evil of his heart brings forth that which is evil. For out of the abundance of the heart his mouth speaks" (Luke 6:45).

The Lord "knows the thoughts of the wise," declares the Apostle (I Cor. 3:20). Again, it is proclaimed that the Word of God is a "discerner of the thoughts and intents of the heart" (Heb. 4:12). While the Lord is able to examine every individual thought expressed by man, this is not the point of these verses. The Word of God is able, through its proclamation, to discover where man's thinking is at variance with the thoughts of God — where God's thoughts are not man's thoughts (Isa. 55:8-9). The discovery of faulty concepts, erroneous views, and vain thoughts is the point.

The Galatians thought men could be justified by the works of the Law (Gal. 3:1-13). That was a faulty concept! The Thessalonians thought that because Christ was coming, they should refrain from earthly duties, and wait for Christ in a state of idleness (II Thess. 2-3). That was an erroneous view! Some of the Corinthian teachers thought that there was no resurrection of the dead (I Cor. 15:12-25). Truly, a false conception!

Concepts must be correct for living to be right. They must be acceptable if life is to be acceptable. One cannot entertain false views and live acceptably in the areas of life directed by those views! It is not enough to be supposedly sincere. Man's thoughts concerning God and His will must be right, or he will live amiss and leave this world only to confront an angry and displeased God.

The Form of Sound Words

The Kingdom of God is one of the orderliness. It is characterized by timeliness and exactness. Whatever God does is marked by precision. When He sent His Son, it was "in the fulness of the time" (Gal. 4:4). When He judges the world by Christ, it will be on a day "appointed" (Acts 17:31). Israel's deliverance from Egypt was precise — on the "selfsame day" before appointed (Exod. 12:51). When Noah entered into the ark, he did so on the "selfsame day" (Gen. 7:13). When the day of Pentecost was "fully come," the church was inaugurated (Acts 2:1). Creation was orderly, and the end of the world shall be exact. Everything God has done or will do is precise, governed by Divine appointment.

God's Word, the means He has ordained to implement His purpose, is characterized by the same exactness that distinguishes Himself. The words of Scripture are "words which the Holy Ghost teaches" (I Cor. 2:13). They portray God's mind, exactly reflecting heavenly things. Spiritual things may only be conveyed in spiritual words — words that are not vague and mysterious, but perfectly expressive of spiritual reality.

It is imperative that men use "sound words" when speaking of the Kingdom of God. "Hold fast the form of sound words," admonished the Apostle (II Tim. 1:13). The reason for the counsel is clear. The only way to maintain a grasp on the things of God is to think properly of them. Hence, the only way to promote proper thoughts of them is to speak correctly concerning them. If unsound or unacceptable words are employed, unsound and unacceptable thoughts will be generated concerning life and death matters. The objective is not to speak the things of God in the most simple manner, but in the most precise manner! It is not only to communicate, but to communicate correctly. No eternal purpose shall have been served if faulty views are fostered by our speaking.

The correct articulation of the things of God enables one to "hold fast the faithful word as he hath been taught . . ." (Titus 1:9). Our grasp of the Gospel is only as firm as our apprehension of the words constituting that Gospel! Learn to say it right! That is one of your greatest contributions to men. Insist upon speaking with the words that "the Holy Ghost teaches." The things of God must not be reduced in expression to the language of the street. It is man's obligation to learn what God said, not to couch the Gospel in simplistic terms that are adapted more to man's ignorance than to the realities they are intended to proclaim!

Words are a container for truth. If they are proper, they will hold a good amount of truth. If they are general and inadequate, they will not be able to convey truth to the hearts of men. Men are admonished to maintain "incorruptness" in their doctrine or teaching (Titus 2:7). Those who represent the King of kings are charged to "teach no other doctrine" (I Tim. 1:13). Exhortations are to be made effective by using "sound doctrine" (Titus 1:9), and we are to avoid anything that is "contrary to sound doctrine" (I Tim. 1:10). Teaching that is sound and without corruption is "good doctrine" (I Tim. 4:6).

If God communicates His purpose through His Word, then an inaccurate representation of that word will result in the obscurement of God's will, and the consequent condemnation of men. When men are carried away with "every wind of doctrine" (Eph. 4:14), and give ear to "diverse doctrines" (Heb. 13:9), they are led away from God and into sin. There can be no connection with God — participation in His salvation — apart from doctrine! The reason for this is evident. We are in a world that has been cursed, and consequently the things of God may only be procured by faith. Faith, on the other hand, must have a word from God — and that word is doctrine, teaching, or instruction.

Every place unsound doctrine was proclaimed, serious repercussions were noted and warned against. The "doctrine of the Pharisees" was to be avoided because of its leavening influence upon men's hearts (Matt. 16:13-14). To be carried about by the inconsistent doctrines of men would result in sure deception (Eph. 4:14). Doctrines originating with men actually nullified worship, according to the word of Christ (Matt. 15:9).

What is God doing? What are men to be doing? What are the implications of the Gospel of Christ? The proclaimed answers to these, and other, questions constitute doctrine. No provision is made for error in doctrine. If men teach in the Name of the Lord, they are required to teach correctly! The Kingdom of God cannot be served with false gospels and strange doctrines! Blessings cannot come from a lie, and eternal life cannot be administered through misrepresentation.

In order to participate in God's salvation and citizenship in His Kingdom, a knowledge of His truth is demanded. That is how God has ordered it! When Jesus came, He spoke the truth. For Him to have done otherwise would have been to betray His mission and cause it to fail. His followers are no less obligated to hold fast the form of sound words and proclaim sound doctrine. Truth cannot be maintained unless it is articulated properly! It will not "free" (John 8:32) unless it is correctly stated.

The church, as "the pillar and ground of the truth," is to hold forth the "word of life." Its message must not constitute a hindrance to men's apprehension of the truth. The church is the custodian of the form of the truth, as well as of the truth itself. In fact, the form of the truth is the only means of expressing the truth. Under the first covenant, men were given a "form of knowledge and of the truth in the law" (Rom. 2:21). When God engraved the ten commandments on tables of stone, He solidified their expression. The words themselves contained the thoughts of revelations of the law. Thinking of God's Law was not possible apart from these words — they were the "form of the truth."

Learning to use the "form of sound words" is the same as using "wholesome words" (I Tim. 6:3). "Wholesome words" are words without flaw; words that are in perfect agreement with the things they represent. They are words as precise as the realities of which they treat. The emphasis here is on the vocabulary used rather than the thoughts conveyed. God has developed a vocabulary — a nomenclature — that transmits to men His mind and purpose. Some of these key words are "atonement" (Rom. 5:11), "reconciliation" (II Cor. 5:19), "sacrifice" (Eph. 5:2), "sanctification" (I Cor. 1:30), "covenant" (Heb. 8:10-13), "death" (Rom. 6:3-4), and "life" (John 17:3). God has invested these words with eternal soundness. It is man's obligation to maintain their form in order to convey and maintain the truth. A failure to do this will result in removing the key of knowledge (Luke 11:52), and the shutting up of the Kingdom of God against men (Matt. 23:13).

The Necessity of Sound Doctrine

While "sound words" refer to the vocabulary used to declare truth, "doctrine" refers to the development of the implications of that truth. "Words" emphasize how it is taught, "doctrine" declares what is taught. Doctrine is an essential part of the Kingdom of God. It is the means God has chosen to bring men into the Kingdom of His dear Son (Col. 1:13).

There are many doctrines in the world, and thus we have an arena of competition. There are "doctrines of men" (Mark 7:7), "doctrines of devils" (I Tim. 4:1), and "the doctrine of Christ" (II John 9). There are objectives behind all of these doctrines. The "doctrines of men" have been originated by men and have objectives that center in men's vanity. The "doctrines of devils" were originated by demonic hosts, and are designed to draw men into perdition. The "doctrine of Christ," on the other hand, proclaims Christ Jesus, the significance of His redemption, and the means by which men may appropriate it. Anyone who speaks in the Name of the Lord has a doctrine — their doctrine is what they say.

Doctrine must be correct. While men are tolerant of "diverse doctrines" (Heb. 13:9), God is not. This is what molds men's minds. This is what provides them with a view of God, and in things pertaining to God, what motivates them.

The Preciousness of the Word

It is the identification of the Word of God with Himself and His objectives that makes it precious. It is not precious because it is scarce, for it has been given to us in abundance. God has spoken freely of His purpose. He has not concealed or veiled it. Deity, His work, the world, man, sin, Satan, heaven, hell, right, and wrong — God has spoken without restraint on all of these things.

He chose Moses to reveal the beginning of all things, as well as the moral reflection of Himself in the Law. He chose the prophets to introduce us to Divine planning, to the coming of a Deliverer, and the accomplishments of the propitiation for sins. The Apostles opened up the earthly ministry of the Lord Jesus, as well as His illuminating words concerning the Kingdom of God. Their words are not few, and they are not mysterious. With consistency of effort, they spoke with great "plainness of speech" (II Cor. 3:12). Because they had "the mind of Christ" (I Cor. 2:16), their aim was to "persuade men" (II Cor. 5:11), not merely to fulfill an obligation. How precious the words that come from such involvement and concern!

Before the Law was given, there "was a man in the land of Uz, whose name was Job" (Job 1:1). He was a man that was "perfect and upright, and one that feared God and eschewed evil." The things he received from God were rudimentary compared to the revelation men now have in Christ (Heb. 1:2), but they were precious to him. With grand perception he cried, "Neither have I turned back from the commandment of His lips; I have esteemed the words of His mouth more than my necessary food" (Job 23:12). He valued the sustenance of the soul above that of the body. Oh that this perception were more common in our day, when the revelation of God is more plentiful, more accessible, more understandable!

Several centuries after Job, a young man became predominant in things pertaining to God. He was known as the "sweet psalmist of Israel" (I Sam. 23:1), the one God took from the sheepfolds and made His servant (Psa. 78:70). With poetic expressiveness he wrote concerning the Divine judgments; "More to be desired are they than gold, yea than much fine gold: sweeter also than honey in the honeycomb" (Psa.

19:10). Not only did he perceive the Word of God as having inherent worth; he also knew it was satisfying to the inner nature of man. It spoke of what man needed, provided what his heart required, and addressed eternal and relevant issues.

It is imperative that the Word of God be so received if it is to profit man. Job and David perceived the truth, and that is what prompted their expressions. The Word of God is precious! It is to be preferred above bodily nourishment! It does transcend the worth of fine gold, and it is satisfying to the soul! That is because it is an expression of God's heart and aim. It is because it is the one thing tailored for fallen man.

How Love I Thy Law

The Word of God, the expression of the truth, must be loved if men are to be saved. The doom of those who do not love the truth is declared by Paul to the Thessalonians, ". . . because they received not the love of the truth that they might be saved. And for this cause God shall send them strong delusion, that they should believe a lie: that they all might be damned who believed not the truth, but had pleasure in unrighteousness" (II Thess. 2:10-12).

The "love of the truth" can be received by all men. That is why those that do not receive it will "be damned." What God proclaims in the Gospel is good, it is lovely, and it is a blessing. To love that truth is to prefer it, to be willing to sell all to obtain it, if necessary (Matt. 13:44). Anything that stands in the way of appropriating the truth will be abandoned if that truth is loved. If, however, men do not choose to love the truth, God will release the floods of delusion upon them that they may believe a lie and be condemned!

The Psalmist declared his love for God's communications (and those things committed to him did not approximate what we have in Christ): "O, how love I Thy law," he declared (Psa. 119:97). "Thy law do I love," he twice exclaimed (Psa. 119:113,163). In a zealous effort to express his heart he said, "I love thy testimonies" (Psa. 119:119), "I love Thy commands" (Psa. 119:127), and "how I love Thy precepts" (Psa. 119:159). Not content to be casual, he stressed the situation: "I love Thy testimonies exceedingly" (Psa. 119:167).

It Frees from Delusion

The enemy of truth is the "father of lies," Satan (John 8:44).

Reaching back into the history of our arch-foe, Jesus said, "He was a murderer from the beginning, and abode not in the truth, because there is not truth in him. When he speaks a lie, he speaks of his own: for he is a liar, and the father of it." As God cannot tolerate the lie, so the Devil cannot tolerate the truth. God "cannot lie" (Titus 1:1), and Satan has "no truth in him." Divine effort centers in the truth, Devilish activity focuses upon the lie.

The only power Satan has is delusion. He cannot overpower or overwhelm any of the sons of Adam that do not submit to his wiles. He has, in fact, been "destroyed" by the King of glory (Heb. 2:14), "spoiled" of his goods, and "made a show of openly" (Col. 2:15). Notwithstanding, his delusion has a captivating power that will bring men down to hell, if they are not freed from it. Their freedom is not accomplished by exorcism, or some mystical power. It is truth that liberates from Satan's dominion. Men are held captive by their thoughts and concepts, as well as by their defiled conscience. That bondage restrains them from coming to Christ, that they might have life (John 5:40).

The success of Satan is unparalleled; he has deceived "the whole world" (Rev. 12:9). Every son of Adam that reached the age of accountability has succumbed to his wiles. Like our ancient parents, the lie has brought results with alarming consistency to all outside of Christ. Into every facet of life, the Devil has woven deception.

There is the "deceitfulness of riches" (Matt. 11:32), designed to lull men into complacency concerning the determined end of all things. Even in religion he has servants that "lie in wait to deceive" (Eph. 4:14). Unrighteousness itself is deceptive, and thus lures many an unsuspecting soul into its snare (II Thess. 2:10). "Many deceivers are entered into the world" (II John 7), and they have set themselves against Christ. Evil men, working under the influence of Satan, "wax worse and worse, deceiving and being deceived" (II Tim. 3:13). False gospels, false Christs, false doctrines — they are all in Satan's arsenal.

It is against this backdrop that our Lord asserted, "If ye continue in my word, then are ye my disciples indeed; and ye shall know the truth, and the truth shall make you free. . . . If the Son shall make you free, ye shall be free indeed" (John 8:32,36). Free from delusion, and thus free from Satan! Liberated from deception, and therefore liberated from satanic bondage (II Tim. 2:26). All sin is the result of delusion! Men are

137

deceived into thinking they can ignore the truth, embrace the cursed, and live as though there was no eternity — that is why they sin. But when the truth is embraced, reality is perceived, and the hold of iniquity loses its grip. The "liberty wherewith Christ hath made us free" (Gal. 5:1) is not license, but freedom from deception. False and erroneous views not only obscure the truth, they enslave to sin!

The mission of Christ essentially deals with the liberation of men. That Sabbath day in Nazareth, when Jesus stood to announce the fulfillment of Isaiah's prophecy, He made that clear. "The Spirit of the Lord is upon me, because He hath anointed me to preach the Gospel to the poor; He hath sent me to heal the broken hearted, to preach deliverance to the captives, and recovering of sight to the blind, to set at liberty them that are bruised" (Luke 4:18). Here was a detailed view of the truth's making men "free" — of the Son making men "free indeed." The "Gospel" preached to the poor was the announcement of liberty; the proclamation of freedom from sin.

The Word of God is the "sword of the Spirit" (Eph. 6:17), and "where the Spirit of the Lord is, there is liberty" (II Cor. 3:17). Liberty from the dominion of sin! Liberty from a defiled conscience! Liberty from condemnation! Liberty from Satan and his delusions! We are no longer the servants of sin when Christ makes us free. Our wills are freed, our eyes are opened, and our hands are strengthened. This freedom is so dynamic that when we "resist the Devil" he flees from us (James 4:7). There is no greater evidence of freedom than this: a fleeing adversary! He cannot abide in a sphere of truth. He could not stay in heaven, and he cannot stay in you if the God of heaven and His Word are dwelling in you richly (Col. 3:16).

All of these things are traceable to the WORDS of God. It is His words that have conveyed to us His thoughts. His words have provided us with insight into the real nature of things. As they were embraced by faith, satanic power was broken, delusion dissipated, and freedom enjoyed. God's children have freedom to serve and worship God, and freedom to deny ungodliness. Thanks be unto God for His Word; His wonderful Word!

10

THE SUPERIORITY OF THE ARTICULATED
WORD TO DREAMS AND VISIONS

The Principle of Light

"Light" is a significant word and concept in the Kingdom of God. God Himself is known as "the Father of lights" (James 1:17), and "the message which we have heard" is that "God IS light, and in Him is no darkness" (I John 1:5). Those that have been "added to the church" (Acts 2:47) are identified as "children of light," and the "children of the day" (I Thess. 5:5). Describing our elevated status in Christ, the Apostle proclaims, "For ye were once darkness, but now are ye light in the Lord" (Eph. 5:8). John wrote that the Lord Jesus was "the Light" (John 1:7), and Christ Himself declared, "I am the light of the world" (John 8:12).

"Light" speaks of illumination — moral illumination. It is not basically a physical phenomenon, but a spiritual one. It has to do with understanding, perception, and insight. Christ was "Light" in that He exposed the world to the Person and plan of Jehovah God. God is "Light" in that it is His nature to open reality to His offspring. He is in-

139

clined to do this, and delights greatly in it. The children of God are "light" because they have been illuminated, and now diffuse light into the world. Whereas they once walked in spiritual ignorance of God and the things of God, now they "know" Him (Heb. 8:11). Like their Lord, they "have their senses exercised to discern both good and evil" (Heb. 5:14). These are the results of "light" — illumination, perception, and discernment. God Himself has opened their understanding to these things. He has not done it in a work of overwhelming power, but in the work of revelation — revelation in words that can be understood, pondered, and taken into the "memory" (I Cor. 15:3).

Historical Dreams

God has communicated with men by means of dreams and visions throughout His dealings with them. A perusal of some of these occurrences will serve to emphasize the superiority of the Word of God. The majority of recorded dreams occurred prior to the inauguration of the New Covenant. That earlier time was, of course, a period of lesser light, rudimentary knowledge, and sparse revelation.

Abimelech, a heathen king, was warned of God in a dream not to take Sarah, the wife of Abraham, to be his wife. If he did so, he would die (Gen. 20:3). Laban, a Syrian, was warned by God in a dream not to speak good or bad to Jacob (Gen. 31:24). A certain Midianite dreamed of the defeat of the Midianites by Gideon (Jdgs. 7:13). In a dream, the chief of the butlers in Egypt, was told of his restoration to Pharaoh's favor while he was in prison. The dream, however, was veiled to him, requiring the interpretation of Joseph, at the time a fellow prisoner (Gen. 40:8-25). The chief of the bakers in the same time, and of the same nation, was told of his imminent death in a dream. It, too, required interpretation by Joseph (Gen. 40:16-23).

Pharaoh, ruler of Egypt, received a revelation of a coming worldwide famine. The dream, however, was not understood, and again required interpretation (Gen. 41:1-32). King Nebuchadnezzar, ruler of Babylon, had a dream that outlined the destiny of the world kingdoms, and told of their ultimate demise and replacement by the Kingdom of God. His dream, however, was blotted from his remembrance. It not only required interpretation, but had to be brought back to the king's mind. Daniel accomplished both of these requirements (Dan. 2:3,28-48). Certain wise men, not Jews, were warned of God in a

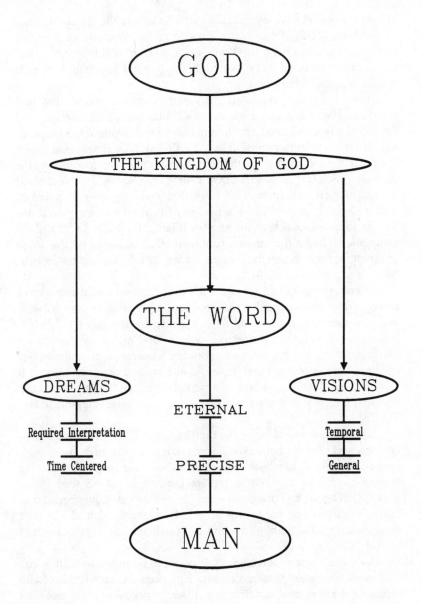

dream to avoid Herod, despotical ruler, who sought the life of the infant Jesus (Matt. 2:12). Pilate's wife, outside of the covenant of promise, had a dream concerning the Lord Jesus, then on trial before her husband. She concluded that Pilate ought not to have anything to do with that "just man" (Matt. 27:19).

There were also righteous men and covenant people that had significant dreams. Jacob dreamed of a ladder "set up upon earth, and the top of it reached into heaven: and behold the angels of God ascending and descending upon it" (Gen. 28:12-16). The dream and vision involved a confirmation of the Abrahamic covenant to him, and a pledge of the companionship of God Almighty. Again, Jacob dreamed of "rams which leaped upon the cattle that were ringstraked, speckled, and grisled." It proved to be a pledge of prosperity during what appeared to be impossible circumstances (Gen. 31:10-13). In his twilight years, Jacob had a third dream confirming that he would be able to go to Egypt for food during the time of famine, and be blessed by Joseph, his own son (Gen. 46:2-4).

Joseph, the son of Jacob, dreamed of sheaves of wheat and stars of heaven. The sheaves and stars represented his brothers and himself, and revealed that they would all bow down to him (Gen. 37:5-10). Solomon the king had a dream in which God asked concerning his preferences as a king. Upon Solomon's statement of a desire for wisdom, God confirmed that he would also receive riches and honor (I Kgs. 3:3-15). Daniel dreamed of a period when the "saints would take the kingdom," and the people of God would have authority (Dan. 7:1-28).

Joseph, husband of Mary, the mother of our Lord, had three significant dreams. All of them provided direction. In the first, he was informed that Mary, to whom he was betrothed, was to give birth to the Son of God. He was not to fear taking her to be his wife (Matt. 1:10-21). The second dream directed him to flee into Egypt because of Herod's edict to slay the infants around Bethlehem (Matt. 2:13). The third dream instructed him to return to Palestine following the death of Herod (Matt. 2:19-22).

There are some observations that ought to be made here. It is true that some today emphasize dreams, and even deprecate those who refuse to attach eternal significance to them. A review of these recorded dreams constrains us to draw several conclusions.

Divine Fellowship Not Required

Whatever may be said of dreams, Divine fellowship was not required for this sort of communication. Not only did Jacob and Joseph have valid dreams, Pharaoh and Nebuchadnezzar did also. Dreams did not necessarily result from a walk with God; they were not an integral part of oneness with Him. It ought to be obvious that such an experience does not constitute a superior manifestation of truth!

An Intrusion of Thought

Dreams are not the product of conscious contemplation or meditation. They are a Divine intrusion into man's thought processes. The will is not involved, the desire is exempted, and preference is not the point. Those that dreamed dreams were not seeking to do so; their thoughts had not been prepared for the dreams. They were placed into their minds at times when they were inactive.

Interpretation Required

The value was not in the dreams themselves, but in the interpretation of them. If words were not spoken during the dream, as in the cases of Solomon and Joseph (Mary's husband), a man of God had to interpret what was dreamed. Joseph and Daniel were known for their ability to interpret dreams. The dreams were profitless until these men opened up what they meant. The dreams, then, were not an end of themselves. It was the objective or message of them that was important.

Dealt with Temporary Situations

Eternal principles were not revealed in dreams. Almost always, they applied to life upon the earth. Redemption was not revealed by a dream. The forgiveness of sins, the inheritance in heaven, the intercession of Christ, the destruction of Satan, and the nailing of the Law to the cross of Christ — none of these were the subject of dreams! The loftier the message, the less dreams occurred! Temporal deliverances, insight into dangerous situations, moral involvements to be avoided, the appropriating of resources required for living in this world — those were the emphases of dreams!

God's Analysis of Dreams

Dreams tend to detract, and appeal to the curiosity in man rather

143

than to faith. This is not to say that they have not occurred, or that they have not had value. The point is that they have a lesser value, and that they promote lesser illumination. They are an inferior mode of Divine communication. We have God's assessment on this: ". . . which think to cause my people to forget my name by their dreams which they tell. . . . The prophet that hath a dream, let him tell a dream; and he that hath my word, let him speak my word faithfully. WHAT IS THE CHAFF TO THE WHEAT? saith the Lord" (Jer. 23:25-28). It is true that false prophets were being denounced here. However, they had employed an inferior means, a mysterious means, to promote their lies — "dreams." God categorically states that such dreams are "chaff" in comparison to His Word!

Dreams Can Be Deceiving

I am careful to point out that there have been legitimate dreams from God. Our objective here is not to deprecate this means of communication, but to identify its relative inferiority. In a commentary on the danger of dreams as the only source of understanding, Isaiah wrote; "It shall be even as when an hungry man dreams, and behold he eats; but he awakes, and his soul is empty; or as when a thirsty man dreams, and behold he drinks; but he awakes, and behold he is faint and his soul has appetite . . ." (Isa. 29:7-8).

Dreams are incapable of satisfying real need. Experience can be emulated, but not produced, by dreams. When truth was communicated through a dream, as in the case of Daniel, it was the interpretation of the dream that ministered spiritual nourishment, not the dream itself.

There Are Superior Means of Communication

One of the most prolific communications ever given to mankind came through Moses, "the servant of God" (Neh. 10:29). It is written, "the law was given by Moses . . . " (John 1:17) — the articulation of the only moral code ever administered from heaven! Apart from Christ Himself, Moses had the greatest social responsibility of any man. His "house" consisted of all Israel, and he was faithful over that house (Heb. 3:2-5).

On one occasion, the authority of Moses was questioned by those closest to him (Num. 12:1-2). Moses was "very meek" above all men which were upon the face of the earth" (Num. 12:3), and therefore did not defend himself. However, the Lord, refusing to let the incident go, "spake suddenly unto Moses, and unto Aaron, and unto Miriam, Come out ye three unto the tabernacle of the congregation." There, before this unique trio, "the Lord came down in the pillar of the cloud, and stood in the door of the tabernacle." Addressing Aaron and Miriam in particular, He said, "Hear now my words: if there be a prophet among you, I the Lord will make myself known unto him in a vision, and will speak unto him in a dream. MY SERVANT MOSES IS NOT SO, WHO IS FAITHFUL IN ALL MINE HOUSE. WITH HIM WILL I SPEAK MOUTH TO MOUTH, EVEN APPARENTLY, AND NOT IN DARK SPEECHES . . ." (Num. 12:4-8).

God here contrasts dreams with conscious, verbal communications. "Mouth to mouth" speaks of directness. To be precise, it means that God's mind was transmitted through His speech to Moses' mind, who, in turn, spoke to men. No interpretation was required, as with dreams, and thus understanding was administered rather than "dark speeches."

Again, the issue is not the validity of dreams. Dreams have always had to give way to prophecy, and often dreamers required prophets to identify the object or meaning of their dreams. Those that despise the Word of the Lord in preference for dreams have betrayed their ignorance, both of God and of the truth of God!

Scriptural Visions

The same general observations apply to visions. This was a phenomenon that found men perceiving persons and things that were not apparent to the senses. They were enabled to see spiritual phenomenon. Some of the men that had visions are, Abraham (Gen. 15:1-17), Joshua (Josh. 5:13-15), Isaiah (Isa. 6), Jeremiah (Jer. 1:11,13), and Ezekiel (Ezek. 1:3; 2:8-9; 10:1-7; 37:1-14,40-48; 47:1-12). Others were Daniel (Dan. 7-8,10) Amos, (Amos 7:1-2,3,7,8; 8:1-2; 9:1), Zechariah (Zechariah 1:8-11,18-21; 3:1-5; 4; 5:1-4; 6:1-8), Zacharias (Luke 1:22), Peter (Acts 10:10-20), and Paul (Acts 16:9; 18:9-10).

In all of these instances, the vision was not the point, but the message of the vision. The thoughts that were conveyed to the minds of men were the advantage, not the experience or witnessing of non-earthly phenomenon.

Both dreams and visions were lesser means of communication. Their message was limited, not exhaustive. Teaching was not accomplished through these means. When Jesus came, and when He sent out His disciples, they were not known for dreaming, but for speaking; not for seeing visions, but for having understanding concerning the Word of the King!

The Precision of the Word of God

While dreams may deal with statues, stalks of corn, and lean and fat cattle, the Word of God deals with particular realities. "Dark speeches" characterize dreams and visions, but not God's Word. Visions dealt with such things as "four beasts," "grasshoppers," flying rolls, and "golden candlesticks"; but the Word of God speaks plainly.

When instructing us concerning the "fruit of the Spirit," the Lord did not speak of valleys of bones, fig trees, lamps with oil, or baskets of bread. He spoke specifically of the realities resulting from the communion of the Holy Ghost (II Cor. 13:14). The mentioning of this fruitage activates the mind with sound conceptions, lofty objectives, and noble aspirations. "Love, joy, peace, longsuffering, gentleness, faith, meekness, temperance . . ." (Gal. 5:22-24). These are the products themselves, not likenesses or figures of them.

The Kingdom of God is now declared in perceptible terms, not dark speeches and mysterious visions. "For the Kingdom of God is not meat and drink, but righteousness, and peace, and joy in the Holy Ghost" (Rom. 14:17). These are the substance of the Kingdom, not parabolic forms of it.

Only the Word of God can be specific. You cannot paint an adequate picture of righteousness. It cannot be thoroughly depicted in a vision, or outlined in a dream. It transcends form and appearance. Only words can bring the real apprehension of spiritual things to men. Man is more mind than body, more thought than sense, more spiritual than flesh and blood!

When God was ready to give the world the Law, He spoke it, and had it written! It was not given in a vision, because a vision or dream could not have been as specific as words. When He determined to bring His "power unto salvation," He placed it in words — the "Gospel of Christ" (Rom. 1:16). No dream, however lofty, could possibly have communicated what the Gospel has given us. The Word of God excels in this respect. It provides direction that is continual. One small network of commands that illustrates this truth is found in I Thessalonians 5:16-22. "Rejoice evermore. Pray without ceasing. In everything give thanks . . . Quench not the Spirit. Despise not prophesyings. Prove all things; hold fast that which is good. Abstain from all appearance of evil." During our entire lifetime, there is not a single moment when these directives are not applicable. It makes no difference where we are, under what circumstances we are laboring, or what our personal accomplishments may be. No dream could convey the power of these words! No vision could transmit the conviction carried by these intelligent proclamations. Jesus said of His words, ". . . the words that I speak unto you, they are spirit, and they are life" (John 6:63). This was never said of a dream . . . never said of a vision. The power of God unto salvation is not a dream! The intrusion of Divine thought into the unconscious mind does not carry with it moral power . . . the Word of God does! The seed of the Kingdom — the thing that produces the fruitage — is God's Word, not dreams and visions (Luke 8:11).

It Declares the Inheritance

The particulars of our inheritance in Christ are proclaimed in "the word of the truth of the Gospel" (Col. 1:5). Any attempt to paint a picture of our inheritance in a dream or vision would come far short of the expressions of it in God's Word.

Think of these specifics. "The saints shall judge the world . . . we shall judge angels" (I Cor. 6:2-3). ". . . but then shall I know, even as I am known" (I Cor. 13:12). ". . . we shall bear the image of the heavenly . . ." (I Cor. 15:48-49). "When Christ, Who is our life, shall appear, then shall we also appear with Him in glory" (Col. 3:4). "If we suffer with Him, we shall also reign with Him" (II Tim. 2:12). "There remains a rest to the people of God" (Heb. 4:9). "And they shall see His face . . . and there is no night there . . . and they shall reign forever and ever" (Rev. 22:4-5).

While dreams and visions tend to generalities, the Word of God deals with specifics. The names of the righteous shall be confessed before God and before the holy angels (Rev. 3:5). Part of the great salvation brought by Christ is "the redemption of the body" (Rom. 8:23). It is at that time, when he comes, that our "vile" bodies shall be "fashioned like unto His glorious body" (Phil. 3:20). When the Lord appears, we shall also "be glad with exceeding joy" (I Pet. 4:13), for "we shall be like Him" and "see Him as He is" (I John 3:2). Everything is not told us about the world to come, but sufficient details are provided to us to whet the appetite and constrain us to become involved in the great enterprise of redemption.

Its Nourishing Capabilities

The concept of spiritual nourishment is set within the context of competition and adversity. In this world, the "man of God" (II Time. 3:17) lives in separation from his homeland. His "citizenship" is in heaven (Phil. 3:10 ASV), and his affections and appetites are anchored in a "better country" (Heb. 11:13-16). While "in the body," those that "are sanctified" (Acts 20:32) are "absent from the Lord" (II Cor. 5:6-9) — the ultimate source of life.

The world, with all of its essential elements, competes with the realm of the unseen. The result is the depletion of spiritual resources. Inner strength (Eph. 3:16) is required to live in a cursed realm! That strength must be "renewed" if spiritual life is to be maintained (Eph. 4:23). That unique benefit of faith was proclaimed by the prophet Isaiah: "But they that wait upon the Lord shall renew their strength . . ." (Isa. 40:31).

In an arena of spiritual conflict, our minds become like sieves. Without regular input, the awareness of spiritual reality gradually dissipates, the heart becomes hard, and enmity with God develops. This is the jeopardy associated with the faith-life: if the faith is not maintained, the life it sustains will fail. While the Savior died "once for all" (Heb. 10:10), faith is not a once-for-all transaction. Faith is, in fact, only as strong as the effort expended by men to maintain it!

Able to Make the Man of God Perfect

But God's Word renews our strength. It is able to make the man of God "perfect, throughly furnished unto all good works" (II Tim. 3:16-17). It appeals to the chief part of man — his mind. That is his faculty of chief utility when it comes to serving the Lord. "With my MIND, I myself serve the law of God," asserted the Apostle (Rom. 7:25). All of our kingdom concepts have been formed by God's Word. Our understanding of the love of God, the grace of God, the longsuffering of God, His power, His wisdom, and His will has been produced by

His Word. No dream has conveyed to us the magnitude of His "great love wherewith He loved us" (Eph. 2:4).

No vision was used to proclaim His wonderful grace. When "the grace of God that bringeth salvation" appeared, it did so in Gospel proclamation. The historical appearance of Christ achieved no lasting results until it was interpreted and proclaimed to the sons of men! Unproclaimed, the Gospel is ineffectual for salvation. A vision of Christ dying on the cross will not save a soul, or bring one to a state of reconciliation. It is the "Gospel" that is the "power of God unto salvation" (Rom. 1:16). Men trust "after" they have "heard the word of the truth," the "gospel" of their "salvation" (Eph. 1:13).

It is the "word of His grace" that is "able to build you up, and to give you an inheritance among all them which are sanctified" (Acts 20:32). Our life toward God is traceable to "every word of God," by which we live (Matt. 4:4). Men are not admonished to go to their bedchamber and seek for dreams if they are to know the will of the Lord, but to "hear what the Spirit SAITH to the churches" (Rev. 2:29). Spiritual strength and stability are developed and maintained by means of the Word of God.

It is by desiring "the sincere milk of the word" that men grow in the grace and knowledge of God (I Pet. 2:2; II Pet. 3:18). Spiritual growth is essential if one is to be saved. This is proclaimed in the parable of the Sower (Matt. 13:3-9,18-23). There are those that hear and do not understand. The Word brings no profit to them in any form. Some receive the Word "with joy," but because they have "no root" in themselves, endure only "for a while." The Word of the Kingdom brought no lasting benefit to them! Still others receive the Word without putting away their lust for other things. Thus the "cares of this world, and the deceitfulness of riches, choke the Word, and it becomes unfruitful." No eternal benefit, in such a case, is gained from the Word of God. In all three of these instances, satisfactory growth did not occur.

The only ones that prove satisfactory are those that bear fruit: i.e., yield good and pleasing results. THEY GROW! The Word of God dwells "richly" in them (Col. 3:16) resulting in a life that is compatible with heaven. They think as God! They perceive as God. They rejoice with Him, and they work in perfect compliance with His will and way.

Only the Word of God can sustain such a growth process. No amount of religious activity can accomplish this requirement. No experience, however wonderful and valid, can sustain spiritual life! Visions, dreams, bodily sensations, etc. — they are all impotent when it comes to the development and advancement of spiritual life.

The reason for this is obvious. We are in an realm that conflicts with spiritual reality. Satan is the "god of the world" (II Cor. 4:4), and as such has corrupted it within and without with sin. The superior life of God cannot be nurtured by the inferior temporalities of this world — religious or otherwise. We must have word from the homeland to renew us! The Word of God is specific, and conveys precise conceptions of the realities faith embraces. This gracious provision has enabled us to "grow in the grace and knowledge of our Lord and Savior Jesus Christ" (II Pet. 3:18).

The Eternality of the Word

Dreams and visions are not meant to be eternal. They deal more with earthly history than with eternal verity, more with general observations than specific realities. But the Word of God is not so. Jesus declared, ". . . my words shall not pass away" (Mark 13:31). The Word of God is the "incorruptible" seed "which lives and abides forever" (I Pet. 1:23). Of old, David cried, "Forever, O Lord, Thy Word is settled in heaven" (Psa. 119:89).

The Sense of Its Eternality

The Kingdom of God is an intelligent Kingdom, dealing with a discernible purpose. It is therefore imperative that men not adopt overly-simplistic views of the "Word of the Kingdom" (Matt. 13:19). God's Word is not "eternal" merely in the sense of longevity. There are very real words of God that will not transfer into the world to come. Men ought not to stumble at this, for it is true. "The flesh lusts against the Spirit, and the Spirit against the flesh" (Gal. 5:17). . . . "I find then a law, that when I would do good, evil is present with me" (Rom. 7:21). . . . "For in this [the body] we groan, earnestly desiring to be clothed upon with our house which is from heaven" (II Cor. 5:2). These words are not "eternal" in the cursory sense of the word. They pertain only to this world, to this time, and to men in the flesh. They have no applicability on the other side of "the veil" (Heb. 10:20), and are not descriptive of the glorified saints!

While some of the Divine affirmations address the temporal conditions of men, they nevertheless fit into an "eternal purpose" (Eph. 3:11). There is an "eternal salvation" that requires their affirmation (Heb. 5:9), and they have been "written" in view of "eternal redemption" (Heb. 9:12). God's Word — the Word of the Kingdom — prepares men for "eternal glory" (II Tim. 2:10), and promises an "eternal inheritance" (Heb. 9:15). From the viewpoint of what the Word of God is designed to implement, it is, therefore, an eternal word!

It Anchors Men to Eternity

Once received and obeyed, the Word of God produces a "hope" that is an "anchor of the soul, both stedfast and sure, and which enters into that within the veil" (Heb. 6:19). It enables men "in the body" to live with a heavenly perspective — to be cognizant of unchanging reality. They entertain no doubts concerning the temporality of this world, or the eternality of "the world to come." They enjoy a fellowship with "the city of the Living God, the heavenly Jerusalem," and "an innumerable company of angels . . . the general assembly and church of the firstborn, which are written in heaven, and . . . God the Judge of all, and . . . the spirits of just men made perfect, and . . . Jesus the Mediator of the new covenant, and . . . the blood of sprinkling, that speaks better things than that of Abel" (Heb. 12:22-24). All of those realities are untainted with earth . . . they are all heavenly in their essence. Corruption and defilement are not found among them. It is, further, the Word of God that has made such a glorious unity possible. It is an eternal Word in that it has united us with eternal personalities and objectives.

Conclusion

God's Kingdom is a moral Kingdom. Heavenly rule concerns the accomplishments of a planned undertaking. Design and reason are woven throughout the fabric of that Divine purpose. As concerns men, God's will is being implemented in a moral arena — this world. Thought, decision, and intelligence are attributes of this Kingdom — in both the King and the constituents of His Kingdom.

The reconciliation of man — the revealed purpose of God — involves the uniting of God's offspring to Himself. That union, because it is an intelligent one, requires understanding on the part of men. For this reason, God has "magnified" His Word above all of His name (Psa.

151

138:2). The Word is the means of bringing men to this required understanding of God and His will. It is an appeal to the mind of man, and can remain a part of him when it is believed.

Dreams were never meant to be a permanent or preeminent means of heavenly communication. They are valid, but not superior. The things revealed by them were limited to this world and time — the time of the curse. They were generally relevant for only a short period of time, and did not deal with eternal issues. Dreams dealt with earthly circumstances, and, with few exceptions, became obsolete with the passing of those that had them.

Visions were an accommodation to man's infirmity, and were limited in the intelligent concepts that they conveyed. Symbols and types were integral in visions, thereby requiring lengthy interpretation. In fact, some visions were never fully interpreted (Ezek. 1). Their purpose was more the creation of impression than the communication of thought. Further, a very general impression was conveyed rather than specific thoughts.

The predominance of God's Word confirms that it harmonizes more completely with His revealed purpose. It is, therefore, superior to dreams and visions — both logically and in the results that it produces.

PART FOUR:
THE PRINCIPLE OF CONSISTENCY

11

THE CONSISTENCY OF GOD'S PERSON

God's Kingdom is identified by God's character, which permeates its entirety. What God purposes, does, or says, is an expression of His Person — His Kingdom is the outworking of His "determinate counsel" (Acts 2:23). For this reason, thoughtful consideration of the Lord lies at the threshold of an understanding of His Kingdom.

Artificial Mysticism Surrounds God

It is unfortunate that men often have conceptions of God and His Kingdom that interfere with spiritual perception. Special training, it is thought, is required to understand the Bible, and secret formulas are sought which can be used to decipher Scriptural doctrines as well as patterns of behavior. God is perceived as doing things without apparent reason, and unintelligent acceptance of proclamation is falsely equated with faith. All of this evidences an inordinate appetite for mystery in an age of revelation. It promotes ignorance in a time when the understanding of God and His purpose is available to men.

While God is infinite and incomprehensible, He is still consistent.

"His understanding is infinite" (Psa. 147:5), and "who hath known the mind of the Lord, that he may instruct Him?" (I Cor. 2:16). In this sense, His judgments are "past finding out" (Rom. 11:33). But what does this mean? Are men to forever be in ignorance concerning their God? Are we shut up to a theology that confounds us with questions instead of instructing us with answers?

God is incomprehensible in that no man of himself may conclude God's mind. God is greater than His offspring, and unless He reveals Himself to them, He cannot be known! His mind and purpose extend beyond the scope of human experience. In this sense, "God made foolish the wisdom of the world" (I Cor. 1:19-20).

As with the "men of Athens," many that have identified themselves with Christ "are in all things too superstitious" (Acts 17:22-23). Their religion is marked more by what they do not know than what they do know. As if that were not enough, this situation is too often viewed as evidence of humility, and even spirituality. This attitude is contrary to the nature and purpose of God's Kingdom as revealed in the "salvation of God" (Psa. 50:23).

God's purpose in Christ is to reveal Himself. There is nothing more characteristic of the Son of God than His revelation of the Father to those that come to Him (Matt. 11:27-29). He graciously opens up God's Person and purpose to those that are willing to "learn" from Him. The "fellowship" that is achieved by living in view of Christ's illumination of the Father is more identified with understanding than ignorance, with nearness than aloofness. The mysticism that surrounds God in the minds of men is artificial — it is not in conformity with His revealed will. It is the product of man's imagination, and militates against the objectives of the Almighty.

Definition of Consistency

Consistency is not, technically speaking, identical with constancy. It is true that God is constant, and that with Him there "is no variableness, neither shadow of turning" (James 1:17).

Consistency speaks of coherence, compatability, and uniformity. God is in agreement with Himself — He always acts in perfect conformity with His character. He never acts in a manner that contradicts Himself or a prior revelation of Himself. His progressive works enlarge upon previous expressions, and complement earlier manifestations.

154

GOD'S PERSONAL CONSISTENCY
REVEALED IN HIS SALVATION

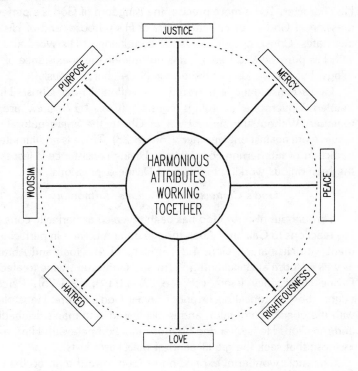

JUSTICE

MERCY

PURPOSE

PEACE

WISDOM

HARMONIOUS
ATTRIBUTES
WORKING
TOGETHER

HATRED

RIGHTEOUSNESS

LOVE

ALL THINGS WORK TOGETHER

DIVINE EXPRESSIONS   DIVINE RESPONSES
DIVINE ATTITUDES   DIVINE COMMITMENTS
DIVINE PURPOSES   DIVINE RECOGNITION

"God is ONE" (Mark 12:29), and, as such, is perfectly united in His character, His works, and His words. There is not, for instance, one God for the sinner, and one for the righteous. God does not act inconsistently with His character toward either.

God's word does not contradict His will; His work does not violate His character. To be more precise, the Kingdom of God is a perfect expression of God — of His character, of His purpose, and of His loves and hates. Consistency involves the correlation of His Word and work with His purpose and Person. It is not merely the coexistence of these things, but the working of them together — harmoniously!

God's consistency is mirrored in creation. Under Christ, His appointed Governor, "all things consist" (Col. 1:17); i.e., are held together. Without the supervision of Christ, the entire natural order would work against one another (Rom. 8:28). There is no ultimate contradiction or interferring competition. Divine consistency is just that — the harmonious working together of Divine expressions!

God's Character and Actions Harmonious

Throughout history, God has been revealed as perfectly consistent. His reactions to Cain and Abel, though different, were in perfect agreement with His nature (Gen. 4:3-15; Heb. 11:4). Noah and Abraham, as well as those at Babel and Sodom and Gomorrah, were treated with Divine consistency (Gen. 6:8; 18:19; 11:1-9; 19:1-25). Perceived aright, these historical occurrences reveal God's nature! He is pleased with the obedience of faith, and is displeased with man's disobedience and rebellion. He is offended by those that compete with Him, as well as those that seek the gratification of their baser lusts.

The most wonderful expression of God toward man occurs in His work of redemption. Here He determined to provide a way for man to return to Himself by addressing the matter of man's sin. In this purpose, He will not work against Himself. He will not repudiate anything that He has said, anything that He has done, or anything that He is, in order to save men! The reconciliation of man shall be accomplished with God remaining both "just" and the "Justifier of him that believes in Jesus" (Rom. 3:26).

God cannot and will not ignore a man's involvement in sin just because he is a "Christian." This is illustrated in the case involving Ananias and Sapphira. Though "added to the church" (Acts 2:47), and

156

having participated in the collection of freely offered monies (Acts 5:1), they were slain by God because of their calloused iniquity (Acts 5:1-11).

Nor, indeed, does He ignore a man's involvement in goodness because of his ignorance of the way of redemption. A case in point is that of Cornelius, a Gentile military man who, though ignorant of the Gospel of Christ, was a "devout man that feared God with all of his house, which gave much alms to the people, and prayed to God alway." A messenger from heaven informed this man that both his "prayers" and his "alms" had "come up for a memorial before God" (Acts 10:1-4).

The explanation for God's recorded reactions, in these instances, is His consistency. He Himself is offended by sin, and loves those that pursue righteousness — thus did He react toward Ananias and Sapphira, as well as Cornelius, in perfect conformity with His character.

The Ways of God

A single Scriptural word that describes God's consistency is His "WAYS." When "He made known His ways unto Moses" (Psa. 103:7), He acquainted Moses with His manners — with the intelligent outworkings of His Person. "The Lord is righteous in all His ways, and Holy in all His works" (Psa. 145:17). This is not because of a mere strict conformity with a righteous standard, but because of rigid conformity with His own nature!

The Kingdom of God is the manifestation of His ways. That revelation has been progressive from Adam to the current "day of salvation" (I Cor. 6:2). The announcement of the appointed overthrow of Satan (Gen. 3:15) was not only the proclamation of Divine purpose; it was a revelation of Divine character — DIVINE CONSISTENCY!

The favorite desire of the Psalmist for the Lord to "show" him His "ways" (Psa. 25:4) was the expression of a quest to know God — to be familiar with Him. David not only desired to know what God was doing, but why He was doing it. This knowledge is entirely within the scope of possibility because of the harmony between God Himself and what He does. The perception of that consistency between God's nature and His expression is what the man after God's "own heart" sought (II Sam. 7:21).

Faith Requires Consistency

Faith cannot anchor in inconsistency. If inconsistency is assumed, faith will waver, and doubt will predominate. That is why those that are not persuaded of God's absolute integrity often question whether or not they are pleasing to Him, even though they have "obeyed the Gospel" (Rom. 10:16; II Thess. 1:8). Perception and understanding, subjective views of faith, require a consistent object!

The harmony between God's Person and presentation is the basis for Scriptural faith. This is why we read of "the law of God" (Rom. 7:22), "the love of God" (Rom. 5:5), the "Christ of God" (Luke 9:20), and the "the church of God" (I Tim. 3:5). There is also "the mercy of God" (Psa. 52:8), "the righteousness of God" (Rom. 3:21), and the "judgment of God" (Rom. 2:2). "The Gospel of God" (Rom. 15:16), "the goodness of God" (Rom. 2:4), and "the longsuffering of God" (I Pet. 3:20), are proclaimed to men! These are proclamations of God's consistency.

The "law of God" is an exact reflection of His Person in the form of a moral code. It fully accords with His character! His "love" is an expression of His yearning for His offspring. The "Christ of God" is the Deliverer appointed by Divine affection, and "the church of God" is the "husbandry" I Cor. 3:9) not only planted by the Lord, but in which He greatly delights. The "mercy of God" is a demonstration of His longing for man — proof that He "is not willing that any should perish, but that all should come to repentance" (II Pet. 3:9).

The "judgment of God" is required by His nature as well as by situations of sin. The "Gospel of God" not only proclaims a satisifed God, but One that has not compromised any of His essential Being to accomplish that satisfaction (Isa. 53:11). The "goodness of God" is not a legal term, but one describing the fervent desire of Him to do good to men instead of evil. That is His preference, and men shall be condemned only because they have ignored the preference as revealed in the Gospel of Christ.

In all of these things, there is perfect harmony in the expression and the Expressor! The perception of this harmony is what stimulates faith. Faith and hope are "in God," not merely in what He has done. While man may speak of believing in peculiar doctrines, the Scriptures speak of believing in God and Christ — PERSONS! Because faith is possible only through the Word of God, there is of necessity a direct correlation between God's Word and His Person — an inseparable union between what God has done, and Who God is! That is consistency!

The Revelation of God

God has revealed Himself in a variety of ways. His "eternal power and Godhead" are made known by the impersonal creation (Rom. 1:20). "The heavens declare the glory of God; and the firmament shows His handiwork" (Psa. 19:1). There is a language being articulated by the material universe in which we find ourselves. "Day unto day uttereth speech, and night unto night shows knowledge" (Psa. 19:2). Nature is an abbreviated index to the Living God! A proper understanding of it will reveal something of God Himself. God has revealed Himself by means of deliberate intrusions into history. The flood, the giving of the Law, the accomplishment and proclamation of the Gospel — these all constituted an unveiling of the Person of God! They were not mere reactions to men, they were expressions of the Divine nature, and thus constituted a revelation of God Himself.

God has graciously revealed Himself to man. This revelation, however, is not primarily an overt one. Further, the physical revelations that have occurred have only been partial — extremely limited. He disclosed Himself to Moses at the burning bush (Exod. 3:2; Acts 7:30), to Israel at Mount Sinai (Exod. 19:18-24), and in the fiery pillar (Exod. 14:24).

In these, and other similar revelations, fear and consternation were often the results. Neither of these conditions delighted the Lord, nor did they serve to implement His primary objective of acquainting man with Himself.

A Revelation to the Understanding

The revelation of God, as to its effectiveness for the individual, takes place primarily in the understanding. By comprehending His nature and His manners, we are brought to understand Him. The Scriptures contain both demonstrations and declarations of God's Person. These are mingled with the proclamation of His "eternal purpose" (Eph. 1:9; 3:11), as fulfilled in Christ. God also unveils an "eternal inheritance" (Heb. 9:15; I Pet. 1:4) that is reserved for those that "receive the atonement."

God has revealed Himself to be "faithful" (I Cor. 10:13), "just" (I

John 1:9), "good" (Psa. 25:8), and unchangeable or immutable (Mal. 3:6; Rom. 11:29; Heb. 6:17-18). On one occasion, Moses fervently besought the Lord, "I beseech Thee, show me Thy glory" (Exod. 33:18). This was a request to know and understand the Lord — to perceive His character and comprehend His Person! The next "morning," God responded with an intelligent proclamation, attended by some arresting phenomena.

There, "in the top of the mount," with Moses holding the tables of the covenant that he had "hewed" earlier, "the Lord descended in the cloud and, stood with him there" (Exod. 34:1-5). In one grand blaze of glory, "the Lord passed by before him" (Exod. 34:6a). When He revealed His "glory," He did not do it with fire, wind, or earthquake! He did it with intelligent words — addressed to Moses' understanding. "The Lord, The Lord God, merciful and gracious, longsuffering, and abundant in goodness and truth, keeping mercy for thousands, forgiving iniquity and transgression and sin, and that will by no means clear the guilty; visiting the iniquity of the fathers upon the children, and upon the children's children, unto the third and to the fourth generation" (Exod. 34:7). God had revealed Himself to Moses!

Neither time nor space permits us to delineate the many aspects of His Person that God has revealed to man. His holiness (Lam. 3:38; Isa. 6:3; John 17:11), love (Psa. 63:3; Mal. 1:2; Eph. 2:4), power (Psa. 52:11; 111:6; Rom. 1:20), wisdom (Psa. 104:24; Dan. 2:20; Eph. 1:8), and impartiality (Deut. 10:17; Job 37:24; Eph. 6:8), are freely proclaimed to His offspring. The design behind these proclamations is not the satisfaction of a mere legal requirement, but the Divine desire to acquaint man with Himself!

Not "Will Not," But "Cannot"

It is revealed that God "cannot deny Himself" (II Tim. 2:13). He cannot act or react in a manner that contradicts what He has revealed of Himself. In a similar proclamation, we read that God "cannot lie" (Titus 1:2), i.e., He cannot fail to do what He has promised! God is not merely disinclined from immorality or a lack of integrity; God is incapable of lying or denying Himself. HE CANNOT DO IT BECAUSE OF HIS NATURE! While man is able to both lie and deny himself, God is not!

He cannot do what He has said He will not do! He cannot fail to do what He has said He will do! He cannot be drawn to those He abhors, and He cannot turn away from those that He loves. When, for instance, He did turn away from His only begotten Son, Whom He loved (Matt. 27:46), it was because "He was made to be sin" (II Cor. 5:21). Only when "He bore our sins in His body on the tree" (I Pet. 2:24) did He become offensive to God — and only then could God turn from Him. HE CANNOT DENY HIMSELF!

The recorded reactions of God to men demonstrate this truth. For God, for instance, to have overlooked the transgression of Adam and Eve, He would have had to "deny Himself." To ignore the self-centered society at Babel (Gen. 11) would have required the same denial. When Israel forsook the Lord at Kadesh, believing the report of the unbelieving spies (Num. 13-14), they barred themselves from entrance into Canaan! It was impossible for God to bring such a people in to the land of promise! He would be required to "deny Himself" to do such a thing!

God's words and actions are, therefore, not only a revelation of His will; they are a revelation of His Person. Properly perceived, they introduce men to God Himself. At no time are His Word or His works in contradiction of His Person. He cannot deny Himself! He cannot contradict His nature! He cannot violate His character!

Divine consistency requires that God's commitments be stedfast. The Kingdom of God cannot be maintained by an inconsistent King! God's commitments make sense when correctly perceived! This is because they are in perfect conformity to His Person!

Perceived in Relative Darkness

Balaam, a mysterious prophet during an age of relative darkness, articulated a truth beyond his own apprehension when he said, "God is not a man, that He should lie; neither the son of man, that He should repent: hath He said, and shall He not do it? or hath he spoken, and shall He not make it good? . . . He hath blessed; and I cannot reverse it" (Num. 23:19-20). Later in history, under the illumination of greater revelation, Samuel said, ". . . the Strength of Israel will not lie or repent: for He is not a man that He should repent" (I Sam. 15:29). God's commitments are irreversible!

Increased Perception with Increased Revelation

The perception of God's faithful commitments increased as God continued to reveal Himself to men. David, a man particularly close to

God during the age of the First Covenant, proclaimed his perception in these words: "The counsels of the Lord stand forever, the thoughts of His heart to all generations" (Psa. 33:11). He understood God's faithfulness by comprehending the steadfastness of His commitments (Psa. 119:89-91).

The Lord Does Not Change

Malachi, delivering a final word during the First Covenant Dispensation, spoke for God: "I am the Lord, I change not . . ." (Mal. 3:6). That revelation was not meant to convey the thought that God did not view things differently, or that He never changed His mind. God has changed His mind in time past, and has inspired men to write of those changes. In Noah's day, the time of unprecedented iniquity, ". . . it repented the Lord that He had made man on the earth, and it grieved Him at His heart" (Gen. 6:6). He did not change His mind concerning the ultimate purpose for which He had made man (Gen. 1:25; Heb. 2:5-8). He did not withdraw His promise of the coming Savior (Gen. 3:15). He did not ignore righteous Noah (Gen. 6:8). This revealed repentance of God was not owing to Divine fickleness, but rather to the Divine nature. He could not have remained God and responded otherwise!

"I am the Lord, I change not!" This is to be viewed in relation to His revealed commitments, as well as His attitudes and responses to the sons of men. He will never contradict what He has promised, nor will He have varying responses to identical situations. He will never respond favorably to a rebellious sinner, nor will He reject and despise a "broken and contrite heart" (Psa. 51:17). He that "believeth not" cannot possibly be favored, and those that "believe and are baptized" cannot possibly be despised (Mark 16:16).

The one that endures "unto the end" cannot be lost (Matt. 24:13), and those that "abide not" in Christ cannot possibly be saved (John 15:6). For these things to occur, God would have to be inconsistent; He would have to "deny" Himself, "change" and repudiate what He Himself has said! His commitments are irreversible because they strictly conform to His Person, and are expressions of His nature. He CANNOT deny Himself!

Divine purpose reflects Divine desire. Unlike man, God is not capable of desiring something that is contrary to His essential being

162

(Rom. 7:15-21). Man has two natures, God has one! Man has inward conflict (Gal. 5:17), God does not. Man often acts contrary to his proper objectives, God does not!

God's Kingdom involves the participation of man in the execution of His will. The participation of man necessarily involves his understanding. Understanding can only grasp what is consistent, harmonious, and not self-contradictory. Therefore, Divine purpose absolutely necessitates Divine consistency. Without it, God's purpose would ultimately be frustrated.

Consistency Required for Perception

A lack of consistency makes perception impossible. To put it another way, faith cannot anchor in inconsistency. Man can only understand that which is fundamentally logical. Logic, on the other hand, demands consistency — that is what makes something logical. The early disciples were often "without understanding" (Matt. 15:16) because of their failure to correlate revealed principles. For instance, it is asserted that the conduct of a man is traceable to the thoughts and perceptions of his heart (Prov. 23:7). The comprehension of this rather simplistic principle would prompt the logical conclusion that evil things that "proceed out of the mouth come forth from the heart," thus "defiling the man" (Matt. 15:18-20). It should also be concluded that the introduction of material things through the mouth into the "belly" cannot possibly work moral corruption (Matt. 15:17). These conclusions, however, can only be drawn when the principle is understood. That principle, further, is understandable because of its consistency. It perfectly accords with God's nature, God's revealed purpose, and the circumstances created by the introduction of sin.

The consistency of God's Kingdom indicates the possibility of comprehension, not the probability of it. It is the possibility which is under consideration here. Things that are "hard to be understood" (II Pet. 3:16) are characterized by logical difficulties. Those difficulties, however, are not owing to any inconsistency. It is the introduction of human reasoning, the dulling effect of sinfulness, and the hardness of man's heart, that makes them "hard to be understood." The "deep things of God" (I Cor. 2:10) have that characteristic because of their closeness to the center of God's purpose. Their discernment requires an aloofness from the world, and intimacy with God. Once those requirements are met, there is no difficulty in making sense out of them.

The point to be established here is that the Kingdom of God is comprised of facts and proclamations that are perfectly united. That is what makes them understandable, and thus accessible.

Satan's Efforts to Portray an Inconsistent God

In the very beginning, the Devil sought to protray an inconsistent God. The Lord God had "commanded the man, saying, Of every tree of the garden you may freely eat: but of the tree of the knowledge of good and evil, you shall not eat of it: for in the day you eat thereof, you shall surely die" (Gen. 2:16-17). That proscription perfectly accorded with reality. Man had been created in God's moral image, thus indicating that his primary fulfillment would be found in intimate association with the Lord. That association would be broken by man's sin. In the light of God's purpose and proscription, it made perfect sense to avoid taking of the forbidden fruit.

Satan sought to make God's prohibition unreasonable and illogical, thereby provoking an invalid conclusion. "In the day you eat thereof, then shall your eyes be opened," said the beguiling serpent. Rather than becoming unlike God, "you shall be as gods, knowing good and evil." In direct contradiction of God's pronouncement, Satan said, " You shall not surely die" (Gen. 3:4-5). This enticement provoked Eve to place the words of God, together with their reasonableness, in the background.

It is written that ". . . .the woman saw that the tree was good for food, and that it was pleasant to the eyes, and a tree desired to make one wise . . . " (Gen. 3:6). These conclusions were prompted by the Devil's affirmation, "Ye shall not surely die" (Gen. 3:4). What she "saw" was not true because it was inconsistent with Divinely appointed objectives.

The tree was not "good for food," it was really not "pleasant to the eyes," and it was not to "be desired to make one wise." Why? Because this was inconsistent with God and His purpose. It centered in this world rather the heavenly realm. It negated Divine purpose, ignored precious communication with the Almighty, and presupposed an unreasonable Divine requirement. Thus did Satan establish his mode of attack upon the sons of men.

164

In Manner of Life

God's inherent and declared consistency continues to be attacked by Satan in the area of conduct — one's manner of life. He zealously seeks to separate the attitudes and deeds of men from Divine consequences — just as in the case with Eve. The indulgence of fleshly appetites with the temporalities of this world is in direct contradiction of Divine purpose. "The Kingdom of God is not meat and drink," asserted the Apostle in confirmation of this principle (Rom. 14:17). Yet, "the father of lies" (John 8:44) continues to "destroy" men's lives by convincing them that fleshly indulgence will bring lawful satisfaction (John 10:11).

Men become involved in "adultery, fornication, uncleanness, lasciviousness . . . murders, drunkenness, revellings, and such like" (Gal. 5:19-21) because they are persuaded it is reasonable. It appears logical to let the flesh dominate. But it is not reasonable! In fact, in view of the revealed purpose of God, it is insane to live in such a manner — it just does not make sense!

In Doctrinal Presentation

The Christian community is plagued with divisions — divisions that are the direct result of inconsistent proclamations. Again, this reflects the activity of our "adversary" (I Pet. 5:8). Inconsistent doctrines require an environment of mystery and ignorance. They can only be accepted by ignoring reason. While reason, of itself, it not the sole source of confirmation, it is included in that process by Divine appointment. It is not possible for a doctrine to be unreasonable and godly at the same time. If God is not unreasonable — and He is not — no teaching associated with Him or His purpose can be unreasonable!

False doctrines "cause divisions and offenses contrary to the doctrine" communicated by the Apostles (Rom. 16:17). Observe that they cause "offenses" that are "contrary" to sound doctrine. The contradiction is found not only in the things asserted, but in the implications that they contain. The corruption of "the word of God" (II Cor. 2:17) involves a corruption of the purpose of God in the minds of men. It produces a conflict between God Himself and what He has expressed.

Examples of Inconsistent Doctrines

God has declared that "He is not willing that any should perish" (II Pet. 3:9), and that He "will [wills to] have all men to be saved, and come to a knowledge of the truth" (I Tim. 2:4). Yet there is a dominant doctrine which views God as willing that some perish, actually decreeing that certain of His offspring be damned. This persuasion is encapsulated in a view of "election" which sees God as determining who will be saved and who will be lost completely independently of a view of their persons and response to Himself. This doctrine essentially posits an inconsistent God — One that acts in a manner contrary to what He was declared Himself to be.

The Lord has emphatically declared that those who walk "in the flesh" and are "carnally-minded" are His enemies, and are excluded from His Kingdom (Rom. 8:6-7; James 4:4; I Cor. 6:9-10). The destroyer of men's souls has, however, authored a doctrine which teaches men that a profession of faith obviates these assertions. Men may live in practical defiance of God, and yet be found acceptable of Him in the "last day" because of their initial obedience to Him. Were this teaching correct, God would be unfaithful. He would have to let people into heaven that He has said could not enter there. In such a case, we would have an inconsistent God!

The Kingdom of God has been conceptually separated from eating and drinking (Rom. 14:17). Involvement in it is not based upon our association with meat and drink. The Devil has, however, developed and perpetrated doctrines that command men to "abstain from meats," associating such abstinence with Divine approval (I Tim. 4:1-2). Such a doctrine presents an inconsistent God.

The Spirit was introduced in association with "remembrance" (John 14:26), and the apprehension of the truth (John 15:26; 16:13). He brings a comprehension of "the love of God" (Rom. 5:5), and produces fruit within the believer that is perceptible and in harmony with Divine purpose (Eph. 5:9). He is not identified with mystery, but with understanding (Eph. 3:16-19). Yet Satan has developed doctrines which have identified the Holy Spirit with strange and mysterious things, unintelligible utterances, and an undiscerned fellowship with God. Such things are contradictory! They are inconsistent with God, God's purpose, and His revelation of the Spirit's mission.

166

Conclusion

God is consistent! He never contradicts Himself, never reverses Himself, never responds in a manner that conflicts with His nature. Further, He governs His Kingdom with perfect consistency. His revealed will is an expression of His character, and never calls for a renunciation of any aspect of that character. He "cannot deny Himself," for to do so would cause Him to cease to be God. His words, His works, and His responses are themselves manifestations of His Person.

This arrangement is conducive to faith, which is, in turn, the means of implementing God's desire for man. It is what enables spiritual understanding, without which fellowship with God is not possible.

Unlike God, the consistency of nature can be countermanded. Natural laws that have been set in motion by the Almighty were, for instance, revoked during the flood of Noah's day (Gen. 7:11-12). Similar revocations occurred in the destruction of Sodom and Gomorrah by fire and brimstone (Gen. 19:24), the sending of the thunder, hail and fire upon Egypt (Exod. 9:23-24), and the parting of the Red Sea for the children of Israel (Exod. 14:21-22). The sun stood still for Joshua (Josh. 10:13), and moved "backward ten degrees" at the word of Isaiah (II Kgs. 20:10-11). All of these were contrary to established laws of nature.

There is, however, no record of God's acting contradictory to His own nature — nor, indeed, is that possible. He is a completely consistent God; harmonious in all His attributes. Thus is the nature of the Kingdom of God determined. It cannot possibly be implemented by either requirements or manners that are not perfectly harmonious with God's revealed nature.

12

THE NATURE OF TRUTH

God is maintaining His Kingdom in the midst of a varying and inconsistent environment. The righteousness of God is being demonstrated in a world overrun by unrighteousness. A holy God is glorified by reconciling unholy man. Spiritual illumination is now taking place where satanic deception is universal. According to Divine intent, truth is being proclaimed in the very realm where the lie has dominated!

The situation described requires that truth, the proclamation of which is the means of Kingdom propagation, be attentively heard and carefully thought upon. God's means are at variance with "the course of this world" (Eph. 2:2). He is not a man, and He does not speak as a man. While the words of men are limited in perspective and duration, God's Word is eternal.

Singularity of the Truth Itself

Truth is preeminent to the informed. It is "the lip of truth" that shall be established (Prov. 12:19), and God is declared to be the "God of truth" (Psa. 31:5). Everything that God does is "truth" (Psa. 33:4).

169

Truth goes before Him, being in eternal association with Himself. As it is written, ". . . mercy and truth shall be before Him" (Psa. 89:14), and ". . . He shall judge . . . His people with His truth" (Psa. 96:13).

Truth has a wide spectrum. It is a large body of interrelated realities. As such, it is singular in nature. Truth is not comprised of a series of unrelated facts. Like God, truth is "one" in essence (Deut. 6:4). This means that it is perfectly united, and never at war with itself.

Truth is the rational and understandable declaration of God's purpose, and the Kingdom of God identifies the execution of that purpose. The various parts of truth are complementary — never contradictory. This is why, in Scripture, "truth" is always mentioned in the singular. We never read of "truths" — it is always "TRUTH"! It is unfortunate that the religion of Christ has been presented as a series of unrelated, and sometimes irrelevant, statements. It is this erroneous concept that has opened the door to division and schism in the body of Christ.

With deliberation, God molds our thinking concerning "truth" by His Word. We never read of "a truth," but rather of "the truth," thus underscoring a body of reality versus a facet of reality. It is the reception of "the love of THE truth" that saves the soul (II Thess. 2:10), and our souls have been "purified" by obeying "THE TRUTH" (I Pet. 1:22). It is "THE way of truth" that is evil spoken of by the wicked (II Pet. 2:2). Willful involvement in sin is most serious when one has "received the knowledge of THE truth" (Heb. 10:26). Returning to the vanities of this world is viewed by James as erring "from THE truth" (James 5:19), and when men lie, they lie "against THE truth" (James 3:14).

This single body of spiritual reality, as perceived within the New Covenant, is called "the truth . . . in Jesus" (Eph. 4:21). It is "the truth" (singular) because it speaks of a single Divine objective — one that is perfectly united in all of its aspects. It reaches its greatest degree of clarity "in Jesus." It is from within the comprehension of that perfectly united spectrum — truth — that we come to love others that have embraced it (III John 1).

Divine Usage

The use of the word "truth" by the Holy Spirit emphasizes its singleness. Our "loins," for instance, are to be "girt about with truth" (Eph. 6:14). This is a term denoting the profitable employment of our thought processes — elsewhere called "the loins of your mind" (I Pet.

INTERRELATIONARY ASPECTS OF TRUTH
EXHIBITED IN SALVATION

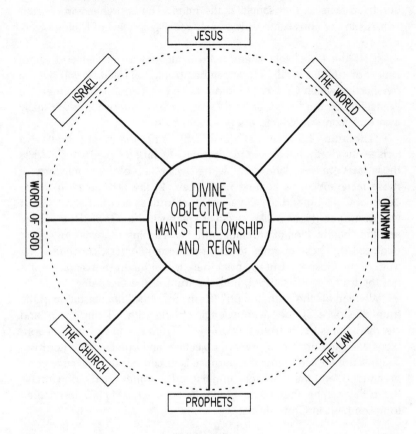

DIVINE INTEGRITY MAINTAINED

REMAINED JUST	MAINTAINED PLAN
EXHIBITED MERCY	NO CONDEMNATION
REMOVED SIN	DISPLAYED WISDOM

171

1:13). When our minds comprehend God's "eternal purpose" and function in harmony with it, they become our chief personal resource. It is the contemplation of this united body of reality — not segmented and unrelated facts — that sanctifies the mind. The apprehension of truth consists in the correlation of heavenly realities in view of Divine objective.

It is "the truth" that liberates the soul, not a peculiar and secret aspect of it (John 8:32). There can be no spiritual freedom without the perspective which God's truth imparts. To put it another way, men are "sanctified by the truth" (John 17:19), i.e., as they become spiritually aware of, consent to, and are governed by it.

"The truth of the Gospel" (Gal. 2:5), is not the mere recitation of facts — the death, burial, and resurrection of Christ (I Cor. 15:1-3). While those facts are true, "the truth" is the declaration of the significance of those facts and of its bearing upon men. In the proclamation of the death of Christ, grand objectives were set forth as accomplished. Satan was destroyed (Heb. 2:14), "we were reconciled to God" (Rom. 5:10, and the "handwriting of ordinances that was against us" was blotted out (Col. 2:14). Those insights, together with many others, constitute "the truth of the Gospel." But my point here is that the truth is single — it is not the truths of the Gospel, but "the truth of the Gospel"!

We read of "the truth of God" (Rom. 3:7), the "manifestation of the truth" (II Cor. 4:2), the "acknowledging of the truth" (II Tim. 2:25), and "fellow-helpers to the truth" (III John 8). Truth is single because it concerns a single purpose, a primary objective, and one Divine enterprise. Truth is not known unless the purpose is discerned, the objective comprehended, and the enterprise understood. In other words, one knows the truth when he knows what God is doing — what He has determined to accomplish in Christ Jesus!

Truth and Diversity

Truth is never diverse — there is not one body of truth for the Christian, for instance, and one for the Hindu. Truth is singular, not plural. This was enunciated by the Lord when He said, "I am the way THE TRUTH and the life: no man comes unto the Father but by me" (John 14:6). Jesus is the embodiment of Divine purpose. In order to come "to the Father," it was necessary that HE be comprehended! It was not enough to grasp a little of what He said, of perceive a portion of

172

what He did. It was Himself that had to be perceived, known, and believed!

Aspects of the Truth

An aspect of the truth is a facet of reality — a particular view of it. Its relevancy is in its association with the body of truth itself.

Take, for instance, the different aspects of Christ's ministry. Although He did many things, they were all for one purpose. He was born, He grew, He ministered among men, He died, He was buried, He arose, He ascended into heaven, and He sat down on the right hand of God. Those are all different things — unique in their manifestation. But they all focused on one end, the accomplishment of God's purpose for man's salvation.

Viewing the reconciliation of man as God's grand objective in Christ, think of the various aspects of that objective. There is the viewpoint of Divine requirement: a propitiation for sin (Rom. 3:25), a Savior "made like unto His brethren" (Heb. 2:17), and the opening of the way to God (Heb. 9:8; 10:18-22). That same enterprise is also perceived from the standpoint of its accomplishments. Christ "put away sin by the sacrifice of Himself" (Heb. 9:26), destroyed the Devil (Heb. 2:14), and "redeemed us from the curse of the Law" (Gal. 3:13). Another aspect of God's purpose is that of provision. Christ is "made unto us wisdom, and righteousness, and sanctification, and redemption" (I Cor. 1:30). Yet another aspect of the Kingdom is the means of appropriating its benefits. Obedience (Heb. 5:9), holiness (Heb. 12:14), and self-denial (Matt. 10:38), together with other factors, are all subpoints of the redemptive enterprise.

All of these aspects, or facets, have proper significance only as they are related to the Divine objective. They do not stand independent of, but united with, that central design.

Illustrated in Christ

The unity of God's purpose in Christ, and so in the truth, is perfectly demonstrated in the Son's earthly life and ministry. He was born of a virgin, born "under the Law" (Gal. 4:4). As a man, He went about doing good, healing all that were oppressed of the Devil (Acts 10:38). He was "crucified through weakness" (II Cor. 13:4), and raised from the dead "by the glory of the Father" (Rom. 6:4). "When He ascended up on high, he led captivity captive" (Eph. 4:8), and "is on the right hand of God; angels and authorities and powers being made subject to Him" (I Pet. 3:22).

But none of these accomplishments is to be isolated from the others. The death of Christ, for example, would be of no value without His resurrection (I Cor. 15:16-20). Nor, indeed, would His resurrection be significant if He did not ascend into heaven. It is the blend of these facts that gives them their efficacy for man's salvation. As they are perceived in the light of God's design for man, they take on eternal significance.

A Practical Illustration

An automobile consists of many different parts: a body, motor, transmission, tires, radiator, interior, electrical components, etc. There is even a further breakdown of its parts. The motor has pistons, valves, rods, etc. One of these components cannot properly be termed an automobile. At best, it is only a portion of the automobile, and has its worth because of that association. Each part is, in this respect, an aspect of the vehicle. Men may become specialists in the building and repair of any one of the parts. However, their specialty has no value unless it contributes to the function of the automobile itself. While there may be an intense interest in one part of the automobile, only the interrelated performance of all of the parts serves its purpose.

So it is with the truth of God. Divine purpose is served when all aspects of the truth are perceived as complementary — harmoniously working together for man's salvation. The objective of "the man of God" (II Tim. 3:16-17), is not merely to become a specialist in some aspect of salvation, but to learn how to "rightly divide the word of truth" in its entirety (II Tim. 2:15).

Scriptural Details

The Word of God — the "seed of the Kingdom" — proclaims details in view of the revealed purpose of God. They deal with domestic issues, social issues, and moral issues. They make mention of personal purity, church polity, and spiritual responsibility. They proclaim what men are to do, and what men are not to do. But the emphasis of Scripture is not domestic matters, social involvements, or moral issues. The pillar of truth is not erected upon external purity, acceptable church government, or the fulfillment of responsibility. These are all facets of a larger

174

body of reality.

Any emphasis of Scriptural detail that ignores the primary purpose of God is erroneous. Aspects of the truth are not intended to be ends of themselves. They are, rather, the means of making the complexity of "the truth" discernible. Without the details, the purpose would not be intelligible to man, and he could not experience participation.

When the Truth Is Perceived, the Aspects Are Perceptible

Spiritual understanding is a preeminent thing in the heavenly Kingdom. Without it, there is no beneficial participation in the Divine enterprise. The initial form of participation — salvation — is accomplished through the "knowledge of the truth" (I Tim. 2:4). Maturity is to characterize man's understanding (I Cor. 14:20), and conformity to the Divine image is realized through man's renewal in "knowledge" (Col. 3:10). All of this underscores the role of perception. It is absolutely critical in the Kingdom of God.

Contrary to the manner of this world, main things are comprehended first. In the light of those primary areas, smaller things come to light. In the words of the Psalmist, ". . . in Thy light shall we see light" (Psa. 36:9). The reason for this is obvious. In God's Kingdom, primary things are heavenly in nature, while secondary things have to do with earthly matters. This truth is reflected in the first and second commandments. The "first commandment," or the primary directive, concerns loving God. The "second" concerns the love of our fellow man (Deut. 6:4-5; 13:3; Mark 12:29-31). Our love for man certainly does not shed a great amount of light upon the obligation to love God. However, our love for God does illuminate the matter of loving our neighbor. "In Thy light shall we see light."

When Things Makes Sense

In Christ, the heavenly Kingdom is identified with a high level of understanding. Prior to Him, men were directed exclusively by precepts and commandments. There was an element of mystery associated with God's rule. This was due to at least two things. First, sin, which had not been "put away" (Heb. 9:26), had a dulling effect upon man's mind. Second, due to the defilement of man's conscience, God could not have intimate fellowship with man. With "the atonement" (Rom. 5:11), however, the shroud of mystery was removed form God's Kingdom.

175

Scriptural Examples of This Principle

In view of the determined destruction of the world, for instance, it makes perfect sense to "live soberly, righteously, and godly, in this present world" (II Pet. 3:11; Titus 2:12). Godly resolve has been produced by spiritual understanding. It is not only the proper thing to do, it becomes a sensible thing to do!

Again, our resolve to "know no man after the flesh" is constrained by our spiritual evaluation of the "love of Christ." "For the love of Christ constrains us; because we thus judge, that if one died for all, then were all dead: and that He died for all, that they which live should not henceforth live unto themselves, but unto Him which died for them, and rose again. Wherefore henceforth know we no man after the flesh . . ." (II Cor. 5:14-16).

Here, a proper view of mankind has been fostered by perception of the death of Christ. His death involved the putting away of the entire natural order. It, together with all of its inhabitants, had already been repudiated by God — cursed of the Almighty (Gen. 3:16-19; Rom. 8:20-23). A comprehension of that reality moves the reconciled to "know no man after the flesh" — i.e., primary associations are not maintained out of mere temporal considerations. This is a reasonable consideration!

Before the New Covenant, refraining from fornication was accomplished primarily by obedience to the commandments. This was, and continues to be, good, and it is not my intention to minimize the value of such a response. It is not bad in any sense of the word. There is, however, a "better way" to cope with this troublesome matter. Reasoning upon the subject, Paul shows the impact of spiritual understanding.

Know ye not that your bodies are the members of Christ? Shall I then take the members of Christ, and make them members of an harlot? God forbid. What? know ye not that he which is joined to an harlot is one body? for two, saith he, shall be one flesh . . . he that committeth fornication sins against his own body. What? know ye not that your body is the temple of the Holy Ghost which is in you, which ye have of God, and ye are not your own? (I Cor. 6:15-19).

176

Observe the reasoning of the Apostle. It is based upon primary considerations; the mundane is judged in view of the transcendent. An understanding of the fact that our response to the Gospel has made us "members of Christ" precludes involvement in fornication. Discernment of the fact that such a transgression results in forbidden union — "one flesh" — will not permit such a relationship! Serious consideration of the indwelling Spirit will cause one to refrain from this appeal to the lust of the flesh. This is a logical conclusion!

Consideration of the Promises

There are two ways to deal with sin and its expressions. One is effectual, and one is ineffectual.

It can be dealt with according to the principle of law, which is for the lawless (II Tim. 1:9). Under this arrangement, an effort is made to refrain from sin because "God said so." Again, this is a valid approach, and is not to be deprecated. It is, however, an inferior one.

The better way is that of perception of the truth. "Having therefore these promises, dearly beloved, let us cleanse ourselves from all filthiness of the flesh and spirit, perfecting holiness in the fear of the God" (II Cor. 7:1). In light of the relationship to Christ and of the function of our body as God's temple, we are better enabled to "flee fornication," for example, as we are told to do (I Cor. 6:18).

God has called us into a special relationship with Himself: "Wherefore come out from among them ("unbelievers," "unrighteous," and "the infidel"), and be ye separate, saith the Lord, and touch not the unclean thing" (II Cor. 6:14-15,17). The real issue here is not what is to be forfeited, but what is to be gained! The experience of Divine fellowship fully justifies the abandonment of any relationship contrary to it.

The comprehension of God's commitments, then, becomes the incentive for personal purity. The fundamental objective is not personal purity itself, but Divine fellowship. That fellowship, however, cannot be experienced in a state of moral defilement. It is, therefore, reasonable to "perfect holiness in the fear of God!"

Resolving Problems by Truth

Problems are an integral part of living in this world. The infection with sin, of life in particular and society in general, has produced an

177

arena of intense conflict and difficulty. Eliphaz, though limited in his apprehension, correctly diagnosed the situation. "Yet man is born unto trouble, as the sparks fly upward" (Job 5:7). Job, responding to the analysis of Zophar, said, "Man that is born of woman is of few days, and full of trouble" (Job 14:1). This is the Scriptural view of problems. They are here — in this world — and they are the lot of every man. No one is exempted from them while he is "in the body."

There are at least two options open to man concerning the existence of problems. He can focus attention on them, and make them, and their resolution, his main concern. This approach is the manner of man in the kingdoms of this world. The other is the manner of the Kingdom of God. The first procedure considers problems as they appear on the surface. The second perceives them in contrast with eternal things, thus diminishing their apparent priority.

Summarizing all of the problems associated with life, and in particular with godliness, Paul wrote, "For I reckon that the sufferings of this present time are not worthy to be compared with the glory which shall be revealed in us" (Rom. 8:17). The same Apostle said, "While we look not at the things which are seen, but at the things which are not seen . . ." The reason for this outlook is that "the things which are seen are temporal; but the things which are not seen are eternal" (II Cor. 4:18). The truth of God is superior to the problems of life!

God's Kingdom involves the emphasis of eternal solution rather than temporary difficulties. The reason — truth is transcendent to problems! The Scriptural emphasis is a proper emphasis — it accords with reality.

The Necessity of Proper Perspective

Perspective considers all of the facets of life, and properly arranges them. The Kingdom of God presents God and His will as preeminent. This is to be the object of our primary concern (Matt. 6:33). Everything, therefore, that is associated with God and our relationship to Him assumes a place of authority.

In a state of spiritual awareness anything that interferes with one's apprehension of God and His will, constitutes a significant problem. If it is not dealt with properly, it will diminish the heart's devotion, and deplete the strength of the soul. Thus are we admonished to cast "down imaginations, and every high thing that exalts itself against the knowledge of

God," and bring "into captivity every thought to the obedience of Christ" (II Cor. 10:5).

As serious as domestic and social issues may appear — and they do, indeed, often appear serious — they are still subservient to the higher issues involving eternal life. The Word of God, together with "all things that pertain to life and godliness" (II Pet. 1:3) are not primarily given for these areas of life. Temporal matters are always peripheral matters in the Kingdom of God. To be sure, they are dealt with, but they are addressed with eternity in mind. For example, in addressing some issues concerning marriage, Peter spoke after this fashion: "Likewise, ye husbands, dwell with them according to knowledge, giving honor unto the wife, as unto the weaker vessel, and as being heirs together of the grace of life; that your prayers be not hindered" (I Pet. 3:7).

Here is the Divine hierarchy, or ranked order, of reasoning on the matter. "Dwell with them according to knowledge, giving honor unto the wife . . ." is the practical view, and the most rudimentary level. You will observe that no details are provided. The fact that husband and wife were "heirs together of the grace of life," viewed the relationship from a higher vantage point. They were mutual stewards of life in this world, and were being summoned to eternal life, where there are no sexual distinctions (Gal. 3:28). There is a spiritual practicality involved also . . . "that your prayers be not hindered." Marital life must not be permitted to inhibit one's quest for glory!

The Role of Divine Instruction

In the Word of God, there is a noticeable absence of detailed instructions concerning every day life. This is particularly true in the writings of the Apostles. They wrote of the requirement for meekness, but did not say how to be meek. They told husbands to be considerate, but did not say how to be considerate. They instructed us to perfect holiness in the fear of God, but did not tell us how to do it. There is a reason for this.

Addressing those in Christ, John wrote, "But the anointing which you have received of Him abides in you, and you need not that any man teach you: but as the same anointing teaches you of all things, and is truth, and is no lie, and even as it hath taught you, you shall abide in Him" (I John 2:27). This declaration reveals much concerning the nature of the Kingdom of God.

179

The intent of these words is not to obviate instruction by godly men. Were that the case, the verse itself would be contradictory, for it was an inspired man that wrote it. Nor, indeed, does it teach us that every man is an island unto himself, receiving private revelations and insights from the "Father of lights." John is here dealing with the perception of implications, and the consequent understanding of details. The "how to" of Kingdom life (which includes the resolution of earthly problems) is not taught by routine or discipline.

Candidly, there are no secret routines that guarantee domestic tranquility or peaceful social relationships. If that were the case, Jesus would certainly have made them known. He Himself did not get along with the Scribes, Pharisees, or Lawyers, as well as others that did not receive His words (Matt. 23:2-29; Luke 11:46-52; John 6:66). He encountered the "problem" of being misunderstood (Mark 9:32; Luke 18:34), and was once considered to be mentally unstable (Mark 3:21). The absence of problems is not an indication of either success or godliness!

Where it is possible, the resolution of earthly circumstances becomes a stewardship of men. On one occasion, Jesus refused to become involved in a family problem that involved the equitable distribution of an inheritance (Luke 12:13-14). In the matter of redemption, men are to "work out" their own "salvation with fear and trembling" (Phil. 2:12). In the "smaller matters" of life, judgment is to be employed (I Cor. 6:1-3). That judgment is associated with evaluation, contemplation, and the choice of good over evil. "Good," in this case, is what contributes to Divine fellowship, while "evil" describes what militates against it.

Valid problem resolution consists, first, in setting our "affection on things above," and seeking "first the Kingdom of God and His righteousness" (Col. 3:1-3; Matt. 6:33). Then, with our vision dominated by eternal realities, we address the lesser things. In such an approach, man's mind is employed, and Divine resources are joined to his own. This is the manner of the Kingdom.

When Shadrach, Meshach, and Abednego confronted the problem of the fiery furnace, two alternatives faced them. They could "fall down and worship the image" set up by king Nebuchadnezzar as soon as they heard "the sound of the cornet, flute, harp, sackbut, psaltry, and dulcimer." That would have saved them from being thrown into the furnace, and thus was one valid form of problem-resolution.

These three men, however, considered more than the circumstances of that day. They contemplated God and His good pleasure. Their reflection upon the Living God and their association with Him, prompted them to ignore the problem. They employed no genius in dealing with it. They refused to think longer upon it, or to reason with the king concerning other possible alternatives. They refused to seek a solution to the dilemma. "We have no care to answer you in this matter," they boldly announced.

God was "able" to deliver them, they confessed. But the ability of God was not the issue. If God chose to deliver them out of the furnace, they would accept it. "But if not," they informed the king, "we will not serve thy gods, nor worship the golden image which thou hast set up" (Dan. 3:14-18). The outcome of their decision verified the correctness of their choice (Dan. 3:19-30).

While all of our difficulties are not remedied so wonderfully, they must all be approached in the same manner. The resolution is really not the preeminent consideration. Rather, the eternal purpose of God is to dominate our view, together with our participation in it.

Conclusion

Truth, like God, is eternal. It is united in all of its aspects as God is united in all of His attributes. There is no contradiction in truth — no competition between the various expressions of truth. There is no such thing as "parallel truths" — a theological expression meant to describe two aspects of the truth that cannot be logically joined together. Expressions that cannot be joined together logically are, of necessity, contradictory to each other. It is no more possible for truth to lack harmony than it is for God to lack consistency. It is, further, the unity of the truth that gives it liberating power. Were it possible to segment the truth and cause its parts to lack harmony, it would become spiritually impotent.

13

THE CONSISTENCY OF DIVINE PURPOSE

We know God by understanding His purpose. "The invisible things of Him" can be, in part, ascertained "from the creation of the world." An intelligent consideration of His creation will reveal His eternal POWER — Divine energy employed in the structuring of the complicated, yet harmonious, realm of nature. A contemplation of the orderliness of the natural creation will introduce one to Divine government and support — His GODHOOD.

In creation, we are introduced to Divine purpose, together with the consistency that permeates it. The reason for the creation of the world is clearly stated; "For thus saith the Lord that created the heavens; God Himself that formed the earth and made it. He hath established it, He created it not in vain, HE FORMED IT TO BE INHABITED . . ." (Isa. 45:18). The earth is not an end of itself. By Divine purpose, it has been united with its inhabitants. A proper view of the "heaven, and earth, and sea" will include "all that therein is" (Psa. 146:6). "I have made the earth, the man and the beast that are upon the ground, by my great power and outstretched arm," God declares (Jer. 27:5). The formation of the earth provided an environment for both "the man and the beast" in general, and man himself in particular (Gen. 1:26-30).

The consistency of that purpose is seen in the harmony of the creation with the requirements of man. The atmosphere of earth, for instance, permits man to breathe. The temperatures are conducive to life rather than death. The sun is near enough to warm the environment, but far enough not to consume it. "Every green herb" is not only pleasing to the eye, but is good for food (Gen. 1:30). The entire natural order blends with God's objective to provide an environment for man — it is consistent with Divine purpose.

The reason for the existence of the whole creation is man. When the salvation of man is complete, and "all things" are gathered together "in Christ" (Eph. 1:10), the heavens and the earth shall be "dissolved" (II Pet. 3:11). Until that time, the rain and the snow will continue to come from heaven to "water the earth," and "make it bring forth and bud, that it may give seed to the sower, and bread to the eater" (Isa. 55:10).

In confirmation that man is God's chief consideration in this arrangement, the Psalmist wrote, "He causes the grass to grow for the cattle, and herb for the service of man: that he [man] may bring forth food out of the earth; and wine that makes glad the heart of man, and oil to make his face to shine, and bread which strengthened man's heart" (Psa. 104:14-15).

God's redemptive purpose pertained to man, and the entire natural order was created with that purpose in mind. He did not make the world to be an object of intense study. The primary objective was not to provide a place for beasts of the field, fish of the sea, and birds of the air. They were all incidental! The primary consideration was man, God's "offspring"! The merging of the Divine activities of the first week of history with that purpose, demonstrates its consistency!

The Singularity of Divine Objective

God has one grand aim, called His "eternal purpose" (Eph. 3:11). He made the world with that objective preeminent. That this purpose involved mankind is shown in the first recorded consultation among the members of the Godhead. "And God said, Let us make man in our image, after our likeness, and let them have dominion . . ." (Gen. 1:26). Man was given charge of the whole earth — a staggering stewardship! "Be fruitful, and multiply, and replenish the earth, and subdue

THE CONSISTENCY OF DIVINE PURPOSE

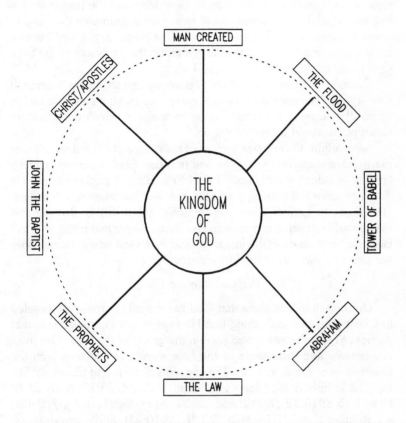

PURPOSE STEDFASTLY MAINTAINED

NOT DISCOURAGED BY FALL   PATIENT WITH ISRAEL
NOT DISCOURAGED BY FLOOD   NO CONDEMNATION
NOT DISCOURAGED AT BABEL   PROMISES UNCHANGED

185

it. . . . Behold I have given you every herb bearing seed . . . and every tree . . ." (Gen. 1:28-30).

There were not multiple purposes in creation, only one! That purpose was revealed in the creation of man. Man was the reason for the natural order! The consideration of him is what prompted the Lord to speak the material world into existence. One purpose, not two! Not one for the sun, one for the waters, and another for the beasts of the field! One purpose! An "eternal purpose"!

You can learn about salvation by properly perceiving the creation (II Cor. 4:4-6). The reason — it was accomplished with man's redemption in mind! The earth was made to be an arena in which the drama of redemption would be accomplished!

Seen aright, the creation testifies of the nature of God. It is His manner to have a single objective — one purpose! God, Who condemns a "double-minded" man (James 1:8; 4:8) is Himself single-minded. He does not serve two primary purposes, but one. Because man is made in His image, he cannot "serve two masters" (Matt. 6:24). It is not that man should not serve two masters, he cannot serve two masters! Why? Because he is made in the image of God — a God whose nature does not permit a division of primary objective!

Prefigured in the Law

Our objective is to show that God has a single purpose as revealed in Christ, and that everything that He says or does complements that purpose. This principle is also seen in the giving of the Law. The commandments and ordinances of the Law were given to men with the redemption of Christ in mind. The concepts of cleansing (Exod. 29:36; Lev. 12:7; Eph. 5:26; I John 1:9), sacrifice (Exod. 23:18; Num. 28:6; Heb. 10:5-8; 10:12), light (Exod. 25:37; Num. 8:2; I John 1:7; 2:10), a high priest (Lev. 21:10; Heb. 8:3; 9:11; 10:21), and a savour pleasing to God (Exod. 29:25; Lev. 23:18; Eph. 5:2; II Cor. 2:15), anticipated the reconciliation of man — God's single objective.

Not only that, they contributed to the clarity of that objective. The law had "a shadow of good things to come" (Heb. 10:1), which introduced that generation to the promised Redeemer. There was not one purpose for the Jews, and another for the Gentiles! "The Law was our schoolmaster, to bring us to Christ" (Gal. 3:24-25). It could not have accomplished that design if it had been basically at variance with

God's single purpose.

Think of the concepts that are unintelligible without the ministry of "the law." "The Lamb of God" (Lev. 9:3; John 1:29,36), "the atonement" (Lev. 17:11; Rom. 5:11), "the holiest" place (Heb. 9:3-8; 10:19), "the blood of the Lamb" (Lev. 23:12-18; Rev. 7:14), "the washing of regeneration" (Heb. 9;10; Eph. 5:26; Rev. 1:5), the "Mediator" (Gal. 3:19; I Tim. 2:5), and "the remission of sins" (Heb. 9:20-22; Rom. 3:25). We owe the comprehensibility and significance of these terms to the ministry of the First Covenant!

Proclaimed in the Gospel

God's objective has not changed in the Gospel. In creation, throughout the dispensation of the Law, and in the "day of salvation," it remains the same! Man has been made to have "dominion" to participate in Divine rule. In the creation he was provided with capacities that would permit such a stewardship. In the Law, the process of thought was activated, together with the development of sound concepts concerning redemption. During that time, an acute awareness of the depth to which man had fallen was fostered. Now, in the Gospel, an even greater degree of clarity is achieved.

God has "made known unto us the mystery of His will, according to His good pleasure which He hath purposed in Himself," declares the Apostle. That revelation proclaims "that in the dispensation of the fullness of times He might gather together in one all things in Christ, both which are in heaven, and which are on earth, even in Him" (Eph. 1:9-10). This speaks of the realization of His purpose for man. The revelation has reached an apex now, for it is in Christ that we also "have obtained an inheritance, being predestinated according to the purpose of Him who worketh all things after the counsel of His own will: that we should be to the praise of His glory . . ." (Eph. 1:11-12).

Here, the single objective of God is described in the words, "predestinated according to the purpose of Him." The realization of His objective for man is culminated "in Christ." A single purpose consummated in a single Person — Christ! God's design for man is realized through him being united with His Son. That is the Divine appointment. The role of the Gospel in this single objective is perceived in a grand overview provided by the Apostle. "In whom [Christ] ye also trusted, after that ye heard the word of truth, the gospel of your salvation; in whom also after that ye believed, ye were sealed with the Holy Spirit of promise, which is the earnest of our inheritance until the redemption of the purchased possession, unto the praise of His glory" (Eph. 1:13-14).

The single objective of God has been progressively introduced to men. In creation a general view was provided, together with insight into the capacities of man. By the Law, the knowledge of sin was introduced, together with a knowledge of how it would be addressed by God. The Gospel announced that sin had been dealt with, that man could fellowship with God now, and that the "ages to come" had been determined for the full realization of man's destiny.

All of these things work together — they are consistent! Without "eternal purpose," there is no reason for creation, the Law, or the Gospel. Further, without creation, the Law, and the Gospel, that purpose would fail of fulfillment! The purpose did not change! God was never diverted from it! He has never had multiple primary purposes! This, I insist, is a revelation of His nature, and consequently is also a revelation of the nature of His Kingdom!

God's Desire to Make Known His Objective

The fact that God has revealed Himself to man demonstrates the existence of His desire to do so. God only does what He wants to do! It is the "good pleasure of His will" that constrained Him throughout His redemptive purpose (Eph. 1:5,9). "He hath done whatsoever He hath pleased," affirmed the Psalmist (Psa. 115:3; 135:6).

It is equally true that God does not contradict His will in His words and works. God made Israel "His people" because it "pleased" Him (I Sam. 12:22). The grevious bruising of Jesus Christ for the iniquities of fallen man "pleased the Lord" (Isa. 53:19), even though it brought Him no personal delight. The Divine appointment of "preaching" as the means of illumination was something that "pleased God" (I Cor. 1:21).

God works "all things after the counsel of his own will" (Eph. 1:11). It is His desire, not mere need, that motivates Him! This is particularly evidenced in the matter of the reconciliation of man, His preeminent objective throughout time. While, from one view, man needed a Redeemer, it was primarily God's will that sent Him, not man's need. "For God so loved the world, that He gave His only begotten Son . . ." (John 3:16). This is the paramount demonstration of the principle — God is primarily motivated by His will.

Illustrated In Historical Appearances

There are two aspects of this truth to be perceived. First, God makes Himself known to men because He desires to do so. Secondly, His appearances are associated with a revelation of His purpose; i.e., He wants to make His will known to men.

When God revealed Himself to Adam and Eve in Eden, He made known His purpose concerning man's recovery (Gen. 3:8-21). "I will put enmity between thee [the serpent] and the woman, and between thy seed and her seed; it [the Messiah] shall bruise thy head, and thou shalt bruise his heel" (Gen. 3:15). At the earliest point of history, therefore, God reveals that redemption would be accomplished by the frustration of Satan, and the infliction of a wound upon man's Deliverer. The Lord made that known because He wanted to — that is His nature; He could not, so to speak, keep it quiet!

Sometime later, the "Lord appeared" to Abraham (Gen. 18:2-33). Again, He made known His objectives concerning Abraham and the world. "Seeing that Abraham shall surely become a great nation, and all the nations of the earth shall be blessed in him" (Gen. 18:18). Beyond Abraham himself and that point in time, God was considering the whole race of man — "the nations of the earth." Not only did God NOT keep His purpose hidden, His nature forbade Him to keep it secret. In a revelation of His goodness He said, "Shall I hide from Abraham that thing which I do?" (Gen. 18:17). He wanted to make His purpose known!

When Jacob "came out of Padanaram," God "appeared unto him." The purpose of that revelation was not simply to impress Jacob with God's greatness — although that was an inevitable result. The Lord desired to make known His objectives to Jacob. In preparation for the coming Redeemer, God was going to raise up a great nation, and He was going to do it through Jacob's posterity. ". . . a nation and a company of nations shall be of thee, and kings shall come out of thy loins; and the land which I gave Abraham and Isaac, to thee will I give it, and to thy seed after thee will I give the land" (Gen. 35:9-12). Again, the nature of God is discerned in His desire to communicate His purpose.

After Moses "fled from the face of Pharaoh," he resided in the land of Midian (Exod. 2:15). It was there that "the angel of the Lord appeared unto him in a flame of fire out of the midst of a bush." Intrigued

189

with the phenomenon, Moses turned aside "to see this great sight." "And when the Lord saw that he turned aside to see, God called unto him out of the midst of the bush, and said, "Moses, Moses." Following the response of Moses. God identified Himself to him. "I am the God of thy father, the God of Abraham, the God of Isaac, and the God of Jacob" (Exod. 3:1-6). But the real intent of this revelation was not merely to impress Moses with the Divine presence, but to reveal Divine objective! Moses was told that God had witnessed, with intense interest, the affliction of His people in Egypt. He had, further, chosen him to bring "the people out of Egypt . . ." (Exod. 3:7-12). He wanted to make His plan known to Moses — that is why He did make it known.

The Revelation of the Gospel

In the Gospel, we have a message for all men everywhere. "Go ye therefore into all the world, and preach the Gospel to every creature," commanded Christ (Mark 16:15). This must not be viewed as a mere duty, or merely as the appointed means by which mankind must be saved. A higher view is necessary.

The Gospel is a body of words that conveys the mind of God to men — particularly His desire. The preeminent fact of the Gospel — the accomplishment of Christ — provides an insight into God's nature as regards men. "Hereby perceive we the love of God, because He laid down His life for us . . ." (I John 3:16). In fact, without that perception, the Gospel is really not gospel. The undergirding reality that makes the message of the Gospel good is that it represents the provisions of a willing God — One that is intent upon saving men because He loves them and wants to save them!

The identification of the Gospel with God's desire is perceived in the terms used by the Apostles. "The Gospel of God" (Rom. 1:1; 15:16; I Thess. 2:8), "the dispensation of the grace of God" (Acts 20:28), "the glorious gospel of the blessed God" (I Tim. 1:11). These words speak of the communication of Divine objective!

God desired to make His purpose known to men, and He was consistent in that determination. From His very first communication to Adam and Eve in the garden — on the same day the fall occurred — until the detailed communication of the "Gospel of Christ," a single purpose has been declared: it is to restore fallen man to Himself. The consistency of Divine objective is seen here. God purposed to reconcile men unto Himself. He announced it to Adam, foreshadowed it in the Law, foretold it in the prophets, and accomplished it in His only begotten Son. He then commanded that His provisions be proclaimed, because He wanted to make it known! He desired for men to comprehend His fathomless love for them! The Gospel is a precise reflection of God Himself — how he thinks, what He has purposed, and how He has wisely implemented that purpose.

The failure to comprehend this rather obvious truth has resulted in gross misconceptions of salvation. Some have concluded that God must be fervently implored in order to be saved. The "mourners' bench" and the "prayer altar" are nothing more than the result of a corrupted view of God. Rigid and lifeless Calvinsim assumes that God appoints men to either heaven or hell, independently of just cause. God is perceived as not loving the world, even though He has clearly proclaimed that He does (John 3:16)! He is set forth as willing that some perish, even though He has pointedly announced that this is not the case (II Pet. 3:9).

These erroneous views are the result of failing to perceive the truth that "God was in Christ, reconciling the world unto Himself, not imputing their trespasses unto them" (II Cor. 5:18-20). "God was in Christ" because this was the perfect expression of His desire! In Christ He not only accomplished what needed to be accomplished; He achieved what He wanted to achieve!

God Does Not Adjust His Purpose to Meet Circumstances

The "kingdoms of this world" are marked by change and inevitable obsoleteness. Earthly kingdoms are unstable, even in the temporal domain for which they are adapted. Their insecure status was proclaimed to Nebuchadnezzar, an ancient king of Babylon, in a mysterious dream. Daniel, a Hebrew prophet who "had understanding in all visions and dreams" (Dan. 1:18), revealed the dream to the king. The dream presented a "great image," the form of which was "terrible." It was the image of a man. There was a progressive degradation of materials in this image from the head to the feet — the more precious metals being at the top and the lesser toward the bottom. The head was constructed of "fine gold, his legs of iron, his feet part of iron and part of clay" (Dan. 2:31-33). One thing, however, that every part of the image had in common — it was to be destroyed. Although its elements had descending

191

degress of value, from the eternal perspective, the common trait of temporality marked every aspect of the image.

The image signified four kingdoms: Babylon, Persia, Greece, and Rome (Dan. 2:38-39, 49; 8:19-21; 10:19-21). Each succeeding kingdom was "inferior" to the one preceding it (Dan. 2:39). Also, these were consecutive kingdoms, each one replacing the previous kingdom. The absence of a consistent purpose, together with the necessity for constant alteration, will make every earthly kingdom obsolete. A Scriptural word indicating the result of inconsistency is "confusion." Confusion is the inevitable result of things not working together.

Inconsistency Necessitates Revaluation

The history of the church contains instances of dramatic changes of perspective. Even in the early church, there were several major alterations. The full acceptance of the Gentiles required a change of view (Acts 10:1-48; 15:3-29). The matter of fleshly circumcision also required revaluation (Acts 15:1-2; Rom. 2:25-26).

Without going into the details, it should be understood that the postapostolic days of the church have also been marked by frequent changes of view among religious men. Godly men have not been noted for embracing the truth, but also for abandoning error. The only reason for this condition is what we must see — it is not enough to merely know that changes have taken place.

Error is perceived at the point it is seen to contradict truth, or reality. In the case of the early church, the exclusion of the Gentiles as recipients of the Gospel was perceived as wrong when it obviously contradicted the Word of the Lord. That is, the position was inconsistent with God's revealed purpose. Peter spoke for all men of understanding when he confessed, "of a truth, I perceive that God is no respecter of persons: but in every nation he that fears Him, and works righteousness, is accepted with Him" (Acts 10:34). For over a decade, the Gospel had not been preached to the Gentiles. That practice was out of harmony with the revelation of God through the Gospel.

The attaching of religious significance to circumcision was also abandoned because it was out of harmony with the nature of the New Covenant. In Christ, circumcision is that "of the heart, in the spirit" (Rom. 2:28-29). The continuance of fleshly circumcision as instituted under the Law was simply incompatible with the nature of the faith of Christ. It was therefore necessary for men to change their mind on that matter. God's will does not change. Whenever men find themselves at variance with God's will, they must change!

The Principle of God's Immutability

The consistency of God and His Kingdom is inseparably associated with His immutability. God, by nature, is incapable of moral change. Right can never become wrong, and wrong can never become right with Him! His "eternal purpose," further, can never become temporal, and primary things can never become secondary, and secondary things can never become primary. Not in God's Kingdom!

"The counsel of the Lord stands forever," proclaimed the Psalmist, "the thoughts of His heart to all generations" (Psa. 33:11). His "counsel" is His determinate will — His "eternal purpose." His thoughts" refer to the revealed details of that purpose to the sons of men. They are never retracted, never made obsolete or supplanted. In an age of limited insight, Solomon confessed, ". . . nevertheless the counsel of the Lord, that shall stand" (Prov. 19:21). Within the progressive revelation of God, Isaiah also spoke the truth of God's immutability. "Yet He also is wise . . . and will not call back His words . . ." (Isa. 31:2). God is immutable, and consequently does not adjust His purpose to meet circumstances. His counsel will stand, and He will not call back His words!

The Role of His Foreknowledge

The determinations of God are made in view of what He knows — and He knows everything (I Sam. 2:3; Prov. 15:3; Isa. 46:10; 48:5-6; Heb. 4:13)! He is never shortsighted in His plans, never caught by surprise, never in a state of consternation.

God, whose understanding is "infinite" (Psa. 147:5), never purposes something that does not precisely meet His objective in mind.

Confirming this principle is Paul's assertion to the Galatians. "The Scripture, foreseeing that God would justify the heathen through faith, preached before the Gospel to Abraham . . ." (Gal. 3:8). Another illustration of the truth is found in God's choice of Abraham.

Shall I hide from Abraham that thing which I do; seeing that Abraham shall surely become a great and mighty nation, and all

193

the nations of the earth shall be blessed of Him? For I know him, that he will command his children and his household after him, and they shall keep the way of the Lord, to do justice and judgment; that the Lord may bring upon Abraham that which He hath spoken of him (Gen. 18:17-19).

A determination that is based upon a consideration of every possible circumstance and variable cannot possibly be altered!

God's foreknowledge was integral to the delivering up of Christ (Acts 2:23). It also has a direct bearing upon the initial calling and ultimate glorification of those that are in Christ Jesus (Rom. 8:28-30; I Pet. 1:2). In salvation God does not ignore man's nature and response, but rather considers them! He not only contemplates man's requirements, but his proclivities. His salvation not only meets every spiritual need of man, it makes an appeal to every valid inclination of man (Acts 17:26-27).

This is why "every one that asks receives; and he that seeks finds; and to him that knocks it shall be opened" (Matt. 7:8). God does not adjust His will to answer the changing quests of men; He provides a salvation which fully meets requirements foreknown to Him.

Demonstrated in Noah

God's revealed purpose for man was that of dominion (Gen. 1:26-27). But man sinned, and came "short of the glory of God" (Rom. 3:23). God's purpose, so far as man was concerned, became buried under the rubble of temporality. Within around 1,600 years, the world became so corrupted that God determined to "destroy man whom I have created" (Gen. 6:7). Surely, now His purpose will change. Man shall no longer have the dominion — after all, he has proved himself unworthy!

But the eyes of the Lord that "run to and fro throughout the whole earth, to show Himself strong in the behalf of them whose heart is perfect toward Him" (II Chron. 16:9), took note of one righteous man in the earth! There, amidst the iniquity and wickedness that had angered the Lord Almighty, there stood a man that was "a just man, and perfect in his generation" (Gen. 6:9). He had not been carried away with the prevailing and overwhelming "wickedness of man" (Gen. 6:5). God took note of that man, and "Noah found grace in the eyes of the Lord" (Gen. 6:8). God's purpose for man was not abandoned, even though He was incensed with him, whose every thought "was only evil continually" (Gen. 6:5b).

After the flood had subsided, and all flesh had died except those "eight souls" in the ark (I Pet. 3:20), "God remembered Noah, and every living thing, and all the cattle that was with him in the ark" (Gen. 8:1). Wonderful grace of God! The word of God reveals the reassertion of God's original purpose — it was not changed!

> And God blessed Noah and his sons, and said to them, Be fruitful, and multiply, and replenish the earth. And the fear of you and the dread of you shall be upon every beast of the earth, and upon every fowl of the air, upon all that moveth upon the earth, and upon all the fishes of the sea; into your hand are they delivered. Every moving thing that liveth shall be meat for you; even as the green herb have I given you all things (Gen. 8:1-3, compared with Gen. 1:28-30).

God did not adjust His purpose to meet the circumstance! It remained the same.

Some Apparent Retractions

There are at several incidents in sacred history, however, which appear to indicate that God does alter His purpose. This section of our study would not be complete without a brief review of them.

God Repents That He Made Man

The unrestrained devotion to self-gratification that characterized the days immediately prior to the flood, caused the Lord to say of men, ". . . it repenteth me that I have made them." It is also stated, "And it repented the Lord that He had made man on the earth, and it grieved Him at His heart" (Gen. 6:6-7). These are arresting words, indeed!

God is not without feeling! He cannot behold His offspring given over to lawlessness without being grieved in His heart. But that grief does not compel Him to alter or renounce His "eternal purpose." He did not abandon His redemptive plan to mortally bruise the head of the deceptive serpent by the Seed of woman! He did not blot out His determined objective that man would have dominion! He did reject that

195

generation, so far as their involvement in that purpose was concerned! He did not repent that He had made Adam! He did not repent that Abel or Enoch had lived! He did not repent that He had made Noah! This was not a grief concerning man in general, but rather of that generation in particular!

In the creation of man, God had knowingly exposed Himself to the possibility of heartbreak and grief! He knew these things, and yet He made man anyway! What a glorious revelation of His nature! Today — in the day of Christ's reign — He is not sorry that He made man! He is happy at the prospect of having a regenerated society presented to Him by His only begotten Son (Isa. 8:18; Heb. 2:13). His purpose has not changed!

God Repents of the Evil Which He Thought to Do

There are at least three occasions where God is said to have "repented Himself of the evil" which He had purposed to do. None of them contradicts the revelation that God does not change, and that He does not "repent" (Mal. 3:6; Num. 23:19; Jer. 4:28; Rom. 11:29).

The first incident occurred at the foot of Mount Sinai. With the inauguration of the First Covenant still fresh in their memory, the Israelites had given themselves over to idolatry, sitting down to "eat and drink," and rising up to indulge in riotous "play" (I Cor. 10:7). Furious at the sight, God confided in His servant Moses, "I have seen this people, and, behold, it is a stiff-necked people: now therefore let Me alone, that My wrath may wax hot against them, and that I may consume them: and I will make of thee a great nation." Those uninitiated in the ways of the Lord would have stood aside, and let the fire burn. But not Moses! God had shown Moses "His ways" (Psa. 103:7).

Immediately, Moses makes an appeal to the nature of God, and to His commitments. With holy boldness he asks, "Lord, why doth Thy wrath wax hot against Thy people, which Thou hast brought forth out of the land of Egypt with great power, and with a mighty hand?" Pleading as a wise lawyer, he fills his mouth with "arguments" (Job 23:4), and produces his "cause" (Isa. 41:21). Egypt would hear of such a judgment and falsely conclude that God brought them out of Egypt "to slay them in the mountains, and to consume them from the face of the earth." Moses also called upon the Lord to "remember Abraham, Isaac, and Israel," God's servants, to whom He had sworn with covenantal oath (Exod. 32:9-13).

It is written, "And the Lord repented of the evil which He thought to do unto His people" (Exod. 32:14). This was not, however, due to Divine fickleness. It was, rather a confirmation of the immutability of His promise, and of the appeal that its remembrance had to Him.

Incidentally, though the destruction of that generation did not occur on that day, it did occur later. God promised Moses, "nevertheless in the day when I visit I will visit their sin upon them" (Exod. 32:35). God was not turned from His purpose. Israel remained His people as a nation, they did inherit the land of promise, but the carcasses of the disobedient still fell in the wilderness (Num. 14:29).

The second incident occurred when King Saul became disobedient to God, not "utterly" destroying "the sinners and the Amalekites" as he was commissioned (I Sam. 15:18). In defiance of the commandment, "he took Agag the king of the Amalekites alive" (I Sam. 15:8). In response to this disobedience, "the word of the Lord" came "unto Samuel, saying, It repenteth me that I have set up Saul to be king . . ." The revelation "grieved Samuel; and he cried unto the Lord all night" in vain (I Sam. 15:11).

Had God altered His purpose? Did this repentance indicate the frustration of God's counsel? God forbid! The choice of Saul as king was only an intermediate choice — until the Divinely-appointed king was of age. That king was David, Saul's successor (I Sam. 16:12-13). Saul was rejected for transgression, and his disobedience grieved the Lord. But there was no interruption of the Divine plan. Israel still remained His people and the Messiah was still appointed to come through them.

A third incident occurred when king David determined to "number Israel and Judah." Although it appeared but an innocent thing on the surface, it proved to be an act of wickedness. Joab, the captain of the host, counselled the king to refrain from this undertaking. "Now the Lord thy God add unto the people, how many soever they be, an hundredfold, and that the eyes of my lord the king may see it," he said (II Sam. 24:2-3). This effort to deter David came because Joab correctly perceived it as an act of unbelief. It was not the size of the nation or its army that had given Israel success, but its favor with God!

We are told that this occasion was prompted by the Lord's anger against Israel. "And again the anger of the Lord was kindled against

Israel, and He moved David against them to say, Go, number Israel and Judah" (II Sam. 24:1). Emphasizing the means used to accomplish this purpose, it is later stated that "Satan stood up against Israel, and provoked David to number Israel" (I Chron. 21:1). On the other hand, when the incident was finalized, David himself took the full credit for the numbering (II Sam. 24:17; I Chron. 21:8).

The situation, duly perceived, seems clear enough. God gave Satan leave, and did not interfere with his provocation — thus was the action credited to God. Satan willingly employed his deceitful ways to bring about the consideration in David — thus was he responsible for its occurrence. David was obviously available for the development of such a thought — thus did responsibility rest with him. The entire event, however, occurred because Israel had angered God with her transgression!

By way of brief diversion, we have here an example of the inner-workings of the Kingdom of God. God is over all, and nothing occurs without His authority or approval. Satan, the enemy of all good, is ever present, ready to do anything he is licensed to do. Man, by his frame of mind, is available for employment in either good or evil, right or wrong, sin or righteousness.

Israel's iniquity, as emphasized by David's sin, resulted in a pestilence that took the lives of 70,000 men (II Sam. 24:15). The pestilence was carried out under the supervision of an angel of God. So intent was this angel upon executing the heavenly commission, that he "stretched out his hand upon Jerusalem to destroy it." This was the city where God had placed His Name (II Kgs. 21:4).

As God witnessed this Divinely-appointed judgment, His nature asserted itself. ". . . the Lord repented Him of the evil, and said to the angel that destroyed the people, IT IS ENOUGH: STAY NOW THY HAND" (II Sam. 24:16). It is a good thing that angels respond more quickly than men! Had the destroying angel been as dilatory in responding as is generally characteristic of men, the holy city would have been decimated.

This repentance of God did not, however, involve a renunciation of His revealed objective concerning men. The coming Messiah was not delayed. The passing of the heavens and the earth were was not accelerated. Israel was not forsaken. This was a temporary judgment, and had no effect upon the overall purpose of God.

God Has Revealed This Aspect of His Nature

In His temporary judgments, God is never so intent upon executing wrath that He will not respond to repentance. This is not an indication of instability, but of mercy — something sorely required in His dealings with men. The type of repentance with which we have just dealt is as necessary to God's nature as that of the immutability of His commitments.

Opening up the tender mercy of God, Moses wrote of Him, "For the Lord shall judge His people, and repent Himself for His servants, when He sees that their power is gone, and there is none shut up or left" (Deut. 32:36; Psa. 135:14). The same principle is repeated in Jeremiah 18:7-8 and 42:9-10. In this usage, "repent Himself" is a synonym for having compassion.

The converse of this principle is also true. When God promises good, disobedience by those to whom it was promised will cause the commitment to be withdrawn. Speaking of a people God had said He would benefit, it is written, "And at what instant I shall speak concerning a nation, and concerning a kingdom, to build and to plant it; if it do evil in my sight, that it obey not my voice, then I will repent of the good, wherewith I said I would benefit them" (Jer. 18:9-10).

God's faithfulness to His purpose is a revelation of His faithfulness to Himself; i.e., He will not contradict His own nature! He is, and has revealed Himself to be, absolutely trustworthy. His purpose does not fluctuate with the change of circumstance. This is the point of Samuel's counsel to Israel: "For the Lord will not forsake His people for His great name's sake: because it hath pleased the Lord to make you His people" (I Sam. 12:22). He would not contradict His changeless Godhood.

The works of God are always accomplished in consideration of the Divine Nature. To put it another way, what God says and does is always a faithful expression of His Person! That is the significance of the phrase, "for Thy name's sake" (I Kgs. 8:41; Psa. 25:11; 79:9; 109:21; Jer. 14:7).

An Eternal Purpose

The reconciliation of man is identified with God's "eternal purpose" (Eph. 3:11). This proclaimed enterprise, like God Himself, is "eternal." It has never been divorced from God's Person. We have no declaration of this purpose having a beginning, or any promise of it ever being renounced — it is an "eternal purpose." It involves Divine activity before the world was formed, and shall consummate in joyful fruition after the world has been removed. It was not conceived in response to the fall of man, but in anticipation of it.

The phrase "the foundation of the world" refers to the deliberate creation of the world. It was made with an objective. It was not an experiment, not a mere expression of unrelated power and wisdom. In the world's creation, God's power and wisdom were joined together in an objective purpose. The Scriptures emphasize that the redemption of man was uppermost in the mind of the Lord when He made the world.

Christ's words were a revelation of things "kept secret from the foundation of the world" (Matt. 25:31). The ultimate inheritance of those in Christ involves a "kingdom prepared" for them "from the foundation of the world" (Matt. 25:34). In His High Priestly prayer, Jesus spoke of God's loving Him "before the foundation of the world" (John 17:24).

The determination of God to present everyone in Christ to Himself "without blame" is said to have occurred "before the foundation of the world" (Eph. 1:4). Christ Himself, in His vicarious role as the Lamb of God, was "foreordained before the foundation of the world" (I Pet. 2:20; Rev. 13:8). The world, then, was made with the reconciliation of God's offspring in mind.

Further, all of the history of the world, foreknown by God, was considered before the enterprise of salvation was foretold or inaugurated.

Conclusion

"As for God, His way is perfect," proclaimed the Psalmist (Psa. 18:30). This is no more evident than in the matter of the salvation of man, which God has "purposed in Himself" (Eph. 1:9). Because that purpose is eternal, and because it is an expression of His Person, it is not possible for it to change without God Himself changing.

His purpose is not altered to fit circumstances, because all of the circumstances were known to Him before He began implementing His purpose. An eternal purpose is becoming of an eternal God! An unchangeable God, further, is magnified by the revelation of an unalterable objective. This condition justifies faith, giving it a solid foundation — the faithfulness of God.

200

14

THE CONSISTENCY OF REVELATION

The Kingdom of God is made known to men by revelation. We cannot, in fact, properly conceive of His Kingdom apart from that revelation. An element of mystery pervades all heathen religions. This is of necessity the case, because they center in those "which by nature are no gods" (Gal. 4:8). The absence of revelation in these religions is one of the reasons for the dominance of fear in them. But it is not so with "true religion" (James 1:27).

A Definition of Revelation

The principle element of revelation is that of opening or uncovering what is hidden. In the case of God's Kingdom, revelation is characterized by Divine intention. It is never accidental, or even incidental. Unlike the kingdoms of this world, there is never a "leak" of Divine information. God makes known what He wants to make known.

Revelation presumes intelligence on the part of the recipient as well as that of the Revealer. The things of God, for instance, cannot be revealed to the brute creation — they have no reason. Nor, indeed, can they be opened up to infants or those incapable of thought and consideration.

In the Kingdom, certain wonderful concepts are integral to revelation. The Revealer must be perceived as having a purpose, as well as possessing a desire to communicate it. On the other hand, the ones to whom the revelation is addressed are seen as possessing abilities capable of receiving the revelation, as well as a need for it.

Revelation, in its loftiest sense, involves the communication of thought. In this capacity, it is addressed to the mind, not the physical senses. The senses are capable of being impressed with a rudimentary revelation. Such was the case with Moses and Israel at Sinai (Exod. 19:16-25; Heb. 12:21), Elijah in a cave in Horeb (I Kgs. 19:8-12), Saul of Tarsus on the road to Damascus (Acts 9:1-8), and Daniel the prophet (Dan. 10:8). These revelations were consistently introductory in nature. They were never an end of themselves. The communication of thought — the Divine objective — followed these occurrences. It is in this sense that I am using the word "revelation."

Examples Confirm Its Association with Thought

"The secret things belong unto the Lord our God," proclaimed Moses, "but those things which are revealed belong unto us and to our children forever . . ." (Deut. 29:29). Experiences and things perceived by the physical sense cannot be passed to our children — only the thoughts concerning them. The heritage to which Moses refers was the Law — an intelligent compilation of Divine thoughts and concepts.

When Peter made an intelligent and accurate confession of Christ as the Son of God, Jesus said; "Blessed art thou, Simon Barjona: for flesh and blood hath not revealed it unto thee, but my Father which is in heaven" (Matt. 16:16-17). Again, the communication of thought — the chief component in perception.

The Apostle Paul, in the presentation of His understanding of God's objective in Christ, wrote, "Whereby, when you read, you may understand my knowledge in the mystery of Christ, which in other ages was not made known unto the sons of men, as it is now revealed unto His holy apostles and prophets by the Spirit; that the Gentiles should be fellow heirs, and of the same body, and partakers of His promise in Christ by the Gospel" (Eph. 3:4-6). The revelation resulted in Paul's discernment of God's objective — something that can only be ac-

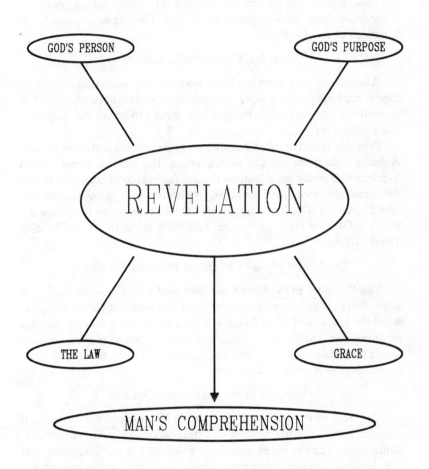

complished by thought, and with the mind.

The religion of Christ has erroneously been identified with mysticism, intrigue, and sensualism. One of our objectives is to expose this abuse and perversion of truth. Such traits belong more to heathenism, and betoken ignorance of God. They have no place in the Kingdom of our God!

What Is a Consistent Revelation?

A consistent revelation is a harmonious one — one that contains no logical contradictions. It does not defy reason, but appeals to it. The consistency of revealed truth does not dignify mystery, but magnifies comprehension.

Properly understood, a consistent revelation will constrain men to embrace it. Its harmony is its attractiveness. The fact that its parts blend together and make sense causes thoughtful beauty to surround it. It is this condition that prompted early believers to "gladly receive the Word" (Acts. 2:41). It is what enabled the Thessalonians to receive the Word of God "in much assurance" and "with joy of the Holy Ghost" (I Thess. 1:5-6).

The Nature of God's Kingdom Requires Revelation

The Kingdom of God has been identified with the reconciliation of men. If man is to be reconciled, he must be informed! He must understand the purpose of God, if God is to be glorified in his redemption! It is inconceivable that man's salvation could be accomplished without God's revelation. If union with God is to come to man, the way must be made plain — it must be revealed!

Illustrated in the Impersonal Creation

The truth of this is seen in the coming liberation of the impersonal creation. Although it has not sinned, it has been made "subject to vanity," contaminated by the sin of man. It is in view of this contamination that "the creature [creation] itself also shall be delivered from the bondage of corruption into the glorious liberty of the children of God" (Rom. 8:19-21).

The whole creation is destined to experience Divine deliverance. There is a mournful note of anticipation being sounded throughout the natural order, as it groans and travails "in pain together until now"

(Rom. 8:22). But no revelation has been given to it! A messenger has not been sent to the birds of the air, the beasts of the field, and the fish of the sea! They are going to be delivered without their personal involvement.

But it is not so with man! He has been made in the image of God, and cannot be delivered without the interplay of his mind and spirit. He is what God's Kingdom is all about. He is not the center of that Kingdom, but the subject of it. In wisdom and prudence, God is dealing with him, gathering out a people for His great Name (Eph. 1:8; Acts 15:14). That sort of enterprize demands revelation, and cannot possibly be implemented without it. Indeed, that is why God has revealed Himself and His will through Christ!

God Cannot Contradict His Person

God delights to have men understand and know Him (Jer. 9:24). This is His nature. For Him to introduce a plan to men that was beyond their comprehension, He would have to deny Himself. Theoretically, only two things can make God's message incomprehensible. It may be conceived of as simply being beyond the reach of man — as dealing with such high and lofty realities that man is incapable of grasping it. It would be like God speaking to us in either a strange and incomprehensible language, or in concepts that are impossible for man to grasp.

The other alternative would be for the message to be illogical, unintelligible, and unsupported by reason. This would render it inaccessible to man, a moral being in the image of God. A man cannot spiritually benefit from what he cannot, to some degree, discern.

Both of these theories contradict God's revealed purpose. God has gone to great lengths to make His purpose intelligible to man. He has brought it within the range of man's mind and understanding. He sent His only begotten Son "in the likeness of sinful flesh" (Rom. 8:3), making Him "like unto His brethren" (Heb. 2:10-17). This arrangement was not only in order that He might be "touched with the feeling of man's infirmities" (Heb. 4:15), and be able to strengthen and succor them in the hour of their temptation (Heb. 2:18) — it was also so that we could "consider the Apostle and High Priest of our profession, Christ Jesus" (Heb. 3:1). Both Christ's Person and words are addressed to our understanding, without which, there would be no purpose for His revelation!

When God made His purpose known, speaking to men first by the prophets, and then by His son (Heb. 1:1), He did so in the langauge of men, not "the tongues of angels" (I Cor. 13:1). The blessing is pronounced upon those that "hear the word of God and keep it" (Luke 11:28). This promise confirms the focus of God's word upon man, and its appeal to his understanding.

The principle is this: what God has revealed does not contradict His Person! It is consistent with His Deity, His Character, and His purpose. There is not a particle of disharmony between what God has said and Who God is!

Perceived in the Giving of the Law

The principle of revelation's consistency with God's Person is exhibited in the Law. There, in tables of stone, an outline of God's character was etched. The Law of commandments was nothing more than a moral reflection of the Living God. It was a rudimentary way of saying, "Be ye perfect as your Father in heaven is perfect" (Matt. 5:48). An examination of the Decalogue will verify this observation.

"Thou shalt have no other gods before me," commanded the Lord. "Thou shalt not make unto thee any graven image, or any likeness of any thing that is in heaven above, or that is in earth beneath, or that is in the water under the earth. Thou shalt not bow thyself down to them, nor serve them . . ." (Exod. 20:3-5). This represented God's own nature. Several centuries later, Jehovah spoke through the prophet Isaiah, "Is there a God beside me? yea, there is no God [beside me]; I know not any" (Isa. 44:8). The commandments forbidding idolatry were a summons to men to reflect the mind of the Lord. God knew no other gods because there are no other gods! The commandment, then, was consistent with His Person and perspective!

"Thou shalt not take the Name of the Lord Thy God in vain . . ." (Exod. 20:7). No man is permitted to lightly use God's Name. When God refers to Himself, He does it with the utmost sobriety. It is never a light matter, never frivolous or meaningless! "But as truly as I live, all the earth shall be filled with the glory of the Lord" (Num. 14:21). When the Lord sought to underscore His commitments, they were often attended with this Divine oath; "As I live" (Isa. 49:18; Jer. 22:24; Ezek. 5:11; 14:16; Zeph. 2:9; Rom. 14:11). Again, the commandment to not take God's Name in vain reflected the Divine image. God takes such usage seriously, and so must man!

"Remember the sabbath day, to keep it holy" (Exod. 20:8). The "first covenant," which revolved around the seen and the tangible, also reflected the Divine nature. "For in six days the Lord made heaven and earth, the sea, and all that in them is, and rested on the seventh day: wherefore the Lord blessed the sabbath day, and hallowed it" (Exod. 20:11). Even though this day has given way to the first day of the week, on which the Lord of glory rose from the dead, it still bears the image of God and His activities during the creation week.

"Honor thy father and thy mother: that thy days may be long upon the earth which the Lord thy God giveth thee" (Exod. 20:12). The respect of God for aged men and women is seen in the special instruction provided for them (Titus 2:2-3). He considers them resources in the work of the Kingdom, and instructs them as such. It was in Christ that the attitude of Deity was perceived toward parents. It is said of Him that "He went down with them [Joseph and Mary], and came to Nazareth, and was subject to them" (Luke 2:51). This is the procedure of the Divine nature in a body of flesh. As such, it is the only proper course for those that bear the Divine image by creation.

"Thou shalt not kill. Thou shalt not commit adultery. Thou shalt not steal. Thou shalt not bear false witness against thy neighbor. Thou shalt not covet thy neighbors wife . . . manservant . . . ox . . . ass, nor anything that is thy neighbors" (Exod. 20:13-17). The apostolic synopsis of these commandments is found in Romans 13:9: "For this, Thou shalt not commit adultery, Thou shalt not kill, Thou shalt not steal, Thou shalt not bear false witness, Thou shalt not covet; and if there by any other commandment, it is briefly comprehended in this saying, namely, Thou shalt love thy neighbor as thyself."

Here is a most glorious reflection of the Lord! It is He that seeks to do good to man, and not evil (Gen. 50:20; Num. 10:19). The Lord "is good" is the frequent proclamation of holy men of God (I Chron. 16:34; Ezra 3:11; Psa. 100:5; Lam. 3:24; Nahum 1:7). It is "every good gift" that "cometh down from the Father of lights" (James 1:17). His "goodness" is repeatedly heralded in Scripture (Rom. 2:4; Zech. 9:17; Psa. 107:8).

The Devil is the "thief" that comes "to steal, and to kill, and to destroy." But God's Son came that men "might have life, and that they might have it more abundantly" (John 10:10). That is in perfect conformity to God's character!

The second table of the law, like the first, was a moral reflection of God. It was consistent with Him, harmonious with His nature, and a mirror of His Person! What a wonderful demonstration of this truth; that God's revelation is consistent with, and does not contradict, His own Person!

Seen in Jesus Christ, the Supreme Revelation

Jesus Christ was "God manifest in the flesh" (I Tim. 3:16), a perfect revelation of His Father. As a man, He was "the brightness of His [God's] glory, and the express image of His Person" (Heb. 1:3). The words and deeds of Jesus were consistent reflections of His Father. He never acted or reacted unlike God. Thus will an intelligent consideration of Him yield an acquaintance with God (Job. 22:21).

The blend of Divine attributes may be seen in Christ's ministry. No single facet of God's character was ignored. That expression of old, "mercy and truth are met together," and "righteousness and peace have kissed each other," is fulfilled in Jesus (Psa. 85:10). Many a soul has supposed that God's righteousness and man's peace with Him are irreconcilable. "Give me mercy, not justice," is the cry of the uninformed.

God, in Christ, is declared to be both "just, and the Justifier of him which believes in Jesus" (Rom. 3:26). In fact, even though the Gospel proclaims the free justification of man (Rom. 3:24), it is also an announcement of the righteousness of God. "For I am not ashamed of the Gospel of Christ: for it is the power of God unto salvation to everyone that believes; to the Jew first, and also to the Greek. For therein is the righteousness of God revealed . . ." (Rom. 1:16-17). Again, it is witnessed, "Whom God hath set forth to be a propitiation through faith in His blood, to declare His righteousness for the remission of sins that are past . . . to declare, I say, at this time His righteousness . . ." (Rom. 3:25-26). In Christ, therefore, "mercy and truth" met together, and "righteousness and peace" kissed each other!

A single demonstration of Divine consistency as revealed in Jesus will suffice. On one occasion in Jesus' ministry, the scribes and the Pharisees "brought unto Him a woman taken in adultery." Subtly they said, "Master, this woman was taken in adultery, in the very act. Now Moses in the law commanded us, that such should be stoned: but what sayest thou?" Here Divine traits were thrown into conflict with one another. How could compassion be ministered when such a clear word from God had been given?

The Law had spoken on this issue, although not exactly as they had said. "And the man that commits adultery with another man's wife . . . the adulterer and the adulteress shall surely be put to death" (Lev. 20:10). Again, "If a man be found lying with a woman married to an husband, then they shall both of them die, both the man that lay with the woman, and the woman . . ." (Deut. 22:22). It is of more than passing interest that only the woman was brought to Jesus!

Jesus ignored the question of these hypocrites. He "stooped down, and with His finger wrote on the ground, as though He heard them not." But these men were not willing to let the matter go. Supposing that they had found a flaw in Him, they "continued asking Him" until "He lifted up Himself." With Divine pungency He said to them, "He that is without sin among you, let him first cast a stone at her!" His words pierced their hearts, "their own conscience" convicting them as they "went out one by one."

Turning to the woman, Jesus asked, "Woman, where are those thine accusers? Hath no man condemned thee?" When she replied, "No man, Lord," He exposed her to the God of heaven. "Neither do I condemn thee: go and sin no more" (John 8:3-11). Mercy and peace met together! Righteousness and peace kissed each other! All of the Divine attributes remained intact!

Christ had not only come to "magnify the Law and make it honorable" (Isa. 42:21), but also to "seek and save that which was lost" (Luke 19:10). "This is a faithful saying, and worthy of all acceptation, that Christ Jesus came into the world to save sinners . . ." (I Tim. 1:15). He had not come to call the righteous, but sinners to repentance (Matt. 9:13). Here, then, was a demonstration of His mission — perfectly consistent with Divine purpose!

Oneness with the Father

"I know Him: for I am from Him, and He hath sent me," proclaimed Jesus (John 7:29). This is something of what He meant when He said, "I and my Father are one" (John 10:30). At no point did Jesus contradict God — His nature or His purpose. His compassion on the multitudes (Matt. 9:36), and indignation with the abuse of the house of God (Mark 11:17) were perfect reflections of God's nature. The entire thrust of

209

Christ's ministry, as well as that of His voluntary death, was in strict keeping with the purpose of God! His oneness with the Father was a oneness of purpose.

Divine Purpose, the Reason for Revelation

The objective of Divine testimony is never novelty. God does not speak with a reason. He is not seeking a casual relationship with man where the act of communication is an end of itself. The point is what is communicated, together with the objective of that communication. God speaks to men through His Word because His purpose involves men. If there were no purpose for man, there would be no revelation to him!

This is confirmed by Paul's declaration of the utility of God's Word. "And now, brethren, I commend you to God and to the word of His grace, which is able to build you up, and to give you an inheritance among all them that are sanctified" (Acts. 20:28). Observe the association of God's word with God Himself, and His objective. God has determined that those that "are sanctified" will have an "inheritance." It is an "eternal inheritance" (Heb. 9:15), and is "reserved in heaven" (I Pet. 1:4). God's revelation — His Word — being consistent with His purpose, prepares men for that inheritance.

"For whatsoever things were written aforetime were written for our learning, that we through patience and comfort of the Scriptures might have hope" (Rom. 15:4). God's revealed word — and there is no other kind — is able to make men "wise unto salvation" (II Tim. 3:15). This result is accomplished by design. It is not simply a coincidence. The Lord has revealed His mind to men in order that they might know how to be saved — how to become involved in His eternal purpose. The Scriptures are not merely a moral code — although that is contained in them. They are a means by which God achieves the enterprise of redemption. That enterprise is the reason for the revelation, and thus the things revealed are consistent with it.

The Purpose Hidden Without Revelation

The purpose of God is of such lofty nature, that it cannot be known unless it is revealed. The Word of God refers to God's objective as "the wisdom of God" (I Cor. 2:7). "But we speak the wisdom of God in a mystery, even the hidden wisdom, which God ordained before the world unto our glory." The Apostle is not stating that he proclaimed something that could not be understood, but something that was not formerly understood. The ASV translates as follows: "But we impart a secret and hidden wisdom of God, which God decreed before the ages for our glorification." Thus the "wisdom of God in a mystery" and "the hidden wisdom of God" are perceived as two views of the same truth. The first phrase emphasizes the former obscurement of the plan. The latter one underscores the wisdom or ingenuity of what was hidden.

The objective of God was "hidden" in Himself! It was a part of His character or Person. Because God was unknown, His purpose was unknown. No amount of intellectual inquiry could discover it. Righteous men could not find it out! Wise angels could not decipher it! It dealt with a facet of God's nature that was hidden to all created intelligences! It involved benefits so transcendent that they could not be imagined, let alone understood. "But as it is written, Eye hath not seen, nor ear heard, neither have entered into the heart of man, the things that God hath prepared for them that love Him" (I Cor. 2:9).

God was not simply successful in hiding His plan from men. Its obscurement was effortless, so far as Deity was concerned. That plan was so high that it was simply beyond the reach of man's natural powers. "But God hath revealed them unto us by His Spirit . . ." (I Cor. 2:10). Well ought we to thank the Lord for that revelation! The centuries of time prior to the revelation of the Gospel demonstrated the inaccessibility of this Divine objective to unilluminated man.

The Hidden Purpose in Patriarchal and Mosaic Dispensations

God's Kingdom has been identified with the accomplishment of His beneficent design for man. This is being achieved in a moral arena that is characterized by thought and decision. In a moral environment, a hidden purpose is an unfulfilled purpose. This is demonstrated in God's dealings during the Patriarchal and Mosaical ages.

The Patriarchal age was the period from Adam to the giving of the Law. During that time, key individuals were predominant in God's dealing with men. They were, furthermore, few and far between (Enoch, Noah, etc.). The purpose of God was so vague during the period, that very limited involvement was realized. The intelligence associated with devotion to God was rudimentary in comparison to that demanded by the greater light of the Gospel.

This is graphically demonstrated in the conduct of Noah following the flood (Gen. 9:18-29). His drunkenness and nakedness was more owing to his ignorance of God's purpose than to moral weakness. The Divine accomplishments among the sons of men prior to the Law were far inferior to those achieved in this "day of salvation." This was not owing to Divine weakness, but to the lack of revelation in that age. Divine objectives that are being fulfilled in a moral environment require revelation.

The Mosaical age encompassed the time from the giving of the Law unto the coming of Christ. During that time, a nation was predominant, in distinction to key individuals. Increased revelation marked that age, and yet the revelation remained rudimentary. Men became more acquainted with themselves than with God in this age. Although He demonstrated His power in signs and wonders, as well as mighty deliverances and preservations, the key element during that time was the demonstration of the need of man!

The moral inferiority of that time was due to the obscurement of Divine purpose. The "carnal ordinances" involving "meats and drinks, and divers washings" (Heb. 9:10), being rudimentary, could not effect a moral change in men. The existence of manners unacceptable from the viewpoint of the New Covenant, was also the result of lesser revelation. Among these things were multiple wives (I Sam. 1:2; 5:13; I Kgs. 11:3), fierce bloodshed (Lev. 20:16; Num. 31:7-17; Josh. 20:6), and the involvement of great men in cursed and unacceptable idolatry (I Kgs. 11:4-10; 14:7-10).

The law was given "that every mouth might be stopped, and all the world become guilty before God" (Rom. 3:19). For this reason, God did not make known His "wisdom" during its administration. Thus did those ancients come short of the ultimate Divine objective. They "received not the promise: God having provided some better thing for us, that they without us should not be made perfect" (Heb. 11:19-40).

Notwithstanding this deficiency, God in His mercy provided a way for His offspring to be accepted — even during those ages of relative darkness. In His grace He gave them a covenant that was external in nature — one that matched their condition. The sign of their identification with that first covenant was in their flesh — circumcision (Gen. 17:4-27; Lev. 12:3). In addition, the promise of a Messiah was given them (Gen. 49:10; Isa. 9:6-7; 11:1-10; 53:1-23; Hag. 2:7; Zech. 3:8;

Mal. 4:2). Faith in that coming Deliverer assured them of participation in His salvation. His death, we are told, effectually dealt with the "transgressions that were under the first testament" (Heb. 9:15). How gracious is God, to make provision for the involvement of men in His ultimate objective, even though they were not advantaged by its knowledge upon the earth!

Permit me to underscore the point here. A hidden purpose cannot be implemented in a moral arena! God's eternal purpose involves the conscious renewal of men (II Cor. 5:17), and their participation in Divine rule (Dan. 7:18,22,27). The fullness of that undertaking was "hidden" until the coming of Christ. It was for this reason that it could not be implemented in earlier ages.

Perceived in the Desire of the Prophets

Divine revelation is consistent with Divine purpose, never contradictory to it! Limited revelation, therefore, is necessarily accompanied by a limitation of the understanding of heavenly objective. This is demonstrated in the holy prophets. "The word of the Lord" came unto these men (Hosea 1:1), as the Lord revealed "His secret unto His servants the prophets" (Amos 3:7).

The revelation received by prophets during those earlier ages, however, was partial — thus they were unable to comprehend the real nature of salvation. This is the intent of the words of Jesus, "For verily I say unto you, That many prophets and righteous men have desired to see those things which ye see, and have not seen them; and to hear those things which ye hear, and have not heard them" (Matt. 13:17; Luke 10:24). Even though the "Gospel of God" was "promised afore by His prophets in the Holy Scriptures" (Rom. 1:2), it was not attended by satisfactory understanding in them that heard it. With keen insight, Peter wrote,

Of which salvation the prophets have inquired and searched diligently, who prophesied of the grace that should come unto you: searching what, or what manner of time the Spirit of Christ, which was in them did signify, when it testified beforehand the sufferings of Christ, and the glory that should follow. Unto whom it was revealed, that not unto themselves, but unto us they did minister the things, which are now reported unto you by them that have preached the Gospel . . . (I Pet. 1:10-12).

The failure of the prophets to discern the manner and time of the promised blessing, was not owing to an arbitrary blinding by God. It was the limitation of the revelation that obscured its fullness. Because the role of the prophets was that of introducing what was for a future generation, their own understanding was limited. The "Gospel" could not benefit them in its intended fullness because it was not yet accomplished in reality. The prophets were introduced to the coming blessing, but it had not yet occurred. Consequently, the revelation of it could only be from the standpoint of Divine intention. This type of revelation is necessarily attended by a lack of comprehension.

Witnessed in the Intrigue of Angels

The message of the Kingdom that is made known to men "by them that have preached the Gospel unto you with the Holy Ghost sent down from heaven" stirs the curiosity of angels. Angels, of themselves "greater in power and might" than man (II Pet. 2:11), "desire to look into" the benefits of redemption (I Pet. 1:12a). They long to comprehend something of its magnitude, but are unable to do so.

Their inability to discern redemption is owing to at least two things. First, the revealed purpose of God does not center in angels, but in man. Speaking of "the world to come," the theme of Apostolic presentation, the Scriptures declare: "For unto the angels hath He not put into subjection the world to come, whereof we speak" (Heb. 2:5). The incarnation also confirms that God's redemptive purpose did not center in angels (Heb. 2:16).

Secondly, the revelation has not been to angels, but to men. It was not the world of angels, but the world of men that God "loved" and "reconciled" (John 3:16-17; I John 4:14; II Cor. 5:18-20). That situation provides an environment of understanding for man, not for angels. In the Kingdom of God, involvement enables comprehension; a lack of involvement renders understanding impossible.

Thus the inability of angels to comprehend redemption. It is certainly not owing to the lack of capacity on the part of angels. They are, in fact, noted for their wisdom (II Sam. 14:17,20) — but not in matters of redemption! Their discernment is unproductive in that.

The Principle Introduced by the Prophets

The principle under consideration is that the consistency of Divine Revelation requires that it not contradict the purpose of God. This requirement is produced by the nature of God, in distinction from a mere moral code. The principle was introduced by the "holy prophets."

The things revealed to the prophets were harmonious with the purpose conceived by the Lord "before the world began." No revelation was independent of that purpose. The emphasis of the prophets' message was "the grace that should come" to those in Christ (I Pet. 1:10). In an introductory manner, they dealt with the "sufferings of Christ and the glory that should follow" (I Pet. 1:11).

God spoke in times past to "the fathers by the prophets," and "hath in these last days spoken unto us by His Son" (Heb. 1:1-2). There is absolute consistency in those messages. The prophets introduced what God was going to accomplish in Christ, and Jesus proclaimed the fulfillment of the central message of the prophets (Luke 4:18).

The prophets did proclaim messages that appeared independent from the goal of man's reconciliation. Among them were the rebuilding of Jericho (I Kgs. 16:34), a drought foretold by Elijah (I Kgs. 17:14), the fall of Ninevah (Nahum), and the judgment of Moab (Jer. 48). These prophecies emphasized the rejection of the Gentile world for the implementation of man's restoration to God. Israel was the nation chosen by the Lord to accomplish His redemptive purpose. Prophecies against the Gentile nations, the nation of Israel itself, or disobedient rulers among the chosen nation were uttered in view of the "eternal purpose," not in ignorement of it.

Expounded by the Apostles

The "Apostles' doctrine" (Acts 2:42) is the most advanced revelation ever provided to man. It interprets all previous revelation and occurrences, as well as the events constituting the Gospel. This is given within the framework of the Divine objective, concerning which the Apostles had fuller illumination. "In other ages" that objective "was not made known unto the sons of men, as it is now revealed unto His holy apostles and prophets by the Spirit" (Eph. 3:5).

The revelation did not consist in a rehearsal of the facts of the Gospel alone, but also in an exposition of the facts' significance. That is, after all, what constitutes a revelation.

The Apostles took the death, burial, and resurrection of Christ, and related those occurrences with the removal of sin, the abolition of the law as a means to righteousness, and the administration of the New Covenant (Heb. 1:3; Col. 2:14; Rom. 10:4; Titus 2:14; Heb. 8:10-13). Jesus Christ was identified with the purpose of God. He was "the Lamb of God" (John 1:29), "the Chosen of God" (Luke 23:35), "His Christ" (Acts 4:26; Rev. 11:15), and the "gift of God" (John 4:10). All of these terms derive their significance from the objective of God, and it alone!

In confirmation of this truth, the Scriptures view Christ's entrance into the world as a means to the accomplishment of the will of God. "Lo, I come to do Thy will, O God" (Heb. 10:7-10). The "will of God" was His "eternal purpose" as revealed by the New Covenant. Jesus came to provide a basis for the implementation of that covenant, promised of old time through Jeremiah (Jer. 31:31-34).

The Apostles took Christ's appearance in this world, His ministry among men, His death and resurrection, and His exaltation to God's right hand, and showed how these events relate to the reconciliation of man. Any inconsistency in their message — any lack of harmony — would have tended to obscure God's design. Such a result would have rendered His aim incapable of discernment, thus frustrating His undertaking.

Consistency Required for Revelation to Be Comprehended

A message that lacks harmony cannot be comprehended — its harmony is what makes it comprehensible. Further, without the possibility of comprehension, there has been no beneficial revelation. Revelation is consistently addressed to the understanding (Luke 24:45; Eph. 1:18; I John 5:20).

The Apostles revealed the consistency of truth in order to make it understandable. The interrelationships of the truth is what makes it discernible. Christ's death, for instance, is of no force without His resurrection. "If Christ be not raised, your faith is vain; ye are yet in your sins" (I Cor. 15:17). Also, if He is not interceding for men, neither His death or resurrection will accomplish the determined result. "Wherefore He is able to save to the uttermost them that come unto God by Him, seeing He ever lives to make intercession for them" (Heb. 7:25). Further, if

216

His life had not been "without sin," His sacrifice would have been unacceptable to God (Heb. 7:26; I Pet. 1:19). It is the understanding of these relationships that makes the belief of the Gospel both possible and effective.

Moral Purity and Consistent Truth

It is God's will that every man "abstain from fornication," and that he "know how to possess his vessel in sanctification and honor" (I Thess. 4:3-4). Admittedly, the sons of men were not too successful in this area prior to "the day of salvation." But following the more complete revelation of God's purpose, the absolute fulfillment of this became possible, and mandatory.

It is the understanding of the situation that makes this requirement achievable. The Apostles reasoned on this wise: "Know ye not that your bodies are the members of Christ? Shall I then take the members of Christ, and make them the members of an harlot? God forbid!" In view of this revelation — that our bodies are the "members of Christ" — involvement in fornication is unreasonable!

The Apostle elaborates further. "Every sin that a man does is without the body; but he that commits fornication sins against his own body." Here man's frame is perceived as a stewardship which is not to be abused. Were there no Divine purpose, sinning against the body would not be possible!

Personal purity is also reasonable in view of the presence of the Holy Spirit. "What? Know ye not that your body is the temple of the Holy Ghost, which is in you, which ye have of God, and ye are not your own?" In the light of this situation, involvement in fornication is to be shunned!

One further aspect of truth makes this form of fleshly indulgence completely unacceptable. "For ye are bought with a price: therefore glorify God in your body, and in your spirit, which are God's" (I Cor. 6:15-20).

When the harmony of the truth is perceived, a moral power is imparted that will result in purity. Without that perception, there is only law — Divine legislation. As was demonstrated during the rule of the first covenant, this did not provide an acceptable incentive. How different it is now — in the time of the revelation of God's purpose!

The Harmony of the Dispensations of Law and Grace

The dispensations of Law and Grace are the subject of Apostolic instruction. The first testament was a "ministration of condemnation" (II Cor. 3:9), resulting in the universal conviction of man (Rom. 3:19). By way of contrast, the new testament is the "ministration of righteousness" (II Cor. 3:9b), accomplishing what a mere moral code was impotent to do. The first covenant was linked to "the giving of the Law" (Rom. 9:4), which contained "the words of the covenant" (Deut. 29:1), written on tablets of stone called "the tables of the covenant" (Deut. 9:11). This covenant was made with Israel at Sinai (Heb. 8:7-9), and it was made "old" by the introduction of the "new covenant" (Heb. 8:13).

It would appear that two covenants so different could not be harmonious. The first covenant produced bondage, the second brought liberty (Gal. 4:22-26). Whereas the new covenant brought righteousness, the first wrought condemnation. The first was written on tables of stone, the second is written on the malleable heart — or inner man — of the regenerate.

While there is an obvious dissimilarity in the covenants, there is, however, a harmony in them. That harmony is found in their association with God's will to reconcile man unto Himself.

Introduction and Acquaintance

The Law introduced us to the purpose of God, the Gospel acquaints us with it. Intrinsic in the Law was an appeal for man to acquaint himself with his Maker. The desire of God for man's fellowship was evident during that earlier dispensation.

"If my people, which are called by my name, shall humble themselves, and pray, and seek my face, and turn from their wicked ways; then will I hear from heaven, and will forgive their sin, and will heal their land" (II Chron. 7:14). "Ho, every one that thirsteth, come ye to the waters, and he that hath no money; come ye, buy, and eat; yea, come, buy wine and milk without money and without price" (Isa. 55:13). Such appeals have the stamp of the Divine nature upon them! God longed for man, fervently desiring his reconciliation.

The dispensation of Law introduced man to God's desire for him, as well as the separating power of sin. "Your iniquities have separated between you and your God," declared the Lord (Isa. 59:2). As men gave heed to these words, they were introduced to the purpose that was then hidden, yet which existed in the mind of God from the beginning of time. There were a few individuals that saw those implications and, as a result "looked for redemption in Jerusalem" (Luke 2:36).

The Gospel acquainted men more fully with that purpose. "God was in Christ, reconciling the world unto Himself" (II Cor. 5:19), was the proclamation of Divine accomplishment. Christ "put away sin by the sacrifice of Himself" (Heb. 9:26), and destroyed "him that had the power of death, that is, the Devil" (Heb. 2:14).

Rather than merely knowing something of what God planned, the new testament brought the knowledge of God Himself. No longer would every man say to his brother, "Know the Lord: for all shall know me, from the least to the greatest" (Heb. 8:11). There is the achievement of Divine acquaintance!

Preparation and Involvement

The Law prepared men for the coming of Christ. It was, in fact, a "schoolmaster to bring us unto Christ, that we might be justified by faith" (Gal. 3:24). This was accomplished by convincing men of sin, for "by the law is the knowledge of sin" (Rom. 3:20). The longing of the heart of man for his Creator was marred by a defiled conscience! Man could not draw near to God because of its contamination. Thus was the coming of a Redeemer made known — One that could deal with this dilemma.

The Gospel enables the achievement of man's involvement, for which the law prepared him. The defiled conscience which prohibited man from drawing nigh to God is now dealt with effectually. "How much more shall the blood of Christ, who through the eternal Spirit offered Himself without spot to God, purge your conscience from dead works to serve the living God?" (Heb. 9:14). There is the involvement which the Law could not accomplish! It was, however, the Law that prepared us for this glorious benefit!

Demonstration and Assertion

During the age of Law, God demonstrated His desire for man. This was seen in the parting of the Red Sea (Exod. 13-15), the overthrow of Jericho (Josh. 6), and the overcoming of mighty armies (II Kgs. 18). After looking at God's dealing with Israel, no one could conclude that man could not be loved by God, or that God was incapable of loving Him. But it was consistently an overt demonstration.

The Gospel introduced a different kind of assertion. Unlike Israel, the church is told, "But ye are washed, but ye are sanctified, but ye are justified in the name of the Lord Jesus, and by the Spirit of our God" (I Cor. 6:11). It is now proclaimed that "he that is joined unto the Lord is one spirit" (I Cor. 6:17), and that even our bodies are "members of Christ" (I Cor. 6:15).

These assertions are addressed to faith, not to sight. While it was obvious that Israel was favored by the Lord, it is not so with the church! God's favor toward Israel was visible in the consistent subduing of her enemies. In Christ, however, the open demonstration does not exist. While there are occasional deliverances and outward confirmations of acceptance, this is the exception, not the rule. Persecution and blood baths have followed the church wherever it has taken its stand for the truth. It started shortly after the day of Pentecost (Acts 8:1-4), and it has not ceased to this day!

The reason for this situation is that our inheritance is not here, but is reserved in heaven for us (I Pet. 1:4). Notwithstanding the present separation of the inheritance from us, we have been joined to the Lord, and are "members of His body, of His flesh, and of His bones" (Eph. 5:30). That language denotes a position of favor and fellowship! It proclaims that man, in Christ, is in the center of Divine purpose. For such, the future is bright! Until the new heavens and the new earth, for which we look, appear, we have the Gospel assertion — far better than mere external demonstration under a regime of Law!

Types and Shadows

The consistency of the Law with the purpose of God is perceived in its types and shadows. Types and shadows refer to likeness of ultimate Divine objectives projected upon the canvas of an external covenant. The scriptural term for this parallel is "shadow." Examples of its usage are, "shadow of heavenly things" (Heb. 8:5), and "a shadow of good things to come" (Heb. 10:1).

These "shadows" were deliberately given by God to represent the realities of salvation. They were an appeal to the heart, not the eye. The elaborate tabernacle worship, for instance, was not intended to merely impress men with pomp and splendor. It contained prefigurements of

220

what was to be accomplished in Christ Jesus.

The tabernacle was a portable tent employed by Israel, in the wilderness, for the service of God. The blueprint for this structure was given by God to Moses in meticulous detail. We are told that "Moses was admonished of God, when he was about to make the tabernacle: for See, saith He, that thou make all things according to the pattern showed thee in the mount." This was required because the tabernacle was to "serve unto the example and pattern of heavenly things" (Heb. 8:5). We have in it a mirror of higher realities and relationships.

The tabernacle was divided into two sections, called by the Apostle, the "first" and the "second," which were separated by a veil (Heb. 10:2-3; Exod. 26). The sections themselves, together with the furniture within them, typified heavenly relationships.

> For there was a tabernacle made; the first, wherein was the candlestick, and the table, and the showbread; which is called the sanctuary. And after the second veil, the tabernacle which is called the Holiest of all; which had the golden censer, and the ark of the covenant overlaid round about with gold, wherein was the golden pot that had manna, and Aaron's rod that budded, and the tables of the covenant; and over it the cherubims of glory shadowing the mercy seat . . . (Heb. 9:1-5).

We have introduced here the concepts of serving God (the sanctuary — Heb. 12:28), and Divine contact (The Holiest — Heb. 10:19-22). We are also introduced to the ideas of illumination (the candlestick — I John 1:7; Eph. 5:8), participation (the table — I Cor. 10:21), and nourishment (the showbread — John 6:35,48). Think of the introduction of a separation that is not total, yet is a regular hindrance (the veil — Heb. 10:20).

In the tabernacle we also confront the thought of pleasing God (the censer — Col. 3:20; Heb. 13:21), Divine provision (the manna — Matt. 4:4), Divine guidance (Aaron's rod that budded — Rom. 8:14), and a written law (the tables of the covenant — II Cor. 3:3; Heb. 10:16). God's mercy, which is over all of His works, was also depicted in the tabernacle (the mercy seat — Heb. 4:16; Jude 21).

All of these concepts owe their origin to God's "eternal purpose." They were not developed under the Law, and then utilized in the New

221

Covenant, but rather were originated in God's purpose, and mirrored in the Law. There is a consistency in revelation!

The Sacrifices

Under the Law, the concept of sacrifice was introduced. The tabernacle, "which was a figure for the time then present," was one "in which were offered both gifts and sacrifices." These offerings were not an end of themselves. They prefigured a "better sacrifice" (Heb. 9:23), and thus were ineffectual to accomplish the remission of sins. "For it is not possible that the blood of bulls and of goats should take away sins" (Heb. 10:4).

They were an introduction to inner cleansing, but by no means accomplished it. Even though the sacrifice of beasts occurred repeatedly, only a "remembrance" of sins resulted (Heb. 10:3). The worshippers, even in a fresh realization of those bloody sacrifices, maintained defiled consciences. Their sense of guilt forbade them to approach a holy God. This is the meaning of the text, "For the law having a shadow of good things to come, and not the very image of the things, can never with those sacrifices which they offered year by year continually make the comers thereunto perfect" (Heb. 10:1).

The "comers" were those attempting to approach God. The perfection which was not achieved was the cleansing of the conscience; the removal of the defilement of guilt. The rivers of blood that were offered on those Jewish altars never placated a single mortal conscience!

Actually, God never was satisfied with those sacrifices. They were only intended to be temporal in their significance. Thus did the man of God proclaim, "Sacrifice and offering and burnt offerings and offering for sin Thou wouldst not, neither hadst pleasure therein; which are offered by the law" (Heb. 10:9; Psa. 40:6). Their worth was in their prefigurement of the sacrifice to come (Heb. 9:26; I Cor. 5:7). Although obedience required their presentation, they had no salvational efficacy. It was the anticipation of Christ's effectual sacrifice that gave meaning to those under law. Without the reality, the shadow would have served no real purpose.

The Priesthood

The first covenant developed the concept of a priesthood — an appointed representative that assured the acceptance of the people. It was the "priests" that "went always into the first tabernacle, accomplishing the service of God. but into the second went the high preist alone once every year, not without blood, which he offered for himself, and for the errors of the people" (Heb. 9:6-7). It is particuarly the "high priest" that is our point here (Exod. 28-30; 35; 40).

Christ is declared to be "a faithful High Priest in things pertaining to God, to make reconciliation for the sins of the people" (Heb. 2:17). He was the Divinely-appointed representative for fallen man. He did not take this honor upon Himself, but was placed in that necessary position by His Father (Heb. 5:8). It is in the role of High Priest that He is to be considered and contemplated by believers (Heb. 3:1). That consideration is to include His representation of the redeemed in the presence of God — now (Heb. 4:14-15).

It will not serve our purpose to elaborate at length upon the magnificent high priesthood of Christ. Suffice it to say that it is the reason why such a priesthood was instituted under the Law. The purpose of God included the Divine representation of fallen man. It is that purpose that was reflected in the Aaronic priesthood. Further, without that reflection, we could not have comprehended the significance of Christ's current ministry in the capacity of our High Priest.

Conclusion

From Genesis through Revelation, God's word is consistent. The purpose of God is not only perceptible throughout the Scriptures; it is the reason for the Word. God's objective has saturated every aspect of His dealing with man. Every word and work of God is an expression of His Person, and consequently, is harmonious within itself.

No single word of God will stand by itself — it must be perceived as an expression of God's "eternal purpose." This is the reason for the affirmation, "All scripture is given by inspiration of God, and is profitable for doctrine, for reproof, for correction, for instruction in righteousness: that the man of God may be perfect, throughly furnished unto every good work" (II Tim. 3:16-17).

The satisfaction of man's curiosity and the establishment of a fruitful society upon earth is not the objective of the Scriptures. The doctrine, reproof, correction, and instruction have to do with the reconciliation of man to God.

The revelation of God consists of Christ's Person, and the Scriptures, or inspired writing. Both are a precise expression of God's purpose, and have derived their origin from that purpose. Christ's Person provides us a demonstration of God in the concrete, so to speak. The Word is a Divine articulation of His objective for man, and of the means whereby man may enjoy participation in it.

There is no self-contradiction in God, Christ, or the Word. No single attribute of God is set against another of His traits. No word or work of Christ contradicts another of His expressions, or any aspect of God's nature. No word of Scripture is in variance with another word, or with the God that gave it. Revelation — all revelation — is absolutely consistent! It is to God's glory and man's advantage that this is the case!

15

THE CONSISTENCY OF GOD'S SALVATION

So far as man is concerned, the preeminent manifestation of God's Kingdom is the reconciliation of man unto Himself. In this great enterprise God involved Himself, His Son, His Spirit, and the angelic hosts. His mercy, righteousness, and wisdom joined together to accomplish a work so transcendent that it will be the cause of praise, "world without end" (Eph. 3:21).

One View — A Completed Work

Man's restoration to God is frequently mentioned as something that has already taken place. "And all things are of God, who hath reconciled us unto Himself by Jesus Christ . . ." (II Cor. 5:18-20); "Even when we were dead in sins, hath quickened us together with Christ . . ." (Eph. 2:1-5); "And having made peace through the blood of His cross . . . And you, that were once alienated and enemies in your mind by wicked works, yet now hath He reconciled . . ." (Col. 1:20-22); "Who hath saved us . . ." (II Tim. 1:9).

The salvation of God is so thorough, so complete, that a valid

225

reason cannot be put forward for not being a part of it. Those who do not embrace it will be summarily condemned — not because it did not adequately meet their need, or that it was not applicable to them, but because they, of their own will, did not accept it! God will do nothing more to effect salvation than He has already done. It is the acceptance of His provision that is now the issue!

Definition of Salvation

"Deliverance" and "preservation" are synonyms for salvation emphasizing what we are delivered from and preserved for.

There are both physical and spiritual deliverances. Perhaps the most visible deliverance was Israel's rescue from the hand of Pharaoh and his armies. That memorable experience, when the Red Sea parted for the Israelites, and closed upon the Egyptians, was called "the salvation of the Lord" (Exod. 14:13). Upon the completion of that mighty rescue, the people of God sang, "The Lord is my strength and my song, and He is become my salvation . . ." (Exod. 15:2). That occasion serves to demonstrate the nature of salvation. The enemy is subdued and God's people are rescued from danger.

In Christ, salvation extends beyond the seen. "The salvation of our God" (Psa. 52:10) now deals with eternal issues, not temporal ones! The term is used no less than 43 times following Christ's exaltation. A careful examination of the texts will reveal that every single one of them refers to a spiritual salvation (Luke 1:69,77; 2:30; 3:6; 19:9; John 4:22; Acts 4:12; 13:26,47; 16:17; 28:28; Rom. 1:16; 10:10; 11:11; 13:11; II Cor. 1:6; 7:10; Eph. 1:3; 6:17; Phil. 1:19,28; 2:12; I Thess. 5:8-9; II Thess. 2:13; II Tim. 2:10; 3:15; Titus 2:11; Heb. 1:4; 2:3,10; 5:9; 6:9; 9:28; I Pet. 1:5,9,10; II Pet. 3:15; Jude 3; Rev. 7:10; 19:1; 12:10).

This "eternal salvation" (Heb. 5:9) proclaims the overthrow of Satan, and the preservation of man. Once this salvation is embraced, Satan is powerless to dominate man, and man is able to enter into personal relation with God.

Salvation also involves spiritual nourishment. "In the day of salvation have I succoured thee," proclaims the Lord (II Cor. 6:2). That is, Satan's subduement and man's liberty not only consist of an initial deliverance, but of continued safety.

In addition, this wonderful word encompasses man's final

226

THE CONSISTENCY OF THE SALVATION
THAT IS IN CHRIST JESUS

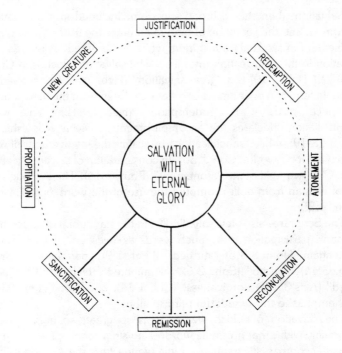

ACCOMPLISHMENT AND UNDERSTANDING

THOROUGH WORK	MAN COMPREHENDED
ACCEPTED RESULTS	REDEMPTION APPREHENDED
DISPLAY OF WISDOM	GOD KNOWN AND UNDERSTOOD

227

deliverance from the temporal order, when the faithful shall be raised from the dead and joyfully inducted into the very presence of the Almighty. It is in this sense that the word is used in Romans 13:11. "Now is our salvation nearer than when we believed."

A Broad Spectrum

Salvation, then, has a broad spectrum. Included in it are Satan's overthrow, and the liberation of man to embrace the truth. There is also the element of spiritual nourishment while in this world, as well as participation in the resurrection unto life. "The salvation which is in Christ Jesus" (II Tim. 2:10) is a "great salvation" (Heb. 2:3). Consequently, no single term can encompass its greatness. Seen from the viewpoint of the price paid, it is "redemption" (Heb. 9:12). The word "reconciliation" declares the accomplishment of Divine fellowship (II Cor. 5:18-19), while "sanctification" proclaims the involvement of man himself in God's work (I Cor. 1:30). In consideration of salvation's effect upon God, we read of the "atonement" (Rom. 5:11). The thorough acquittal of man from guilt prompted the use of the word "justification" (Rom. 4:25).

The Scriptures also view salvation from the standpoint of experience — man's participation in it. Such words as "washed" (I Cor. 6:11), "born again" (John 3:3,5), "purged" (II Pet. 1:9), "partakers of Christ" (Heb. 3:14), "raised" (Eph. 2:6), "illuminated" (Heb. 10:32), "converted" (Acts 3:19), "forgiveness" (Col. 1:14), and "obey Him" (Heb. 5:9), emphasize this wonderful participation.

The salvation of which we speak is so great, so high, so unfathomably wide, that no single word — no single concept — can adequately encompass its greatness. Little wonder that the Apostle said of it, "I . . . cease not to give thanks for you, making mention of you in my prayers, that . . . the eyes of your understanding being enlightened; that ye may know what is the hope of His calling, and what [is] the riches of the glory of His inheritance in the saints, and what is the exceeding greatness of His power to usward who believe . . ." (Eph. 1:16-19). Again, it is written; "That He would grant you, according to the riches of His glory, to be strengthened with might by His Spirit in the inner man; that Christ may dwell in your hearts by faith; that ye, being rooted and grounded in [His] love, may be able to comprehend with all saints what is the breadth, and length, and depth, and height; and to know the love of Christ, which passes knowledge" (Eph. 3:16-21). That is the "great salvation" of which we speak!

Its Centrality in Scripture

The subject of the prophetic messages of old was the "salvation" which is now proclaimed through the Gospel (I Pet. 1:9). The thrust of the Apostolic message also concerned this theme. "Neither is their salvation in any other: for there is none other name under heaven given among men, whereby we must be saved" (Acts 4:12). They proclaimed Jesus as the "Captain of our salvation" (Heb. 2:10), and "the Author of eternal salvation" (Heb. 5:9). The hope which sustains the soul and protects the mind is called "the hope of salvation" (Eph. 6:17; I Thess. 5:8).

"The Gospel of Christ" is God's power "unto salvaton" (Rom. 1:16), and "with the mouth confession is made unto salvation" (Rom. 10:10). The "end," or objective, of our faith, is "salvation" (I Pet. 1:9), and we are admonished to "work out your own salvation with fear and trembling" (Phil. 2:12).

Salvation is nowhere mentioned incidentally by the Apostles! No inspired man ever approached it with indifference or disinterest. It is always primary, central, and critical. This is the theme of the Apostles' doctrine! They were not social reformers, domestic problem solvers, or political revolutionists. They were appointed to proclaim "the way of salvation" (Acts 16:17) — to announce the destruction of Satan (Heb. 2:14), the spoiling of Satanic powers (Col. 2:14), and the remission of sins (Luke 24:47). Everything they had to say related to that theme — nothing was divorced from it!

Incidentally, with unwavering consistency, when the Apostles left the exposition of salvation to deal with other matters, it was due to the carnality of the church (Jude 3-25; II Pet. 2-3). Even in these instances, however, the Apostolic objective was to get the people back to a proper view of, and participation in, salvation — the proper emphasis!

The Heart of All Scripture

The salvation of man is the heartbeat of prophecy, the objective for which the Law made preparation, and the quest of all truly informed individuals. The book of Genesis is no more potent than when the coming "Seed" is foretold (Gen. 3:15), the blessing of "all families of the earth"

229

(Gen. 12:1), and the "gathering of the people" unto the coming Shiloh (Gen. 49:10). The eye of faith perceived the coming Lamb of God in the paschal lambs slain the night Israel spoiled Egypt, and was brought out with a strong arm (Exod. 12). The priesthood of Leviticus shouted to man of the coming High Priest, Christ Jesus (Lev. 21:10). The promise in the book of Numbers of entrance into a promised land foreshadowed a "better land" pledged in Christ (Num. 13). The emphasis upon the written Law in Deuteronomy prepared men for the writing of God's law upon the heart (Deut. 5).

The anticipation of the coming salvation erupted in Job's longing for a "Daysman" (Job 9:33), the "Covert" of Isaiah (Isa. 32:2), and the "Sun of righteousness" of Malachi (Mal. 4:2). Zechariah wrote of the "Branch" of righteousness (Zech. 3:8), Haggai proclaimed the "Desire of all nations" (Hag. 2:7), and Daniel declared a coming "Messiah" (Dan. 9:25). THE SALVATION OF MAN! The Word of God is nothing without that theme!

The Apostles took up the refrain in the light of the fullest revelation ever given to man. Their fundamental theme was the salvation of man! Personal deficiencies were a lament in view of this great salvation (Rom. 7). Immorality was firmly denounced as antithetical to the salvation of Christ (I Cor. 6:9-11). The world was pronounced "evil" in view of redemption (Gal. 1:4). The zealous and personal activity of men for God was identified with working out one's own "salvation with fear and trembling" (Phil. 2:12).

Were it possible to remove the theme of salvation, the prophets and the Apostles would have nothing to say, no counsel to give, no hope to offer! There would be no need for Christ, the church, or religious enterprises of any sort! It is never viewed as secondary, optional, or of no consequence. Salvation is central in the Scriptures.

Its Harmony with God's Character

God's Kingdom is a perfect expression of His nature and demonstration of His character. More of God and His rule is comprehended in the saving of man than in any previously-known Divine activity. The reconciliation of man through Jesus is not a mere accommodation to the need of man; it is an expression of the Person of God. He is what He represents Himself to be in the Gospel. It is not the language of hyperbole — no exaggeration — that we have in the good news of a "ransom for all" (I Tim. 2:6). Think of the terms associated with salvation. "The grace of God" (I Pet. 5:12), the "love of God" (Rom. 3:21). How the mind is stirred by the contemplation of the "longsuffering of God" (I Pet. 3:20; II Pet. 3:15), and the "will of God" (Col. 4:12)! It is God Himself that is reaching out for man in Christ Jesus. He does love man! His grace and favor are toward man!

He has maintained His integrity and righteousness in providing a ransom for His offspring! His longsuffering toward men is not merely a tolerant attitude — it is a revelation of His Person! The "abundant mercy" that is offered those that have "sinned and come short of the glory of God" is an expression of God's heart! It is true — He is "not willing that any should perish, but that all should come to repentance" (II Pet. 3:9).

In redemption we have a perfect expression of God's nature. That is the reason for its absolute consistency. For it to be otherwise would require inconsistency in the Lord Himself.

There are several conclusions that are dictated by these observations. 1. No man can question the applicability of the Gospel to himself without questioning the integrity of God. 2. God does not have to be begged in order for salvation to be appropriated. Faith and obedience consistently obtain the promised benefit. 3. God is no more pleased than when His redemptive provision is received by faith. 4. God is not more displeased than when His provision of eternal life is rejected.

Meeting Divine Demands

The perfect harmony of salvation with God's Person is seen in the way it exactly meets Divine demands. Nothing that is necessary has been omitted. God has been completely "satisfied" with the price, and is joyful over the results of its acceptance. A salvation that did not address every facet of the Divine nature could not be consistent with it! So far as the basis for man's acceptance by God is concerned, nothing remains to be done! Here the genius of the Kingdom is perceived.

He Will Not Acquit the Guilty

God has revealed an aspect of His nature that is not to be ignored. At Sinai, when "the Lord descended in the cloud, and stood" with Moses, He "proclaimed the name of the Lord." He unveiled His Person to Moses, opened up what He was like, and exposed that meek man to

231

the Divine nature. Incorporated in that revelation was this word, "and that will by no means clear the guilty" (Exod. 34:5-7). What a revelation is this! God cannot call guilt anything other than "guilt"! He cannot overlook it, ignore it, or treat it lightly. That is His nature! He cannot and will not simply forget involvement in sin.

Until the vicarious sacrifice of Christ, sin remained. Though the guilt was often unacknowledged by men, under the convicting hand of the Law, the whole world was "guilty before God" (Rom. 3:19). No one was cleared of guilt, no conscience purged, no reconciliation accomplished! God could by no means "clear the guilty"!

In Christ, however, this aspect of God's nature was satisfied. Perfect consistency! Man's guilt was laid upon Christ, in order that God's righteousness might be imputed to man. The guilt was not ignored, but dealt with in "wisdom and prudence" (Eph. 1:8). As it is written, "For He [God] hath made Him [Jesus] to be sin for us, Who knew no sin; that we might be made the righteousness of God in Him" (II Cor. 5:21). God did not "clear the guilty," but justified "the ungodly" (Rom. 4:5). Thus is salvation consistent with His Person!

He Will Have Mercy

God also revealed to Moses that He was "merciful and gracious . . . keeping mercy for thousands" (Exod. 34:6-7). In an even more exact statement of the case, the Lord said to Moses, "I will be gracious, and will show mercy on whom I will show mercy" (Exod. 33:19). The point here is not an arbitrary or discriminatory conferring of mercy upon selected individuals. Rather, we have here an assertion that God's desire always accompanies His mercy. It is never revealed as an expression of legality, but of Divine will. In other words, God's mercy is an expression of His desire, not of mere pity.

If salvation is to be consistent with God's Person, it must provide for the expression of mercy. In mercy the need of man and the desire of God meet together! Man's condition requires Divine tenderness and consideration, without which he will surely perish! On the other hand, God desires to show compassion and lovingkindness — that is His nature! "But God, Who is rich in mercy, for His great love wherewith He hath loved us, even when we were dead in sins, hath quickened us together with Christ, (by grace are ye saved)" — Eph. 2:4-5. This mercy has been bestowed upon man without any compromise of the Lord's character. He forfeited nothing in order to show mercy, but retained all of His essential attributes. Divine consistency!

The Lamb of God

That day when Abraham climbed mount Moriah with his only son, to offer him as a sacrifice unto God, his heart was heavy, but his faith was keen and perceptive. God had commanded him, "Take now thy son, thine only son, whom thou lovest, and . . . offer him . . . for a burnt offering" (Gen. 22:2). As they made their way up that mountain, Isaac asked a heart-rending question. "Behold the fire and the wood: but where is the lamb for a burnt offering?" In a grand assertion of faith, Abraham proclaimed the very nature of God. "My son, God will provide Himself a lamb for a burnt offering" (Gen. 22:7-8).

Abraham's confession embraced more than he perceived in that age of twilight revelation. It is as though God spoke through him, unable to conceal the intense Divine anticipation of a Savior for man! Indeed, in Christ Jesus God did "provide Himself a Lamb"! Jesus was "the Lamb of God that takes away the sin of the world" (John 1:29). God selected Him, offered Him, and bore the unfathomable grief of loss and separation.

In the book of Revelation there is an underlying emphasis on God's "Lamb" — His provision for Himself (Rev. 5:6,8,12,13; 6:1,16; 7:9,10,14,17; 12:11; 13:8; 14:1,4,10; 15:3; 17:14; 19:7,9; 21:9,14,22,23,27; 22:1,3). That "Lamb" so completely fulfilled the requirements of God, that those who embrace the Lamb, are given power to overcome the world! God provided Himself a Lamb in order that all of His attributes might remain intact. They now work together for the benefit of fallen man! Wonderful consistency!

The Blood of the Covenant

When man sinned, death enveloped him. As it is written, "Wherefore, as by one man sin entered into the world, and death by sin; and so death passed upon all men for that all have sinned" (Rom. 5:12). That death resulted in man being cut off from His God. Adam and Eve died the day they sinned, in that they were separated from the Living God. "Dead in trespasses and sins," is on the spiritual tombstone of humanity (Eph. 2:1,5; Col. 2:13).

At the very threshold of human history, God demonstrated that the taking of innocent life was required for the sustaining of the life of sinful man. Before driving Adam and Eve out of the Garden, God made "coats of skin, and clothed them" (Gen. 3:21-24). Everytime those "coats" were considered by the guilty pair, recollection was stirred of an innocent victim suffering for their transgression!

Later, the second son of the created couple, Abel, "brought of the firstlings of his flocks and of the fat thereof. And the Lord had respect unto Abel and to his offering" (Gen. 4:4). Once again, an innocent living victim was offered to God in behalf of an alienated soul!

Under the first covenant, God developed the significance of these innocent victims. It was the "blood" that was emphasized. "For the life of the flesh is in the blood: and I have given it to you upon the altar to make an atonement for your souls: for it is the blood that maketh an atonement for the soul" (Lev. 17:11). Man, who had died toward God, could now approach unto God by being identified with guiltless life!

The blood of those beasts was called "the blood of the covenant." Moses, it is written, "took the blood, and sprinkled it upon the people" (Exod. 24:8). The sprinkled blood symbolically conferred upon the people an acceptable relationship with God. Spiritual life was, so to speak, simulated in the old covenant. The slaying of an innocent victim, and the sprinkling of its blood typified the bestwoal of that victim's innocence upon the people. With Israel, it was but a shadow of reality. In Christ, we have the reality.

We are "made the righteousness of God in Him," proclaims the Apostle (II Cor. 5:21). That transaction is accomplished by the "blood of the everlasting covenant" (Heb. 13:20) being "sprinkled" upon us. This "sprinkling" is spiritual in nature, and results in an awareness or conviction of Christ's righteousness. Before Jesus returned to heaven, He told His disciples that He was going to send the Holy Spirit to carry on the heavenly ministry. The Spirit would, among other things, convince the world of righteousness, because Christ went to His Father (John 16:8-10). The persuasion of Christ's absolute sinlessness before God gives reality to the acceptance of His sacrifice by God.

Those possessed of this conviction "know that we were not redeemed with corruptible things, as silver and gold . . . but with the precious blood of Christ, as of a Lamb without blemish and without spot" (I Pet. 1:19). Our acceptance by God is based upon the merit of Another! That is the significance of the "blood of the covenant."

The evening of our Lord's betrayal, He instituted a memorial without parallel. It was designed to provide man's memory with the very truth of which we have been speaking — that God approves of us because of the sacrifice of His Son. As he took the cup that night, He said, "Drink ye all of it; for this is my blood of the New Testament, which is shed for many for the remission of sins" (Matt. 26:27-28). It was the voluntary forfeiture of His life on our behalf that made the covenant blessing possible.

The point to be seen here is that Divine demands were met by "the blood of the new testament." Guilt was addressed effectually, thus enabling God to bless man as He desired to do.

God Is Pleased

Integral to the will of God is His satisfaction, or good pleasure. He cannot confer a blessing against His will, or in a state of displeasure. The curse is consistently associated with the Lord's dissatisfaction. Onan, son of Judah through "a daughter of a certain Canaanite," was slain because he "displeased the Lord" (Gen. 38:10). The murmuring Isrealites so displeased God that he sent a fire "among them, and consumed them that were in the uttermost parts of the camp" (Num. 11:1). Other plagues and curses were said to have occurred because God was "displeased" (II Sam. 11:27; I Chron. 21:7; Zech. 1:2). Blessings cannot be conferred while God is not pleased!

Unwilling to let man go, God dealt with His own displeasure in the saving of man. He will not ignore the fact that man has sinned! He cannot simply clear him of guilt with an act of sovereign will. He cannot be pleased with man while man walks contrary to His law. Here, the wisdom of our God bursts forth! Because He loves the world, and desires to do good unto them, He sends His only begotten Son into the world. Jesus comes on a mission to provide a just basis for man's acceptance.

While in this world, Jesus was "despised and rejected of men; a man of sorrows, and acquainted with grief." As if that were not enough, "He was wounded for our transgressions, He was bruised for our iniquities: the chastisement of our peace was upon Him; and with His stripes we are healed" (Isa. 53:1-6). He assumes the responsibility for every vile thing ever committed by man! Every wicked thought, every act of rebellion, all disobedience — the responsibility for it all was laid

235

upon Him — "in His body on the tree" (I Pet. 2:24).

Never before had sin in any form touched His Person. He was in every sense "separate from sinners" (Heb. 7:26). He had never in any way transgressed or contradicted the Law of God. Yet in His death, God "laid on Him the iniquity of us all" (Isa. 53:6). As that iniquity touched His undefiled spirit, it constrained His Father to forsake Him (Matt. 27:46). The sufferings inflicted at the hands of men were nothing to compare with bearing our sins and being forsaken by God. He "made His soul an offering for sin" (Isa. 53:10).

It is, however, the reaction of God to this experience that will determine whether or not it is valid. It is written — and God be praised for it — "Yet it pleased the Lord to bruise Him; He hath put Him to grief . . . the pleasure of the Lord shall prosper in His hand" (Isa. 53:10).

Jesus was openly declared to be God's Son at the very beginning of His earthly ministry. "This is My Beloved Son, in Whom I am well pleased," confessed the Father at Jesus' baptism (Matt. 3:17). He was further "declared to be the Son of God with power by the resurrection of the dead" (Rom. 1:4). The resurrection confirmed Christ's Sonship, and proved the acceptance of His sacrifice. Jesus Himself experienced satisfaction in the fruit of His death (Isa. 53:11) — and so did His Father! An exalted Christ proves the acceptance of the atonement! His obedience "unto death" became the ground for God to highly exalt Him, and give Him "a name which is above every name" (Phil. 2:8-9).

This is the truth depicted by the Apostles' doctrine concerning Christ's entrance into heaven. "Neither by the blood of goats and calves, but by His own blood He entered in once into the holy place, having obtained eternal redemption for us" (Heb. 9:12). It was God that accepted the atonement! The redemption price was paid to God Himself — and it has been accepted! Thus God blesses man with salvation in perfect agreement with His nature. Blessedness comes from His good pleasure!

The Gospel of the Blessed God

Twice in Scripture, God is called "blessed" — both times following the entrance of "the Man Christ Jesus" into heaven (I Tim. 2:5). "According to the glorious gospel of the blessed God . . ." (I Tim. 1:11). ". . . Who is the blessed and only Potentate, the King of kings, and

236

Lord of lords . . ." (I Tim. 6:15).

The term "blessed," as used in these texts, denotes intelligent happiness or joy. It is the term used in the beatitudes — a word depicting a beneficial condition that is discerned and enjoyed. Such is the case with Jehovah as regards the death of Christ.

By Christ's death Satan has been cast down (Heb. 2:14), the Law that was contrary to us taken out of the way (Col. 2:14), sin put away and condemned in the flesh (Heb. 9:26; Rom. 8:3), and a mighty deliverance accomplished (Gal. 1:4). God is joyous over the achievement! The Divine mission has been fulfilled — and that without any Divine compromise whatsoever! Now God, Who "delighteth in mercy" (Micah 7:18) can show it justly, freely, and without reservation! While He did not delight in "burnt offering" (Psa. 51:16), He does delight in Christ's offering. It is written that "Christ also hath loved us, and hath give Himself for us an offering and a sacrifice to God for a sweetsmelling savour" (Eph. 5:2).

God is joyful about Jesus' accomplishment! Jesus Himself is pleased with it! It remains for man to be pleased with it — for him to receive the glorious Gospel of the "blessed God."

Its Perfect Adaptability to Man's Need

One of the major aspects of salvation's consistency is its perfect adaptability to man's need. To discern its value and lay hold of it, man must willingly confront his need. Man's true awareness of his "need" will accord with and reflect heaven's perception of that need.

The End of the Law

The Law not only brought "the knowledge of sin" (Rom. 3:20); it removed any ground for boasting and confidence, rendering "all the world . . . guilty before God" (Rom. 3:19). Its merciless finger pointed at man's transgression — willful transgression — and shouted "guilty" with an authority that could not be gainsayed!

The entire thrust of the Law was against man's unregenerate nature. It is called "the handwriting of ordinances that was against us" (Col. 2:14). It was delivered against the backdrop of man's alienation, and addressed man as distant from God. It did show man a way back to God — a valid way. Of the commandments it was said, "The man that does them shall live in them" (Gal. 3:12; Rom. 10:5; Lev. 18:5). While this was a legitimate offer — one which, if fulfilled, would have been honored by God — no man could perfectly fufill the Law. He was defiled within by an appetite for sin, and the law chaffed against his soul. The same words that pointed out what he should and should not do, also proclaimed that he had miserably failed on every count. Thus "the commandment which was ordained unto life" was "found to be unto death" (Rom. 3:10).

The Law made no provision for failure, offered no remedy for sin, and opened no door for hope. No mistakes were permitted, no failures, no forgetfulness! It was an exacting taskmaster, demanding perfection on all points, and permitting absolutely no deviation. It was this condition that James described when he wrote, "For whosoever shall keep the whole law, and yet offend on one point, he is guilty of all" (James 2:10). Oh, how man needed deliverance from the principle of justification by the works of the Law!

Salvation meets this need! Jesus took the handwriting of ordinances that was against us "out of the way, nailing it to His cross" (Col. 2:14). In a powerful proclamation of this aspect of Christ's death, Paul elsewhere wrote, "Having abolished in His flesh the enmity, even the law of commandments, contained in ordinances . . ." (Eph. 2:15). An undeniable emphasis is perceived in this language: "took it out of the way" — "nailing it to the cross" — "abolished."

This is by no means intended to teach that men are now without law or Divine restraint. Christ has brought an end to the Law as a means to righteousness. As it is written, "For Christ is the end of the law for righteousness to every one that believes" (Rom. 10:4). The righteousness that makes a man acceptable to God is no longer the result of personal achievement. Whereas the Law spoke of the righteousness of works, the Gospel of salvation speaks of the "righteousness of faith" (Rom. 4:11). It is also called "the righteousness which is of faith" (Rom. 9:30), and "the righteousness which is of God by faith" (Phil. 3:9). Faith, not works, is counted for righteousness (Rom. 4:5; Gal. 3:6), or "imputed" for righteousness (Rom. 4:22). This is the sense in which Christ "is the end of the Law for righteousness. . . ."

When Christ "Himself purged our sins" (Heb. 1:3), He ended "the ministration of condemnation" (II Cor. 3:9) for everyone that would receive that atonement. With sin removed, the Law had no more that it

238

could do! Righteousness, as God counts it, is now a matter of receiving and acting upon the Gospel. Merit is, in a manner of speaking, attached to faith in Christ. "Whosoever believes in Him shall receive remission of sins," proclaimed Peter (Acts 10:43). Where there is remission of sins, righteousness has been realized.

"The Law is not made for a righteous man, but for the lawless and disobedient, for the ungodly and sinners, for unholy and profane . . ." (I Tim. 1:9). Those in Christ have been removed from this category of men, and thus the Law is no longer "for them" — i.e., its condemning role is no longer applicable to them. In this sense also, Christ has made an "end of the Law" — ending its resounding condemnation of all men.

The Purging of the Conscience

Man, being made in the image of God, cannot escape the effect of his sin upon his own person. One of his chief resources — his mind — is defiled by his involvement in transgression. This defilement results in a fear that forbids him to voluntarily confront the Living God. This effect was seen in the sin of our parents, Adam and Eve. When they deliberately violated the Divine prohibition, they "hid themselves from the presence of the Lord God amongst the trees of the garden" (Gen. 3:8). They could not bear to face Him. By their own confession they were "afraid" (Gen. 3:10). This was the unavoidable result upon an intelligent being of involvement in sin.

One of the most graphic expressions of a defiled conscience is provided by David, following his greivous transgressions of adultery and murder (II Sam. 11).

> Have mercy upon me, O God, according to Thy lovingkindness: according to the multitude of Thy tender mercies blot out my transgressions. Wash me thoroughly from mine iniquity, and cleanse me from my sin. For I acknowledge my transgression: and my sin is ever before me . . . Make me to hear joy and gladness; that the bones which Thou hast broken may rejoice . . . Restore unto me the joy of Thy salvation . . . (Psa. 51:1-14).

This was the cry of a contaminated conscience.

A defiled conscience can only surface when God is considered. Apart from that consideration, deadness pervades the conscience of the

239

transgressor. This condition was aptly described by Jeremiah the prophet. "Were they ashamed when they had committed abomination? Nay, they were not at all ashamed, neither could they blush . . ." (Jer. 6:15). An Apostolic representation of the same truth is found in Ephesians 4:19; "Who being past feeling have given themselves over unto lasciviousness, to work all uncleanness with greediness." Paul also identified this condition when he wrote of latter-day apostates; ". . . having their conscience seared with a hot iron . . ." (I Tim. 4:2). The salvation of God does not provide a remedy for this state.

There must be a recovery from this condition before the Gospel will exert its drawing power. Such a recovery was sought when Paul "reasoned" with Felix "of righteousness, temperance, and judgment to come." When Felix was confronted with these realities, "he trembled, and answered, Go thy way for this time; when I have a convenient season, I will call for thee" (Acts 24:25). The defilement of his conscience took place at that time, prohibiting Felix from making further inquiry into the Gospel. It is this condition that is confronted and solved by the "faith of the Gospel" (Phil. 2:27).

Under the law, "worshippers" approached God by external ordinances. They were called "comers" because they meticulously obeyed the laws concerning religious service. Yet, their approach to God obtained no eternal advantage for them. Their only advantage pertained to their stewardship of God's oracles (Rom. 3:1). The closer they came, so to speak, the more contaminated their conscience became. Their sacrifices, rather than placating their conscience, stirred up a "remembrance" of "sins every year" (Heb. 10:1-3). The "ordinances of Divine service" (Heb. 9:1) of the first covenant only served to emphasize that man was not acceptable to God! To put it another way, "it is not possible that the blood of bulls and goats should take away sins" (Heb. 10:4).

The "Gospel of your salvation" (Eph. 1:13) effectively addresses this need. Those that "come unto God by" Christ (Heb. 7:25) experience a purging of the conscience — something that could not be achieved under the Law. Phrases denoting this spiritual experience are "make the comers thereunto perfect," "worshippers once purged," and "no more conscience of sins" (Heb. 10:1-2).

The proclamation of the Gospel is, "How much more shall the blood of Christ, Who through the eternal Spirit offered Himself without spot to God, purge your conscience from dead works to serve the Living God?" (Heb. 9:14). This is the cleansing of which John wrote; ". . . the blood of Jesus Christ His Son cleanses us from all sin . . . cleanse us from all unrighteousness" (I John 1:7,9). This cleansing results in a spiritual awareness of the truth of the Gospel. Jesus really did "put away sin by the sacrifice of Himself" (Heb. 9:26). The belief of that truth, coupled with conformity to the demands of the Gospel, frees the conscience from guilt.

In view of the Divinely-appointed objective for man, one of his greatest needs is that of a purged or cleansed conscience. This must not be a mere salving of the conscience, but a purifying that is the result of the apprehension of reality. The blood of Christ achieves this.

The Renewal of the Mind

When "judgment came upon all men unto condemnation" (Rom. 5:18), God repudiated the entire natural order. It was cursed so that no aspect of it could blend with the "world" or "ages" to come. The body, or tabernacle, of man is of that cursed order — together with the "will" and the "fleshly mind" (John 1:13; Col. 2:18).

For those in Christ, this situation has introduced a principle of deterioration. The things of God, if not given due attention, will actually fade from the mind. Also, strength of heart wanes even while engaged in heavenly enterprises. Thus did the Apostle speak of "weariness" (II Cor. 11:27). Without required renewal, it is quite possible for the believers to become "wearied" and to "faint" in their "minds" (Heb. 12:3). Mere religious discipline cannot sustain the strength of the inner man! While we are in this world Divine strength is required to renew and refurbish our spirits.

It is written, "But they that wait upon the Lord shall renew their strength; they shall mount up with wings as eagles; they shall run, and not be weary; and they shall walk, and not faint" (Isa. 40:31). The Apostles' doctrine defines this work more precisely. "And be not conformed to this world: but be ye transformed by the renewing of your mind . . ." (Rom. 12:2). The association of this salvation is a matter of revelation: ". . . according to His mercy he saved us, by the washing of regeneration, and the renewing of the Holy Ghost" (Titus 3:5).

The continuity of this work, as well as its initiation, is also proclaimed. "And have put on the new man, which is renewed in knowledge after the image of Him that created him" (Col. 3:10);

241

". . . and be renewed in the spirit of your mind . . ." (Eph. 4:23). The willing exposure of the mind to the truth of God brings a restoration of inner strength. That is the meaning of the words, "That He would grant you, according to the riches of His glory, to be strengthened with might by His Spirit in the inner man" (Eph. 3:16).

This strength is only useful in things pertaining to the kingdom of God. While it meets a required need of man, it is impossible to exploit it, or to capitalize upon it for earthly advantage. Thus, not only is the need of man supplied, but the glory of God is protected. Wonderful consistency!

Something to Embrace

In God's Kingdom, relinquishing the love of this world is required in order to embrace the next one. Yet, to abstain from the forbidden is not an end of itself. In fact, it is of no value before God if not attended by laying hold on eternal things. It was this activity that characterized the saints of old time. "These all died in the faith, not having received the promises, but having seen them afar off, and were persuaded of them, and embraced them, and confessed that they were strangers and pilgrims on the earth" (Heb. 11:13). They were not "strangers and pilgrims" by Divine decree, but by personal preference. Having seen the good promises of God by faith, they preferred them, consequently rejecting the things of this world, and assuming the role of wayfaring men.

Those that "seek first the Kingdom of God," while they are in a strange land, are fully justified in their radically-strange behavior, as it is perceived by the worldly mind. They have "embraced" eternal things by faith, which is the "substance of things hoped for, and the evidence of things not seen" (Heb. 11:1). Their desire to have possessions is met in Christ Jesus. As it is written, "For all things are yours; whether Paul, or Apollos, or Cephas, or the world, or life, or death, or things present, or things to come; all are yours" (I Cor. 3:21-22). These "things" are embraced by faith — by a conviction of their reality and a preference for them.

Hope for the Future

Although Satan attempts to get man to live only for the present, the quest for the future is an integral part of true wisdom. Throughout history, the men who perceived this world correctly, hoped for the

242

future. Although the ages prior to the salvation of Christ were marked by an absence of clarity concerning the future, men still hoped in the Lord — i.e., they relied upon God to answer the cry of their hearts.

"In Thee, O Lord, do I hope," cried the Psalmist (Psa. 38:15). Although the full grounds for a justified hope for the future had not yet been revealed, Solomon declared that "the righteous hath hope in his death" (Prov. 14:32), and Jeremiah pronounced a blessing on "the man that trusteth in the Lord, and whose hope the Lord is" (Jer. 17:7).

An optimistic anticipation of the future is a must for the man of God! "We are saved by hope," proclaims Paul (Rom. 8:24), underscoring the present benefits of it. The prevalence of this hope in God's purpose for man is seen in the Apostolic statement: "Ye are called in one hope of your calling" (Eph. 4:4). It was the desire of the Apostle that men's eyes be opened to this "hope" (Eph. 1:18) — that they might comprehend it and rejoice in it. The reason for this is quite obvious — hope is integral to salvation; to the purpose of God. "The hope that is laid up" in heaven for the faithful (Col. 1:5) is not simply an optional benefit. There is no salvation without it! The spiritually informed man realizes his need for this hope, and rejoices in its possession.

An Intercessor in Heaven

Prior to the accomplishment of redemption, righteous men longed for a representative in heaven. Job lamented, "Neither is there any daysman betwixt us, that might lay His hand upon us both" (Job 9:33). A "daysman" would represent God to man, and man to God. Such an individual was as necessary to God as he was to man. He would clarify God's message to man, and represent man favorably to God.

In a limited sense, Moses was such an individual. He was the "mediator" in whose hand the Law was ordained by angels (Gal. 3:19). He brought God's word to the people, and presented the people to God. But he by no means fulfilled the need of mankind in this area.

Isaiah prophesied of a Messiah that would make "intercession for the transgressors" (Isa. 53:12). He also proclaimed that, apart from the coming Savior, "there was no man . . . no intercessor" (Isa. 59:16). Here was something that was needed if man was to be acceptable with his God.

As we have already mentioned, the intercession of Christ is integral to salvation. "Wherefore He is able also to save them to the uttermost that come unto God by Him, seeing He ever lives to make intercession for them" (Heb. 7:25). In an inspired overview of the implementation of salvation, Paul wrote, "Who is he that condemns? It is Christ that died, yea rather, that is risen again, Who is even at the right hand of God, Who also makes intercession for us" (Rom. 8:34).

The intercession of Christ does not consist of fervent pleas for God to ignore His own holiness in the acceptance of man. Rather, it is accomplished by His APPEARANCE before His Father in our behalf. From that position of Divine favor, He pleads the efficacy of His sacrifice for sin (Heb. 10:12-14). His very presence constrains God to anticipate the reception of "His brethren (Heb. 2:17).

The Communion of the Holy Ghost

Until the appearance of "the new heavens and the new earth, wherein dwelleth righteousness" (II Pet. 3:13), Divine fellowship can only be enjoyed by faith. Christ dwells in the heart "by faith" (Eph. 3:17) — i.e., only to the degree that we discern and appropriate the significance of His Person and work.

We are not, however, warranted in supposing that this indwelling by faith is not real. It is real! It is a genuine spiritual experience — but it is not sensually perceived or complete in its scope. It is accomplished within our spirit, which constitutes one third — and the determinative — part of our being. Man is comprised of "spirit and soul and body" (I Thess. 5:23) — in that order of priority! The soul, or physical life, of man, together with his body, is not immediately affected by salvation. Both of them tend away from the things of God, and must be brought under subjection. The "soul and the body" constitute the lower part of our nature, and have been irrevocably tainted with sin. They shall be redeemed at the resurrection of the dead. Our tenure in the "present evil world," among other things, is to be devoted to making our spirits compatible with the coming resurrection body.

The Holy Spirit of God is given to those that are in Christ — to them that "obey Him" (Acts 5:32; I John 3:24; 4:13). The Spirit leads men in the work of subduing of the flesh. "For if ye live after the flesh, ye shall die: but if ye through the Spirit do mortify the deeds of the body, ye shall live" (Rom. 8:14). This leadership is accomplished through the Word of God, which is the Spirit's sword (Eph. 6:17). It is also performed from within the believer, where the Holy Spirit's enablement is found (Eph. 3:16). Without the Word of God, the Spirit's leading would be unintelligible, and consequently ineffectual for those made in God's image. Without being performed from within, there would be no awareness of it or participation in it.

The union of man's spirit with God's Holy Spirit is not theoretical but actual. "He that is joined to the Lord is one spirit," proclaims the Word (I Cor. 6:17). With that union comes a oneness of purpose. There can be no Divine fellowship apart from a common objective. That commonness consists of man participating in God's objective, not God aiding man in his mundane objectives.

This is the "fellowship of the Spirit" (Phil 2:1) and "the communion of the Holy Ghost" (II Cor. 13:14) of which the Apostles wrote. Jesus alluded to this spiritual unity in His words to the Apostles; "If a man love Me, he will keep My words: and my Father will love him, and we will come unto him, and make our abode with him" (John 14:23). This is accomplished by the indwelling of the Holy Spirit as perceived in the words, "In Whom [Jesus] ye also are builded together for a habitation of God through the Spirit" (Eph. 2:22).

The Harmony of Salvation with God's Revealed Objectives

God's declared undertaking in Christ is to bring "many sons to glory" (Heb. 2:10). Reconciliation — the removal of enmity and the agreement of the reconciled ones — is required for the realization of that purpose. Those that are at variance with God cannot walk with Him — in this life or the one to come! Two cannot walk together except they be agreed — and this is particularly true of God and man (Amos 3:3).

Reconciliation is an integral part of salvation! "God, who hath reconciled us unto Himself by Jesus Christ . . . God was in Christ, reconciling the world unto Himself . . ." (II Cor. 5:18-19). "And that He might reconcile both [Jew and Gentile] unto God . . ." (Eph. 2:16). "And you, that were once alienated and enemies in your mind by wicked works, yet now hath He reconciled in the body of His flesh through death . . ." (Col. 1:21-22).

The Gospel is the proclamation of this accomplishment. If believed, it will produce an experiential reconciliation within man. He will begin to see things the way God sees them — Jesus, sin, the world, and the inheritance laid up in heaven, will be perceived in truth. This is what is involved in man being reconciled by God, and how sorely the perception of it is needed! Such received reconciliation may also be perceived as the writing of the law upon the heart (Heb. 8:10-13), the result of which is agreement with God.

Salvation restores what was lost in Eden — the knowledge of good and evil. It is said of those that avail themselves of the "things that accompany salvation" (Heb. 6:9), that they, "by reason of use, have their senses exercised to discern both good and evil" (Heb. 5:14). It is not their involvement in iniquity that exercises their "senses" (spiritual faculties), but their apprehension of the truth. Iniquity is then perceived by way of contrast with righteousness. It appears evil by way of contrast with the "good and acceptable and perfect will of God" (Rom. 12:1-3; Eph. 5:10).

Resisting the Devil

In the beginning, Satan was not resisted. The fall of men occurred because of a failure to draw back from that early confrontation of the adversary. From that time until now, the failure of men in general to resist the devil is seen in this single statement, ". . . the devil, which deceives the whole world" (Rev. 12:9).

Unresisted, the Devil will lead men into Hell! It is absolutely necessary that they be not "ignorant of his devices" (II Cor. 2:11). To "resist" means to refuse to do what Satan tempts them to do — that they perceive his intent, and ignore his enticements. Such resistance requires strength of soul, clearness of vision, and firmness of persuasion.

Salvation wonderfully meets this need. Those that live by faith have this promise, "Resist the Devil, and he will flee from you" (James 4:7). This resistance is accomplished indirectly — not by an immediate confrontation of the Tempter. Warning us of the ferocity of our opponent, Peter wrote, "Be sober, be vigilant; because your adversary the devil, as a roaring lion walks about, seeking whom he may devour; whom resist stedfast in the faith . . ." (I Pet. 5:8-9).

Stedfastness in the faith provides such a clarity of spiritual vision that Satan's enticements are neutralized, losing their attractiveness and power. When our "affection" is set on "things above, not on things on the earth" (Col. 3:2), we, like our Lord, learn to "choose the good and refuse the evil" (Isa. 7:15-16). Such discernment cannot be learned by rote or mere catechism. While such procedures enable us to begin in this area, it is our experiential fellowship in the truth that frustrates the tempter!

Reigning in Life

Man was made to have dominion — that is why God created him! Because of this, there is an underlying desire in man to rule. "The lust of the flesh, and the lust of the eyes, and the pride of life" (I John 2:16) are nothing more than a Satanic appeal to this desire. Unlike the Divine objective for man, these appeals are centered in self. It is the lust of one's own flesh and eyes that is the sin, as well as the pride or sinful exaltation of personal and unregenerate life.

In Christ, however, there is a legitimate provision for man's reign. "For if by one man's offence death reigned by one; much more they which receive abundance of grace and of the gift of righteousness shall reign in life by One, Jesus Christ" (Rom. 5:17). This reign begins now, as, by faith in Christ, men subdue the tendencies resident in their mortal bodies. It will be consummated in the world to come, when death shall have been swallowed up of life.

For the saint of God, the future is bright with the prospect of reigning. "If we suffer, we shall also reign with Him . . ." (II Tim. 2:12), proclaims the Apostle. This is the time when we shall "judge the world" and "angels" (I Cor. 6:2-3). "To him that overcomes will I grant to sit with Me in My throne, even as I also overcome, and am set down with My Father in His throne" (Rev. 3:21).

Admittedly, these promises soar beyond the sphere of current experience. But they are true, and they shall come to pass for those that keep the faith. The desire for rule and authority is met in Christ — now, by dominion over a personal proclivity to sin; in the world to come its experience will not have the present limitations.

The Requirement for a Universal Offer

Salvation's consistency requires that it be offered — legitimately offered — to all men. First, salvation is portrayed as being for the "world." "For God so loved the world . . ." (John 3:16). "For God sent not His Son into the world to condemn the world; but that the world through Him might be saved" (John 4:42; I John 4:14), and Jesus is called the "bread of God" which "gives life to the world" (John 6:33). He also declared Himself to be "the light of the world" (John 8:12; 9:5).

Whoever is included in the phrase "the world" is included in salvation's provision. We are told that the Devil "deceives the whole world" (Rev. 12:9), and that "the whole world lies in wickedness" (or, under the dominion of the wicked one (I John 5:19). The perimeter of deception is the same as that of salvation! Salvation reaches as far as the effects of wickedness! The potential of the blessing can be no less broad that the extent of the curse. John wrote, "And He is the propitiation for our sins: and not for ours only, but also for the sins of the whole world" (I John 2:2).

The point is that it was not merely a portion of the world that was deceived by Satan, but all of it. The view that Christ died for only part of those deceived ones, as Calvinism's "limited atonement" teaches, belies John's declaration that His death propitiated the sins of the "whole world." Thus the Calvinistic doctrine of salvation being available to only a part of the deceived world of men is false.

All Have Sinned

Not only were all men deceived by Satan, all men responded to the deception. "All have sinned and come short of the glory of God," asserts the Spirit (Rom. 3:23). In further confirmation of this, the Apostle credits the universality of death to the universality of sin; ". . . and so death passed upon all men, for that all have sinned" (Rom. 5:12).

The Apostolic interpretation of Christ's death was this; "Christ came into the world to save "sinners" (I Tim. 1:15). He Himself said that he came to call "sinners" to repentance (Matt. 9:13; Mark 2:17; Luke 5:32).

Christ entered the world bearing the likeness of those He came to save (Heb. 14-18). Over sixty-five times, God's Word refers to Jesus Christ as "the Son of man." Even after He had been exalted into heaven, this term was applied to Him by Stephen as he was about to enter into the Divine presence (Acts 7:56). It was "the Son of man" that had "power on earth" (Mark 2:10), and "the Son of man" that was betrayed into the hands of men (Matt. 17:22). In that capacity He was "delivered up" (Luke 24:7), and raised from the dead (Mark 9:9). His presentation to the world as the Divine remedy for sin is one of "the Son of man" being "lifted up" (John 3:13-14; 12:32-34).

The salvation of God must, in its provisionary aspect, be for all men, or it can be for no man. If provision has not been made for every man, then no man can be assured of its applicability to himself! The need applies to all men, and so does the salvation!

Whosoever Will

The closing verses of God's revelation to men sounds a universal note that cannot be denied. Wherever there is a hungry heart, a searching spirit, or a thirsting soul, Divine encouragement is provided. "And the Spirit and the bride say, Come. And let him that hears say, Come. and let him that is athirst come. And whosoever will, let him take the water of life freely [without restraint or limitation]" (Rev. 22:17).

The Holy Spirit gives the summons through the Gospel. Everywhere it is preached in truth, a universal invitation is given. No one can possibly conclude that he is exempted! "COME"! The invitation is not to some men — it is to all men! The Holy Spirit knows of no man not included in the summons! The salvation has been "prepared before the face of all people" (Luke 2:31). Cursed be the one that preaches any other kind of Gospel (Gal. 1:8-9)!

The bride — Christ's church — also says "COME"! This is not a limited invitation, but one to all men! All men are perceived as sinners — all men are urged to come and be reconciled to God!

Anywhere there is a thirsty soul — one that has realized the emptiness of the world, and its inability to satisfy the need of God's offspring — there is a positive note of hope. "Let him that is athirst come. And whosoever will, let him come and drink of the water of life freely." As those words are heard, they seem to echo the words of our Lord as He stood and cried on that great day of the feast; "If any man thirst, let him come unto Me, and drink" (John 7:37).

The heart of God has always pulsed with a desire for every man to come to Him. The prophets proclaimed this desire. "Ho every one that thirsts, come ye to the waters, and he that hath no money; come ye, buy, and eat; yea, come, buy wine and milk without money and without price . . . incline your ear, and come unto me: hear, and your soul shall live" (Isa. 55:1-3).

It is not to be denied there are many voices in the world calling for the allegiance of man. But above the din of those discordant notes, there sounds a clarion call from heaven! It is to all men everywhere, and declares a salvation for the whole world — a consistent salvation that meets the real need of every man!

249

16

JESUS — THE IMPLEMENTER OF DIVINE OBJECTIVES

The introduction of Jesus Christ into history began the final stages of God's work upon the earth. The purpose announced in Eden, foreshadowed in the Law, and heralded by the prophets is brought to its culmination in Jesus. The times of His preeminence are the "last days" of Isaiah (Isa. 2:2). The revelation of God and His will that is being accomplished by Him is said to be occurring during "these last days" (Heb. 1:2). This period is also called, "the last times." "Who verily was foreordained before the foundation of the world, but was manifest in these last times for you" (I Pet. 1:20).

The word "last," however, is not meant to emphasize the end of the world, but rather the culmination of Divine objective. While it is true that the heavens and the earth shall pass away at the close of this time, their demise is not to be the object of our attention. Spiritually informed people do not merely look for the end of the world, they look for the manifestation of "the world to come" and their involvement in it. The only way to consider God's aim is to concentrate on Jesus!

251

Jesus the King

A great deal of religious controversy exists over whether or not Jesus is King now. One segment of the Christian community believes that He will become King — another part of it contends that He is a reigning King at this time. The varying views that are associated with this controversy have been prompted more by the "tradition of men" (Col. 2:8), than a consideration of the Scriptures.

Pilate asked Jesus twice concerning His kingship. "Art Thou the King of the Jews?" he asked in the "judgment hall." Later he again asked, "Art Thou a King, then?" Jesus gave specific answers to both questions. To the first He replied, "My kingdom is not of this world. . . ." To the second He replied, "Thou sayest that I am a King. To this end was I born, and for this cause came I into the world. . . ." Observe that He did not say He was going to return to the world to be King, but that He was born — that He came into the world — for that purpose. That is an end of all controversy!

The Apostle Peter proclaimed Christ's Kingship on the day of Pentecost. Taking the "keys of the Kingdom" which had been given to him by the King (Matt. 16:19), he unlocked the door of entrance into God's Kingdom by proclaiming its King. "Men and brethren, let me freely speak unto you of the patriarch David," urged the Apostle. He spoke of him being "a prophet, and knowing that God had sworn with an oath to him, that of the fruit of his loins, according to the flesh, He would raise up Christ to sit on his throne." Peter further proclaimed, "Therefore, let all the house of Israel know assuredly, that God hath made that same Jesus, whom ye crucified, both Lord and Christ" (Acts 2:29-36). He was the "Lord" which David "foresaw," and of which he prophesied concerning his throne. He was also "Christ" — the one anointed of God in fulfillment of the Davidic covenant.

As a King, "all things have been delivered" unto Him by His Father (Luke 10:22). He is, and is proclaimed to be, "Lord of all" (Acts 10:36). "All power in heaven and earth" has been given unto Him (Matt. 28:18), and He has been exalted "far above all principality, and power, and might, and dominion, and every name that is named, not only in this world, but also in the one to come" (Eph. 1:21). He has "gone into heaven, and is on the right hand of God; angels and authorities and powers being made subject unto Him" (I Pet. 3:22).

252

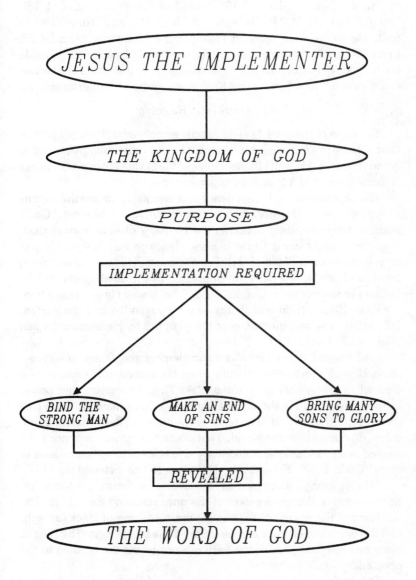

He is "Captain" (Heb. 2:10), "Head of the church" (Col. 1:18), "King" (Matt. 21:5), "Prince" (Acts 3:15; 5:31), and "Ruler" (Micah 5:2). He has already received His appointed Kingdom (Acts 22:29; Luke 19:12-27), and is currently reigning "until His enemies be made his footstool" (I Cor. 15:25). The supposition that these conditions could exist without Jesus being King is unworthy of further attention.

Why He Is Now Reigning

The reign of the Lord Jesus is directly associated with the purpose of God. That is, in fact, why He is reigning — in order to implement that grand objective. He is the Implementer of the Divine enterprise of man's reconciliation, and it is under His supervision.

The objective of God is not peace and tranquility among the nations of the earth — it does not concern prosperity and social equity! God's purpose unquestionably concerns the recovery of man from the fall. Everything about Jesus Christ is associated with that design. He was born for this reason (Matt. 1:21). For this cause, He "went about doing good, and healing all that were oppressed of the devil" (Acts 10:38). He died to recover men (Col. 1:21-22). That is why He was raised from the dead (Rom. 4:25) and that is why He ascended into glory (Heb. 1:3; 9:24). The consummation of this plan is why He is coming again (Heb. 9:28; I John 3:2).

God exalted Jesus in order to implement the Divine objectives. Jesus Himself proclaimed his truth when He prayed to His Father — a time when it was with great clarity. "As Thou hast given Him power over all flesh, that He should give eternal life to as many as Thou hast given Him" (John 17:2). The term "power over all flesh" describes absolute dominion over the world. That dominion, however, is not to be viewed in a political sense. Objectively, He rules to bring "many sons to glory" (Heb. 2:10). Subjectively, He reigns to "give eternal life."

This is being accomplished by Divine authority, but not independently of the involvement of the ones receiving eternal life. The subduing of the enemy of their souls, the conferring of inner strength, and the imparting of grace and peace are done by the King. The King of glory has been exalted for this very reason: to get the blessing to the obedient!

This truth was demonstrated on the day of Pentecost, when Jesus began the ministry of giving "gifts to men" (Eph. 4:8-11). The events of that inaugural day constituted a revelation of Christ's reign. "Therefore being by the right hand of God exalted, and having received of the Father the promise of the Holy Ghost, He hath shed forth this, which ye now see and hear" (Acts 2:33). He was implementing God's purpose! The Apostles, who were the objects of His empowerment, spoke of salvation, of reconciliation, forgiveness, and the reception of God's Spirit (Acts 2:38-41). The reign of King Jesus was underway!

Whose Son Is He!

The significance of Jesus is directly associated with His Sonship. This is reflected in His ministry. He did not simply come into the world, He came with a predetermined objective.

On one occasion Jesus asked the Pharisees, "What think ye of Christ? whose Son is He?" (Matt. 22:42). This was not a mere academic question. It was addressed to the scholars of the day — the Pharisees — that sat in "Moses' seat" (Matt. 23:2). They were to be expounders of the Law, who, like the priests of old time, "read in the book of the Law distinctly, and gave the sense, and caused them to understand the reading" (Neh. 8:8). But instead of fulfilling this much required role, they "shut up the kingdom of God against men" and did not permit those to do so that were making an effort to "enter in" (Matt. 23:13).

Our Lord's probing question exposed their basic ignorance of God. But it also provided an opportunity for them to break out of their traditional restrictions. He did come to save sinners, and the Pharisees were certainly in that category. Their honest consideration of the question could have opened the door to the apprehension of the truth.

The answer to the inquiry, "Whose Son is He?" will reveal the role of Jesus in God's eternal purpose. The proper identification of Jesus constitutes a recognition of what God is doing — the objective He is implementing. Note the academic answer of the Pharisees; it was void of understanding. "They say unto Him, the Son of David" (Matt. 22:42). From the viewpoint of scholarship, their answer was correct — but it was not scholarship the Lord sought, but discernment (Matt. 12:23; 15:22; 20:30-31; 21:9; John 7:42; Rom. 1:3; II Tim. 2:8). His answer to them revealed their failure to apprehend the truth of His Person and Role in the Heavenly objective. "How then doth David in spirit call Him Lord, saying, The Lord said unto my Lord, Sit Thou on my right hand, till I make Thine enemies Thy footstool? If David then call Him Lord, how is He his Son?" (Matt. 22:43-44).

By way of contrast, this is the term ascribed to Jesus by two discerning blind men that followed Him. "Thou Son of David, have mercy on us," they cried. Before the day was over, they were no longer blind, but "their eyes were opened" by the Prince of life (Matt. 9:27-30). They had perceived the significance of that title — they sensed His mission, His work, His representation of the God of all the earth!

"Whose Son is He"? The question stands at the threshold of understanding and of the church. It is equivalent to asking, "Whom does He represent?" "Whose work is He doing?" "Whose likeness does He bear?" "Whose mission is He fulfilling?" Here we may expect to find a revelation of both His Person and position — indeed, the preeminent position — in the Kingdom of God. The Kingdom cannot be understood or apprehended apart from Jesus Christ!

Son of Abraham

Jesus is also called "the Son of Abraham" (Matt. 1:1). It must be observed that He is not merely "a son of Abraham" like Zacchaeus (Luke 19:8-9), but "the Son of Abraham" — his relationship is unique! His role as the Seed of woman is to deliver the fallen race from Satan. His capacity as the "Seed of Abraham" emphasizes His function as Blesser. Through Him the Abrahamic blessing would be conferred upon believers.

God had committed Himself to the blessing of all people. To Abraham he said, ". . . and in thee shall all families of the earth be blessed" (Gen. 12:3). Of old time, in a dialogue among the Members of the Godhead, it was said, "Shall I hide from Abraham that thing which I do; seeing that Abraham shall surely become a great and mighty nation, and all nations of the earth shall be blessed in him?" (Gen. 18:17-18). Again, at the sparing of Isaac and the discovery of a Divinely-provided sacrificial ram, it was said to Abraham, "And in thy seed shall all the nations of the earth be blessed . . ." (Gen. 22:18). The promise was reiterated to Abraham's son Isaac, in assurance of its fulfillment; ". . . and in thy seed shall all the nations of the earth be blessed" (Gen. 26:4).

The "blessing" of which God spoke was not mere earthly prosperity. It was not the improvement of the temporal order — it had already been cursed! His revelation concerning this blessing is specific, requiring no conjecture. "Unto you first God, having raised up His Son Jesus, sent Him to bless you, in turning away every one of you from his iniquities" (Acts 3:26). This "turning" becomes a personal confirmation of the bruising of Satan, and is a prelude to Divine fellowship. Although the magnitude of the Abrahamic blessing was not fully known in ages past, it "is now revealed to His holy apostles and prophets by the Spirit" (Eph. 3:5).

The Seed of Abraham was to be the means of blessing all nations — the whole world. How wonderfully this has been fulfilled in Christ Jesus. The "Gospel of Christ" is to be preached to "every creature," as His followers go "into all the world" (Mark 15:15). In joyful anticipation, He commanded His disciples to "Go ye therefore, and teach all nations, baptizing them in the Name of the Father, and of the Son, and of the Holy Ghost: teaching them to observe all things whatsoever I have commanded you . . ." (Matt. 28:19-20). While the proclamation of "repentance and remission of sins" was to begin at Jerusalem, it was to be "preached in His name among all nations" (Luke 24:47).

There is no continent, no society, no remote area of the earth in which this Gospel is not to be preached! Every nation, every creature, is to hear of God's intention to bless them — to turn them away from their iniquities. This salvation was prepared "before the face of all people" (Luke 2:31), and its "good tidings of great joy" is "to all people" (Luke 2:10).

The Apostles proclaimed that Christ is the promised "Seed" of Abraham (Gal. 3:16). He is God's means of fulfilling His intention to bless men by remitting their sins. Jesus has no saving significance apart from this purpose. He offers no benefit to men that is separate from that declared objective. The very term "the Seed of Abraham" identifies His wonderful ministry!

Son of David

In his "book of the generation of Jesus Christ," Matthew refers to Jesus as "the Son of David" (Matt. 1:1). In addition to the discerning blind men that perceived Him as David's Son (Matt. 9:27; 20:30,31), "a woman of Canaan" likewise so addressed Him (Matt. 15:22). When the Lord fulfilled Isaiah's prophecy by coming to Jerusalem, "sitting upon an ass, and a colt the foal of an ass," the people acknowledged

Him as "the Son of David" with their shouts of acclamation (Isa. 62:11; Zech. 9:9; Matt. 21:5-9; Mark 11:10). The Apostle taught that He was "made of the seed of David according to the flesh" (Rom. 1:3).

This term is intended to further reveal the role of Jesus in accomplishing God's objective to restore man to a position of favor. While the term, "Son of Abraham" contemplates Him as the means of blessing "all nations," "Son of David" emphasizes His Kingship. He was the One that was raised up to sit upon David's throne (Acts 2:29-36; II Sam. 7:12; Psa. 132:11). His rule was to be one of "righteousness" (Isa. 32:1), under which the will of the Lord would be accomplished.

The point is that God recognized Him as King; as it is written; "But unto the Son He [God] saith, Thy throne, O God, is for ever and ever" a sceptre of righteousness shall be the sceptre of Thy Kingdom. Thou hast loved righteousness and hated iniquity; therefore God, even Thy God, hath anointed Thee with the oil of gladness above Thy fellows" (Heb. 1:8-9).

Clear association is made between all aspects of Christ's Person and the salvation of men. "God, Who at sundry times and in divers manners spake in time past unto the fathers by the prophets, hath in these last days spoken unto us by His Son . . . Who . . . by Himself purged our sins," and "sat down on the right hand of the Majesty on high" (Heb. 1:1-3). At the point where He "sat down on the right hand" of God, He assumed the reins of the Kingdom! The sceptre was then placed in His hand, and He commenced a rule of righteousness — one that would consummate in the giving of eternal life to those given to Him (John 17:2). His reign involves the subduing of His adversaries — those determined to inhibit the work of salvation.

Christ is a different order of king, just as He is a different order of man. He is the "Second man," and the "Last Adam" — terms denoting His unique manhood. Ezekiel, long after David had died, wrote of the Messiah as "David." "And I will set up one shepherd over them, and He shall feed them, even my Servant David; He shall feed them, and He shall be their shepherd. And I the Lord will be their God, and My Servant David a Prince among them; I the Lord have spoken it" (Ezek. 34:23-24). "And David My Servant shall be King over them . . . and My Servant David shall be their Prince for ever" (Ezek. 37:25-26).

Jesus is not the King over a geographical area, but over an enterprise! He does not rule to establish military superiority, but to lead men safely from earth to glory! His might is not for purposes of display, but for the implementation of God's desire for men! There is no reason for His rule apart from salvation — no benefit to men in separation from reconciliation to God. He has overthrown unseen enemies, ministered spiritual benefits, and opened the way for man back to God. All of this has been accomplished by the King — the Son of David!

Son of God

The most significant title of Jesus is "the Son of God." There is no term that more precisely identifies Him or His purpose. He has been "declared" by the resurrection to be "the Son of God" (Rom. 1:4). The opening of Christ's earthly ministry was attended with a voice from heaven that declared, "This is My Beloved Son" (Matt. 3:17). When Jesus was transfigured in a "high mountain apart" — when His inner glory burst through His flesh — the heavenly voice spoke again; "This is My Beloved Son" (Matt. 17:5).

The magnitude of this revelation is seen in Christ's response to Peter's confession in Caesarea Philippi. It was there that Peter said, "Thou art the Christ, the Son of the Living God." Confirming that this was not the result of mere intellectual analysis, Jesus said, "Blessed art thou Simon Barjona: for flesh and blood hath not revealed this unto thee, but My Father which is in heaven" (Matt. 16:16-17). Peter's words were not an academic response, but the evidence of a burst of insight. Though the understanding quickly dissipated, Peter saw Jesus in that moment of time as God's only begotten Son! Just as Satan showed Jesus the kingdoms of the world and the glory of them "in a moment of time" (Luke 4:5), so God the Father showed Peter His Son and His glory, so to speak, in a moment of time!

Jesus had already proclaimed "no man knows the Son but the Father" (Matt. 11:27). Luke's Gospel states it even more precisely; "No man knows Who the Son is but the Father" (Luke 10:22). Jesus' Sonship was not apparent — not something that could not be missed. Isaiah had prophesied that such would be the case. "He hath no form nor comeliness; and when we shall see Him, there is no beauty that we should desire Him. He is despised and rejected of men . . ." (Isa. 53:2-3). He was the "Stone which the builders rejected," not being able to identify Him with God's promised salvation (Matt. 21:42).

One of the clearest demonstrations of the obscurity of Christ's Sonship is seen in John the Baptist. Here was a man "filled with the Holy Ghost, even from the mother's womb" (Luke 1:15) — not your ordinary man! In addition to this, he was contemporary with Jesus. In fact, Jesus was John's "cousin" on his mother's side (Luke 1:36).

John was specifically raised up to "prepare the way of the Lord" (Mal. 3:1; Matt. 3:3). John had come, "baptizing with water," in order to play a significant role in making the Lamb of God "manifest to Israel." Here was Jesus of Nazareth — his own cousin — and yet he had not yet perceived Him as God's Son! John's mother, Elizabeth, had been given the revelation of Jesus' Sonship — the knowledge was in the family (Luke 1:41-45). Yet, the erosion of time had seemed to obscure this most wonderful revelation. Mary herself had lost her hold upon it by the time Jesus was twelve years old (Luke 2:48-50). Now the insight is lacking, even in John, Christ's harbinger.

John twice confessed his failure to recognize Jesus; "Behold the Lamb of God, which takes away the sin of the world . . . And I knew Him not . . . I saw the Spirit descending from heaven like a dove, and it abode upon Him. And I knew Him not . . . And I saw, and bare record that this is the Son of God" (John 1:30-34). This obtuseness was not the result of John's simplicity, but of Christ's lack of external uniqueness. John did know that He was righteous in a superior sense (Matt. 3:14), but was unable to see Him as the Son of God until the sign of the descending Spirit was given him.

Paul spoke for all those "in Christ" when he said, "Wherefore henceforth [from this time forward] know we no man after the flesh: yea, though we have known Christ after the flesh, yet now henceforth know we Him no more" (II Cor. 5:16). The fleshly view of Christ as a miracle Worker, mighty Healer, unrestricted Feeder of the multitudes, and authoritative Teacher is not sufficient. Unless the significance of His works are perceived, the truth of His Sonship will be missed. His unparalleled works authenticated His claim of immediate association with Jehovah and His purpose. No matter how astute the man — no matter how superior his intellectual abilities — Jesus of Nazareth cannot be perceived as the "only begotten of the Father, full of grace and truth" (John 1:14) without Divine influence!

No man ought to stumble at this truth, as though it denied the sufficiency of the Scriptures. The Scriptures derive their power from Divine influence. They are "the record God has given of His Son" (I John

260

5:10), "and so also is the Holy Ghost, Whom God hath given to them that obey Him" (Acts 5:32). We have Jesus' own words on this matter. "No man knows Who the Son is" (Luke 10:22)! Let none hesitate to embrace them, or suppose that an acceptance of them constitutes a compromise of the completeness of the Scriptures. God did not eliminate Himself from the Kingdom when He gave the Scriptures! They are His means of making men "wise unto salvation" (II Tim. 3:15). He reveals this truth to men's hearts through the written Word, as He did to Peter throughout the Living Word — that Jesus is the Son of God!

John explained the reason for His Gospel with these words; "But these [Divine signs] are written, that ye might believe that Jesus is the Christ, the Son of God; and that believing ye might have life through His Name" (John 20:31). Moreover, "Whosoever shall confess that Jesus is the Son of God, God dwells in him, and he in God" (I John 4:15). Those are arresting words, particularly to one that has been blinded by an erroneous consideration of Jesus. They are true words, and are to be embraced with the whole heart! Jesus said only the Father knew Who the Son is — and He told Peter that a persuasion of the truth concerning His identity was evidence of Divine revelation. John teaches us here that the joining of God and man — personally — is evidenced by a confession of this truth. The confession is not a mere recitation of facts. The only confession honored in heaven is one that has been prompted by faith. "For with the heart man believes unto righteousness, and with the mouth confession is made unto salvation" (Rom. 10:10). The involvement of the heart connotes perception, insight, and understanding. Unless that accompanies the acknowledgment of Christ's Sonship, there has been no confession of Him as "the Son of God."

The effect of this confession is witnessed by these words; "Who is he that overcomes the world, but he that believes that Jesus is the Son of God" (I John 5:5). One is overcoming the world when he successfully resists Satan, avoids his delusion, and embraces the truth. In such a case, the "fashion of this world" does not delude, and the command-ments of the Lord are kept without grief or chaffing (I John 5:3). The conclusion ought to be obvious and inescapable. Those that are not overcoming the world do not believe that Jesus is the Son of God!

There is yet another arresting word concerning this matter. "He that believeth on the Son of God hath the witness in himself . . ." (I John 5:10). This is where the effectual witness must be if assurance is to be possessed! Divine attestation consists of an inner witness that conforms with the written record. It speaks of an assurance, a confidence, a persuasion that Jesus is God's Son — the express Image of His Person, and the only means of becoming a part of His "eternal purpose."

God with Us

Matthew, in his record of the Savior's birth, declared the fulfillment of Isaiah's prophecy. "Now all this was done, that it might be fulfilled which was spoken by the prophet, saying, Behold, a virgin shall be with child, and shall bring forth a Son, and they shall call His name Emmanuel, which being interpreted is GOD WITH US" (Matt. 1:22-23). God with us! What a word is this! He Who "inhabits eternity" (Isa. 57:15) among the rebel race!

Jesus was "the Word" that was "with God" and "was God"! In His precreation capacity, He made "all things; and without Him was not anything made that was made" (John 1:1-3). In essence, there is no separation between Him and God. Before the foundation of the world, "He counted it not robbery to be equal with God" (Phil. 2:6). There was no variance in Their will or work! Perfect agreement existed between Them. The creation of man was the result of their Divine agreement — "Let US make man in OUR image" (Gen. 1:26). Two Persons, one heart! Two individuals, one will!

When Jesus entered into the world, He entered as the perfect expression of God the Father. His attitude toward sinners was God's attitude. He came to "seek and save that which was lost" (Luke 19:10) because it was a Divine desire. God's heart longed for man — He was not content to have His offspring forever separated from Himself. They must be retrieved — that is why Christ Jesus came into the world! When He had "compassion" on the multitudes (Matt. 9:36; 14:14) He was expressing the heart of the God of heaven, who is "full of compassion" (Psa. 86:15; 111:4; 112:4; 145:8).

He was "God manifest in the flesh" (I Tim. 3:16). His ministry was not to show the potential of man, but to reveal the greatness of the God man's sin had hidden! His role was not to unveil what man could have been, but how God felt about man — how greatly the Father loved the world! Here, in Jesus of Nazareth, was God among men — among

262

them to bless, not to curse!

The "Rock" upon Which the Church Is Built

Christ's Sonship is such a pivotal truth, that the church is built upon its reality. In a greatly-misunderstood text of Scripture, we have the response of Jesus to Peter's grand confession. "And I say also unto thee, that thou art Peter, and upon this rock I will build My church; and the gates of hell shall not prevail against it" (Matt. 16:18).

The Roman Catholic heresy supposes the rock upon which Jesus built His church was Peter himself. And they are not alone in this view. Throughout church history, there have been men inclined to it. Without devoting a lot of space to answering this tradition, let us briefly examine the logical results of embracing it.

If the church — the assembly of those called out of the world — is built upon Peter, we are faced with several incongruities. 1. We have a temporal foundation. 2. The foundation of the church is itself imperfect, requiring an atonement. 3. Christ Himself is superseded by one of His disciples. 4. The foundation rock of the church is different from the "Stone which the builders rejected" (Psa. 118:22; Mark 12:10). 5. God, Who has taught us to think of Deity as the "Rock" (Deut. 32;4; Psa. 18;2; 71:3; I Pet. 2:3), now makes the most important "rock" in the history of the world a mortal man. 6. Jesus, in such a case, does not build with man, but on man.

It was the confession Peter made that would be the foundation of the church — that Jesus Christ was the Son of God! "Confession is made unto salvation" (Rom. 10:9-10) — I will build My church! "Whosoever shall confess that Jesus is the Son of God, God dwelleth in him, and he in God" (I John 4:15) — I will build My church! "Who is he that overcomes the world, but he that believeth that Jesus is the Son of God" — I will build My church! "For the Son of God, Jesus Christ, Who was preached . . . for all the promises of God in Him are yea, and in Him Amen, unto the glory of God by us" (II Cor. 1:19-20) — I will build my church!

Peter, like James and John, was a "pillar" in the early church (Gal. 2:9). He did not, however, make any significant contribution to the faith of Paul. In Paul's words, "But of these who seemed to be somewhat . . . they who seemed to be somewhat in conference added nothing to me" (Gal. 2:6). This is by no means a derogation of Peter,

James, and John. It but indicates that Jesus had personally instructed Paul in such an efficient manner that even the Apostles could provide him no significant insight he had not already received. In such a case, Paul was not built upon Peter or his teaching, but on the reality of Christ's Sonship. This was ministered to him in complete separation from Peter.

"The gates of hell [hades] shall not prevail against it," proclaimed the Master, of the unassailable rock of His Sonship (Matt. 16:18b). These are the gates of death which have closed upon the entirety of mankind to this day. Jesus is the only individual ever to have entered into that region Who, of His own will and power, has returned in triumph. He alone has "the keys of hell [hades] and of death" (Rev. 1:18). The individual Peter, the sanctified church, and all men in general, will emerge from the region of the dead at the voice of the Son of God (John 5:28-29). Until that voice has sounded, the "gates of death" shall indeed prevail over all men — the church included. No man can come back from the dead at will, and no man can raise another at will!

When Jesus "descended into the lower parts of the earth" (Eph. 4:9), He entered into a temporary confinement. The third day, He arose victorious, the "gates" notwithstanding. Peter Himself proclaimed the glory of Christ's Sonship; "Whom God hath raised up, having loosed the pains of death: because it was not possible that He should be held by it" (Acts 2:24). Were He not the Son of the Living God, it would have been possible for Him to be restrained by death. It was His Sonship that was being held in question while He remained among the dead. And when God raised Him, He was "declared to be the Son of God with power . . ." (Rom. 1:4).

In conclusion, recognizing Jesus as the Son of God becomes the foundation for the entire matter of salvation. If He is not the Son of God, the whole superstructure of reconciliation falls to the ground.

No Significance Without God the Father

Jesus has no redemptive significance apart from His immediate relationship to His Father. Jesus was never meant to be a replacement for the Father. With the revelation of the Son, the Father did not move to the background. The Divine purpose still belongs to God! It is God that was offended, and the atonement was presented to Him. Jesus was

"His Christ," and "the Lamb of God." In Him men gain "access unto the Father" (Eph. 2:18), and are "reconciled" to God (II Cor. 5:18-20). The Father "sent the Son to be the Savior of the world" (I John 4:14), and Jesus is our "Advocate with the Father" (I John 2:1).

The "Lord's Christ"

The term "Christ," or "Messiah," emphasizes Jesus' appointed ministry. He was elected of God (Isa. 42:1) to accomplish the basis for man's salvation. He was "anointed," or officially designated and set apart, for this purpose. It was "Christ" — God's designated representative — that "died for the ungodly" (Rom. 5:6). In that capacity He was "raised from the dead" (Rom. 6:4), and sound preaching proclaims Him as the "Christ," God's chosen One (I Cor. 1:23). "Christ is the end of the Law for righteousness" (Rom. 10:4), and it is He that "died for our sins" (I Cor. 15:3). As "Christ," He is our "life" (Col. 3:4), and all "spiritual blessings" are in Him (Eph. 1:3).

He is not only our Christ, but "the Christ of God" (Luke 9:20). God raised "Christ" to sit on the appointed throne (Acts 2:30). He was the Father's anointed One! This is why it is written, "Christ pleased not Himself," but made God the center of His devotion (Rom. 15:3).

Jesus came into the world to give clarity to God the Father. "I honor My Father," He declared (John 8:49). He did not seek His personal exaltation. In His own words, "And I seek not Mine own glory . . ." (John 8:50). His objective was to manifest the Father from whom man had been alienated, and to provide an acceptable means of return to Him. Thus is it written, "He that honors not the Son, honors not the Father which hath sent Him" (John 5:23). It is inconceivable that such an individual — one that does not honor the Son — will inherit everlasting life!

Christ demonstrated unquestionable devotion to His Father's will. "I seek not mine own will, but the will of the Father which hath sent Me" (John 5:30). In another affirmation of this attitude He proclaimed, "I am come in My Father's name . . ." (John 5:43). Jesus said of His death, "No man taketh it [My life] from Me, but I lay it down of Myself. I have power to lay it down, and I have power to take it again. This commandment have I received of My Father" (John 10:18).

Had Jesus failed in His commission to "lay down His life" (John 10:15,17; 13:37,38; 15:13) God would have been disgraced! His in-

265

tegrity would have suffered damage, and His purpose overturned. My point here is that the devotion of Jesus was required for the accomplishment of God's will. It was not achieved without stedfastness on Jesus' part. He "set His face stedfastly" to fulfill God's will (Luke 9:51) and sweat "as it were great drops of blood falling to the ground" rather than fail in His mission (Luke 22:44). He was determined to do what He had been sent to perform.

The Father Honors the Son

I must remind you of the purpose for this rather lengthy treatise. The Kingdom of God is inseparably associated with the implementation of Divine objective. That aim has been revealed as the reconciliation of man unto God, and is being achieved under the administration of Jesus Christ, God's only Son. Jesus has no relevancy apart from this purpose. He is not available for the solution of earthly difficulties that have no bearing on salvation. He is not the universal problem-solver. Rather, He is the "Savior of the world" (I John 4:14). Any other view of Him is foreign to Scripture, and to be zealously avoided.

It is in the capacity of Savior that God "honors" the Son. Jesus confessed this when He said, "If I honor Myself, My honor is nothing: it is My Father that honors Me" (John 8:54). God honored Jesus by glorifying Him — raising Him from the dead, and setting Him at His own right hand (John 16:14; Acts 17:31; I Thess. 1:10).

I cannot help but observe the marked contrast between the Head of the church and many that bear His Name. While He sought not His own glory, but that of His Father, myriads are capitalizing upon religion by vaunting their names and filling their coffers. How must the Father of glory view such activities? It is not a new thing, but it is a curse! Even in the day of the Apostles it was said, "For I have no man likeminded, who will naturally care for your state. For all seek their own, not the things which are Jesus Christ's" (Phil. 2:20-21). Such an attitude has no place in the Kingdom of our God and of His Christ!

Honoring the Son and Honoring the Father

The Father and the Son are inseparable. In the greater illumination of the New Covenant, God cannot be properly contemplated without the consideration of Jesus. Equally true, neither can Jesus be correctly discerned without a spiritual awareness of the Father. "He that has seen

Me," proclaimed Jesus, "has seen the Father" (John 14:9).

All men must honor the Father. This is accomplished by giving proper honor to His Son. It is written that the Father judges no man, but has committed all judgment "unto the Son: that all men should honor the Son, even as they honor the Father. He that honors not the Son honors not the Father which hath sent Him" (John 5:22-23). The responsibility for the administration of God's Kingdom has been given to Christ Jesus — all judgment has been committed to the Son. In the awareness of this reality, "all men should honor the Son"! Their response to God's Son indicates their attitude toward God Himself.

The way to give honor to the Son is to respond to Him by faith. He calls everyone that is thirsty — that is unable to be satisfied by the course of this world, and that craves the approval of God — to come to Him. "If any man thirst, let him come unto Me and drink" (John 7:37). In the coming, Jesus is honored — and when He is honored, God is honored! He died to reconcile us to God (Col. 1:21)! He is honored when men respond to the admonition "Be ye reconciled to God" (II Cor. 5:20). When the atonement is received (Rom. 5:11), both the Son and the Father are honored.

God cannot be properly honored without receiving Jesus (John 1:11), and Jesus cannot be received and obeyed without honoring the Father. Unfavorable and incomplete responses to the Son of God constitute a denial of the Father, and consequently dishonor Him. God has given us a "record" concerning His Son. If any man refuses to believe that Gospel record, he has made God "a liar" — the ultimate dishonor (I John 5:10-11).

Jesus Brings Us to God

Do not lose sight of Christ's role: He is the One that is implementing God's purpose. That objective will not be accomplished without Him, and men will not enjoy participation in it without accepting Him. This is the concern of God's Kingdom.

The objective of Christ's substitutionary death is summed up in these words; "For Christ also hath once suffered for sins, the Just for the unjust, that He might bring us to God . . ." (I Pet. 3:18). The writer of Hebrews phrased it differently — but it is the same truth; "For it became Him [the Father] in bringing many sons to glory, to make the Captain of their salvation perfect through suffering" (Heb. 2:10).

The "bringing" is not coercive — it is not the result of Divine force. There have been times in history when God reeled rebels in, so to speak — like the case of Sennacherib, king of Assyria. "Because thy rage against me and thy tumult is come up in Mine ears, therefore I will put My hook in thy nose, and My bridle in thy lips, and I will turn thee back by the way thou camest" (II Kgs. 19:28-29; Isa. 37:29). But this was not the hook of salvation — it was that of condemnation. Rather than bringing that evil king to God, it pulled him away from God. To put it another way, it restrained Sennacherib from performing his evil desires against the people of God. But salvation is not after this order!

Christ brings to God those that "follow" Him (John 10:4,27; Luke 9:23), that obey Him (Heb. 5:9; I Pet. 1:2), that "press toward the mark," extending intense effort (Phil. 3:7-14). His "bringing" assures that our efforts are not "vain in the Lord" (I Cor. 15:58). Men's efforts assure that He will have someone to "bring"!

The bringing of "many sons to glory" may be viewed in at least two ways. First, Jesus brings us by preparing the way, and going before us. As the "Forerunner," He has entered into heaven "for us" (Heb. 6:20). The sons must be brought along a sanctified way — one that has been traversed by an accepted One! It is this action that constitutes the preparation of a "place" for the ones being brought (John 14:2,3). The point is that from heaven He is bringing men to heaven. Heavenly appeals are employed instead of earthly proddings. The look is preferred to the goad!

Secondly, He brings by Divine guidance. He is "the Good Shepherd" (John 10:3,4) — "good" because wisdom and love are combined in His shepherding. He wants to bring us to God, and He knows how to do so without compromising His Deity or man's humanity.

Isaiah foretold the magnanimity and divine ability of this Shepherd: "He shall feed His flock like a shepherd: He shall carry the lambs with his arm, and carry them in his bosom, and shall gently lead those that are with young" (Isa. 40:11). Here the emphasis is on His tenderness and ability. The Divine objective is to bring the sons home — to get the redeemed to heaven.

He will safely guide them into heaven's haven! He has been appointed by God to this office. Anyone and everyone that "believes on His Name" (John 1:12) has been given to Him by the Father. He will feed them (Psa. 23:1-2; John 10:9), guide them (Psa. 23:3; John 10:3,4), protect and preserve them (Jer. 31:10; Ezek. 34:10; Zech. 9:16; John 10:28). These are the Divinely appointed means by which Jesus brings men to heaven.

The Erroneous "Jesus Only" Doctrine

The unitarian view of the Godhead represents an error of unspeakable magnitude. Purported "evangelicals" that have embraced this concept have chosen to refer to it as the "Jesus only" doctrine. This view proclaims that only One Person is involved in the Godhead. That single Person has been manifested in three different ways; as Father, Son, and Holy Spirit. These are perceived as three offices or functions instead of three distinct personalities. The parallel is made of a man performing three different roles — John Doe the carpenter, plumber, and teacher. The "Name" of God is proclaimed to be "Jesus," to the exclusion of all other supposed names. Baptism, for instance, is valid only if accompanied by the words "in Jesus' name." The words of Jesus Himself concerning baptism ("in the Name of the Father, and of the Son, and of the Holy Ghost" Matt. 28:19) are said to be a reference to titles of Jesus. The fulfillment of His commandment is declared to have taken place when Peter commanded those that receive the Word of God to be baptized "in the name of JESUS" (Acts. 2:38).

Not only does this doctrine evidence an inexusably cursory view of the Word of God, it betrays a fundamental ignorance of the Person of Jesus Christ. In the Scriptures, the word "name" is not meant to connote a mere earthly appellation. It is a term describing the character of the person possessing it, and often is used as a description of the person himself. Adam's wife was called "Eve" (Living) because she was the "mother of all living" (Gen. 3:20). Abram's name was changed to "Abraham" (Father of a great multitude) because God made him "a father of many nations" (Gen. 17:5). Sarai, Abraham's wife, had her name changed to "Sarah" (Princess) because God determined He would "bless her, and she shall be a mother of nations; kings of people shall be of her" (Gen. 17:5).

The "name of the Lord" identifies His Person, His character, His attributes! When the Lord proclaimed His "Name" to Moses, He did not simply recite the word "Jehovah!" He declared His nature! "And the Lord stood with him, and proclaimed the name of the Lord. And the

Lord passed by before him, and proclaimed, The Lord, The Lord God, merciful and gracious, longsuffering, and abundant in goodness and truth, keeping mercy for thousands, forgiving iniquity and transgression and sin, and that will by no means clear the guilty; visiting the iniquity of the fathers upon the children, and upon the children's children, unto the third and to the fourth generation" (Exod. 34:5-7). It is obvious that the declaring of God's Name was the revelation of His Person!

There are numerous references to the "name" of the Lord — and all of them provide insight into His Person and will. God told Moses His name was "Jealous" because He was "a jealous God" (Exod. 34:14). When asked by Moses what to say to those asking the name of his God, the Lord provided the name "I AM THAT I AM" (Exod. 3:13). Later, on the banks of the Red Sea, Israel declared in song "the LORD is His name" (Exod. 15:3). David spoke of "His name JAH" (Psa. 68:4). Isaiah, in a prophetic picture of the coming Messiah, wrote, "and His name shall be called Wonderful, Counsellor, The Mighty God, The Everlasting Father, The Prince of Peace" (Isa. 9:6). He also said that the coming Savior's name would be "Immanuel" (Isa. 7:14; Matt. 1:23). In another revelation of Deity, Isaiah said, "the Lord of hosts is His name" (Isa. 47:4), while Amos declared "the God of hosts is His name" (Amos 4:13; 5:27). Zechariah said of the Messiah, "whose name is The Branch" (Zech. 6:12).

The point to see in all of these texts is that the Name of the Lord is a means of revealing what He is like — how He works, how He reacts to men, and what dictates His manners.

The unitarian dogma is not an innocent departure from the mainstream of Christian doctrine. It is a heresy of monumental proportions. It constitutes a flagrant denial of the very "rock," or foundation, of salvation! Jesus is "the Christ the Son of the Living God" (Matt. 16:16-18). This is the fountain from which the water of life springs. If this is denied, there is no hope of eternal life! Here are the strong and clear words of the Apostle; "He that believeth on the Son of God hath the witness in himself: he that believeth not God hath made Him a liar, because he believeth not the record that God gave of His Son. And this is the record, that God hath given us eternal life, and this life is in His Son. He that hath the Son hath life; and he that hath not the Son of God hath not life" (I John 5:10-11).

The concept of salvation is completely destroyed by corrupting the truth that God sent His Son into the world to reconcile men to Himself. That Deity vacated heaven during Jesus' earthly ministry is so inconceivable that only Satan could seduce men into believing it — and yet this is required if there is only one Person in the Godhead.

It will do no good to claim Divine omnipresence for Jesus while He was in the world. Jesus Himself declared that He was "straitened" while "in the flesh" (Luke 12:50; I John 4:2,3). That was occasioned by the emptying of Himself for the redemption of man (Phil. 2:6-7)!

The acceptance of the delusion that a single Individual comprises the Godhead would force us to unreasonable conclusions. Christ's prayers would then have been to Himself, even though He addressed them to the "Father" (Matt. 11:35; 26:39). He would have come to fulfill His own mission, even though He emphatically denied that such was the case (John 5:30; 15:10). We would also be required to believe that He is both Vine and Husbandman, when He taught us that He was the Vine, and His Father the Husbandman (John 15:1).

Jesus said, "My Father is greater than I" (John 14:28! He revealed that His Father taught Him (John 8:28), and that He spoke that which He had "seen" with His Father (John 8:38). He honored His Father (John 8:49), and received a commandment from Him to lay His life down and take it up again (John 10:18). His Kingdom was "appointed" to Him by the Father (Luke 22:29), and the redeemed shall be confessed by Him to the Father (Matt. 10:32). Jesus is the Divine Implementer of God's will — and He is accomplishing that implementation as "The Son of God"!

The Man Christ Jesus

In anticipation of the Savior of men, the prophet Isaiah said, "And A MAN shall be as an hiding place from the wind, and a covert from the tempest; as rivers of water in a dry place, as the shadow of a great rock in a weary land" (Isa. 32:2). This language foresaw Divine protection for penitent men. Paul declared the fulfillment of the prophecy. "For there is one God, and one Mediator between God and men, THE MAN Christ Jesus" (I Tim. 2:5). That Mediator fulfills the need of man, and man provides a ministry for the Mediator. Man cannot deal with God without the Mediator, and there is nothing to mediate without man! The Mediator is only required because of men!

God's provision of a Mediator for man — and for man alone — is a

271

commentary on the value He has attached to him. The value is not the result of man's achievement, but because of his potential. That potential has its realization in intimacy with the Living God!

From the viewpoint of promised provisions, the Savior is preeminently "Christ." From the vantage of the effect of His work, He is mainly "Jesus" — the Deliverer. Viewing the same Wonderful Lord from the standpoint of those for Whom He was made known, He is "THE MAN"! "The Man Christ Jesus" — what a marvelous revelation!

Jesus represented a new order of man — a new kind of man. Adam was the "first man," but Jesus was "THE SECOND MAN." Obviously, this is not a chronological designation. Sequentially, Cain was the second man (Gen. 4:1). "Second," in Scripture, speaks of a new order — a new kind.

In the tabernacle, the "second veil" was a different kind of veil (Heb. 9:3). Its separation was of a higher order than the entry veil. The "second" section of the tabernacle was of a different order. Into it went the High Priest alone, and that only once a year (Heb. 9:5-10). The "second" convenant — the new testament — was a different type of covenant, "not according" to the previous one (Heb. 10:9; 8:9). The "second death" is one of another order — eternal condemnation (Rev. 2:1; 20:6).

Jesus, as "the second Man" is "the beginning, the Firstborn from the dead" (Col. 1:18). As He Himself testified to the church at Laodicea, "These things saith the Amen, the faithful and true witness, the beginning of the creation of God" (Rev. 3:14). The emphasis here is not on "creation," but on "beginning." It is not that Jesus Christ was "created," as the Jehovah's Witnesses falsely teach. He was the first of a new creation — a new order of man. His personal "goings forth have been from of old, from everlasting" (Micah 5:2).

Jesus was the God-man; a union of heaven and earth. The "fullness of the Godhead dwelt in Him bodily" (Col. 2:9). He "was tempted in all points like as we are" (Heb. 4:15), and yet had the Holy Spirit without "measure" (John 3:34). Heaven and earth brought together in a single Person. How glorious the wisdom of God!

Those in Christ Jesus are possessed of a dual nature. This is called the "old man" and the "new man" in Scripture (Col. 3:9). The "old man" is the unregenerate part of man, the "new man" is the result of being "joined to the Lord" (I Cor. 6:17). Put in another way, those that are in Christ Jesus have a heavenly "treasure" in an "earthly vessel" (II Cor. 4:7). They have been made "partakers of Christ" and of "the Divine Nature" (Heb. 3:14; II Pet. 1:4) while yet "in the body." This never occurred prior to the enthronement of Jesus! As the "Second Man," He heads up a new order of men — those that shall eventually blend with eternity, and reign with Him!

The "Last Adam"

Not only was Jesus the first of a new order, He was the "last" of the old order! The Adamic order is no longer recognized by God! It has been put away by means of a vicarious death. That is the affirmation of God! "God sending His own Son in the likeness of sinful flesh, and for sin, condemned sin in the flesh" (Rom. 8:3). Those that "walk in the flesh" and "mind the things of the flesh" are excluded from the Kingdom of God, and "cannot please" Him (Rom. 8:8,13; II Pet. 2:10).

The removal of condemnation is the firstfruits of God's purpose! Integral to man's reconciliation to God is his separation from the natural order — his denial of ungodliness and worldly lusts (Titus 2:12).

The consideration of fallen man is essential to the concept of "the Last Adam." It is also an inseparable part of God's "eternal purpose." No man, no Jesus! No man, no salvation! Even though fallen and blighted by sin, the coming of Jesus has verified man's value to God!

Divine Objectives and Their Implementation

Jesus has been appointed by God to implement His objectives for men. The affirmations of Christ confirm this to our hearts. We must make an association between what Jesus did and what God desired. If we fail to do this, we shall have missed the purpose for the Savior, who came to do His Father's will.

The Son of God left no doubt concerning this point. To a group of wondering disciples He said, "My meat is to do the will of Him that sent Me, and to finish His work" (John 4:34). Again He declared, ". . . I seek not Mine own will, but the will of the Father which hath sent me" (John 5:30). In a concise statement of His personal objectives, the Lord said to the multitudes, "For I came down from heaven, not to do Mine own will, but the will of Him that sent Me" (John 6:38).

He glorified God by finishing the work that He was given to do. That

273

is what He confessed to His Father the night of His betrayal: "I have glorified Thee on the earth: I have finished the work which Thou gavest Me to do" (John 17:4).

He Came In His Father's Name

The devotion of Jesus to His Father's will is in all of His personal testimonies. On one occasion, when "the Jews sought the more to kill Him" (John 5:18, He confessed, "I am come in My Father's name . . ." (John 5:43). Another time, as He "walked in the Temple in Solomon's porch," He said to the gathering of Jews, ". . . the works that I do in My Father's name, they bear witness of Me" (John 10:25). The phrase, "in My Father's name," identifies the reason for Christ's words and works. He was on a mission from the Father. What He said carried all of the weight of God's voice thundering out of heaven. There was not one particle of difference between what Jesus said and did and what God wanted said and done! The Father would have done nothing different, said nothing different! Jesus was consumed with the will of God — He honored no other will, not even His own (Luke 22:42).

Jesus' words are never to be considered independently of God. His speech was in conformity with His commission to "seek and to save that which was lost." God is glorified by an awareness of this truth. This is witnessed by Jesus' words to His own countrymen: "When ye shall have lifted up the Son of man, then shall ye know that I am He [the Messiah], and that I do nothing of Myself; but as My Father hath taught Me, I speak these things" (John 8:28). "I speak to the world those things which I have heard of Him" (John 8:26), He declared. Again He affirms His dependency upon His Father; "For I have not spoken of Myself; but the Father which sent Me, He gave Me a commandment, what I should say, and what I should speak . . . whatsoever I speak therefore, even as the Father said unto Me, so I speak" (John 12:49-50). The weight of these words cannot be ignored by inquiring minds.

Jesus was not a novel wonder-worker! He worked the works of God — i.e., He was accomplishing God's objective. What Jesus did was not a mere Divine reaction to temporary circumstances. There was eternal design in what He wrought! His works blended with God's "eternal purpose" for man. "I must work the works of Him that sent Me," He declared (John 9:4). So precisely did those works reflect the purpose of

God that Jesus could say, "Believe Me that I am in the Father, and the Father in Me: or else believe Me for the very works' sake (John 14:10).

This chapter's rather lengthy introduction has served to demonstrate that Jesus Christ cannot be properly contemplated without a preeminent consideration of God. God's Kingdom is incomplete without God's Son — its Implementer. Further, Jesus serves no real purpose apart from His implementation of God's redemptive objectives!

God's Requirement for an Implementer

God does nothing superfluous. If He sends His Son to reconcile the world unto Himself, it is because there is no other possible way to accomplish that objective. If He appoints an Intercessor, it is because One is required. He is all-wise and all-powerful, and those attributes have merged in the accomplishment of man's salvation. Nothing has been provided that is not necessary. The existence of the Heavenly Implementer confirms His Divine requirement!

The Lord is holy and exalted. Man's sin — and "all have sinned" — has placed a moral gulf between him and God. This situation demands someone to "stand in the gap" that sin created (Ezek. 22:30). A third party is required that will perfectly execute God's purpose, and yet be able to identify with the needs of the fallen ones. Jesus Christ perfectly fufills this need! The nature of the "high and lofty One that inhabiteth eternity" has created this requirement (Isa. 57:15).

"I the Lord your God am holy," God said to Israel (Lev. 19:2). His character is untainted with iniquity, spotless and pure. The holiness of God, apart from Christ, prohibits His immediate fellowship with man. To Israel, Joshua said, "Ye cannot serve the Lord, for He is holy, He is a jealous God" (Josh. 24:19). "Who is able to stand before this holy Lord God?" (I Sam. 6:20) is still a universal question.

The holiness of God is the reason why sin brings alienation from Him (Eph. 4:18; Col. 1:21). God will not compromise His holiness in order to resolve the problem of man's alienation. On the other hand, He will not compromise His character by abandoning His undertaking to restore man. The sending of Jesus solved these difficulties — both the alienation of man and the justice of God.

Man's Obtuseness Concerning God

Sin has so dulled man's spiritual capacities that he is unable of himself to apprehend the Lord's person or blessing. "God is great, and we know Him not" (Job 36:26), is an appropriate confession for all ages! In a blazing condemnation of the entire race of man, Paul confirmed "There is none that understands [God], there is none that seeks after God" (Rom. 3:11). The concept introduced here is not that man is incapable of understanding God, but that he is unwilling! The capacity is there — God put it there — and God wants to be known!

The stirring words of the prophet Isaiah serve to illustrate the dilemma created by man's transgression; "And there is none that calls upon Thy name, that stirs up himself to take hold of Thee: for Thou hast hid Thy face from us, and hast consumed us because of our iniquities" (Isa. 64:7). The judgment was that men did not arouse themselves Godward, not that they could not!

Prior to Jesus, there were a few men that excelled their peers in their desire to know God: Noah, Abraham, Isaac, Jacob, Joseph, Moses, and the prophets. But God desired not just a few representatives from among men, but "all men" (II Tim. 2:4; Titus 2:11). A marked insensitivity toward God, however, was found throughout mankind.

This situation called for the introduction of a Third Party — One that would implement God's revealed desires. Four millennia of time yielded no change in the situation. Man was still dull toward God, still insensitive concerning His great desires. He sorely required one like unto Himself that would unveil heavenly realities, and make them discernible to him. Man's discernment was also required by God — else He would not have provided One. Jesus Christ was His appointed remedy for the situation!

The Inadequacy of Overt Demonstration

Some might contend that an unquestionable demonstration of Divine power would awaken man from the lethargy to which sin had reduced him. An overt demonstration that could be clearly perceived by the senses — surely this would provide adequate stimulation! The Divine record, however, shows that this is not the case.

The most universal display of Divine intervention is the Noahic flood. There was nothing that approximated this revelation in prior history, and there has been nothing after it. In the flood, the complete order of nature was shaken. The "windows of heaven were opened," and for forty days and forty nights the skies emptied themselves. The "fountains of the great deep" were "broken up," as the earth shook and convulsed under the mighty judgment of God (Gen. 7:11-12). If a visible demonstration could enable men to remain holy and have intimacy with the Living God, the flood had met the need.

The stark reality of the case, however, is that within approximately one century God had been forgotten, and man again became the center of his own attention. The attempt to "build a city and a tower whose top may reach into heaven," and the determination to "make us a name" occurred within memory of the flood. Noah and Shem, the progenitor of the promised Seed, were still alive (Gen. 9:28-29; 11:10-11). Yet their experience — unequalled in the annals of time — was not sufficient to induce man's involvement in God's purpose.

Signs, Wonders, and Israel

The nation of Israel served to dramatically demonstrate the inadequacy of physical phenomena to implement God's objective. In their deliverance from Egyptian bondage, for instance, ten plagues of unspeakable magnitude occurred. In all of these plagues, the land of Goshen, where the Israelites were held captive, was exempted. Thus a twofold witness of God's mighty power was given. First, in the cursing of Egypt, and second in the protection of Israel. Yet in all of Egypt, this action did not produce a single expression of faith!

Following their departure from Egypt, Israel passed through the Red Sea on dry ground (Exod. 14:22), saw the Egyptian armies drowned in the same waters (Exod. 14:23-30), and were fed miraculous bread from heaven — for forty years (Exod. 16:4-31). They twice drank rivers of water out of a rock (Exod. 17:5-7; Num. 20:8-11), and saw the sun stand still for a day (Josh. 10:12-14). Yet these very people were noted for their hardness of heart and dullness of spirit. In fact, we are admonished not to be as they were (I Cor. 10:6-11). It is evident that external demonstrations of Divine power cannot accomplish God's ultimate objective for man! Therefore, Jesus was sent to be the Divine Implementer!

The Binder of the Strong Man

In order for the purpose of God to be achieved, the "adversaries of the Lord" must be broken (I Sam. 2:10). The enemy of God and opponent of man — Satan — must be effectually subdued if men are to be rescued! He had successfully deceived "the whole word" (Rev. 12:9). Who will subdue him?

As we look to the sons of men, we can find no one capable of fulfilling this requirement. Adam could not do it — sin entered by him (Rom. 5:15-19). Abraham, who lied, is disqualified (Gen. 12:13; 19:20), as well as Moses, who struck the rock to which he was to speak (Num. 20:10). David, who himself was seduced, cannot subdue the temptor (II Sam. 11:1-27). These represent the most righteous of our race — and yet they are powerless to subdue our enemy!

Jesus proclaimed that deliverance could not be achieved until Satan was bound. "But if I cast out devils [demons] by the Spirit of God, then the Kingdom of God is come unto you. Or else how can one enter into a strong man's house, and spoil his goods, except he first bind the strong man; and then He will spoil his house" (Matt. 12:28-29). Satan is the "strong man" to which Jesus refers, and the world is his "house." Men are the "goods" which Satan has captivated, and Jesus is the "One" who is addressing that situation. When He came into the world, He entered the strong man's house. His earthly ministry began, and His death and resurrection consummated, the binding of the strong man. The objective was to liberate captive man in order that God's purpose might be fulfilled!

The binding of Satan is not merely a judicial binding — i.e., it was not simply accomplished by the enactment of a Divine law. There was action involved — Divine works. Satan is now under very real restriction. He was not bound from heaven, but from earth. The Man from heaven entered Satan's house to bind him! God often restrained him from heaven, as in the case of Job (Job 1-2), but the Kingdom of God involves loftier objectives than were known in Job's twilight age. The effectual subduement of Satan would require a face-to-face confrontation — in his domain. The Incarnation set the stage for that confrontation.

Although Satan was directly confronted by Jesus, his binding was accomplished indirectly. The subduing of wicked spiritual forces is not achieved by hand-to-hand combat. Victory or defeat involves truth and error, right and wrong, good and evil. The Devil cannot be bound by simply tying his hands behind his back, so to speak. As a spirit — a wicked spirit — he is now subdued indirectly. In the end of time, he will be cast into the lake of fire.

The binding of Satan and the destruction of Satan are terms for the same reality. The achievement can be viewed from several different angles — all of which focus on the accomplishments of Jesus, the Divine Implementer.

In Christ's death, He dealt a decisive blow to the Prince of this world. Concerning His Manhood and consequent death, it is written, "He also Himself likewise took part of the same [flesh and blood]; that through death He might destroy him that had the power of death, that is the Devil" (Heb. 2:14). "Through death" — an indirect defeat!

Jesus, being "separate from sinners" and "undefiled" (Heb. 7:26) did not die of moral necessity. "The soul that sins, IT shall die," — that was the judgment of God (Ezek. 18:4,20). Here was a Man that did not fit into that category. Apart from the purpose of God, there was no reason for this Man to die. In fact, His death was voluntary, and an act of His will. "No man takes it [My life] from Me, but I lay it down of Myself," Jesus declared. That dark day on Golgotha, Jesus dismissed His own spirit as He expired — Satan did not take it from Him (Luke 23:46).

Satan had no claim on Jesus — he could not keep Him in the grave. Jesus, in His death, represented all men everywhere. Satan himself cannot contradict or dispute what has been done. An innocent Man, with the sins of the world laid upon Him, has voluntarily laid down His life, and endured the abandonment of God Almighty. All that are joined to Him in His death (Rom. 6:16) participate in His victory. That death becomes the point of Satan's destruction. He has been effectually bound by means of the death of God's Lamb!

Spoiling Principalities and Powers

"Principalities and powers" had blinded the world for four millennia, maintaining "gross darkness" over the people (Isa. 60:2). Here were the "rulers of the darkness of this world" (Eph. 6:12), achieving consistent success in their diabolical work since the day Adam and Eve were driven out of the garden. No man, no work, no power, had been able to abort their efforts or free their captives. Even godly men throughout history lamented the fact that they had been influenced by these perpetrators of spiritual ignorance (Psa. 32:5; Isa. 6:5; Jer. 14:7; Dan. 9:5; Hosea 14:3; Micah 7:9).

It was not altogether due to the strength of these principalities and powers, however, that they had achieved such universal success. It was

279

also because of the weakness of man — his nature had been corrupted, and the Divine Image marred by his involvement in sin.

All men were potentially freed from Satan's grasp when Jesus laid down His life, and took it up again. Speaking of the accomplishments of Christ's death, the Apostle wrote,

> And you, being dead in your sins and the uncircumcision of your flesh, hath He quickened together with Him, having forgiven you all trespasses; blotting out the handwriting of ordinances that was against us, which was contrary to us, and took it out of the way, nailing it to His cross; and having spoiled [stripped and plundered] principalities and powers, He made a show of them openly, triumphing over them in it [the cross] (Col.2:13-15).

The authority of these principalities, which man's enslavement to sin had demonstrated, was broken at the cross. There sin was successfully dealt with — in view of God's purpose. No individual embracing that atonement (Rom. 5:11) can be held captive by Satan or his hierarchy of wicked personalities. Jesus, by stripping them of their authority, indirectly freed all of their slaves. It only remains for man to be united with that death in baptism (Rom. 6:3-4; Col. 2:12-13), and united with that cross by faith (I Cor. 1:17-18; Gal. 6:14).

Captivity Led Captive

The liberation of man from the tyranny of Satan is also identified with Christ's ascension. Quoting from the sixty-eighth Psalm, Paul writes, "Wherefore He saith, When He ascended up on high, he led captivity captive, and gave gifts to men" (Eph. 4:8; Psa. 68:18). The Psalm itself was one of triumph that proclaimed the scattering of God's enemies (Psa. 68:1). It doubtless had reference to those days when the ark went before the people of God in anticipation of victory (Num. 10:35-36).

But the Apostle's point is not to interpret the meaning of the Psalmist, but to apply the principle that it sets forth to the return of Christ to heaven. Jesus returned to His Father's house as the undisputed Conqueror of the region of darkness. Satan, sin, and death had now lost their power for everyone that would "receive Him."

Christ's defeat of the enemy is evidenced in the effects of salvation.

Men in Him can "resist the Devil, and he will "flee from" them (James 4:7). Sin no longer has dominion over them, for they are "not under the law, but under grace" (Rom. 6:14). And death now belongs to them; as it is written, "For all things are yours; whether . . . death . . . all things are yours" (I Cor. 3:22).

When Jesus returned from the region of the dead, and began His ascent from Olivet to glory, with the clouds as His chariots and the winds as His steeds, those saints that had passed on before, "not having received the promises," were left with a hope not possessed before! What shouting there must have been in Paradise, reverberating throughout those hidden chambers, "The Sun of righteousness has arisen with healing in His wings" (Mal. 4:2)!

The Accuser of the Brethren Cast Down

Prior to the "day of salvation" (I Cor. 6:1-2), Satan was a regular attendant before God's Throne. He came there to accuse and malign those that trusted in God. Some insight is granted into this condition in the book of Job. We are told that there "was a day when the sons of God came to present themselves before the Lord, and Satan came also among them." This situation occurred two times (Job. 1:6; 2:1). Both times, Satan reproached Job, of whom God said, "Hast thou considered my servant Job, that there is none like him in the earth, a perfect and upright man, one that fears God and eschews evil?" (Job 1:8).

With diabolical hatred, Satan responded, "Doth Job fear God for nought? . . . But put forth Thine hand now, and touch all that he hath, and he will curse thee to thy face" (Job 1:9-11). The account reveals that Satan was given "power" over all that Job had. In a unique demonstration of his wicked nature, he immediately effected the destruction of Job's wealth and children — but Job did not curse God. A second attempt was made after a similar period of accounting before the Almighty, and was also met with failure (Job 2:3-10). Here was "the accuser'" at the height of his permission and power!

But the situation has changed now that Jesus has been exalted to God's right hand. In an obvious reference to the Lord's Christ, the result of redemption is proclaimed in Scripture. Jesus, during His initial ministry upon earth, said that He "beheld Satan as lightning fall from heaven" (Luke 10:18). John reveals to us that this was the result of his being overcome and cast out of the heavenly domain. "And there was war in heaven: Michael and his angels fought against the dragon; and the dragon fought and his angels, and prevailed not; neither was their place found any more in heaven. And the great dragon was cast out, that old serpent, called the Devil, and Satan, which deceives the world: he was cast out into the earth, and his angels were cast out with him" (Rev. 12:7-9).

The attempt to place that event in the future betrays a very fundamental ignorance of Christ and His accomplishments. This is specifically identified with the redemption of Christ — there is no question about it. A loud voice sounded "out of heaven," providing us with an inspired interpretation of this event. "Now is come salvation and strength, and the Kingdom of our God, and the power of His Christ; for the accuser of the brethren is cast down, which accused them before our God day and night. And they overcame him by the blood of the Lamb . . ." (Rev. 12:9-10).

This perfectly coincides with Christ's announcement on earth that the Kingdom of God had come, as evidenced by His dismissal of demonic powers (Luke 11:20). THE STRONG MAN HAD BEEN BOUND, thus permitting the implementation of God's purpose. There was no man that could accomplish this but Jesus!

Now, instead of "the accuser of the brethren" being before our God day and night, saints have an Advocate there — One that "ever lives to make intercession for them" (Heb. 7:25). Satan has not only been bound; his position has been filled by One that loves us and gave Himself for us (Gal. 2:20)!

Delivered from the Power of Darkness

God, through Christ, has liberated men from the grip of spiritual ignorance. "The Father," Paul asserts, is the One "Who hath delivered us from the power of darkness . . ." (Col. 1:13). Note — we have been delivered from the power of darkness, not from darkness itself. This introduces a moral situation — one which requires the action of man. The rulers of darkness have no authority in the realm of faith. They are impregnable in the arena of unbelief! The deliverance which has been wrought by Christ must be apropriated by faith. That is, after all, "the victory" (I John 5:4-5).

Thus Jesus has effectively bound the strong man. Satan is powerless "in Christ." It remains for man to capitalize upon his demise by a reception of and obedience to the Gospel.

Making an End of Sin

Daniel prophesied of Christ, that one of His objectives was to "make an end of sins" — i.e., to conclude their dominion over men (Dan. 9:26). This would be accomplished by assuming the responsibility for their sins, and paying the penalty for them. There are several inspired phrases that portray this marvelous accomplishment.

Destroying the Works of the Devil

The Son of God, John states, was manifested for a particular purpose: "that He might destroy the works of the devil" (I John 3:8). The "works of the devil" are the fruits of his labors. They are the results of temptation, allurement, and enticement to the unlawful. He, too, is implementing a purpose — an evil one — and his works are his endeavors to achieve that objective.

These "works" are destroyed by cleansing — by the removal of the guilt that they generate in the conscience of men. The fact that men have sinned cannot, and will not, be removed; but the impact of that fact is destroyed by Christ's atonement. Satan's objective is thus frustrated, and his works are for naught. All those in Christ receive this benefit. Thus has our Lord made an "end of sins."

Made a Curse for Us

The Law of God, because of sin, had brought a curse upon all mankind. Under its abrasive ministry "all the world" had become "guilty before God," and every self-justifying mouth had been "stopped" (Rom. 3:19). That guilt must be dealt with if man is to be received by God.

It is written, "Christ hath redeemed us from the curse of the Law, being made a curse for us: for it is written, Cursed is every one that hangs upon a tree" (Gal. 3:13). The curse, once put upon our Lord and borne by Him, cannot be again visited upon those who flee to Him for refuge from it. "There is therefore now no condemnation to them which are in Christ Jesus, who walk not after the flesh, but after the Spirit" (Rom. 8:1). Jesus has delivered all such from the curse.

A Propitiation

A "propitiation," as we have said, is a covering — a merciful covering. The root of the word is found in the Law, specifically in the Tabernacle arrangements. There, in the most holy place, was the "ark of the covenant" (Exod. 25:16; Num. 10:33; Heb. 9:4). Within that "ark" were the "tables of the covenant" (Heb. 9:4). Covering it was a "mercy seat" — a propitiatory — upon which atonement for sin was made (Lev. 16:14). Thus was an appeal made to the mercy of God as regarded the transgression of the Law.

Jesus is man's "propitiation" — the covering of mercy. "Christ Jesus, Whom God hath set forth to be a propitiation through faith in His blood . . ." (Rom. 3:25). "And He is the propitiation for our sins; and not for ours only, but also for the sins of the whole world" (I John 2:2). "Herein is love, not that we loved God, but that He loved us, and sent His Son, to be the propitiation for our sins" (I John 4:10).

As God views men through Christ, He cannot see their sins. That is what has freed Him to bless man and walk with Him. But that Divinely provided Covering applies only to those that have "faith in the blood" — that are persuaded of the truth and effectuality of Jesus' sacrifice. This is also God's provision for Himself — one that enables Him to righteously confer the benefits of the New Covenant upon men.

Purging the Conscience

The experiential side of the "end of sins" is found in the purging of the conscience (Heb. 9:14). The alienating effects of guilt are thus removed, enabling the recipient to come near to God with a "true heart in full assurance of faith, having his heart "sprinkled from an evil conscience," and his body "washed with pure water" (Heb. 10:22). In such a case, there is "no more conscience of sins" (Heb. 10:2).

The washing of our bodies with "pure water" refers to the individual's obedience in baptism. Baptism is the "form of the doctrine" (Rom. 6:17) — a physical enactment of spiritual reality. There is a very real death to sin that occurs at that time, and a union with the Lord's Christ accomplished. Accompanied by faith, obedience in baptism will result in a cleansed conscience — "the answer of a good conscience toward God" (I Pet. 3:21). The spirit of alienation and enmity will be removed, and the "Spirit of adoption" will prompt the cry of a child at ease before God — "Abba, Father" (Rom. 8:15; Gal. 4:6). Those with a purged conscience feel at home with God, and are not even fearful of the day of judgment (I John 4:17).

No Law, No Transgression

We are categorically told that Jesus "abolished in His flesh the enmity, even the law of commandments contained in ordinances" (Eph. 2:15), ". . . and took it out of the way, nailing it to His cross" (Col. 2:14). He is truly "the end of the Law for righteousness to everyone that believeth" (Rom. 10:4).

In Christ, we stand liberated from the condemning ministry of the Law. It is now written in our heart, and is no longer contrary to us (II Cor. 3:3; Heb. 8:8-13). The past transgressions of men no longer can keep them from God — not if they receive the atonement.

It was this reality that prompted the Apostolic observation, "Because the Law works wrath; for where no law is, there is no transgression" (Rom. 4:15). This is not a proclamation of license — not an announcement of man's release from obligation to God. Such a doctrine would be perversion of Scripture. The meaning of this word is simply this; those joined to Christ, in whose hearts the Law has been inscribed, are not viewed as transgressors by God! They are perceived as "sons" (I John 3:1-3), and rightly so. To be in Christ, you must be taken from under the dominion of the law. You simply cannot be under Law and in Christ at the same time. Wonderful truth! Where no [condemning] law is — and that is where men are "in Christ" — there is no transgression; no cause for condemnation!

Where sins are forgiven, the Law cannot work! The remission of sins places men beyond the reach of the Law, beyond its condemnation, beyond its judgment! When Jesus "washed us from our sins in His own blood" (Rev. 1:5), He ended the "ministration of condemnation" for the washed ones (Acts 22:16; II Cor. 3:9). "Where there is no Law, there is no [record of] transgression" — no condmenation!

The Captain of Salvation

The word "captain" identifies a leader or a ruler (I Sam. 9:16; 22:2). More than that, however, it speaks of initiative — often military initiative. A "captain" is not a mere figurehead; it is one that is active in the development of strategies and leadership.

"God Himself is our Captain," proclaimed Abijah as he stood upon Mount Zemaraim (II Chron. 13:4,12). The acknowledgment of God as their Captain changed the perspective of the battle. "O children of Israel, fight ye not against the Lord God of your fathers; for ye shall not prosper," said that ancient warrior. God was their captain!

In the matter of man's salvation, the Lord Jesus Christ is at the forefront. The responsibility for leadership has been given to Him by the Father, together with all authority in heaven and earth. God, in His preparation of the "Captain of our salvation," made Him "perfect through sufferings" (Heb. 2:10). He was schooled in the arena of conflict, and seasoned for spiritual leadership by feeling in His spirit the pain of suffering. "For in that He Himself hath suffered being tempted, He is able to succor them that are tempted" (Heb. 2:18).

For every weakening temptation, there is appropriate Divine strength, and it is ministered by Jesus Christ, the "Captain" of our "salvation." Salvation, then, is not automatic — it is not a once-for-all experience. Salvation has a Captain, whose function is to assure the success of that salvation in those that believe.

The Author and Finisher of Faith

Salvation as a whole, or any aspect of it, requires the involvement and supervision of the Lord's Christ. Take, for instance, the matter of "our faith" — the means by which salvation is appropriated. Faith is not something dropped down from heaven — it is the apprehension of what is in heaven! Faith itself is not a gift, it is the means of appropriating the gift of eternal life (Rom. 4:23). Jesus is the "Author" of faith because He is the object which it embraces. He is the custodian of eternal life, and He dispenses it to those that believe. He teaches men so that they come to an understanding of God and eternal life (I John 5:20). It is in this sense that He is faith's "Author."

Christ is the "Finisher" of our faith because He will return to bring the "end of our faith, even the salvation of our souls" (I Pet. 1:5). This is the salvation that is "ready to be revealed" (I Pet. 1:5). When that salvation, which includes the "redemption of the body" (Rom. 8:23), is experienced, Jesus shall have finished our faith — brought it to fruition. But it shall not be accomplished without Him! As the Implementer of God's purpose He accomplishes these things.

286

The Good Shepherd

"I AM THE GOOD SHEPHERD," proclaimed the Lord. This function is also required if God's purpose is to be realized. The sheep do require a Shepherd, and a "good" One has been provided from heaven.

Contrary to some contemporary analyses, the sheep do not require a Shepherd because they are stupid, and prone to lose their way in the maze of life. This teaching has a semblance of spirituality in it, but it constitutes a reproach to God! Were this the case, God's creation of man in His own image would have little significance. The impact of faith upon the heart would also be something less than efficacious. If faith does not make us discerning, of what worth is it? The salvation of God brings man's capacities to their peek, and those that have participated in it are anything but wandering and stupid!

One of the responsibilities Jesus fulfilled as the "Good Shepherd" was that of laying down His life "for the sheep" (John 10:10-13). He was bruised by the enemy in order that man might be freed! He grappled with Satan, that devouring "wolf," and thus liberated the sheep! These sheep were open to Satan's abuse because of their involvement in sin. That is what made them vulnerable. Jesus, by taking their sins upon Himself, fulfilled His Father's commandment to "lay down" His "life for the sheep" (John 10:14-15).

The "Good Shepherd" also knows the sheep — is acquainted with their handicaps and liabilities. "I am the Good Shepherd, and know My sheep" (John 10:14). He knows them by experience — having walked where they walked — and is therefore able to nourish them.

He also "goes before them, and the sheep follow Him, for they know His voice" (John 10:5). He went before them in temptation (Heb. 4:15), suffering (Heb. 2:10,18), death (Heb. 2:9), and the ascension (Heb. 6:20)! And He shall go before us when we stand before the God of judgment (Matt. 10:32; Rev. 3:5).

The Counsellor

Isaiah said that the coming Messiah would be called "Counsellor" (Isa. 9:6). Prior to Jesus, "there was no counsellor" (Isa. 41:28) — no one that could properly direct men into a saving acquaintance with the Almighty.

Christ is not a Counsellor in earthly problems, but in eternal matters.

We have an example of some of His counsel to the church at Laodicea. It pertained to God's ultimate purpose for man, and by no means turned man's attention to temporal considerations. "I counsel you to buy of Me gold tried in the fire, that you may be rich; and white raiment, that you may be clothed, and that the shame of your nakedness not appear; and anoint thine eyes with eyesalve, that you may see" (Rev. 3:18).

We have here a summary of Divine provisions. Treasure that will endure the destruction of the world and bring true wealth for the soul, a covering that removes the shame caused by sin, and the enablement to perceive things unseen. It is not possible to negotiate the course to heaven without these spiritual commodities, and they are all obtained by Divine counsel. Jesus is that Counsellor!

The Faithful Witness

A reliable Witness is also required if man is to obtain glory — One that will give us an understanding of the Father and of the things pertaining to life and godliness. Hear the joyous proclamation: "and from Jesus Christ, Who is the Faithful Witness . . ." (Rev. 1:5). And again, "These things saith the Amen, the Faithful and True Witness . . ." (Rev. 3:14).

He is "faithful" because He speaks when He ought to speak and what He ought to speak! He is the "Witness" because His testimony is firsthand. He gives us heaven's perspective! He has come and given us an understanding of "Him that is true," and He has provided it as One that is with Him that is true!

His assessments are true, and His remedies are correct! He assessed the seven churches of Asia, and provided them remedies that would be accepted in heaven (Rev. 2-3). The tutelage of this Counsellor is imperative if men are to be brought to God. He is, again, perceived to be the Implementer of God's purpose!

The Way

The appointed means by which man comes to God is a Person, not a discipline! To be sure, there is personal discipline involved. That is what self-denial and bearing the cross concerns (Luke 9:23). However, unless the endurance of inconvenience and hardship is directly associated with following Christ — with embracing His atonement — it counts for nothing before God. God's purpose cannot be realized in one in separation from His Son.

Jesus said, "I am the way . . . no man comes to the Father, but by Me" (John 14:6). Jesus has no Divine utility for anyone apart from that one's coming to the Father. Oh, that this were known by the multitudes today. Jesus is wholly innaplicable to those with no interest in coming to the God of heaven — appearing before Him in favor. He is the way — the only way — to God, the appointed means of appropriating His favor.

Coming by the appointed "Way" involves hearing Christ (Matt. 17:5; Eph. 4:26), following Him (Matt. 10:38; 16:24), obeying Him (Heb. 5:9), and forfeiting everything that inhibits a knowledge of Him (Phil. 3:7-14).

Conclusion

The redemptive plan is the Father's; the Son is responsible for implementing it. There is no reason for Jesus — for God manifest in the flesh — apart from that Divine objective!

I have labored to show the perfect sense of this arrangement. Here is where man receives hope — here is where the things of God become accessible to him. He could not fulfill God's objective for himself, and thus required a Daysman that could accomplish the requirement.

17

JESUS — THE ADMINISTRATOR

Over twenty-five times the Lord said to Israel, "and ye shall know that I am the Lord." In addition, the reason for Divine injunctions was often said to be "that ye might know that I am the Lord" (Deut. 29:6). Again it is written, "that thou mightest know that the Lord, He is God" (Deut. 4:35). This is the language of Divine objective — the heart of God's Kingdom!

The knowledge of God reaches its highest potential in the salvation that is in Christ Jesus. Here God is seen, and His objectives perceived, most clearly. There is less mystery, fewer areas of vagueness, and more lengthy development of Divine motivations.

The writings of the New Testament are considerably less in volume than those of the Old Testament.

Quantitatively, the New Testament writings contain only 41 percent of the number of books in the Bible, 28 percent of the number of chapters, 31 percent of the number of pages, 34 percent of the verses, and 30 percent of the words. Yet, who would dare to declare that it had less content, fewer truths, or decreased insights?

Where understanding is prevalent fewer words are required, less demonstration is necessary, and the requirement for rules is diminished. In confirmation of this, the Apostle summed up the social aspects of the Decalogue: "For this, Thou shalt not commit adultery, Thou shalt not kill, Thou shalt not steal, Thou shalt not bear false witness, Thou shalt not covet; and if there be any other commandment, it is briefly comprehended in this saying, namely, Thou shalt love thy neighbor as thyself" (Rom. 13:9).

The prevalence of "spiritual understanding" (Col. 1:9) during this "day of salvation" is completely attributable to the Lord Jesus Christ — God's Administrator! He has, by His death and resurrection, produced the basis for the opening of the "eyes of the understanding" (Eph. 1:18), and now He is administrating an "understanding" through the appointed means of His Word (I John 5:20).

In Christ, Men Free to Receive the Blessing

Under the Law, with no provision for the remission of sins, God could not bless men as He does in Christ. Man, in general, did not have a heart to serve God. Even when the children of Israel were at the peak of willingness, they fell woefully short of the Divine objective. In his rehearsal of the covenant God made with Israel at Horeb (Deut. 5:1), Moses reminded the people of their commitment. "And ye said, Behold, the Lord our God hath showed us His glory and His greatness, and we have heard His voice . . . speak thou unto us all that the Lord our God shall speak unto thee; and we will hear it, and do it" (Deut. 5:27). Noble aspiration, indeed!

Moses recalled God's assessment of the situation: "I have heard the voice of the words of this people, which they have spoken unto thee: they have well said all that they have spoken. O that there were such a heart in them, that they would fear Me, and keep my commandments always, that it might be well with them forever" (Deut. 5:28-29). God, Who requires purity of heart, could not confer the blessing of eternal life on those people!

The situation, however, has changed in Christ. He has been appointed to announce the liberation of man. That day in an obscure synagogue in Nazareth, "where He had been brought up," Jesus proclaimed His mission. Having been given "the book of the prophet Isaiah," He opened it, and "found the place where it was written, The

292

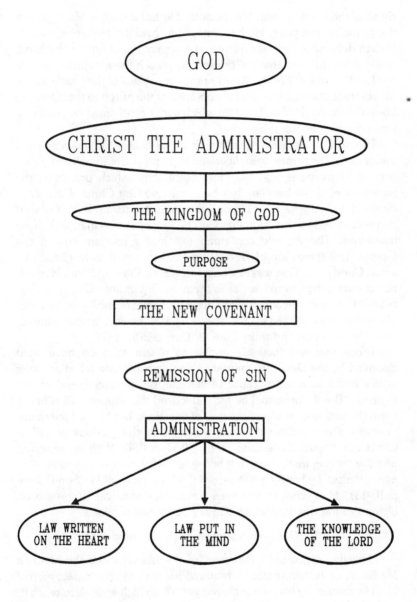

293

Spirit of the Lord is upon Me, because He has anointed Me to preach
the gospel to the poor; He has sent Me to heal the brokenhearted, to
preach deliverance to the captives, and recovering of sight to the blind,
to set at liberty them that are bruised, to preach the acceptable year of
the Lord" (Luke 4:17-19). Isaiah's prophecy spoke of the proclamation
of "liberty to the captives, and the opening of the prison to them that are
bound" (Isa. 61:1). The freedom which Jesus proclaimed was real — it
was not just a figure of speech.

This was not political freedom or moral license. It was a spiritual
freedom in which men were liberated to appropriate the Divine provision of forgivenesss and the Holy Spirit. Sin, which prohibited the
reception of these benefits, has been removed by Christ. God "condemned sin in the flesh" of His only begotten Son (Rom. 8:3). The condemnation was so thorough that God no longer credits man with those
trespasses. The Apostle confirmed this in his proclamation of the
Gospel. "All things are of God, Who has reconciled us to Himself by
Jesus Christ . . . God was in Christ reconciling the world unto Himself,
not imputing their trespasses unto them . . ." [but unto Christ] (II Cor.
5:18-19). It only remains for man to accept this reconciliation by belief
of an obedience to the Gospel. That is what is involved in that admonition, "be ye reconciled unto God" (II Cor. 5:20).

Those that feel they are unable to obtain salvation have been
deceived by the Devil. All men are able to appropriate salvation; their
failure to do so is not because of inability, but deception and unwill-
ingness. "But if our gospel be hid," declared the Apostle, "it is hid to
them that are lost: in whom the god of this world has blinded the minds
of them which believe not, lest the light of the glorious gospel of
Christ . . . should shine unto them" (II Cor. 4:4). With sin removed
and the "strong man" bound, it but remains for man — any man — to
assert himself by believing the record God has given of His Son (I John
5:10-11). Men who do not avail themselves of salvation have been
blinded to the freedom which Christ's death has obtained.

The Administration of the Blessing

Until the appointed destruction of the heavens and the earth, a
Mediator, or Administrator, is required for man to appropriate eternal
life. He cannot, by his own achievement, climb high enough to reach it,
and God, because of His infinite holiness, cannot compromise His

character to give it. The blessing must come through an Administrator! Someone must confer the benefit in behalf of God. Jesus is that Administrator!

Think of the many affirmations of this truth. We have "peace with God through our Lord Jesus Christ" (Rom. 5:1). The gift of "eternal life" is declared to be "through Jesus Christ" (Rom. 6:23). The "kindness" that has been exhibited by God toward man has been "through Christ Jesus" (Eph. 2:7). He is the Divine Administrator!

We enter into the spiritual presence of God "by the blood of Jesus" (Heb. 10:19), coming unto God "by Him" (Heb. 7:25). Our spiritual sacrifices are made acceptable to God "by Him" (Heb. 13:15). Men are "rooted and built up in Him" (Col. 2:7) with no hope of spiritual stability apart from intimacy with Him.

A New Kind of Mediator

The righteousness of God and the defilement of man necessitated a mediator. The requirement is not one of mere formality, but of practicality. The objective of the mediator is to stand between two parties. Here are the facts: 1. The superior party has been offended by the inferior one. 2. A reconciliation is desired by the one offended. 3. The claims of the offended one are to be apprehended. 4. The needs of the offending ones must be met.

The concept of a meditor presumes that there is a benefit to be ministered and a willingness for it to be conferred. Kindness and consideration are the environment in which the mediator operates. Wrath and indignation are what is avoided by having a mediator.

Moses As Mediator

The first appointed mediator between God and men was Moses. While the word "mediator" is not used in the writings of "Moses and the prophets" (Luke 16:29), the concept was developed under the old covenant. Paul spoke of Moses when he wrote, ". . . and it [the Law] was ordained by angels in the hand of a mediator" (Gal. 3:19). Moses brought the "words of the covenant" (Deut. 29:1), or the "tables of the covenant" (Deut. 9:9-15), to the people. He mediated the Law! John, writing of the role Moses played as mediator, said, "For the law was given by Moses . . ." (John 1:17).

There is a close affiliation between Moses and the Law which he mediated. This is perceived in the various references made to the Law by Jesus and the Apostles. Jesus referred to those that proclaimed the Law as those that "sit in Moses' seat" (Matt. 23:2). He also said to the doubting multitudes, "Did not Moses give you the Law . . .?" (John 7:19), again referring to it as "the Law of Moses" in John 7:23. Paul, in one of his early defenses, also mentioned "the law of Moses" (Acts 13:39), and the writer of Hebrews wrote of those that "despised Moses' Law" (Heb. 10:28).

Moses mediated between two unreconciled parties — Jehovah God and Israel. Though chosen by God (Deut. 7:7) and blessed by Him, Israel was basically at variance with God. An atonement had not been made for their sin, their thoughts and ways were at variance with God's, and their primary concerns were focused on themselves.

When they came out of Egypt and faced the Red Sea, their rebel-hearts surfaced; "For it had been better for us to serve the Egyptians, than that we should die in the wilderness" (Exod. 14:11-12), they cried. Later, when finding bitter waters, they murmured at the waters of Marah (Exod. 15:23). Again, they murmured because of the lack of food (Exod. 16:2,3), and for want of water at Rephidim (Exod. 17:2-7). They continued to murmur when the unbelieving spies brought back a report that contradicted God's promise to give them Canaan (Num. 14:1-5).

Not content with Moses, they also murmured against him and his brother Aaron (Num. 16:41-50). A second time they murmured because of the lack of water at Meribah (Num. 20:1-12). The history of this people is cluttered with expressions of rebellion and enmity. Moses upbraided them when he said, "Ye have been rebellious against the Lord from the day that I knew you" (Deut. 9:24). In his valedictory, his memory became his enemy as he confessed, "For I know thy rebellion, and thy stiff neck: behold while I am yet alive with you this day, ye have been rebellious against the Lord; and how much more after my death" (Deut. 31:27).

The church is admonished to zealously avoid being like Israel. They are not notable examples for those that live by faith! "We should not lust after evil things, as they also lusted. Neither be ye idolators, as were some of them. . . . Neither let us commit fornication, as some of them committed. . . . Neither let us tempt Christ, as some of them also tempted. . . . Neither murmur ye, as some of them also murmured . . ." (I Cor. 10:6-10). The curses brought against them were a commentary on the magnitude of their transgression. "And fell in one day three and twenty thousand . . . were destroyed of serpents . . . and were destroyed of the destroyer. . . . "

These things occurred because no reconciliation had been accomplished. There were overt blessings — water, bread, and meat; but they were alienated from God! God led them, fed them, and protected them — but they rebelled against Him! He gave them His Law, making it unquestionably plain, and they straightway broke it! They were unreconciled to Him, and that condition required a mediator — else they would have been destroyed!

Moses' mediatorship was primarily to God in behalf of the people. Apart from the "giving of the Law" and its associated ordinances, he brought little to the people from God. His "rod" seemed to serve their desires more than the words of his mouth which had been provided by God.

More than once God's anger waxed hot against these people. It was His appointed mediator, Moses — knowledgeable of the Divine ways — that turned His fierce anger from them.

The giving of the Law provided the most arresting physical environment for Divine communication the world had ever seen. "The earth shook, the heavens also dropped at the presence of God: even Sinai itself was moved at the presence of God, the God of Israel . . . the hill of God is as the hill of Bashan; an high hill as the hill of Bashan. Why leap ye, ye high hills? this is the hill which God desireth to dwell in. . . . The chariots of God are twenty thousand, even thousands of angels: the Lord is among them, as in Sinai, in the holy place" (Psa. 68:8,17).

Over 700 years after the giving of the Law, Habakkuk wrote, "God came from Teman, and the Holy One from mount Paran. Selah. His glory covered the heavens, and the earth was full of His praise, and His brightness was as the light . . ." (Hab. 3:3-4). It was an event without parallel, as those mountain ranges lit up with the glory of God and the earth convulsed at His presence. Surely it was something that would never be forgotten! Would not the fear of the Lord control the nation of Israel?

An alienated heart cannot maintain a remembrance of truth! This is illustrated in Israel's conduct following the display of God's glory in the giving of the law. Before Moses had come down from the mount, they had become involved in idolatry (Exod. 32:6; I Cor. 10:7). God, witnessing their actions "said unto Moses, I have seen this people, and, behold, it is a stiffnecked people: now therefore let Me alone, that my wrath may wax hot against them, and that I may consume them: and I will make of thee a great nation" (Exod. 32:9-10). It is fortunate for Israel that Moses was not like many leaders of our day. In such a case, he would have piously said, "the will of the Lord be done." Instead, Moses pled for the people. "Lord, why doth Thy wrath wax hot against Thy people, which Thou hast brought forth out the land of Egypt with great power, and with a mighty hand?" After reminding God that the Egyptians would conclude that He had delivered Israel only to destroy them, Moses said, "Turn from Thy fierce wrath, and repent of the evil against Thy people. Remember Abraham, Isaac, and Israel. . . ." The Divine response — "And the Lord repented of the evil which He thought to do unto His people" (Exod. 32:11-14).

A second similar occasion occurred when Israel rejected the faithful testimony of Joshua and Caleb, seeking to stone them with stones. Again the Lord told Moses He would "smite them with a pestilence, and disinherit them, and will make of thee a greater nation and a mightier than they." Again, Moses mediated for the people, pleading, "Pardon, I beseech Thee, the iniquity of this people according unto the greatness of Thy mercy . . . And the Lord said, I have pardoned according to thy word" (Num. 14:10-20).

Benefits for Rebels

The Divine provision of benefits for rebels is an Old Testament concept. The condition existed then because of a lack of man's reconciliation to God. Further, the benefits that were given were temporal, not eternal. Eternal blessings cannot be ministered to alienated hearts — that would involve a contradiction of God's character.

The Divine provisions that were given to Israel were all external — temporal. Deliverance (Exod. 14-15), water (Psa. 78:16), bread (John 6:31), meat (Psa. 78:25-30), raiment (Deut. 8:4), a physical tabernacle (Heb. 8-9), and military victory (Num. 21:1-3,21-32,33-35). Notwithstanding all of these advantages, they remained rebellious and obstinate. Moses correctly called them "rebels" when they "provoked his spirit, so that he spake unadvisedly with his lips" (Psa. 106:33;

Num. 20:10). "Rebels," "rebellious" (Deut. 9:7,24), "stubborn" (Psa. 78:8) "stiffnecked" (Exod. 32:9), "stiffhearted" (Ezek. 2:4), "disobedient" (Rom. 10:21), "gainsaying" (Rom. 10:21) — some of the terms ascribed to that ancient people!

Thus was Moses' mediatorship one of heartbreak to him, and pacification to the people. No eternal benefits, and no involvement with God for the people. Their only hope was for Moses to stand between them and the God from Whom they were estranged!

Several brief observations are in order. 1. Overt demonstrations of Divine power have no lasting effect upon the hearts of even a covenanted people. 2. God is incensed by the rebellion of those to whom He has revealed Himself. 3. Moses stood between a holy God and an unholy people. 4. Without Moses the mediator, Israel would surely have been destroyed. 5. The temporal benefits provided to Israel were due more to Moses and his mediatorship than to Israel's receptivity toward God's word.

A Mediator of One

In Christ, we have a new kind of Mediator — One that ministers under a new set of Divinely ordered circumstances. In his declaration of the glorious provisions of the new covenant, Paul writes, "Now a mediator is not the mediator of one, but God is one" (Gal. 3:20). He is making a comparison between the mediatorship of Moses, and that of the Lord Jesus Christ. Moses was a mediator of two — God and the people. He mediated a covenant that depended upon the accomplishments of both God and the people. In his mediatorship, the accomplishments of God were a response to the achievements of the people: "Ye shall therefore keep My statutes, and My judgments: which if a man do, he shall live in them: I am the Lord" (Lev. 18:5). The plan was straightforward: perfect obedience brought the blessing — and there was no promise of the blessing until there was complete obedience! No Savior was provided. No remedy for transgression. No allowance for errors of judgment! Life was to be had, but must be earned under the Law!

But in the case of the New Covenant, "the inheritance" is not of the law, but by promise, or Divine commitment. "For if the inheritance be of the law, it is no more of promise: but God gave it to Abraham by promise" (Gal. 3:18). The Law was actually an intermediate provision, given to prepare men for the promised Savior. "Wherefore then serves the

Law? It was added [to the Abrahamic promise] because of trans-gressions, till the Seed should come to Whom the promise was made; and it was ordained by angels in the hand of a mediator" (Gal. 3:19).

Under the "old testament" (II Cor. 3:14). The covenantal promise of life was made to Israel, conditioned on their perfect obedience. Under the new covenant, the promise "was made" to the "Seed," Jesus Christ. "Now to Abraham and his Seed were the promises made. He saith not, And to seeds, as of many; but as of ONE, And to thy Seed, WHICH IS CHRIST" (Gal. 3:16). Now those that are "in Christ" obtain the promise — not by virtue of their fulfillment of the law — but because of their union with Christ. "And if ye be Christ's, then are ye Abraham's seed, and heirs according to the promise" (Gal. 3:29). Since the resurrection of Christ, eternal life is never declared apart from Him!

In the promise of the covenantal blessing to Abraham, no one stood between God and him. There was no mediator like Moses to insure that the promise would be fulfilled to Abraham. God made the commitment without a "daysman." "Seeing that Abraham shall surely become a great and mighty nation, and all the nations of the earth shall be blessed in him" (Gen. 18:18). Under the Law, God's distance from the people required the presence of an earthly mediator between Him and the peo-ple. But in the convenantal promise of universal blessing, no mediator was employed!

Jesus did not come into the world as the result of mediatorial pleading! He was not sent because God was urged to send Him! The coming of the Savior was not contingent upon obedience, seeking, or devotion to the Law! Were that the case, He never would have come! A mediatorless promise was given to Abraham! Wonderful truth!

God and Man Reconciled

In a very real sense, Jesus is the Mediator of "One," He is not bridg-ing the gap between two alienated parties. He has reconciled men to God by means of His vicarious death, thus making us "one" in Him (John 17:11,21,22; I Cor. 6:17)! His mediatorship is not necessary because of a moral gulf between God and man, but because of the in-compatibility of the eternal order with the temporal one. While we are "at home in the body, we are absent from the Lord: (For we walk by faith, not by sight)" (II Cor. 5:6-7). This is the condition that requires our Mediator!

300

Christ's mediation, further, applies only to those that are "in Him" (Col. 2:6-10; I John 2:5-10) — to those that have already been "reconciled" (II Cor. 5:18-20; Col. 1:21). Jesus is not pleading for those that are alienated from God! "I pray not for the world, but for them which Thou hast given Me" (John 17:9). He is ministering covenant benefits to those that have been reconciled to God by His death! Their faith appropriates what He gives by mediation!

The Willingness of Believers

While Israel was not willing, those in Christ are identified by willingness to please God. How often it is expressed in Scripture. "We are . . . willing rather to be absent from the body, and to be present with the Lord" (II Cor. 5:8); ". . . for to will is present with me . . ." (Rom. 7:18); "So then, with my mind, I myself serve the law of God" (Rom. 7:24). Under the new covenant, the very concept of obedience requires willingness. It is "with the heart" that "man believes unto righteousness" (Rom. 10:10) — an expression denoting voluntary submission. Under such an arrangement, the commandments of God "are not grievous" (I John 5:3) — something which could not be said under the "ministration of condemnation" (II Cor. 3:9). It is, after all, the one that "loves" Christ that "keeps His words" (John 14:15,23).

The unique willingness of those in Christ is not an indication of their superior achievement, but of the effectiveness of Christ's achievement. The "Gospel of Christ" — the announcement of reconciliation — constrains willingness in all that believe and obey it! It is in this sense that it is said to be "the power of God unto salvation to everyone that believes" (Rom. 1:16). It is powerless to all others!

Sons of God

Christ is the Mediator between God and His sons — quite different from the situation in which Moses found himself. Jesus does not bring water to rebels, nor plead for the stiff-necked! God's people are not noted for being "stubborn," "stiff-hearted," and "alienated." There is, unfortunately, much ministering in our day which assumes that this is the case — but it is not. There is now a very real union between God and man. In Christ, men are "joined to the Lord" (I Cor. 6:17), and made "joint-heirs" with Him (Rom. 8:17).

One of the terms that most precisely reflects this relationship is "sons of God." This is absolutely unique to the new covenant — the "day of salvation." Hosea foretold a time when it would "come to pass, that in the place where it was said unto them, ye are not my people, there it shall be said unto them, Ye are the sons of the Living God" (Hosea 1:10). That was, however, a truth attended with great mystery in those days. The statement stands alone among the prophets; no other inspired man under the old covenant mentioned it.

Now, under the new covenant, those who through faith and obedience embrace the Son are called "the sons of God." "Behold, what manner of love the Father hath bestowed upon us, that we should be called the sons of God. Beloved, now are we the sons of God . . ." (I John 3:1-2). Those that are led by the Spirit of God in the holy work of subduing fleshly inclinations are properly called "the sons of God" (Rom. 8:14). Devotion, further, to the matter of shining as lights in the midst of a "crooked and perverse nation," constitutes a revelation of "the sons of God" (Phil. 2:15).

There is some disagreement among conservative theologians concerning whether the people of God are really the sons of God or not. The utter foolishness of such questioning is seen in the many assertions — plain assertions — that God has made concerning the subject. Jesus is bringing "many sons" to glory (Heb. 2:10), and it is "because ye are sons" that God hath sent forth the Spirit of His Son into your hearts, crying, Abba Father" (Gal. 4:6). If God recognizes those in Christ as "sons," who would dare to make Him a liar (I John 5:10) by questioning the reality or accuracy of His affirmation?

As the "sons of God," those in Jesus become His "brethren." Thus is it written, "For both He that sanctifieth [Jesus] and they who are sanctified [those "in Him"] are all of One [the Father]: for which cause He [Jesus] is not ashamed to call them [believers] brethren" (Heb. 2:11).

Those that are "joined to the Lord" have come into an area of blessing that is unequalled. The greatest godly men of prior ages coveted the status of the sons of God in their time, but did not realize it. Abraham was "the friend of God" (James 2:23), David was a "man after" God's "heart" (I Sam. 13:14), and "Among those that are born of women there is not a greater prophet than John the Baptist: but he that is least in the Kingdom of God is greater than he" (Luke 7:28). This greatness is not due to personal achievement or superiority. In Christ — and in Him alone — we have been exalted to the status of God's sons. While

John was a giant standing in the valley of unfulfilled prophecy, even the "least in the Kingdom of God" stands upon the mountain of reconciliation. Excellence accompanies that position because men have been united with their Mediator.

What a glorious thing has transpired in Him! He now takes the things of God and, through the Spirit, gives them to His own "body" (I Cor. 12:27; Col. 1:18). What was impossible for Moses is both possible and reasonable in Christ. He now accomplishes what formerly was a logical impossibility — the ministration of benefits to God's reconciled sons. Thus, in practicality, He is a "mediator of one."

Mediating the Purged Conscience

The provisions of the new covenant have been clearly identified by both the prophets and the Apostles. The provisions consist of a Divine reaction to the appropriation of Christ's work by faith. 1. "I will put My laws into their minds, and write them in their hearts." 2. "I will be to them a God, they shall be to Me a people." 3. "And they shall not teach every man his neighbor, and every man his brother, saying, Know the Lord: for all shall know Me from the least to the greatest." The reason for the conferment of these blessings is also stated: "For I will be merciful to their unrighteousness, and their sins and their iniquities will I remember no more" (Heb. 8:10-12; Jer. 31:31-34; Heb. 10:16-17).

Jesus now ministers these convenantal benefits to His "brethren." Both the greatness and the effectuality of His mediation are seen in the ministration of the "purged conscience" (Heb. 9:14). Legally, this is achieved by His blood; practically, it is accomplished by His Mediatorship. In this sense, "He is the Mediator of a better covenant" (Heb. 8:6) — "the Mediator of the New Testament" (Heb. 9:15), or "Jesus the Mediator of the New Covenant" (Heb. 12:24).

The purging of the conscience (Heb. 9:14) results in the knowledge of God (II Pet. 1:2), which is the "knowledge of salvation" in its fullest sense. God, in such a case, becomes "my salvation" (Psa. 27:1; 62:2; 118:14; Isa. 12:2). Salvation is then associated with God's Person rather than mere external deliverance, as it was with Israel on the banks of the Red Sea (Exod. 15:2).

It is "the blood of Christ" that cleanses the conscience from the contamination of "dead works." But let us not miss the point here: if Christ were not alive and mediating the New Covenant, there could be no purifying of the conscience! It is not the intellectual embracement of a mere historical fact that purges it, but the ministration of that reality by a living Christ! "How much more shall the blood of Christ . . . purge your conscience . . . And for this cause He is the Mediator of the New Testament . . ." (Heb. 9:14-15).

When the heart has been persuaded of the effectuality of Christ's death, and when that persuasion is followed by obedience to the Gospel, the "knowledge of salvation" is ministered by Christ. The Apostles referred to this "knowledge" in their use of the terms "assurance" (Col. 2:2; Heb. 6:11; 10:22), "confidence" (Eph. 3:12; Heb. 3:6,14), and "peace" (Rom. 15:13; Col. 3:15). John spoke of the "knowledge of salvation" when he wrote, "Beloved, if our heart condemn us not, then have we confidence toward God" (I John 3:21). Jesus is the Mediator of this benefit.

Receiving the Atonement

Another view of the purging of the conscience focuses on man's acceptance of "the salvation of our God" (Psa. 98:3). Again, this activity is identified with the Mediator of the New Covenant. "And not only so, but we also joy in God through our Lord Jesus Christ, by Whom we have now received the atonement" (Rom. 5:11).

Without Jesus "the atonement" could not have been wrought or received! He is necessary for both its accomplishment and its reception. He accomplished it in His death; He ministers it by His life at God's right hand. As it is written, "For if, when we were enemies, we were reconciled to God by the death of His Son, much more, being reconciled, we shall be saved by His life" (Rom. 5:10). Under Christ's supervision, the "atonement" becomes accessible to men through faith. Were He not governing the Kingdom of God, men would strive in vain for experiential reconciliation. They could not appropriate the atonement, nor would God acknowledge it. The reception of reconciliation requires the ministration of a living and reigning Christ!

Hearts Purified by Faith

The relief of the conscience from guilt is also associated with saving faith. Faith, in this case, is the persuasion of the truth of God's testimony concerning His Son (I John 5:10-11).

In a discerning analysis of the conversion of the Gentiles, Peter interpreted their experience of salvation. "And God, which knoweth the hearts, bare them witness, giving them the Holy Ghost, even as He did unto us; and put no difference between us and them purifying their hearts by faith" (Acts 15:8-9). Though there were external manifestations of the Spirit at the house of Cornelius (Acts 10:44-46), they were only incidental. The real value of that occurrence is found in the purifying of their hearts "by faith." It is a reproach to the Savior and His redemption to become enamored of the appearances of that epochal occasion. Such appearances were not even consistent during the first century of the church — but the purifying of the heart by faith was! It is that consistent work that is to be emphasized!

The purification of the heart and the purging of the conscience refer to the same thing. Purifying the heart emphasizes the appropriation of redemptive benefits, while the purging of the conscience emphasizes the removal of sin's contamination. Christ is the preeminent consideration in both views, and they are accomplished under His administration. From the Father's right hand, Jesus administers this cleansing by means of the truth of the Gospel. It is His life that gives the Gospel its power, and His authority that makes it applicable to man.

Purified by Obedience

Obedience is an integral part of faith, and is indispensable to the realization of a pure heart, or purged conscience. Using the "keys of the kingdom" (Matt. 16:19), Peter unlocked our understanding on this matter. "Seeing ye have purified your souls in obeying the truth through the Spirit . . ." (I Pet. 1:22). Salvation so intimately and vitally involves man, that his own actions play a significant role in its accomplishment. This exposes as a fable the view of man being unable to contribute to the realization of salvation. The purification of the heart is identified with man's obedience to the Gospel.

Man's obedience, however, is not independent of Divine influence. It is accomplished "through the Spirit," as He works in concert with man's spirit. His use of His sword — the Word of God (Eph. 6:17) — brings spiritual truth within the grasp of faith, thus making saving obedience possible.

The role of Jesus the Administrator in accomplishing this is vital. Before His death, He promised His Apostles that He would send the

305

Spirit. "When the Comforter is come Whom I will send you from the Father . . ." (John 15:26a). Again he testified, "Nevertheless I tell you the truth; It is expedient for you that I go away: for if I go not away, the Comforter will not come unto you: but if I depart, I will send Him unto you" (John 16:7). The basis for the sending of the Spirit was the sacrifice of Christ. This is the emphasis of Jesus' words in John 14:26: "But the Comforter, which is the Holy Ghost, Whom the Father will send in My name. . . ."

It is "through" the Spirit that obedience — personal conformity to the truth — is rendered. Man's initial entrance into God's Kingdom occurs when, in baptism, he experiences the "answer of a good conscience toward God" (I Pet. 3:22). This is his introduction to the purging of the conscience. It is administered by the authority of the reigning Christ, through the illumination of the Holy Spirit, by means of one's obedience to the truth.

The Confession of Sin

The mediation of a purged conscience depends upon man's acknowledgment of personal sin. "IF we confess our sins, He [God] is faithful and just to forgive us our sins, and to cleanse us from all unrighteousness" (I John 1:9). This is not a mere formality; it is something that involves man's comprehension. God's Kingdom is operating within a moral environment — among His intelligent offspring. The benefits of the Kingdom cannot be realized without the personal involvement of those for whom they are prepared.

John teaches us that personal benefit from God's justness and faithfulness depends upon our action — quite a different view from that of much contemporary theology. My point here, however, is that Jesus mediates this cleansing — it is His blood that relieves the conscience of guilt, and His reign of authority that brings it to a conclusion. To be more precise, it is the persuasion of the atoning efficacy of His blood that relieves the conscience of the sense of alienating guilt.

Boldness Before God

Yet another view of the purged conscience, or purified heart, is seen in our approach to God through Christ. Those "in Christ" are exhorted to "come boldly unto the throne of grace . . ." (Heb. 4:16). This boldness is proper, and acceptable with God. As it is written, "Having therefore, brethren, boldness to enter into the holiest by the blood of Jesus . . . let us draw near . . ." (Heb. 10:19-22). "Having" boldness speaks of its availability to the believer, not necessarily of its realization. The redeemed are urged to possess what is theirs in Jesus!

This "boldness" is not brashness or presumption. It is the result of an awareness of one's acceptance with God in Christ. John put it this way, "Beloved, if our heart condemn us not, then have we confidence toward God" (I John 3:21). This confidence enables us to approach the Living God by faith, even though we have "sinned and come short of the glory of God" (Rom. 3:23). We do not ignore our sin, or pretend that we have not committed it. We come to God, through Christ, fully aware of our sin, yet not condemned in our conscience by it. This is the result of the mediation of Christ.

Writing the Law Upon the Heart

The promised covenant proclaimed, "I will put my law in their inward parts, and write it in their heart" (Jer. 31:33). The writer of Hebrews proclaimed this as a present reality in Christ. "But this Man [Jesus], after He had offered one sacrifice for sins forever, sat down on the right hand of God . . . Whereof the Holy Ghost also is a witness to us; for after that He said before, This is the covenant that I will make with them after those days, saith the Lord, I will put My laws into their hearts, and in their minds will I write them . . . Having therefore, brethren, boldness to enter into the holiest by the blood of Jesus . . ." (Heb. 10:12-21). The current rule of Christ is thus identified as the time when God is writing His law upon men's hearts.

In his contrast of the old and new covenants, Paul makes a comparison of the types of inscriptions under both. The redeemed, he confirms, "are manifestly declared to be the epistle of Christ ministered by us [the Apostles], written not with ink, but with the Spirit of the Living God; not in tables of stone, but in fleshly tables of the heart" (II Cor. 3:3).

The law written in tables of stone mirrored the type of covenant it represented. It was one without comprehension, freedom, or growth. Those tables were "stony" — like the hearts of those to whom it was addressed (Ezek. 11:19; 36:26). They did not see the implications of the Law, and were unable to successfully adapt it to their lives.

That same law is now inscribed upon "fleshly tables of the heart" —

hearts that are pulsating with Divine life (Gal. 2:20). It is now possible to have the "senses exercised to discern both good and evil" — without a meticulous list of approvals and prohibitions (Heb. 5:14). The law must be written in the heart, for instance, for one to successfully ". . . follow that which is good" and "abstain from all appearance of evil" (I Thess. 5:15,22) [Observe the absence of details in those Apostolic instructions.] However, those that have the law written upon the "fleshly tables of the heart" can "grow in the grace and knowledge of our Lord Jesus Christ" (II Pet. 3:18). How else, for example, could one ever hope to obey the exhortation, "Follow peace with all men, and holiness, without which no man shall see the Lord" (Heb. 13:14)?

The "Apostles' doctrine" (Acts 2:42) is not a manual of procedures that identifies acceptable conduct, but a spiritual interpretation of Christ and the salvation which He has wrought. With a consistency befitting of the Kingdom of God, "do's and don'ts" are presented incidentally. They are never the principal message or primary emphasis. It was not so, however, with the old covenant. The details of acceptable conduct were preeminent. The Apostolic emphasis reveals a new covenant, written in a new manner — upon the heart.

To Will Is Present with Me

"But if you are led by the Spirit, you are not under the Law," proclaimed the Apostle (Gal. 5:18). That leading is not mystical, but facilitated through a willing and discerning heart. The Spirit leads neither the ignorant nor the stubborn! Those possessing such traits "quench" and "grieve" the Spirit (I Thess. 5:19; Eph. 4:30). It is the "willing" that are given the promise of good (Isa. 1:18-19).

Willingness is but another view of the law being written upon the heart and placed in the mind. It is the underside of agreement. Believers are quick to admit that their achievement has not measured up to their wills. Their failures, however, are attributable to the weakness of their flesh, not the subbornness or reluctance of their wills. Paul put it well when he wrote, ". . . for to will is present with me: but how to perform that which is good, I find not" (Rom. 7:18). That dilemma is created by the conflict of the flesh and the Spirit — not by a basic variance between the individual believer and his God. As it is written: "For the flesh lusts against the Spirit, and the Spirit against the flesh; and these are contrary the one to the other: so that you cannot do the things that ye would"

(Gal. 5:17).

The spirit of man has experienced reconciliation, but his fleshly, or earthly, nature has not. The body, together with the parts of man's person that are wed to it, has yet to be renewed in the resurrection (Rom. 8:23). Until that time, an irreconcilable conflict exists between the old and new natures of the believer. The agreement of the will, however, makes one leadable and acceptable to God in Christ.

David was in agreement with the Lord, and found delight in His commandments. How often he affirmed this to be true. "I myself delight in Thy statutes" (Psa. 119:16,65); "I delight in Thy commandments" (Psa. 119:47); "I delight in Thy law" (Psa. 119:70). Paul spoke for every person "in Christ," when he said, "For I delight in the law of God after the inward man" (Rom. 7:22). This "delight" prompts a hunger and thirst for righteousness (Matt. 5:6), and cannot be satisfied with the baubles of this world.

Thy Law Do I Love

When the law is placed within the mind, and inscribed upon the heart, a deep love for it is realized. Israel "despised" God's judgments (Ezek. 20:16), His "statutes" (Ezek. 20:24), and His "Law" (Amos 2:4). Conversely, David spoke for believers when he said, "O how I love Thy law" (Psa. 119:97); ". . . Thy law do I love" (Psa. 119:113,163); ". . . I love Thy testimonies (Psa. 119:119); "I love Thy commands above gold" (Psa. 119:127). With a total lack of pretense he spoke with the Lord God, ". . . consider how I love Thy precepts" (Psa. 119:159).

John referred to this experience when he said, "For this is the love of God, that we keep His commandments: and His commandments are not grievous" (I John 5:3). Paul spoke of it as receiving "the love of the truth" (I Thess. 2:10). The enjoyment and satisfaction that are found in the words of His mouth evidence that the Law is upon the heart.

God's covenantal promise was, "I will put my laws into their hearts, and in their minds will I write them" (Heb. 10:16). While delight and love are the results of the law being written upon the heart, a devotion to its consideration evidences its writing upon the mind.

Meditation in the precepts and statutes of God (Psa. 119:15,23,78) is an activity in which the God of heaven finds great delight. Not only did David, for instance, "love" the Law of the Lord; it was his "meditation all the day" (Psa. 119:97,99). The contemplation of God's perspectives as revealed in His Word was the Psalmist's chosen occupation. Little wonder He was a man after God's own heart — a man in whom God greatly delighted (Acts 13:22).

Paul, in keeping with God's superior revelation in Christ, wrote; "So then with the mind I myself serve the law of God . . ." (Rom 7:25). The law had been written in his heart — that is why he could delight in it. This reality, however, is not a replacement of the Scriptures, but a means by which they are embraced.

Mediating the Knowledge of God

The old covenant was not characterized by the "good knowledge of the Lord" (II Chron. 30:22). Israel, with whom that covenant was made (Heb. 8:9), drew back from the covenant-making God because they were ignorant of Him and His ways. Their reaction to the giving of the words of the covenant at Mount Sinai, demonstrated the impact of that ignorance. "And they said unto Moses, Speak thou with us, and we will hear: but let not God speak with us, lest we die" (Exod. 20:18-19). The lack of knowledge of God — an ignorance of Him — dictated this response. God was not speaking to slay them, but to make covenant with them!

The new covenant, which incorporates the knowledge of God by its constituents, produced results that were in keeping with God's "eternal purpose." Men may now "come" to Him (Heb. 4:16), "draw near" (Heb. 10:22), and "live by every word of God" (Luke 4:4) — characteristics quite different from those found under the old covenant!

They Shall All Know Me

Under the old covenant, there were few individuals that possessed the knowledge of God. The masses were ignorant of Him, and thus alienated from Him. But it is not so under the new covenant. Of the new covenant, Jeremiah prophesied, "for they shall all know me, from the least of them unto the greatest of them, saith the Lord" (Jer. 31:34). Paul confirmed that this has been fulfilled in Christ when he said of the new covenant, "For this is the covenant . . . for all shall know Me, from the least to the greatest. . . . In that he saith A new covenant, He hath made the first old. Now that which decayeth and waxeth old is ready to vanish away" (Heb. 8:10-13).

310

Unlike the old covenant, the new one is not characterized by only a few individuals being acquainted with God. Under the old order, the priest — not the people — accomplished "the service of God" (Heb. 9:6). The high priest appeared "alone" before the Lord, and that only once a year (Heb. 9:7). Special prophets were also required for the discernment of God's will (II Chron. 26:5; 36:12; Jer. 7:25).

God is known by the perception of His will and objectives. These have been revealed in the Person of Christ and the words of Scripture — both of which are available to every man "in Christ." Those that possess the "excellency of the knowledge of Christ Jesus" (Phil. 3:8), and have availed themselves of "the scriptures which are able to make" them "wise unto salvation" (II Tim. 3:15) are "increasing in the knowledge of God" (Col. 1:10).

This knowledge is so common in the new covenant, that those who do not possess it have cause of shame. "Awake to righteousness, and sin not; for all have not the knowledge of God: I speak this to your shame" (I Cor. 15:34). A deliberate involvement in sin is the only thing that will inhibit the knowledge of God — that is how profuse it is under the new covenant! There is, further, no excuse for being overcome by sin under Christ. This is the perspective from which God says, "They shall all know Me."

Giving Us An Understanding

Jesus is the Mediator of the knowledge of God. It is He that "is come, and has given us an understanding, that we might know Him that is true, and we are in Him that is true, even in His Son Jesus Christ. This is the true God and eternal life" (I John 5:20).

Jesus does not minister an academic understanding of God. God cannot be known in that manner. Divine tutelage flows out of man's union with Deity. Those that are reconciled have been "baptized into Christ" (Gal. 3:27), "joined to the Lord" (I Cor. 6:17), and made "partakers of Christ" (Heb. 3:14). They have also been made "partakers of the Divine nature" (I Pet. 1:4). "He that abides in Christ, he has both the Father and the Son" (II John 9). This is a relationship of faith, and out of it the knowledge of God is ministered by Christ.

The understanding of God — or the knowledge of God — "is life eternal" (I John 5:20b). Men are spiritually alive to the degree that they comprehend the God of their salvation — to the extent of their spiritual

311

discernment of God's purpose in Christ Jesus! Confidence, assurance, and boldness are all results of this understanding. The academic recitation of Gospel facts is not the evidence of the knowledge of God. Rather, embracing and conforming to those facts evidences its possession! Where these exist, Jesus has ministered "an understanding"!

The requirement for Christ's ministration of the knowledge of God is seen in His own words; ". . . neither knows any man the Father, save the Son, and he to whomsoever the Son will reveal Him" (Matt. 11:27). Luke's gospel states it in these words, ". . . and no man knows . . . who the Father is, but the Son, and he to whom the Son will reveal Him" (Luke 10:22).

Sin has resulted in the obscurement of God. This obscurity has been produced by the moral gulf between Himself and those outside of Christ. Man has become self-centered, and thus cannot comprehend God. It is not that God is unknowable, or that man is incapable of knowing Him, even though transgression has made it appear as though these things were true.

The remission of sins refurbishes man's powers of discernment, enabling him to comprehend the One in Whose image he has been made. From within, Christ takes His Word, and imparts an understanding of the Father. This knowledge involves a comprehension of His overall objective, and is ministered from an eternal perspective. It cannot, further, be passed from man-to-man. It must be the result of Divine fellowship.

The Benefits of the Knowledge of God

The inestimable value of the knowledge of God can be seen in its benefits. This knowledge is expressed by the Scriptures and expounded by the Lord Jesus. Without His ministration, the Scriptures are nothing more than a dead letter. Without the Scriptures, Jesus has no comprehensible base from which to minister. In the new covenant, Jesus and the Word are complementary — one is never considered in isolation from the other. Thus are the Scriptures called "the Word of Christ" (Col. 3:16).

Escaping the Pollutions of the World

This world — the temporal order — having been defiled by sin, is a "present evil world" (Gal. 1:4). Those enamored of it become defiled and corrupt, and consequently disqualified for Divine fellowship. The mandate from heaven is this, "keep" yourself "unspotted from the world" (James 1:27). "All that is in the world," declares John, "is not of the Father" (I John 2:16). An effective separation from its contaminating influence must occur if men are to reach heaven!

The knowledge of God is the means through which this separation is achieved. "For if after they have escaped the pollutions of the world through the knowledge of the Lord and Savior Jesus Christ . . ." (II Pet. 2:20).

This "escape" is not accomplished like that of Lot's deliverance from Sodom. It is written that "while he lingered, the men laid hold upon his hand, and upon the hand of his wife, and upon the hand of his two daughters; the Lord being merciful to him: and they brought him forth and set him without the city" (Gen. 19:16). That was a deliverance reflective of the times — a period when the knowledge of God was at a minimum level. But men do greatly err when they suppose spiritual deliverance is accomplished in this manner during this "day of salvation" (II Cor. 6:2).

The "knowledge of the Lord and Savior Jesus Christ" compels one to voluntarily come out of the world order. Such an individual is said to have "fled for refuge to lay hold upon the hope set before" him (Heb. 6:18). The greater glory of the world to come draws men away from the course of this world. The knowledge of the Lord, so to speak, puts heaven in man's eye!

Grace and Peace Ministered

Grace and peace are essential in the economy of faith — the new covenant. An awareness of God's favor and lovingkindness, together with an assurance of our acceptance with Him (Rom. 5:1) must be possessed by those that have abandoned the "fashion of the world" (I Cor. 7:31). The supply of grace and peace, further, is increased in direct proportion to our spiritual involvement in the Kingdom. The more we are devoted to the denial of "ungodliness and worldly lusts" (Titus 2:12), and the closer we get to the "salvation ready to be revealed" (I Pet. 1:5), the more grace and peace are required.

In the matter of the ministration of grace and peace, the role of the knowledge of God is again seen as a critical one. "Grace and peace be multiplied unto you through the knowledge of God, and of Jesus our

Lord" (II Pet. 1:2). Those that "acquaint" themselves with the Almighty (Job 22:21) so delight Him, that His lovingkindness and settled peace are copiously given to them.

Grace depicts a God who smiles. We have in Noah an historical example of the effect of such a situation. It is written that he "found grace in the eyes of the Lord" (Gen. 6:9). His preservation from God's wrath and indignation was only a small representation of what is "prepared for them that love" God (I Cor. 2:9). In Christ, grace not only involves preservation; it also is associated with the enjoyment of eternal benefits and blessings. "And the grace of our Lord was exceeding abundant with faith and love which is in Christ Jesus" (I Tim. 1:14).

Peace enables the heart to remain stable under stress. The peace of God is said to "keep your hearts and minds through Christ Jesus" (Phil. 4:7). It is evidenced when the heart is "not troubled," even though tribulation is being experienced "in the world" (John 14:1,27; 16:33).

Both grace and peace are experienced to the degree that the knowledge of God is possessed. That is the appointed vehicle by which they are ministered.

All Things Pertaining to Life and Godliness

Divine resources are necessary for the sustaining of spiritual life. God's purpose in Christ is to bring "many sons to glory" (Heb. 2:10) — to get them from earth to heaven. In His Kingdom an adequate provision and allocation of resources has been made for achievement of that purpose. The race is long, the terrain is rough, and His people are in enemy territory. They must draw upon heavenly supplies in order to successfully navigate through Satanic straits, and finish their course!

"According as His Divine power hath given us all things pertaining to life and godliness through the knowledge of Him . . ." (II Pet. 1:3). "Life" refers to spiritual life — reciprocity to God. "Godliness" is the expression of that life in a godless world, amidst both internal and external handicaps. Everything that is necessary for the maintenance of "life and godliness" is granted "through the knowledge of Him."

Those that stand aloof from God, not availing themselves of the redemption that is in Christ Jesus, have, in the most charitable view, severely handicapped themselves. They have cut off resources required to live unto God! On the other hand, those that "count all things but loss for the excellency of the knowledge of Christ Jesus" (Phil. 3:8) have, by that very attitude, guaranteed the supply of required spiritual resources.

Conclusion

Christ Jesus is God's appointed Administrator. No spiritual blessing or benefit is realized independently of Him. His rule and reign, from this perspective, is the administration of the benefits of the new covenant. He is indispensable to both God and man. In this "day of salvation" God cannot bless man without Jesus, and man cannot receive the blessing apart from Him.

18

JESUS — THE CENTRAL OBJECT INTO WHICH ALL WILL BE GATHERED

The consideration of Jesus is essential to the comprehension of the Kingdom of God. "All things," we are told, "were made by Him, and without Him was not anything made that was made" (John 1:3). Not only is He the Source of the creation, however, He is also the Object of it. The creation was neither incidental or experimental. The Word of God is specific on this point. "For by Him were all things created, that are in heaven, and that are in earth, visible and invisible, whether they be thrones, or dominions, or principalities, or powers: all things were created by Him and for Him" (Col. 1:16).

Jesus Christ — "God manifest in the flesh" (I Tim. 3:16) — is the primary consideration in the creation of all things. Everything was made in contemplation of the government which has been placed upon His "shoulder" (Isa. 9:6). An intelligent appraisal of the impersonal creation is not possible apart from a perception of Jesus Christ. All things that are made can be properly perceived only through an understanding of Him and His redemptive accomplishments!

As I have before stated, man's reinstatement in God's favor, and his consequent dominion over the "world to come," is the objective that God is implementing (Heb. 2:5-8). It is obvious that this purpose has not yet been fully realized. "Thou hast put all things in subjection under his [man's] feet. For in that He put all things under him, He left nothing that is not put under him. But now we see not yet all things put under him."

We do, however, "see Jesus, Who is made a little lower than the angels for the suffering of death, crowned with glory and honor; that He by the grace of God should taste death for every man" (Heb. 2:8-9). A glorified man now sits at the right hand of God — exalted and reigning. He is ruling to bring "many sons to glory" (Heb. 2:10). He is, further, the "forerunner" of the coming sons — an example of their fulfilled destiny. The entire enterprise of salvation centers in Him, and Him alone.

The Gathering of the People

Jacob spoke of Jesus when he prophesied, "The sceptre shall not depart from Judah, nor a Lawgiver from between his feet, until Shiloh come; and unto Him shall the gathering of the people be" (Gen. 49:10). According to this prophesy, Judah would remain predominant "until" a Divinely scheduled event. The tribe of Judah, out of which Jesus "sprang" (Heb. 7:14), was identified as God's "lawgiver" (Psa. 60:7). The emphasis here is not so much on Judah as it is upon authority — rule and law — which postulates the existence of rebellion. Jacob's prophecy provides a contrast between the old and new covenants. Both covenants were in the future during his time.

The old order addressed a covenant people that were alienated from God, though chosen by Him. They did not have the mind of God, and thus were required to literally set God's commandments before their eyes at all times. "And thou shalt bind them for a sign upon thine hand, and they shall be as frontlets between thine eyes. And thou shalt write them upon the posts of thy house, and on thy gates" (Deut. 6:8-9). This condition was to continue until the appearance of "Shiloh."

The New Emphasis

"Shiloh" comes from a root word meaning tranquil and secure. It also includes the idea of joy — the result of safety. After Jacob's death, and following Israel's entrance into Canaan, there was an assembly of

318

JESUS — CENTRAL OBJECT INTO WHICH ALL WILL BE GATHERED

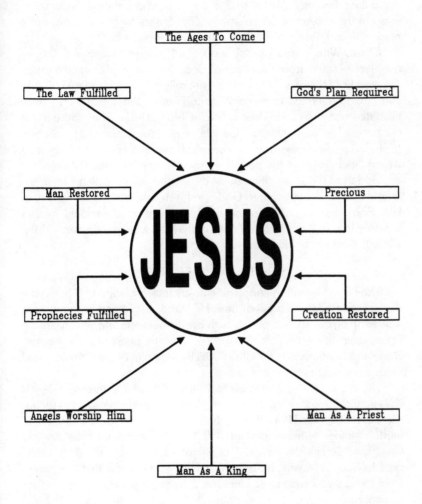

Israel at a place called "Shiloh." There "the land was subdued before them," and "Joshua divided the land unto the children of Israel according to their divisions" (Josh. 18:1,8-10). This event, though typical of it, was not the subject of Jacob's prophecy. He spoke of a person, not a place: "unto HIM shall the gathering of the people be."

Christ, Who "is our Peace" (Eph. 2:14) is man's spiritual Shiloh — the place of safety from the wrath of God. "Having made peace through the blood of His cross," He became the rallying point for mankind. "By Him," God intended to reconcile unto Himself those that were "once alienated and enemies in their minds" (Col. 1:20-21). The "gathering of the people" — both Jew and Gentile — is accomplished in God's Son (Eph. 2:13-15). Unlike the old covenant, the new covenant includes a willing "gathering" of the people — they "come" to their "Shiloh."

God used Caiaphas, high priest during the year in which Christ "offered Himself without spot to God," to foretell the gathering ministry of His Son. "And . . . he prophesied that Jesus . . . should gather together into one the children of God that are scattered abroad" (John 11:52). God be thanked for our "Shiloh"!

Gathering All Things Together

The Divine intention concerning Jesus is clearly stated: "That in the dispensation of the fulness of time He [God] might gather together in one all things in Christ, both which are in heaven, and which are on earth; even in Him" (Eph. 1:10). The Apostle peers into the ages to come and announces that "Christ" will be the point of commonality and value for everything.

The reconciliation accomplished by Christ is large in scope. In his elaboration upon it, Paul taught that "by Him" God intended to "reconcile all things unto Himself; by Him, I say, whether they be things in earth or things in heaven" (Col. 1:20b). The intention of the Apostle was not to declare the necessity of personalities in heaven being reconciled to God. "Heaven" here speaks of the natural order that is separate from the residence of man. The term is frequently used in this manner in Scripture. "Heaven and earth shall pass away" (Mark 13:31; Luke 21:33); "And the heaven departed as a scroll when it was rolled together . . ." (Rev. 6:14); "And sware by Him that . . . created heaven, and the things that therein are . . ." (Rev. 10:6); "And I saw a new heaven . . . for the first heaven . . . passed away" (Rev. 21:1).

The sin of man defiled all creation — even the created "heaven and those things that are therein." Though not personally involved in the rebellion, "the creature [creation] was made subject to vanity." The curse was not due to the adverse will of the creation — "not willingly." It was the anticipation of the ultimate gathering of all things into Christ that constrained God to subject it to "vanity" in "hope." The achievement of Jesus includes the deliverance of the "creature" [creation] itself "from the bondage of corruption into the glorious liberty of the children of God" (Rom. 8:20-21).

God has determined to gather "all things" together in His only begotten Son! He is the proclaimed Center of all things, and eternal significance is in Him, and Him alone. God has begun the "gathering" already; it shall be consummated at the manifestation of the new heavens and the new earth, "wherein dwelleth righteousness" (II Pet. 3:13).

His Absolute Requirement

The purpose of God cannot possibly be fulfilled without Jesus. No mortal will realize the objective for which he was created unless he embraces the Son of God through faith, and obeys His Gospel! "Neither is there salvation in any other: for there is none other name under heaven given among men whereby we must be saved" (Acts 4:12). This is "the name of Jesus Christ of Nazareth" (Acts 4:10). His "name" identifies His Person — particularly in the capacity of a man. It is as a man that He saves us (I Tim. 2:5). He was born as a man (Gal. 4:4), lived as a man (Heb. 2:18), and through "weakness" He was crucified and died as a man (II Cor. 13:4). He arose from among the realm of dead men, and ascended into heaven as "the Man Christ Jesus." His "name" speaks of that whole spectrum of commissioned experience.

He alone had been invested with the responsibility to "accomplish" a decease "at Jerusalem" (Luke 9:31), and He alone has been given the authority to give eternal life to those united with that death. Moses gave the Law; the prophets heralded a time of universal blessing; but "grace and truth came by Jesus Christ" (John 1:17).

Salvation cannot be realized by merely adhering to a set of moral principles and examples! Over fifteen hundred years of moral futility proved that, of himself, man is not capable of achieving perfection before God. Having searched heaven and earth, the witness is given from the Throne that He alone is able to "save them to the uttermost that come unto God by Him" (Heb. 7:25).

Only Foundation

The relationship between God and man must be built upon the Person of Jesus. "For other foundation can no man lay than that is laid, which is Jesus Christ" (I Cor. 3:11). His accomplishments form the foundation for man's acceptance with God.

The earthly aspect of His mission was finalized when the people were "sanctified through the offering of the body of Jesus Christ once for all" (Heb. 10:5-10). That "offering" became the ground or basis for man's acceptance. It was laid "once," and is potentially effectual "for all." Because of its stability and consistency, it will never be laid again.

God, Who could not keep quiet concerning His intense desire for man, moved Isaiah to foretell the nature of this Foundation. "Therefore thus saith the Lord God, behold, I lay in Zion for a foundation a stone, a tried stone, a precious corner stone, a sure foundation: he that believes shall not make haste" [be put to flight by the enemy] (Isa. 28:16).

The "stone" speaks of a ledge of rock that cannot be dislodged or made ineffectual — a stone "for a foundation." Man's relationship to the Living God will be built upon this Foundation! A "tried stone" is one that has passed through the same area of testing that caused the fall of the ones being reconciled. It is "precious" because of its effectuality, and "sure" due to its eternal stability.

Under the new covenant, the key issue is not the moral responsibility to be obedient, and there is no acceptance apart from that obedience. Man is, however, accepted because of the Foundation. His lifetime is to be spent appropriating the "excellency of the knowledge of Christ Jesus," or in the winning of Christ (Phil. 3:8). Those that emphasize duty and include Christ have distorted the Foundation. It is the Foundation that is to be emphasized, with the inclusion of duty!

No Man Comes to the Father But by Him

It is possible to develop an empty tradition using the shell of true words. Thus it is with this very truth: "I am the Way, the Truth, and the Life: no man comes unto the Father but by Me" (John 14:6). That is not intended to be a mere creedal statement — it, rather, proclaims that provision has been made for men to actually come to the Father! It presumes that there is a desire to approach unto God, to receive His approbation, and to be received into His favor.

Further, this is not merely a legal requirement. In the world, objectives can be accomplished by ignoring man-made laws. Thus do men gain wealth by theft and dishonesty, etc. But this condition does not exist in the Kingdom of God. Men cannot come to God illegally, so to speak. They must come "lawfully," as the Apostle indicates (II Tim. 2:5). They cannot begin to approach the Father except by Christ.

Without Him, Man Can Do Nothing

Even though man has been reconciled to God, he is not free from restraint. He is free, yet not independent; at liberty, but without license! In Christ, man becomes a liberated dependent — a freed slave. He is made free in order to conform to the truth by doing what is right.

This was in the Lord's mind when He said to His disciples, "I am the Vine, ye are the branches: he that abides in Me, and I in him, the same brings forth much fruit: for without Me ye can do nothing" (John 15:5) — i.e. "nothing" relevant to fruitfulness to God. Men can build empires — political, financial, or religious — without Christ! They may also achieve personal wealth and fame independently of "the Vine."

Anything that is not immediately associated with God's "eternal purpose" is really "nothing" — destined for destruction. Peter tells us that "the works" of man that are in "the earth" shall be burned up at its destruction (II Pet. 3:10). All such works can be achieved "without" Jesus!

A considerable amount of confusion has been produced in this area by the religious claims of men. Denominational empires have been successfully built by those claiming to have been led and empowered by Christ. Yet, these are often at variance with the revealed purposes of God. Their existence by no means contradicts Christ's assertion that without Him, nothing can be done!

Spiritual fruit results from comprehending God's purpose in Jesus. It is fruit that will "remain" after the passing of the heavens and the earth (John 15:16). A simple test of the sort of things that are accomplished "with" Christ is this: whatever survives the passing of the heavens and the earth is accepted with God. These are the accomplishments of which Jesus spake when he said, "without Me, ye can do nothing!"

God's Attitude Toward Him

The consideration of God's attitude toward Christ is a critical one. If we are to be "followers of God as dear children" (Eph. 5:1), we must be united with Him in this matter. One cannot be "acceptable to God" (Rom. 14:18) and entertain a persuasion of Jesus that differs form His. Unity with God on this issue will result in salvation; variance will result in condemnation!

God views Christ within the context of His purpose regarding man. The fact that Jesus is His "only begotten Son" is not the determining factor in His consideration. As regards salvation, it is the achievement of the Son that is the point of Divine contemplation.

In his prophecy of the coming Messiah, Isaiah spoke of One in Whom "the Lord is well pleased for His righteousness' sake." With Divine anticipation, it was foretold that "He will magnify the law, and make it honorable" (Isa. 42:21). "Well pleased," in this case, is a term denoting God's thorough satisfaction with the accomplishments of His Son.

When Jesus was first revealed as the Son of God, the Father's pleasure in Him was audibly expressed from heaven. The heavens had not reverberated with Divine speech since the day when Israel had received the Law in Horeb. It is as though there was no occurrence upon earth that merited Divine commentary.

That day when Jesus' cousin, John the Baptist, plunged Him beneath the baptismal wave, God could not hold His silence! He saw His "eternal purpose" beginning to take shape as the ministry of His Son was launched. For the first time in almost 1,500 years, the "voice of the Lord" that "shakes the wilderness" (Psa. 29:8) penetrated the environment of Satanic deception. "This is My beloved Son, in Whom I am well pleased," proclaimed "a voice from heaven" (Matt. 3:17). Jesus was, in God's estimation, fully qualified to embark upon the ministry of reconciliation!

Approximately three years later, toward the close of Jesus' earthly ministry, "He took Peter and John and James, and went up into a high mountain to pray" (Luke 9:28). As He prayed, His inner glory, concealed from the vision of men in the body, overcame His flesh, and "the fashion of His countenance was altered, and His raiment was white and glistening" (Luke 9:29).

324

At Sinai, in the presence of God, "the skin" of Moses' "face shone," affected from without by Divine glory (Exod. 34:29). But it was different with Jesus. The glory that He had laid aside in His humility (Phil. 2:7) surfaced in a Divine union that none of the sons of men had ever before realized. There, in unequalled spiritual communion, even the clothes of Jesus became saturated, as it were, with glory!

In the grand conclusion of this unparalleled experience, the voice heard three years before again penetrated the sky: "This is My beloved Son, in Whom I am well pleased; hear ye Him" (Matt. 17:5). Perhaps a little more than 30 years later, and shortly before his martyrdom, Peter recalled that heavenly testimony. "We" were "eyewitnesses of His majesty," he recounts. "For He received from God the Father honor and glory, when there came such a voice to Him from the excellent glory, THIS IS MY BELOVED SON, IN WHOM I AM WELL PLEASED" (II Pet. 1:17). Peter's words confirm the continued pleasure of the Father in the Son.

The only question that remains is whether or not men are "well pleased" with the Son. If they are, they are in the will of the Lord. If they are not, they are at variance with the Living God, and, consequently, without "the hope of glory" (Col. 1:27).

At God's Right Hand

The centrality of Jesus is also perceived in His current location at God's right hand. A great deal is made of this in the Apostles' doctrine. In the conclusion of his gospel, Mark writes, "So then after the Lord had spoken unto them, He was received up into heaven, and sat on the right hand of God" (Mark 16:19). Luke provides us with some of Christ's final words; "Hereafter shall the Son of man sit on the right hand of the power of God" (Luke 22:69).

The writer of Hebrews proclaims that He "sat down on the right hand of the Majesty on high" after He "had by Himself purged our sins" (Heb. 1:3). At least three other times, the same writer affirms this reality (Heb. 8:1; 10:12; 12:2), thereby emphasizing its importance.

This truth was announced on the day of Pentecost (Acts 2:33), and as Stephen was about to make the transition from this world to the next, he saw Jesus "standing on the right hand of God" (Acts 7:55,56). Christ's presence at God's right hand is associated with the absence of condemnation (Rom. 8:34), the display of Divine power (Eph. 1:20), and the location of "the things above" (Col. 3:1).

This is the place of favor, of rule, and of acceptance! The current position of Christ is itself a witness of God's attitude toward Him. "All power in heaven and earth" has been given to the One on the Father's right hand (Matt. 28:18). Peter proclaims that Jesus is "gone into heaven, and is on the right hand of God; angels and authorities and powers being made subject to Him" (I Pet. 3:22). A dispensation of authority with that magnitude demonstrates a measure of Divine favor and good pleasure that is without equal.

Kingdom Given to Him

The Kingdom of God is the only one recognized by heaven. All other kingdoms are destined to become "the kingdoms of our Lord and His Christ" (Rev. 11:15). This Kingdom "shall break in pieces and consume all these [worldly] kingdoms, and it shall stand forever" (Dan. 2:44b). Its final revelation began during the earthly ministry of Christ, was inaugurated on Pentecost after King Jesus had assumed its reins, and it shall be consummated when He comes again (II Tim. 4:1).

In a parable that mirrored His own exaltation, Jesus said, "A certain nobleman went into a far country to receive for himself a kingdom, and to return" (Luke 19:12). In confirmation of the fact that He was speaking of Himself, He later revealed that His Father had "appointed" a kingdom to Him (Luke 22:29). Paul taught that reconciliation to God consisted of a translation "into the Kingdom of God's dear Son" (Col. 1:13). Christ has charge of the enterprise of salvation. He is governing the heavenly Kingdom in order to bring many sons to glory.

His current government will continue until God has "put all enemies under His feet. The last enemy that shall be destroyed is death" (I Cor. 15:25-26). At that time, the work of reconciliation shall be complete, and the reconciled and the Reconciler shall begin the ages to come "together." Speaking of that commencement, the Apostle wrote, "Then comes the end, when He shall have delivered up the Kingdom to God, even the Father; when He shall have put down all rule and authority and power" (I Cor. 15:24). The enormous sacrifice entailed in a "Man" assuming the control of the Kingdom is seen in this Apostolic affirmation; "And when all things shall be subdued unto Him, then shall the Son also Himself be subject unto Him that put all things under Him, that God may be all in all" (I Cor. 15:28). He Who "thought it not robbery to

326

be equal with God" (Phil. 2:6) shall bear the effects of man's reconcilia-tion throughout eternity. He has received the Kingdom in full knowledge of this! His great heart anticipates the time when He shall have "delivered up the Kingdom of God" by the acknowledgment, "Behold I and the children which God hath given Me" (Heb. 2:13).

God's Servant

God has always had servants — individuals appointed to ac-complish a heavenly objective. Abraham was God's appointed "servant" to father a nation that would bring forth the Messiah (Gen. 26:24). Moses was the "servant" of God, selected to give the Law (Num. 12:7), and Caleb served the Lord by pioneering the entrance in-to Canaan (Num. 14:24). God referred to Job as "My servant Job" because he represented an upright influence in his day (Job 1:8; 2:3). The prophets were called "His servants the prophets" (Amos 3:7), and "My servants the prophets" (Zech. 1:6) because they proclaimed the mind of God to their generation.

When it came to the matter of reconciling men to God, however, these servants were inadequate. The work was too large for them. Pro-phetically, Isaiah, himself the servant of God (Isa. 20:3), announced the coming of a Servant of a higher order. "Behold MY SERVANT, Whom I uphold; Mine elect, in Whom My soul delights; I have put My Spirit upon Him: He shall bring forth judgment to the Gentiles . . . He shall not fail nor be discouraged . . ." (Isa. 42:1-6).

The "judgment" which he would bring forth was not one of con-demnation. He proclaimed, "for I came not to judge the world, but to save the world" (John 12:47). This salvation was the Divine judgment of God — He had judged men worthy of Divine consideration, and had thus provided for their salvation in His Son! Matthew proclaims that Christ's redemptive work was the fulfillment of Isaiah's prophecy (Matt. 12:17-21). He came to serve God by providing a means for the nations of the world to come to God.

God's Anointed

The Word of God has taught us to identify anointing with "consecra-tion" to Divine appointments (Exod. 28:41; 30:30; I Sam. 10:1). Both kings and priests were anointed according to God's direction (I Sam. 15:17; Exod. 29:29). Among men, respect was to be had for the Lord's "anointed (I Chron. 16:22; Psa. 105:15). This requirement was not due to the particular merit of those who were anointed. Rather, it was in the prospect of the coming Redeemer that significance was attached to those early anointings, or Divine appointments.

The greatest responsibility ever committed to anyone by God fell upon Jesus — the redemption of man! The Lord God "anointed" Him for the activity, appointing Him to a work which no other Person or dispensation could accomplish (Isa. 61:1; Luke 4:18).

The early church recognized this appointment, as evidenced in their prayer; "For of a truth against the holy Child, Whom Thou hast anointed . . ." (Acts 4:27). The Apostles proclaimed His Divine anointing; "How God anointed Jesus of Nazareth with the Holy Ghost and with power . . ." (Acts 10:38).

Beginning of the Creation of God

The Apostles, according to the will of God, have revealed God's ultimate objective for men. It is a grand objective, and is worthy of all acceptance. "For whom He did foreknow, He also did predestinate to be conformed to the image of His Son, that He might be the Firstborn among many brethren" (Rom. 8:29). Theologians have been divided over the meaning of these words. Some have chosen to believe that God has arbitrarily, and without apparent cause, selected some to go to heaven. Others believe that individuals are not the object of Divine determination, but a class of individuals — those that come to Him by Christ (Heb. 7:25). Generally speaking, the latter is the correct view; but it certainly does not exhaust the text.

The point of declaration is not who is predestinated, but the objective of the predestination. "The Lord knows them that are His" (II Tim. 2:19). However, He has not made men privy to that information. Instead, He informs them to "depart from iniquity" (II Tim. 2:19), which is the designated means of becoming identified with His purpose.

Observe the revealed intention of God: it is to conform men "to the image of His Son" — to make them like Jesus! The reason for this determination is also revealed: "that He might be the Firstborn among many brethren." Jesus is to the redeemed what Adam is to sinners. He is the "Firstborn" (Heb. 12:23), God's "First begotten" (Heb. 1:6; Rev. 1:5) — the first One of a new order of men. A new race has been begotten in Christ — a race that thinks and acts like God! This new order of men is referred to as a "new creature" [creation] (II Cor. 5:17; Gal. 6:15), and Jesus is the "Firstborn" of every [such] creature" (Col. 1:15). This is the truth proclaimed in Revelation 3:14; "These things saith the Amen, the faithful and true Witness, the Beginning of the creation of God."

Jesus served God because He wanted to. The Father's will was His "meat," or source of inner nourishment. Jesus did not obey God because He "had to," but "for the joy that was set before Him" (Heb. 12:1-2). Satan had "nothing" in Him — no foothold, or area through which inroads could be made (John 14:30).

God has determined that everyone that receives His Son will be conformed to His likeness. That is the Divinely appointed result of faith — it will be the fruition of a consistent walk "in the light as He is in the light" (I John 1:7).

There is no mystery about this reality. Men are wasting precious time trying to determine whether or not God has selected them for salvation. They make their "calling and election sure" by devoting themselves to the activities God has appointed for men. "And beside all this, giving all diligence, add to your faith virtue; and to virtue knowledge; and to knowledge temperance; and to temperance patience; and to patience godliness; and to godliness brotherly kindness; and to brotherly kindness charity . . . Wherefore the rather, brethren, give diligence to make your calling and election sure: for if ye DO THESE THINGS, YE SHALL NEVER FALL" (II Pet. 1:5-10).

God has already announced His determination for those that have received His salvation. They will ultimately and completely be "like" His Son (I John 3:2). That reveals how precious His own Son is to Himself! He is the central object into which all will be gathered!

Precious to Those That Believe

The new covenant has added the spiritual dimension to man's relationship with God. The elements of joy and satisfaction are associated with the discernment and acceptance of Christ's role in the "salvation of our God" (Psa. 52:10). The personal involvement of the believer is brought into harmony with the revealed purpose of God. Not only is Jesus central in God's redemptive objective, He Himself is the heart and core of the believer's experience. "Unto you therefore which believe He is precious . . ." (I Pet. 2:7).

Access to God

The remission of sins has freed man to love God with all his heart, soul, mind, and strength. That love values the accessibility of its Object, the Living God. Thus is Christ, through Whom we have access to God, of inestimable value. "For through Him we both [Jew and Gentile] have access by one Spirit unto the Father" (Eph. 2:18). Access to God is a practical view of "peace," which was achieved by Christ's redemption. "And [Jesus] came and preached peace to you which were afar off [Gentiles], and to them that were nigh [the Israelites]" (Eph. 2:17). Christ "made peace through the blood of His cross" (Col. 1:20), which is the basis for man's "access," or authorization to "draw near" (Heb. 10:22).

Man's access to God is realized "by faith" — by means of a persuasion of its reality. Faith is not an end of itself, but is the means of appropriating the benefits of the new covenant. Paul provides an inspired recognition of this situation in Romans 5:1-2: "Therefore, being justified by faith, we have peace with God through our Lord Jesus Christ: by Whom we have access by faith into this grace wherein we stand, and rejoice in hope of the glory of God." God has been accessed when "this grace" has been appropriated. Grace, in this case, is associated with obtaining "all things that pertain to life and godliness" — resources required to live acceptably in this world.

The Hope of Glory

God's purpose in Christ begins in this world and terminates in the next. The primary objective of His salvation is not realized in the realm of the temporal, but in the sphere of the eternal. The inheritance to which God summons man is "reserved in heaven," completely separated from the cursed order (I Pet. 1:4). Until the inheritance is possessed, those in Christ live "in hope of eternal life" (Titus 1:2). This "hope" is so vital, that salvation is said to be obtained by it. "For we are saved by hope," declares the Spirit to the churches (Rom. 8:24). The object of this hope is unseen — one that has not yet been realized (Col. 1:5).

The "one hope" to which we have been called (Eph. 4:4) is God's determination to conform the called to the "image of His Son" (Rom. 8:29). A single word which portrays this conformation is "glory." The completion of that conformity will occur when the saints are "glorified" (Rom. 8:30b). Glorification consists of the absence of everything cursed. It will take place when "mortality is swallowed up of life" (II Cor. 5:4), and "death is swallowed up in victory" (Isa. 25:8; I Cor. 15:54). The resurrection of the dead is identifed with this glorification.

Until the "redemption of the purchased possession" — the resurrection of the body (Rom. 8:23; Eph. 1:14) — believers are "waiting for the hope of righteousness" by faith (Gal. 5:5). Their possession of Christ, Who dwells in their "hearts by faith" (Eph. 3:17), is God's pledge of glorification. In Apostolic language, it is "Christ in you, the hope of glory" (Col. 1:27). How precious He is!

Sun of Righteousness

Another aspect of Christ's preciousness is the remedial effects of His ministry. Sin has blasted the race of man, leaving "wounds and putrifying sores" upon his spirit. A deterioration of soul, as well as that of the body, became prevalent, and he continued to "come short of the glory of God" (Rom. 3:23).

Toward the conclusion of the time when God spake "unto the fathers by the prophets" (Heb. 1:1), hope was declared for man's condition. Malachi, who stood at the beginning of a period of four hundred years of Divine silence, foresaw a healing for the infection of iniquity. "But unto you that fear my name shall the Sun of righteousness arise with healing in His wings [rays]" (Mal. 4:2). What a wonderful promise! The warmth of Divine grace would restore spiritual health to men.

Jesus would fulfill the prophetic word of David; ". . . I will yet praise Him Who is the health of my countenance" (Psa. 42:11). Again he said, "God be merciful to us and bless us, and cause His face to shine upon us . . . that Thy way be known upon the earth, Thy saving health among all nations" (Psa. 67:1-2). God's "saving health" comes from the acceptance of Christ's atonement for sin. The persuasion of the effectuality of His sacrifice will lift the countenance, and produce an inner health that will enable a recovery from sin!

A Covert

In a promise of spiritual safety, God spoke through Isaiah of a coming "Man" that would provide refuge from the storms of this life. Isaiah prophesied, "And there shall be a tabernacle for a shadow in the daytime from the heat, and for a place of refuge, and for a covert from storm and from rain" (Isa. 4:6). Again, he declared, "And a Man shall be as a hiding place from the wind, and a covert from the tempest; as rivers of water in a dry place, as the shadow of a great rock in a weary land" (Isa. 32:2).

That "man," is "the Man, Christ Jesus" (I Tim. 2:5). Those that are united to Him by faith cannot be spiritually harmed by any of the above dangers. In Him they are "not appointed to wrath, but to obtain salvation" (I Thess. 5:9). Jesus is also perceived to be a protective "covert" from the impending wrath of God, which shall be poured out upon the wicked "without mixture" (Rev. 14:10).

It is also written, ". . . he that is begotten of God keepeth himself, and that wicked one toucheth him not" (I John 5:18). Those that are "born of God" (I John 2:29) "keep" themselves by hiding in Christ — taking refuge in the "covert" God has provided for the soul. This is accomplished when they voluntarily die to the course of this world, choosing to deny "ungodliness and worldly lusts" as directed by God's grace (Titus 2:12). As it is written, "For ye are dead, and your life is hid with Christ in God" (Col. 3:3). This safety causes the redeemed to properly consider Jesus as "precious."

The Ages to Come

From a broad perspective, there are two basic sets of ages. 1. All time from the beginning of creation until the enthronement of Christ. These ages were characterized by an obscurement of God's plan to reconcile man to Himself through Jesus Christ. ". . . (the mystery of Christ), which in other ages was not made known unto the sons of men, as it is now revealed unto His holy apostles and prophets by the Spirit" (Eph. 3:5). "Even the mystery which hath been hidden from ages and from generations, but now is made manifest to the saints" (Col. 1:26).

2. All ages from the inauguration of the new covenant forward. "Unto Him [God] be glory in the church by Christ Jesus throughout all ages, world without end" (Eph. 3:21). These latter "ages" also have two parts; the current "day of salvation," and the boundless horizon of the future. "That in the ages to come He might show the exceeding riches of His grace in His kindness toward us through Christ Jesus" (Eph. 2:7). The "ages to come" are also addressed by the intriguing

words, "world without end." It is this collection of "ages" that is the subject of this section.

Eternity

God's purpose concerns eternity. This is the realm inhabited by God (Isa. 57:15), and from whence the Lord Jesus came (Micah 5:2). We are "taught of God" (John 6:45) to identify Him with boundlessness; ". . . even from everlasting to everlasting, Thou art God" (Psa. 90:2). His Kingdom is also to be so considered; "For Thine is the Kingdom, and the power, and the glory, forever" (Matt. 6:13). Time, as we know it, is but an interlude during which God's wisdom and grace are being demonstrated to heavenly intelligences (Eph. 3:10).

Eternity is woven throughout every aspect of salvation. Redemption may only be comprehended within the context of eternity! The primary gift provided for men through Jesus is life — "eternal life" (Rom. 6:23; I John 2:25). God's purpose in Christ is "eternal" (Eph. 3:11). His salvation is said to be "with eternal glory" (I Tim. 2:10), and He has obtained "eternal redemption" for us (Heb. 5:9). The object for which the saints long is an "eternal inheritance" (Heb. 9:15). The consolation generated by a reception of the Gospel is an "everlasting" one (II Thess. 2:16).

The judgment of all men will have eternal consequence: thus is it called "eternal judgment" (Heb. 6:2). Even the punishment of the wicked is identifed with eternity. Sodom and Gomorrah, we are apprised, "suffered the vengeance of eternal life" (Jude 7). The wicked shall be punished with "everlasting destruction" (II Thess. 1:9), elsewhere called "everlasting fire" (Matt. 18:8) and "everlasting punishment" (Matt. 18:25).

The "ages to come" is a term which makes eternity more comprehensible to men in the flesh. It represents eternity from the standpoint of progression; upward and onward, so to speak. The world to come" (Heb. 2:5) perceives eternity from the standpoint of the environment. In both cases, there is obvious preeminence. True issues are eternal issues! Temporal matters are always secondary, and tend to distract from the more critical and central issues of eternity.

The eternal ages shall be marked by a continued centrality of Jesus. He shall remain the central One into which all is gathered. This is evidenced by numerous glimpses into the "everlasting Kingdom" given by revelation (Dan. 4:3; 7:27; II Pet. 1:11).

His Confession of the Saints

The participation of the saints in the "ages to come" will commence by Jesus' acknowledgment of them before God. "Whosoever therefore shall confess me before men, him will I confess before My Father which is in heaven" (Matt. 10:32). Those that were not ashamed to identify themselves with God's Son in this world, will enjoy His acknowledgment of them before His "God and Father." The "children of God" (Gal. 3:20; I John 3:10; 5:2) are never contemplated independently of Christ. They owe their present identity as "children" or "sons" to their unity with the "only begotten Son."

The lofty position to which believers are called involves an heirship of "all things" (I Cor. 3:21). They are called the "heirs of the Kingdom which He hath promised to them that love Him" (James 2:5), and "heirs of God" (Rom. 8:17). The connection of their heirship with eternity is seen in the summary statement of the Apostle: "That being justified by His grace, we should be made heirs according to the hope of eternal life" (Titus 3:7).

The centrality of Jesus in our inheritance is apparent. Those that are "sons" are "joint-heirs with Christ" (Rom. 8:17). They have been called into an eternal participation with Jesus, Whom God has "appointed the Heir of all things" (Heb. 1:2). No reward, however small or large, will be separate from Him!

Conclusion

God's "eternal purpose," at all points and from every perspective, revolves around Jesus. Man's involvement in that purpose begins as he, by faith, embraces the Son. It continues as he maintains fellowship with the Son, and it shall consummate in an uninterruptible union with Him as an heir. God be praised for His Son, Jesus Christ!

PART SIX:
THE ROLE OF THE CHURCH

19

THE CHURCH NOW — THE PILLAR AND GROUND OF THE TRUTH

Introduction

The consideration of the church is integral to the contemplation of the Kingdom of God. God has given Jesus to the church (Eph. 1:22), Christ loved and gave Himself for it (Eph. 5:25), and the Holy Spirit enlivens it (Rom. 14:17; 15:13). The prophets foretold it (Psa. 22:22; Heb. 2:12), and the Apostles proclaimed its foundation (Eph. 2:20). The church is at the heart of the work of God (Eph. 3:21), the custodian of the Gospel (Eph. 6:15), and the habitation of God through the Spirit (Eph. 2:22). It is never mentioned casually. Its advantages are proclaimed, and its faults and failings are rebuked with unwavering consistency. The church is the focus of Divine attention. This situation makes it imperative that God's offspring develop and maintain a proper view of and relationship to it.

Identifying the Church

Of itself, the term "church" has little eternal significance. It comes from the root word *ekklesia* which has the general meaning of "an assembly" — a body of people separated from the masses and devoted to a specific purpose. The word also bears the connotation of "called out," indicating that the objective for which they were gathered together was determined outside of themselves — they but embraced the purpose.

The word ekklesia is used in variety of ways in the Scriptures. Luke used it to identify a riotous gathering that opposed the preaching of Paul (Acts 19:32,41). He also employed it to describe a body of people lawfully assembled for consideration of the affairs of state (Acts 19:39). Stephen used it to describe the Israelites in their wilderness wanderings (Acts 7:38). Its preeminent use, however, pertains to those who, by faith and obedience, have embraced the atonement of Christ (Eph. 5:24,25,27,29).

In the latter usage, "the church" is the body of people separated from the world in order to fellowship with God through Christ. Their separation is the result of their response to a heavenly summons, referred to as the "heavenly calling" (Heb. 3:1). This "calling" is accomplished by the Gospel (II Thess. 2:14a). It has an upward thrust, and is therefore called a "high calling" (Phil. 3:14). Those that have "obeyed the Gospel" (Rom. 10:16) comprise "the church." While "in the world," they are being oriented for glory by their submission to God's will.

The church is the extension of Christ upon the earth — His "body" (Eph. 1:23; Col. 1:24). It was His central consideration when He died. As it is written, He "loved the church and gave Himself for it" (Eph. 5:25). It is His personal "house" — those to whom He ministers Divine benefits (Heb. 3:6). God contemplates His Son in eternal association with the church, and therefore she is called "the bride, the Lamb's wife" (Rev. 22:17). Because Jesus Himself is constructing the church, a "spiritual house" in which God resides (I Pet. 2:5; I Tim. 3:15a), groups of believers are also called "churches of Christ" (Rom. 16:16). Rather than being a mere appellation, this portrays them as being identified with Jesus. That identification began when they obeyed the Gospel; it continues by their devotion to the truth, and shall consummate by them being joined to Him forever.

Its Relevance

The relevance of the church is found in God's salvational purpose in

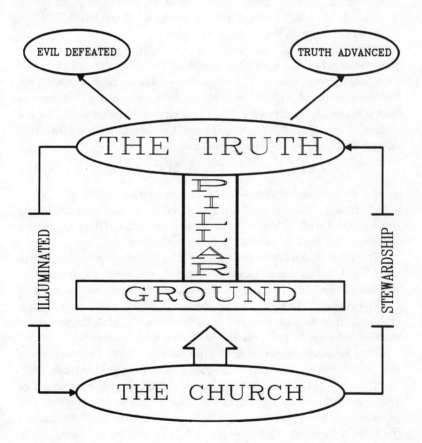

337

Christ. It really has no other significance. Its members are a "holy priesthood," appointed "to offer up spiritual sacrifices" to God (I Pet. 2:5). The work of God is perceived as being accomplished through the church, thereby bringing glory to Him (Eph. 3:21). The church exists for participation, not merely to be blessed. Divine blessings are intended to equip the church for involvement in Divine work. Herein is found its relevance.

As "the church of God," the redeemed participate in the "work of God." As the "body of Christ," they become the means by which He accomplishes His will. The church is, therefore, as relevant as the work of God; as pertinent as the ministry of Jesus!

The "Kingdom of God" and "the church," though related, are not synonymous terms. God's Kingdom is an enterprise, the church is an assembly of personalities. The Kingdom is a Divine reign involving the implementation of an "eternal purpose," the church is a revelation of that purpose. God, through Christ, is achieving His purpose "by the church" (Eph. 3:10). There is no reason for the church apart from that objective. This is what gives it relevance.

An Unilluminated Church, A Contradiction

An uninformed church — one that is fundamentally ignorant of eternal realities — cannot glorify God. Contrary to some contemporary notions, God is not glorified by His own obscurement. Glory, by its very nature, is the result of revelation or manifestation.

The chief stewardship of the church, the "word of reconciliation" (II Cor. 5:19), is called the "glorious gospel" because of its revelatory attributes (II Cor. 4:4; I Tim. 1:1). Through it, the mind and purpose of God has been made known to men. Indeed, the new covenant — "the ministration of the Spirit" — is "rather glorious." It excels the first covenant — the Law — in its disclosure of God's will to men.

That purpose is summarized by the Apostle; "Unto Him be glory in the church by Christ Jesus throughout all ages, world without end" (Eph. 3:21). The nature of this glory is perceived in the statement of Divine intention: "To the intent that now unto the principalities and powers in heavenly places might be known by [means of] the church the manifold wisdom of God" (Eph. 3:10). Those that are "partakers of the heavenly calling" bring glory to God in their manifestation of the wisdom of God. This is achieved by means of their participation in the primary demonstration of His wisdom — His "great salvation" (Heb. 2:3).

A church that is ignorant of the reconciliation, therefore, contradicts the purpose of God. It obscures God's glory rather than revealing it, and draws a veil over the greatest manifestation God has ever given of Himself — that under the new covenant. God has ordained the church as custodian of the covenant. If it is not made known by her, God has no other means of making it known, and, consequently, no other means to glorify Himself "by Jesus Christ."

Another word for illumination is enlightenment. This is elsewhere called "spiritual understanding" (Col. 1:9), and means the perception of the significance and implications of God's provision in Christ. The concept postulates one passing from a state of spiritual ignorance into one of understanding and discernment.

Paul elaborates upon this concept to the Ephesian church, showing that it is an incongruity for the people of God to be ignorant of Him. The Apostle's prayer for them was "that the God of our Lord Jesus Christ, the Father of glory, may give unto you the spirit of wisdom and revelation in the knowledge [or understanding] of Him: the eyes of your understanding being enlightened. . . ."

This enlightenment results in a comprehension of what had been previously undiscerned. The purpose and nature of God becomes clearer to the heart in fulfillment of Divine purpose: ". . . that ye may know what is the hope of His calling, and what [is] the riches of the glory of His inheritance in the saints, and what is the exceeding greatness of His power to usward who believe, according to the working of His mighty power" (Eph. 1:17-19). Paul prayed for the enlightenment of the Ephesians because it was in keeping with Divine objective.

Called by Means of Illumination

There comes a time when it is profitable for one to recall his entrance into the Kingdom of God's "dear Son" (Col. 1:13). It was the time when he became "a new creature" in Christ (II Cor. 5:17), and the "answer of a good conscience" was experienced (I Pet. 3:18). The time of one's conversion (Acts 3:19; 15:3) is also a time of illumination. Thus did the Apostle stir the remembrance of lethargic Jewish believers: "But call to remembrance the former days, in which, after ye were illuminated . . ." (Heb. 10:32). At that time they perceived their own state as sinners, God's great love in Christ, and the availability of that love through the belief of the Gospel. It was a time of enlightenment, when the veil of obscurity was taken away from their hearts (II Cor. 3:14).

A salvation begun by illumination only to be later characterized by obtuseness is a contradiction. God has joined salvation and illumination together, and they cannot be separated without one becoming alienated from God. An unilluminated church is one that has denied its calling, and repudiated the means by which it was once called into the fellowship of God's Son (I Cor. 1:9).

Man's initial participation in salvation is accomplished by means of spiritual enlightenment. The Divine fellowship for which salvation is wrought is also maintained by the same means. The lack of maturity in Christ evidences a failure to comprehend the realities of the Kingdom. The Apostle said, "For this cause I bow my knees unto the Father of our Lord Jesus Christ . . . that He would grant you . . . to be strengthened with might by His Spirit in the inner man . . . that ye . . . may be able to comprehend with all saints what is the breadth, and length, and depth, and height; and to know the love of Christ which passeth knowledge, that ye might be filled with all the fulness of God" (Eph. 3:14-19).

The phrase, "that ye might be filled with all the fulness of God," is a metaphor for Divine fellowship. The Lord's spiritual intimacy with His people results in their conformity to Himself — "filled with all the fulness of God." Divine communion will consistently yield an improvement in man's character.

The Means of Growth

Divine fellowship is the objective view of the effect of spiritual enlightenment. Spiritual growth is the subjective view of its result. Men "grow up" into Christ by means of faith — exercised through "the eyes of" their "understanding" (Eph. 1:18). The fundamental means of advancement in redemption is that of comprehension, not morality. Moral improvement is recognized by God when it is the result of discernment. Those that have achieved this type of growth are said to have their senses exercised to "discern both good and evil" (Heb. 5:14). Morality that is accomplished by rote, or mere fleshly discipline, has no eternal value.

The spiritual progress of believers is identified with the truth — the objective statement of heavenly reality. As the truth is articulated, it is brought within reach of the mind. Apart from that articulation, saving truth cannot be comprehended. The Apostle alluded to this process when he said, "but speaking the truth in love, may grow up into Him in all things . . ." (Eph. 4:15). The use of "love" refers primarily to a love of the truth itself (II Thess. 2:10). It is out of that attitude that truth may be considerately spoken to others. Reality thus proclaimed will provoke advancement toward the "mark for the prize of the high calling," by clarifying the hope of that calling.

The Concept of Stewardship

Collectively, the church is God's steward, or custodian, of His truth. Stewardship is an expression of the dominion for which man was made. It speaks of responsibility and management. In Scripture, a steward was one that had charge of a household or estate. In a poignant statement to His disciples, Jesus said, "Who then is that faithful and wise steward, whom his Lord shall make ruler over His household? . . . Of a truth I say unto you, that He will make him ruler over all that He has" (Luke 12:42-44).

Prior to this utterance, Jesus had alerted His disciples to the necessity of readiness. "Let your loins be girded about, and your lights burning; and ye yourselves like unto men that wait for their lord, when he will return from the wedding; that when he comes and knocks, they may open unto him immediately." He pronounced a blessing on servants that were found "watching" at the return of their lord. "Verily I say unto you, that he shall gird himself, and make them sit down to meat, and will come forth and serve them. And if he come in the second watch, or come in the third watch, and find them so, blessed are those servants" (Luke 12:35-39). Jesus associated service with stewardship — with spiritual rule or responsibility. Under the new covenant, a servant was not to be a mere slave, but one that was given responsibility in a key Kingdom area (Luke 12:43-44).

Stewardship is also identified with accountability. A steward has been given the goods of another, and is responsible for handling them in a manner pleasing to their owner. In a parable that revealed the nature of God's Kingdom, Jesus revealed this truth. "For the Kingdom of heaven is as a man traveling into a far country, who called His own servants, and delivered unto them His goods . . ." (Matt. 25:14-30). This was the well known parable of the "talents." Following its proclamation, a Divine commentary was provided. "When the Son of man shall come in His glory, and all the holy angels with Him, then shall He sit upon the throne of His glory: and before Him shall be gathered all nations." The accountability which followed was awesome, resulting in the salvation of some, and the damnation of others (Matt. 25:31-46). This was a commentary on Kingdom stewardship — the allocation of Divine resources to men, together with the responsibility to handle them acceptably in prospect of the day of accounting.

The primary area of responsibility for the church is that of the truth of God. The "church of the Living God" is the "pillar and ground of the truth" (I Tim. 3:15). It is to make manifest the purpose and revelation of God to the minds of men. It is to introduce men to heavenly substance and its conflict with the world. The members of Christ's church are "kings" as regards their stewardship (Rev. 1:5; 5:10. In Jesus they are able to speak the Gospel with all of the authority of heaven — they have been made under-rulers over Christ's house!

Truth's effectiveness is now dependent upon the faithfulness of its steward, the church. It can be spoken or concealed, plentiful or scarce, flourishing or failing — it is up to the steward. This condition does not exist because God is weak, or because the truth, of itself, is impotent. This is the manner of God's Kingdom. In Christ, He has brought men into His purpose as participants. Admittedly, the situation has introduced an element of restriction — but that element was imposed by God, not man. The restoration of man includes a period of temporary handicap. That period, however, can be addressed successfully by a faithful and willing church. God has provided resources that will support diligent effort — but the steward must appropriate them by faith.

The Requirement of a Steward

The proper emphasis of the church is not its organization, but its stewardship. It is the "pillar and ground of the truth." Believers are to maintain their relationships as "good stewards of the manifold grace of God" (I Pet. 4:10-11). To receive grace is marvelous — to be a steward of it in its diversity is sobering! Faithfulness is to be the watchword of the church! The Divine requirement for stewards is clearly stated in Scripture. "Moreover it is required in stewards, that a man be found faithful"

(I Cor. 4:2).

The Emphasis Is on the Steward

Conceptually, God's truth cannot be separated from its stewards. It is as apparent as its stewards are faithful. Jesus has actually dispensed His goods to His church, and it is responsible for handling them correctly. Such an arrangement requires that the emphasis be placed upon the steward — upon the custodian of the truth. That is the appointed means of establishing the truth. The church is the "pillar and ground of the truth."

When Christ "went about doing good," He was the heavenly steward among men. He was sent to "bear witness unto the truth" (John 18:37). God placed the emphasis upon His Steward: "This is my Beloved Son . . . hear ye Him" (Matt. 17:5). Truth could not be obtained independently of Him.

When the Son returned to heaven, He charged His Apostles with the responsibility of ministering the truth — they received the Divine stewardship. "Preach the Gospel to every creature" (Mark 16:15); "Go therefore and teach all nations . . . teaching them to observe all things, whosoever I have commanded you . . ." (Matt. 28:19-20). He determined to build His church "upon the foundation of the Apostles and prophets" — His stewards (Eph. 2:20). Men would be judged according to their response to these men — the emphasis was upon His stewards. The truth "in Jesus" (Eph. 4:21), because of this stewardship, was called "the Apostles' doctrine" (Acts 2:42).

Paul's stewardship of and identification with the Gospel constrained him to call it his Gospel; "In the day when God shall judge the secrets of men according to MY Gospel" (Rom. 2:16). Speaking in behalf of those that brought the message of the Gospel, he wrote to the Thessalonians, "Whereunto He called you by OUR Gospel, to the obtaining of the glory of our Lord Jesus Christ" (II Thess. 2:14).

In God's Kingdom — an economy of truth — the rejection of His stewards constitutes a rejection of their stewardship. Thus, a rejection of Jesus is a rejection of the "grace and truth" which came by Him (John 1:17). A refusal to accept the Apostles is a refusal to embrace the Gospel of salvation which they proclaimed. To despise the members of the body of Christ is to despise their ministration of "nourishment," which is designed to "knit together" and produce "the increase of God"

343

(Col. 2:19). In this sense, the emphasis is on the steward.

When Truth Fails

It is possible for truth to fail — to cease functioning and lose its strength. This condition is not caused by any deficiency in the truth itself — God forbid! Rather, God has ordained that the truth be communicated by the intelligent expression of men. Angels do not proclaim it to the world, as they themselves do not comprehend it (I Pet. 1:12). Jesus will not return to the world to minister it among men. He shall remain in heaven until the fulfillment of all prophecy (Acts 3:21). The dead will not be raised to proclaim it, as their word would carry no more weight than that of those remaining in the earth (Luke 16:31). Men must declare the truth, or it will not be made known.

In the time of Isaiah there was a lack of truth. God denounced His people for permitting such a condition to arise. "Yea, truth fails: and he that departs from evil makes himself a prey: and the Lord saw it, and it displeased Him that there was no judgment" (Isa. 59:15). It was not that truth was beyond them, but that men were not availing themselves of it — thus its power was lost. When there is no proclamation of or regard for the truth, its fruits may not be experienced.

Truth is essentially associated with expression; "Thy WORD is truth" (John 17:19); ". . . speaking the truth . . ." (Eph. 4:15); ". . . the word of truth . . ." (Eph. 1:13; Col. 1:5; II Tim. 2:15; James 1:18). It is not possible to form a valid idea about heavenly things apart from the Word of God! Thus, when the truth of them is not declared by the church, sound concepts of spiritual realities become impossible. This condition results in the failing of the truth.

Whether it is a failure to "preach the Word" (II Tim. 4:2), or the turning "away their ears from the truth" (II Tim. 4:4), the result is the same; truth is rendered ineffectual — it fails! This situation places a solemn obligation upon the church, God's custodian of the truth. It is its responsibility to proclaim the truth with godly consistency.

Perilous Times Shall Come

The scarcity of truth produces perilous times — periods of intense danger. The Apostles spoke of such times, and their words carried a note of alarm. "This know also, that in the last days perilous times shall come" (II Tim. 3:1-6). The danger did not consist of imminent physical harm, but of spiritual jeopardy. Protection from those perilous times could not be achieved by fleeing to safety, as in the destruction of Jerusalem (Matt. 25:16-19). Rather, it was to be found in the truth; "But continue thou in the things which thou hast learned, and hast been assured of . . ." (II Tim. 3:14).

Elaborating upon those days of danger, Paul identified them with a lack of devotion to the truth. "Preach the Word . . . for the time will come when men will not endure sound doctrine . . . and they shall turn away their ears from the truth and be turned unto fables" (II Tim. 4:1-4). The proclamation of the truth is what holds it up and causes it to produce spiritual results.

If Satan can deceive the church into closing its mouth, the truth will be "fallen in the street, and equity cannot enter" (Isa. 59:14). The time of the "dark ages" in history abundantly demonstrates this principle. With Bibles chained to the monasteries of papal Rome, the "lip of truth" dried up (Prov. 12:19). The result was a prevailing ignorance of the Living God that was reflected in all of society. Literature, art, and social advancement had the stamp of spiritual death upon them. Truth failed and fell in the streets, and perilous times were introduced. The church, by its devotion to its stewardship of truth, can help avert the occurrence of such tragedy.

The Advancement of Truth and the Defeat of Evil

The time of the first covenant was marked by military exploits, bloodshed, and war (Joshua 10:5-24; 11:17). The Israelites were commissioned to drive the inhabitants out of the land of Canaan, and to possess it by carnal warfare (Deut. 7:1-5).

The new covenant, however, is not according to this manner. The weapons provided the church are "not carnal, but mighty through God to the pulling down of strongholds." These "strongholds" are citadels of error that interfere with the apprehension of the knowledge of God. "Casting down imaginations, and every high thing that exalts itself against the knowledge of God, and bringing into captivity every thought to the obedience of Christ" (II Cor. 10:4-5). The church, as the "pillar and ground of the truth," is to make inroads into the kingdom of darkness by its faithful and discerning proclamation of the truth! This is the appointed means of advancing the truth and defeating evil.

Nothing is automatic, or accomplished without effort, in the

345

Kingdom of God. The foundation of man's acceptance by God was accomplished by the zealous effort of Jesus Christ. Effective declaration of that accomplishment is by the zealous effort of redeemed men. The prophet declared that God's purpose would be achieved by Divine zeal; "The zeal of the Lord of hosts will perform this" (Psa. 9:7). That zeal, however, consumed the heavenly Steward. It was prophesied of Jesus that He would be "clad with zeal as a cloak" (Isa. 59:17). When He "dwelt among us" (John 1:14), His disciples observed His energetic ministry and "remembered that it was written, the zeal of Thine house hath eaten Me up" (John 2:17). God's Kingdom is revealed when His Divine resourcefulness and devotion are exhibited in men.

A realization of this principle burned in the heart of the Apostle. He knew that God did not, in His salvation, work through casual and indifferent efforts. If the reconciliation of men to God was to be realized experientially, God's stewards must have God's zeal — it must consume them! Thus did Paul earnestly request of the church, "Praying always . . . for me, that utterance may be given unto me, that I may open my mouth and speak boldly . . . that therefore I may speak boldly, as I ought to speak" (Eph. 6:19-20).

The table of salvation has been "prepared" in the presence of the church's enemies — enemies among men and among the spirit-world. If there is not a bold proclamation, the forces of evil will prevail. The intense energy of Satan cannot be successfully thwarted by a half-hearted effort by the church.

The Word Having Free Course

God's redemptive purpose and the "word of reconciliation" were closely united in the mind of the Apostle. He could not conceive of God's undertaking being achieved without proclamation of the Gospel. How fervently he besought the Thessalonians; "Finally, brethren, pray for us, that the Word of God may have free course, and be glorified, even as it is with you: and that we may be delivered from unreasonable and wicked men . . ." (II Thess. 3:1-2).

The "free course," or running, of God's word is connected with its proclamation. It cannot run to fulfill God's pleasure where it has not been declared! Paul's desire to be delivered from inhibiting men was not one for mere personal well-being. He saw wicked men as capable of hindering the spread of the truth, and thus solicited the prayers of discerning hearts. He was united with the Lord in the desire for the salvation of "all men" (II Tim. 2:4).

The church, in my judgment, is ill-advised to become engrossed in the social issues of our day at the expense of the truth. If truth fails, it is the church's fault, for she is its custodian and steward! If the Word of truth is to move freely among men, the church must speak it, and be delivered from wicked and unreasonable men in order that she might do so.

Whose Mouths Must Be Stopped

Not only must truth be proclaimed with zealous effort, it is also imperative that religious error be subdued. Just as Israel had to subdue the land of Canaan (Deut. 20:20), so must the church subdue the proclamation of dogmas that separate men from God. This task is more necessary than pleasant, and thus men must be exhorted to engage in it.

It is an unfortunate reality that spiritual "gainsayers" exist — men that speak reproachfully of the truth. Such are called "unruly and vain talkers," who "subvert whole houses, teaching what they ought not, for filthy lucre's sake." Their existence presents a challenge to Christ's church. They are not to simply be ignored in hope that they will go away. Nor, indeed, are the redeemed to be so naive as to think that the positive declaration of the Gospel will automatically put false prophets to flight.

We have an Apostolic word on this — it was part of their "doctrine." "For there are many unruly and vain talkers and deceivers, specially they of the circumcision, whose mouths must be stopped" (Titus 1:10-11). In his instruction concerning the appointment of elders, Paul told Titus that "a bishop" was required to hold "fast the faithful word as he hath been taught, that he may be able by sound doctrine both to exhort and convince the gainsayers" (Titus 1:7-10). This activity would result in the silencing of the subverters.

The church must come to grips with its reponsibility to confront contrary doctrines that shut up the Kingdom of God, and restrain men from entering it (Matt. 23:13; Luke 11:52). Thus will it follow the example set by the Apostles, who did not hesitate to expose error by shining the light of truth upon it (II Tim. 2:14-18; I John 4:1-5; II John 7-11; III John 9-10; Jude 4-11).

347

Controversy

The offensiveness of controversy is not reason to avoid it. The Kingdom of God is essentially involved therewith. Even the Law made provision for "matters of controversy" (Deut. 18:8; 19:17), teaching men that it was not be avoided. Scripture records that Michael, an angel of great authority, "when contending with the devil, disputed about the body of Moses" (Jude 9). Controversy, or disputation, is thus not unknown in the heavenly places (cf. Dan. 10:11-14). God Himself is a God of controversy. He had a "controversy" with Israel (Isa. 34:8; Hosea 4:1; 12:2; Micah 6:2), as well as with "the nations" (Jer. 25:31). The Kingdom of God, therefore, is no stranger to dispute and controversy.

What Is Controversy?

Controversy does not involve merely different views, but conflicting ones — not varying perspectives, but antithetical ones. Not all differences are conflicting in nature, as the Apostle taught; "for one believes that he may eat all things: another, who is weak eats herbs . . . One man esteems one day above another: another esteems every day alike. Let every man be fully persuaded in his own mind" (Rom. 14:2-6). It is out of order to make these kinds of differences matters of controversy. Valid controversy involves differences of eternal consequence; varying views that have a direct bearing upon the salvation and damnation of men.

Like Christ, truth has a discriminating effect. It was said of our Lord, that "there was a division among the people because of Him" (John 7:43) . . . "There was a division therefore again among the Jews for these sayings" (John 10:19). Thus was His truth often proclaimed in the arena of disputation (Acts 9:29; 15:2; 17:17).

While Paul was in Ephesus, "he went into the synagogue, and spake boldly for the space of three months, disputing and persuading the things concerning the Kingdom of God" (Acts 19:8). Having met with considerable opposition in the synagogue, he did not abandon the practice of disputation, but rather "separated the disciples, disputing daily in the school of one Tyrannus" (Acts 19:10).

Contrary to carnal analysis, controversy does not cause division; division produces controversy. Disputation does not bring about separa-

348

tion, but is rather evidence of its existence.

A proper involvement in controversy requires discernment of the truth. Reality must be blended with man's spirit before it can be successfully defended. Jesus put it in these words; "If any man will do [wills to do] His will, he shall know of the doctrine, whether it be of God, or whether I speak of Myself" (John 7:17). Without that experiential knowledge, disputation is confined to the realm of flesh, and is thus unlawful.

Let the church press the battle by boldly confronting religious error with the truth. Righteous disputation will show the illogical nature of error — it simply cannot blend with truth. Truth cannot be supported without toppling dogmas that do not permit it to be embraced.

The Sin of Silence

All manifestations of the Kingdom of God are by articulation. Truth has never been embraced where it was not uttered. God "spake in time past unto the fathers by the prophets," and in these "last days" He has spoken unto us by His Son" (Heb. 1:1-2). Jesus came speaking — teaching and proclaiming the purpose of God. "I speak to the world those things which I have heard of Him," He declared (John 8:26). The preeminent role of the Holy Spirit is found in what He says. "He that has an ear, let him hear what the Spirit says unto the churches" (Rev. 2:7,11,17,29; 3:6,13,22). Man's withdrawal from God (Heb. 10:39) is arrested by hearing what "the Holy Spirit says" (Heb. 3:7,15; 4:7).

A silent church cannot be in harmony with a speaking God, a teaching Jesus, and an exhorting Spirit. The Gospel must be proclaimed, and the Word is to be preached with reproof, rebuke, and exhortation (II Tim. 4:2). The conversion of sinners and the edification of saints is accomplished by speech — "words of faith and doctrine" (I Tim. 4:6). The words God spoke through the Psalmist are still true; ". . . open thy mouth wide, and I will fill it (Psa. 81:10). Let no individual that has named the name of Christ be content to be silent, to hold his peace, or to have his tongue cleaving to the roof of his mouth (Ezek. 3:26). In view of the great salvation that has been provided in Christ, and of the activities of God toward men such an attitude is sinful!

A Betrayal of the Stewardship

The Gospel has been placed in the hands of the church — she is the pillar and ground of its truth. Its power is unleashed when it is preached, for it has "pleased God by the foolishness of preaching to save them that believe" (I Cor. 1:21). Undeclared, the Gospel has no power. It is the "power of God unto salvation to everyone that believes," but "How shall they call upon Him in Whom they have not believed? and how shall they believe in Him of Whom they have not heard? and how shall they hear without a preacher?" (Rom. 10:14-17).

A silent church has betrayed its stewardship. It has buried its talent in the ground, so to speak, and shall be judged for doing so (Matt. 25:18-19,24-30). The true expertise of the church is to be found in its discernment and proclamation of the Word of God. She is primarily the "pillar and ground of the truth" — God's means of getting his saving truth to men.

The requirement of faithfulness in stewards (I Cor. 4:2) is introduced by the prophets. In strict conformity with His character, God revealed how He views an unfaithful steward. His revelation to Ezekiel is startling to a lethargic church, and thus needs to be proclaimed. "When I say unto the wicked, Thou shall surely surely die; and you give him not warning, nor speak to warn the wicked from his wicked way, to save his life; the same wicked man shall die in his iniquity; but his blood will I require at thy hand" (Ezek. 3:18).

The same point is made concerning watchmen, charged with the responsibility of alerting the city to possible attack. "But if the watchmen see the sword come, and blow not the trumpet, and the people be not warned; if the sword come, and take any person from among them, he is taken away in his iniquity; but his blood will I require at the watchman's hand" (Ezek. 33:6). God then declared that He had appointed Ezekiel to be a "watchmen unto the house of Israel." Failure to warn the people of impending judgment would result in the judgment of the prophet (Ezek. 33:7-8).

Paul alluded to this principle of responsibility in his letter to the Corinthians. "For if I do this thing [preaching the Gospel] willingly [if I speak of myself], I have [right to a worldly] reward: but if against my will [if by Divine appointment], a dispensation of the Gospel is committed unto me" [I will be held accountable for having proclaimed it] (I Cor. 9:17). Little wonder he exclaimed, ". . . for necessity is laid upon me; yea, woe is unto me, if I preach not the Gospel" (I Cor. 9:26). His was a Gospel stewardship!

350

This Kingdom principle is also applied to "the church of the Living God, which is the pillar and ground of the truth." Woe unto her if she does not execute her responsibility — if she does not hold up the truth! She is to hold it up under the fierce attacks of men and demons! With unrelenting zeal, her efforts are to be poured into the "manifestation of the truth" (II Cor. 4:2). If she proves unfaithful in this awesome stewardship, the souls of the condemned will be required at her hand!

Conclusion

God's Kingdom is one of truth. It involves the effectual dissemination of that truth by those that have embraced it. In His wisdom and prudence, the Lord has deposited the truth with His church. That truth will run only as far as the church carries it; it will grow only to the extent that His people proclaim it. The "elect angels" (I Tim. 5:21) cannot proclaim it. The Holy Spirit will not pierce the heavens with a thunderous announcement! If the church does not preach it, it will not be preached. It is in her care!

20

THE CHURCH NOW — LABORERS
TOGETHER WITH GOD

Under the first covenant, as well as in prior ages, God worked for man; under the new covenant God works with and in man. This represents a marvelous relationship — one into which prophets inquired, and that angels view with intense interest (I Pet. 1:10-12). God did not make man to be a mere object of attention; a pawn, so to speak, to be used by Divine manipulation. Birds of the air and beasts of the field would have sufficed for an enterprise of that nature, but not man.

Illustrated in Enoch

Prior to the flood, "whereby the world that then was, being overflowed with water perished" (II Pet. 3:6), Enoch "walked with God" (Gen. 5:22,24). It is apparent that he maintained a Divine perspective of the unparalleled evil that surrounded him. Jude provides us with a prophecy given by Enoch, "the seventh from Adam." His words revealed his reaction to the wickedness of his day. "Behold, the' Lord comes with ten thousands of His saints, to execute judgment upon all, and to convince all that are ungodly among them of all their ungodly deeds which they have ungodly committed, and of all their hard speeches which ungodly sinners have spoken against Him" (Jude 14-15).

Enoch's walk "with God" resulted in an accurate appraisal of his generation. He apparently was not a smiling, positive-thinking, prophet, with an appealing presentation and a polished appearance. His reaction to the world was a godly one, not a calculating one. In this way Enoch labored together with God. His view was God's view; his reaction was heaven's reaction!

God and Man under the New Covenant

God now dwells within man, in distinction to coming upon him. "God dwells in us, and His love is perfected in us. Hereby know we that we dwell in Him, and He in us, because He has given us of His Spirit" (I John 4:12-13). "And he that keeps His commandments dwells in Him, and He in him. And hereby we know that He abides in us, by the Spirit which He has given us" (I John 3:24). In Christ, men are "joined to the Lord," and become "one spirit" with Him (I Cor. 6:17).

God does not join Himself to man to sympathize with him, but to enable him to participate in heavenly activity. God is a Worker, and His uniting with men results in His expression through them. It is God "which works all in all" (I Cor. 12:6), working in believers "to will and to do His good pleasure" (Phil. 2:13) — enabling them to execute His purpose. In God's Kingdom, effectual labor is accomplished "according to His working, which works in" men "mightily" (Col. 1:29).

Jesus promised, "If a man love Me, he will keep My words: and My Father will love him, and We will come unto him, and make Our abode with him" (John 14:23). His covenantal promise is, "I will dwell in them, and walk in them" (II Cor. 6:16). In His high priestly prayer, shortly before His betrayal, Jesus prayed, "That they all may be one; as Thou, Father, art in Me, and I in Thee, that they also may be one in Us . . . I in them, and Thou in Me, that they may be made perfect in one . . ." (John 17:21,23).

Saving Men

The extent to which men in Christ labor with God is perceived in their participation in the salvation of men. No man joined in the accomplishment of salvation's foundation — Jesus did that "alone," or

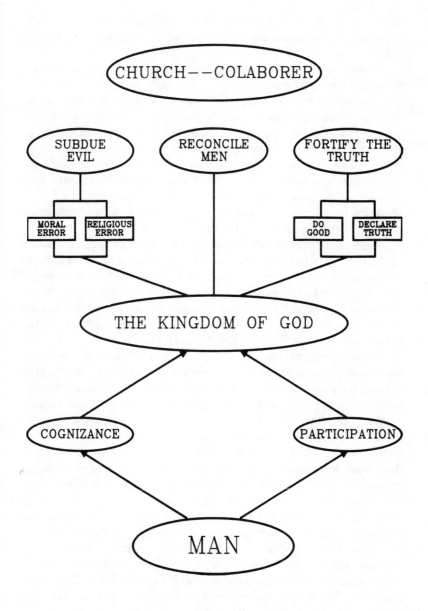

"by Himself" (Isa. 63:3; Heb. 1:3). However, men do become involved in the effectual administration of that salvation. They become "laborers together with God" (I Cor. 3:9).

Paul spoke of his desire to reach his kinsmen according to the flesh, the Jews. He stated that his purpose was to "provoke them to emulation . . . which are my flesh, and might save some of them" (Rom. 11:14). He again affirmed this intention to the Corinthians. "To the weak became I as weak, that I might gain the weak: I am made all things to all men, that I might by all means save some" (I Cor. 9:22). In this attitude he was obedient to Christ's commission to him: ". . . the Gentiles, unto whom now I send thee, to open their eyes, and to turn them from darkness to light, and from the power of Satan unto God . . ." (Acts 26:18). Those are arresting words, indeed, and yet they are precisely correct! Paul was a laborer "together with God"!

In an admonition to young Timothy, Paul again stressed this matter. "Take heed unto yourself, and unto the doctrine; continue in them: for in doing this you shall both save yourself and them that hear you" (I Tim. 4:16). To be joined to the Lord is to be joined to His work! As He dwells in His people, He continues to "work salvation in the midst of the earth" (Psa. 74:12), even employing their sanctified abilities in the enterprise! They are "laborers together with God"!

The conversion of some of the Corinthians had brought division in their home — some were in Christ, some were not. In his doctrine concerning that sensitive situation, Paul again brings up the matter of man's participation in the work of salvation. "For what do you know, O wife, whether you shall save your husband? or how do you know, O man, whether you shall save your wife" (I Cor. 7:16). The words are certainly clear enough; it is their conflict with false concepts that cause men to draw back from them. They are unable to conceive of men saving anyone. But such a reaction is altogether unwarranted. In Christ, men are made "laborers together with God."

James also reveals this aspect of the Kingdom of God. His words are challenging, and are to be embraced by faith. "Brethren, if any of you do err from the truth, and one convert him; let him know that he who converts the sinner from the error of his way shall save a soul from death, and shall hide a multitude of sins" (James 5:19-20). Converting the sinner! Saving a soul! The removal of sins! — these are results attributed elsewhere to God Himself (Acts 3:19; Matt. 18:11; Isa. 38:17).

356

The new covenant, however enables men to unite with God in these things. They thus become, "laborers together with God."

Jesus admonished His disciples to petition God to "send forth laborers into His harvest" (Matt. 9:37). He perceived a great work that required immediate attention — but resources were very scarce. "The harvest [of men's souls] truly is great, but the laborers are few: pray therefore the Lord of the harvest, that He would send forth laborers into His harvest" (Luke 10:2).

It is not that the Lord's hand is "shortened, that it cannot save" (Isa. 59:1). There is still "no restraint to the Lord to save by many or by few" (I Sam. 14:6). The "day of salvation," however, requires a ministry of joint labor — men with God, accomplishing the work of the Kingdom! The harvest of men's souls will not be reaped without the efforts of godly laborers, and they will not be sent into the harvest apart from the petitions of men. This is the "manner of the Kingdom" (I Sam. 10:25).

God Without the Church — Contradicts Divine Purpose

The church is so closely associated with God that He can longer be correctly viewed apart from it. This is His "family" (Eph. 3:14-15), consisting of His "sons" (I John 3:1-3). The church is "God's husbandry," "God's building" (I Cor. 3:9), and His "habitation" (Eph. 2:22). It has been identified as "the city of God" (Heb. 12:22), the "flock of God" (Acts 20:28), and "the temple of God" (I Cor. 3:16). It is not possible to entertain a proper view of the Living God without the inclusion of the church. He has made it an integral part of Himself, His purpose, and His work!

A view of God that excludes the church contradicts the revealed purpose of the "first covenant." The period during which it was in force was a Divinely appointed interlude. God's primary objective was never intended to be achieved by the law. In the words of Apostle, "For if the inheritance be of the Law, it is no more of promise: but God gave it to Abraham by promise" (Gal. 3:18).

This observation might prompt one to question the appropriateness of the Law. We are told the reason for its administration. "Wherefore then serves the Law? It was added because of transgressions, till the Seed should come, to Whom the promises were made . . ." (Gal. 3:19). The prevalence of transgression was more known to God than to man. Before the Son of God — "the Seed" — came into the world, it

357

was necessary to develop man's awareness of iniquity. God determined to do this by identifying sin as contrary to Himself. Thus would man, made in the image of God, be able to perceive the reason for his alienation. The law was a "schoolmaster to bring us unto Christ, that we might be justified by faith" (Gal. 3:24) — to prepare us for His salvation.

But let us not miss the point here. The Divine prospect of a people — the church — being joined unto Himself, required that they be convicted of sin. This would prepare them for the perception of the "commandments contained in ordinances" (Eph. 2:15). The law was not established to illuminate God's intentions, but to prepare men for them. Those intentions centered in the church, that would work together with Him.

The Message of the Prophets

The "holy prophets" (II Pet. 3:2) frequently spoke of the church. While their words were attended by mystery, they have become understandable in the light of the Gospel. The church is built upon the "foundation of the Apostles and prophets" (Eph. 2:20). They were given glimpses into the purpose of God that provoked their earnest inquiry and diligent search. They sensed, by faith, that the good things of which they prophesied pertained to future generations — the church!

Peter, in his elaboration of this consideration, said, "Of which salvation the prophets have inquired and searched diligently, who prophesied of the grace that should come unto you [the church]: searching what, or what manner of time the Spirit of Christ which was in them did signify, when it testified before hand of the sufferings of Christ, and the glory that should follow. " It "was revealed" to them, Peter continues, that their prophecies of salvation were not for themselves, but "unto us [the church] they did minister . . ."

The Gospel is an elaboration of the message of the prophets. It is the "report" of what they saw in obscurity, and is declared "with the Holy Ghost sent down from heaven" (I Pet. 1:10-12). In his defense before King Agrippa, Paul proclaimed that he said "none other things than those which the prophets and Moses did say should come: that Christ should suffer, and that He should be the first that should rise from the dead, and should show light unto the people [the Jews], and to the Gentiles" (Acts 26:22).

Remove the church from religious thinking, and there is no objective

358

purpose for the prophets or their message. The church has always been foremost in God's mind and heart. His inspiration of the prophets, therefore, included hints and allusions to it. This was the "city of God" of which David spake (Psa. 46:4; Heb. 12:22), "the branch of the Lord" of Isaiah (Isa. 4:2; John 15:1-2), and the "flock of God" of Ezekiel (Ezek. 34:15; I Pet. 5:2). It is God's "heritage" of Joel (Joel 3:2; I Pet. 5:3), the "vineyard" of Jeremiah (Jer. 12:10; I Cor. 3:9), and the "called" of Isaiah (Isa. 62:12; Rom. 8:28).

The prophets dealt with issues of their time, but their primary role pertained to the "day of salvation." A division between God and the church reproaches the prophets, negates their message, and makes God a liar. A man can no more have dealings with God apart from the church that he can have a Bible without prophets!

The Accomplishments of Christ

The church is a primary consideration in the accomplishments of Christ. The church is His "body" — those through whom His life and intentions are expressed (I Cor. 12:27; Eph. 4:12). He is "the Savior of the body," and its "Head," from "Whom all the body by joints and bands having nourishment ministered, and knit together, increases with the increase of God" (Col. 1:18; 2:19). The ministration of Christ is exclusively through the church. The spiritual sinews, nerves, and joints, through which Divine strength and succor are administered, are all in the church. There can be no participation in them apart from one's addition to Christ's body, the church.

God provided forgiveness through Christ loving "the church" and giving "Himself for it; that He might sanctify and cleanse it with the washing of water by the Word. That He might present it to Himself a glorious church, not having spot or wrinkle, or any such thing; but that it should be holy and without blemish" (Eph. 5:25-27). The effects of His sacrifice focused upon the church. It was in prospect of it that He gave Himself. His objective was to purify it from sin by means of its embracement of His atonement. The Word communicates the truth of His vicarious provision, and baptism is the appointed means of being washed within (Acts 22:16). The Divine objective will be ultimately realized when the church is joined to Him eternally, without any moral imperfection.

The Calvinistic perversion of Ephesians 5:25ff to support its error of "limited atonement," or "particular redemption," is just that — a corruption of text. When Paul speaks of Christ's loving and giving Himself for the church, he contemplates the ultimate efficacy of His sacrifice. It is made abundantly clear elsewhere by Scripture that Christ, as well as the Father, loved the whole world, and that the Son died for it. It is simply a matter of the universal love and sacrifice being personally accepted by the individual.

The Gospel

"The Gospel of God" (Rom. 15:16) is the announcement of His provision of salvation in Christ. The church has been "called" by (II Thess. 2:14) and "begotten" through the Gospel (I Cor. 4:15). The "hope" which it has embraced is revealed by the Gospel (Col. 1:23), and it is "the Gospel" to which it has subjected itself (II Cor. 9:13). The Gospel is the means of establishing the church (Rom. 16:25), and "the truth of the Gospel" continues with it alone (Gal. 2:5).

The "Gospel of Christ" is God's appointed means of calling, illuminating, and sanctifying the church. Without the church, the Gospel has no lasting fruit. Were it possible to sustain a relationship to God outside of the church, the Gospel would be meaningless and useless. There can be no Gospel without the church as its fruitage, and no reconciliation to God apart from the Gospel of His Son.

In the light of the Gospel, there are two basic categories of men. Men are now identified as "believers" (I Tim. 4:12) and "unbelievers" (II Cor. 6:14), "saved" (II Cor. 2:15) and "lost" (II Cor. 4:3), "reconciled" (II Cor. 5:20) and "alienated" (Col. 1:21), "illuminated" (Heb. 10:32) and "deceived" (Titus 3:3). They are either "servants of righteousness" (Rom. 6:18) or "servants of sin" (Rom. 6:17).

There are also two types of Divine responses — one for each of the above categories. "He that believes and is baptized shall be saved; he that believes not shall be damned" (Mark 16:16). "He that believes on Him is not condemned: but he that believes not is condemned already" (John 3:18). "Whosoever will save his life [maintain purely selfish interests] shall lose it; but whosoever shall lose his life for my sake and the gospel's [deny himself], the same shall save it" (Mark 8:25).

Every man shall receive one of these commitments — there is no neutral ground. Life eternal or everlasting punishment (Mat. 25:46) — there are no other alternatives!

360

God's commitments of blessing are all made to the church — to those that have been "justified by faith" (Rom. 5:1). There are no promises of good to those that have not been "added to the church"! All the "better promises" (Heb. 8:6) are applicable in Christ alone — and only the church has been identified with Him. "For all the promises of God in Him [Jesus] are yea (affirmative), and in Him Amen (agreement with and satisfaction in) by us" (II Cor. 1:20).

If there were no church, there would be no promises in Christ! Exclusion from the church results in an exclusion from God's commitments for good. Any consideration of a relationship to God without the church is a contradictory one — it conflicts with the revelation of Himself, His intentions, and His salvation.

The Church Without God — A State of Spiritual Impotence

Without a vital union with the Living God, the church would be nothing more than a lifeless institution. Such a condition would exclude the possibility of accomplishing the work of God. He can no more work through a dead church, than Satan can work through a living one.

The spiritual life of the church has resulted from her unity with God, not from an increase of information. Of itself, information — even heavenly information — cannot impart life. It must be coupled with faith if profit is to be realized. This principle is taught by the writer of Hebrews. "For unto us was the Gospel preached, as well as unto them [the Israelites]: but the word preached did not profit them, not being mixed with faith in them that heard it" (Heb. 4:2). The amount of truth given to Israel was much less than that given to the church. Notwithstanding, had it been received by faith, it would have profited them.

Old Testament Religion

A religion that is of the old testament order is inexcusable in this "day of salvation." A new covenant has been ratified by the blood of Christ, and with its inauguration, the first covenant was obviated. As it is written, "In that He says, A new covenant, He has made the first old. Now that which decays and waxes old [the first covenant] is ready to vanish away" (Heb. 8:13).

The old covenant was one of works — of man's accomplishment. Men selected the sacrifice, slew it, prepared the altar upon which it was offered and offered it. They performed the washings, kept the light

361

burning, and presented the sweet smelling incense. Those under the old covenant were identified with God because of outward associations: circumcision, shedding of blood, divers washings, and "carnal ordinances." Life was promised to them upon the basis of perfect obedience to the moral code.

The church cannot operate under such an arrangement. It works from within an accepted state, not in order to obtain one (Eph. 1:6). It goes about doing the will of God because it is alive, not in order to obtain life. Old Testament religion — very prevalent in our day — is an admission of the absence of the Living God.

Working Together with God

Those that are "workers together with God" are involved in an "eternal purpose." It is not possible to work "with God" without knowing what He is doing, or His intentions among men. His Kingdom is an intelligent one, involving man's will and the understanding. It is axiomatic that to "do the will of God" you must understand it; "Wherefore be ye not unwise, but understanding what the will of the Lord is" (Eph. 5:17). It is the responsibility of the church to comprehend the objectives of God, and then to participate in them.

Planting, Watering, and Increase

The activity of the church in the Kingdom of God is represented by two efforts — planting and watering. Planting is the proclamation of the Gospel of salvation in order to convert sinners. Watering involves the nourishment of believers — their orientation for glory. Both are identified with hearty effort, and both can yield profitable results. The church is responsible for being productive in both areas.

Paul credited the progress of the Corinthians to three things: planting, watering, and increase. "I have planted, Apollos watered; but God gave the increase" (I Cor. 3:6). By this the Apostle meant that he brought the word initially to them (Acts 19:1-4; II Cor. 10:14), and Apollos nurtured and strengthened them in the faith (Acts 19:1). The fruitage of these endeavors, however, was produced by God. As Paul later confessed, "Not that we are sufficient of ourselves to think anything of ourselves; but our sufficiency is of God" (II Cor. 3:5).

Herein is a wonderful truth! Firstly, the labors of both Paul and Apollos blended perfectly with God's redemptive purpose. In their word and work, they were not at variance with God. Secondly, God identified Himself with their labors. In their conversion, God used the Gospel Paul preached, and in their growth He used the words Apollos ministered. They were "laborers together with God."

In God's Kingdom, "work" implies involvement. One cannot "walk" in good works (Eph. 2:10) without his heart and soul being affected. Thus were apostolic labors often accompanied with "tears" (Acts 20:19,31; II Cor. 2:4). A labor of understanding cannot be accomplished by routine or repetition. To be accurate, Kingdom laborers cannot be produced by mere traning. If there is no involvement — no joyful discernment of Divine purpose — no amount of regimentation can produce a laborer for God's harvest.

In a fervent appeal to a deficient Corinthian church, Paul revealed how deeply he was involved in the work of the Kingdom. "We then, as workers together with God, beseech you also that you receive not the grace of God in vain" (II Cor. 6:1). It made a difference to the Apostle whether or not the Corinthians responded to God's grace. He could not simply preach the word and forget about its implications. If God's grace is received, men will be saved; if it is rejected, men will be damned. This was not just a doctrinal point with Paul — he saw the reality of those alternatives, and identified it with his preaching.

He was in fellowship with the God that "so loved the world that He gave His only begotten Son" (John 3:6). He could no more be passive about the Corinthians than God was. If God invested the life of His Son, Paul could not take lightly the proclamation of that investment. He was a "worker together with God." This is, further, the only type of worker that is acceptable in God's Kingdom.

Ministers of God

The close association of God with the church is seen in the way "every man" is apprised of His salvation. "Who then is Paul, and who is Apollos, but ministers by whom ye believed, even as the Lord gave to every man" (I Cor. 3:5). God's ministers are men, not angels; personalities, not arresting phenomena! This is the means employed by the Almighty God to effect His salvation among men — men that are "ministers."

The Kingdom of God, however, centers in God Himself, not in men. Thus those that deliver the good news are not to be the object of

363

men's attention. In the words of the Apostle, they are to be accounted "as the ministers of Christ, and stewards of the mysteries of God" (I Cor. 4:1). "Ministers of Christ" are subordinant to Him, sent by Him, and representatives of Him. Their mouth, when filled with the truth, is His mouth; their words are His words. He will save and succor men by what they say — they are His ministers. This appellation is not intended to exalt the ministers, but to underscore what they say.

The Apostles approved themselves as "ministers of God" in their responsibility, as well as by the results of its fulfillment. "But in all things approving ourselves as the ministers of God." Their reaction to adversity revealed the source of their ministry (II Cor. 6:4-5). The nature of their preaching manifested that its content was truth (II Cor. 3:7). The reaction of men to their message also justified their assertion that they were the "ministers of God" (II Cor. 3:8-9). They were laborers together with God!

Oracles of God

When representing the Living God, "I think" is never sufficient as a preface to instruction. God works with men only as they speak "the truth in love" (Eph. 4:15). In God's Kingdom, the issues are too serious for men to be unsure of their message!

We have a mandate from God on this matter, and it is quite clear. "If any man speak, let him speak as the oracles of God . . ." (I Pet. 4:10) — there must be perfect unanimity between God's purpose and the speaker's words! If it is not God's message, it is not to be delivered in His Name! The idea here is not that of simply speaking in accord with Scripture — although that is a requirement. It is, rather, that of being God's spokesman.

The man that speaks "as the oracles of God" is to God what Aaron was to Moses. Thus did God say to Moses, "And you shall speak unto him, and put words in his mouth: and I will be with your mouth, and with his mouth, and will teach you what you shall do. And he shall be your spokesman unto the people: and he shall be to you instead of a mouth . . ." (Exod. 4:15-16).

The church is God's "spokesman" to the world; it is His "mouth." As such, its words must be precise, setting before men the will of its God. If this is the case, God will stand behind that word, honoring it by men's salvation and edification.

It is in this sense that Jesus' words to the Apostles are to be understood: ". . . and whatsoever you shall bind on earth shall be bound in heaven: and whatsoever you shall loose on earth shall be loosed in heaven" (Matt. 16:19; 18:18). And again, "Whose soever sins you remit, they are remitted unto them; and whose soever sins you retain, they are retained" (John 20:23). It was their capacity as Christ's "oracles" that prompted those words.

An Inactive Church and an Active God — a Contradiction

God is intensely active. Jesus said of Him, "My Father works hitherto . . ." (John 5:17). The accomplishment of a basis for man's salvation is called "the works of Him" (John 9:4). His will, wisdom, creativity, and strength, are employed in this great undertaking. Infinitely more Divine "work" is evidenced in redemption than in the natural creation!

God "works in you," believers are told (Phil. 2:13), and holy men prayed that He would express Himself even further in men. "Now the God of peace . . . make you perfect in every good work to do His will, working in you that which is well pleasing in His sight" (Heb. 13:21). It is God that "works all in all" (I Cor. 12:6).

An inactive church is a contradiction of terms. An individual or a group of individuals cannot be joined to a working God without becoming involved in the work. At the point the church ceases to work, its involvement with God ceases.

The work of the church, however, must be spiritual — it must contribute to the eternal welfare of men and the glory of God. Carnal displays, however religious they may appear, are of no use in God's Kingdom. They are a hindrance, and thus are cursed by God. Thus were Israel's empty rituals an abomination to Him. "Bring no more vain oblations; incense is an abomination unto Me; the new moons and sabbaths, the calling of assemblies, I cannot [tolerate them] away with [them]; it is iniquity, even to the solemn meeting. And when you spread forth your hands, I will hide mine eyes from you . . ." (Isa. 1:13-15).

It Is High Time to Awake

A lethargic church is summoned to awake — to shake itself from the dust of earth that has gathered around it. This is no time to be lulled into complacency. God's people are to know the times as well as of their mission. "And that, knowing the time, that now it is high time to awake

365

out of sleep: for now is our salvation nearer that when we believed" (Rom. 13:11). We are progressing toward the culmination of God's purpose. The church is to be determined not to be found asleep when the Lord comes. What He says unto one, He says "unto all, WATCH" (Mark 13:37).

The "night" of obscurity is "far spent," and "the day is at hand; let us therefore cast off the works of darkness, and let us put on the armour of light" (Rom. 13:12). Involvement in works that spring from an ignorance of God brings spiritual sleep. We "awake" by determinedly casting away from us anything and everything that inhibits the expression of Divine life.

An inactive church must recover itself from the snare of the devil, and recapture heavenly insight. When spiritual vision is obscured, it is not restored by a simple prayer or casual resolution. An inactive church is admonished of the Lord, "Awake, you that sleep, and arise from the dead, and Christ will give you light" (Eph. 5:14).

This requires effort — the effort of faith. God will not have His church idle, insensitive to His objectives. It is to be awake and alert because He has ordained to work through it in the accomplishment of His will. He cannot and will not work through a slumbering people! If the church insists on sleeping, it will forfeit the saving light that is ministered by Christ.

But this is not what the Lord wants — He is not content to let the church sleep on, as it were. Instead He shouts to her, Awake"! "Awake to righteousness, and sin not" (I Cor. 15:34)! "Arise from the dead," (Eph. 5:14) and I will illuminate you, and fortify you for the work to which you have been called!

Conclusion

The strength of the church is to be found in its association with and involvement in the revealed will of God. Heaven and earth are joined together in the church and its appointed work. The words of Azariah the son of Oded, are applicable here. "The Lord is with you while you are with Him; and if you seek Him, He will be found of you; but if you forsake Him, He will forsake you" (II Chron. 15:2).

The presence of the Lord is promised only while men are engaged in His work. It was in prospect of the preaching of the Gospel to all nations that Jesus said to His disciples, "And lo, I am with you alway, even unto the end of the world" (Matt. 28:20). That promise still applies to His church. As it labors together "with God," it can confidently say, "the Lord is my Helper, and I will not fear what man shall do unto me" (Heb. 13:5).

If you, reader, are a part of Christ's church, a member of His body, then put your hand on the plow and throw yourself into the work of the Kingdom! "Be ye stedfast, unmovable, always abounding in the work of the Lord, forasmuch as ye know your labor is not in vain in the Lord" (I Cor. 15:58). Men shall reap eternal wages only if they "faint not" (Gal. 6:9). You have been called into the fellowship of God's dear Son (I Cor. 1:30), and that is a fellowship associated with intense activity.

21

THE FUTURE AND THE CHURCH —
JOINT-HEIRS WITH CHRIST

The Kingdom of God is associated with an "eternal purpose" (Eph. 3:11), the "ages to come" (Eph. 2:7), the "world to come" (Heb. 2:5), and the "world without end" (Eph. 3:21). God's Kingdom concerns an objective that reaches back "before the world began" (II Tim. 1:9; Titus 1:2), and forward to "new heavens and new earth wherein dwells righteousness" (II Pet. 3:13). The love of God — the preeminent expression in His Kingdom — is characterized by "breadth, and length, and depth, and height" (Eph. 3:18). It is a great Kingdom!

In order to comprehend somewhat of the greatness of God's objective rule, it is necessary that "the eyes" of the "understanding" be "enlightened" regarding its benefits (Eph. 1:17-20). Men cannot dwell in the sphere of mediocrity and hope to participate in this Kingdom — it is too large in scope for the mediocre, too high for the slothful, too deep for the casual thinker. It pertains to a rule and dominion that has been appointed for men. Men do well to seek it "first" (Matt. 6:33), and to "strive to enter the strait gate" that stands at its threshold (Luke 13:24).

Man, Made to Have Dominion

Man was not created to be a vassal; he was made to have dominion! Contrary to the opinion of several religious bodies, the primary objective for man's creation was not the worship of God. In Christ, the "hour" has come "when the true worshippers" do worship "the Father in spirit and in truth" (John 4:23). The fact is, however, that the Scriptures do not affirm this to be the primary reason for the creation of man. There were myriads of angelic personalities already engaged in the worship of God before man was ever formed (Psa. 103:10-21; 148:2). Man was made to have dominion!

God has not left Himself without a witness in this matter. He inspired Moses to record the reason for man's existence. "And God said, Let us make man in Our image, after Our likeness: and let them have dominion over the fish of the sea, and over the fowl of the air, and over the cattle, and over all the earth, and over every creeping thing that creepeth upon the earth" (Gen. 1:26-27). Dominion over the natural order — a responsible stewardship, indeed!

David, in his inspired interpretation of man's existence, wrote; "You made him to have dominion over the works of Your hands; You have put all things under his feet . . ." (Psa. 8:6-8). Man's creation was not a Divine experiment — it was the expression of an objective purpose! He was made to have dominion — dominion over the works of his Creator's hands!

God's Image and Capacities

The writer of Hebrews, commenting on this revealed purpose, points out that man's rule is not yet apparent — the purpose has not been fulfilled. "You made him a little lower than the angels . . . and did set him over the works of Your hands: You have put all things in subjection under his feet . . . He left nothing that is not put under him . . ." (Heb. 2:7-8). Then, bringing the economy of salvation into view, he says, "But now we see not yet all things put under him." His dominion has not yet been brought to fruition (Heb. 2:8).

But this is no cause to suppose that the purpose has been abandoned — it has not. God has provided a pledge of His intentions in Jesus — the "express image of His Person" (Heb. 1:3). The full potential of the Divine purpose is seen in Him — now! "But we see Jesus,

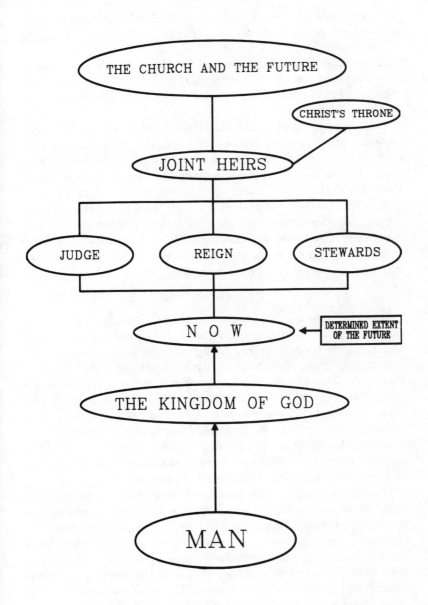

Who was made a little lower than the angels for the suffering of death, crowned with glory and honor . . ." His rule has its fruit in the bringing of "many sons to glory" (Heb. 2:10).

The subject being considered in the above text is "the world to come," a world that has been appointed for men, not angels. "For unto the angels has He not put in subjection the world to come, whereof we speak" (Heb. 2:5).

The capacities of man have been marred by his own rebellion. They have not, however, been destroyed, but still retain their potential. One of the functions of salvation is to ultimately restore the fullness of God's image in man. This is being demonstrated in "the Man Christ Jesus." Here is a glorified man, ruling and reigning as the representative of men. The recognition of Him in this capacity is to be one of man's primary considerations in embracing the Divine commitment, ". . . we shall be like Him, for we shall see Him as He is" (I John 3:2). The Apostle has more than the resurrection body in view! Grace is bringing man into the purpose for which he was created!

Prophetic Promises

God, Who greatly delights to reveal His will to men, refused to conceal His objective from them. Even while they remained in a state of alienation, He spoke to them, through the prophets, concerning His gracious intentions. An example of this introductory insight is found in Psalms 49. "Nevertheless man being in honor abides not: he is like the beasts that perish . . . Like sheep they are laid in the grave; death shall feed upon them . . ." As the spirit of the Psalmist was caught up in contemplation, a ray of heavenly illumination enlightened his understanding. In a sudden burst of anticipated triumph he cried, "the upright shall have dominion over them in the morning" (verse 14). How his heart must have longed for the light to expand!

Later, the Prophet Isaiah spoke of a hope that would boggle the mind of the oppressed. He was moved by God to write of the sure retribution for abuse of the godly. The establishment of equity would include an acknowledgment of wrong on the part of those that afflicted Israel. "The sons also of them that afflicted you shall come bending unto you; and all they that despised you shall bow themselves down at the soles of your feet; and they shall call you, The city of the Lord, The Zion of the Holy One of Israel" (Isa. 60:14). There is a note of triumph here;

the language of rule and reign! God was making His purpose known.

During the latter part of the Babylonian captivity, some unusual insight was given to the Prophet Daniel. God revealed that circumstances and surroundings do not have to stifle insight and understanding. In His reference to the Messiah, and His unending government, He wrote; "Until the Ancient of days came, and judgment was given to the saints of the Most High; and the time came when the saints possessed the Kingdom" (Dan. 7:22). This was an announcement of God's determination to bring His purpose for man to its consummation!

Again, Daniel provides some stimulating detail concerning the heavenly intention for the "saints." "And the Kingdom and dominion, and the greatness of the Kingdom under the whole heaven, shall be given to the people of the saints of the Most High . . ." (Dan. 7:27). The extent of that dominion parallels the revealed purpose of Genesis 1:26: ". . . and let them have dominion . . . over all the earth. . . ."

Let no one doubt the magnitude of God's endeavor in Christ! Man, in Him, is being schooled for dominion in the ages to come. Let the redeemed so account of themselves as kings in training and rulers in preparation!

Involved in the Judgment

Every man shall be judged — this is the Divine appointment (Heb. 9:27). The people of God shall not be excluded from this duty of reckoning. They "must all stand before the judgment seat of Christ" (Rom. 14:10; II Cor. 5:10). Lives are to be lived in preparation for that great day, so that an appearance may be made with "boldness," and not with fear (I John 4:17).

There is, however, more to the time of judgment than this. The saints shall participate in the judgment. Redemption is not only preparing them to be judged, it is grooming them to be judges! Jesus challenged men to become judges! In a stirring rebuke of the indifferent of His day He said, "When you see a cloud rise out of the west, straightway you say, there comes a shower; and so it is. And when you see the south wind blow, you say, There will be heat; and it comes to pass. You hypocrites, you can discern the face of the sky and of the earth; but how is it that you do not discern the times? Yea, and why even of yourselves judge you not what is right?" (Luke 12:54-57). Jesus still asks men this question! What answer shall be given Him by our generation?

373

The church is summoned to "judge" the truth of Apostolic doctrine — to evaluate it and receive its implications (I Cor. 10:15). The church is not to blindly embrace what they have been taught, but to use their spiritual capacities in the sacred work of evaluation and acceptance or rejection, as the case requires (I Cor. 11:13,31; 14:29; Phil. 1:9).

The Judgment of the World

Throughout history, the church has often been deficient in the area of sound judgment. It has permitted the rise of false prophets, the perversion of conduct, and the spread of iniquity (Rev. 2:4,14-15,20; 3:2,15-16). More than once, the church's greatest enemies have risen from within her (Acts 20:29-30; II Pet. 2:1-2). The reason for this condition is the lack of judgment on the part of the church! It has not exercised its appointed prerogatives.

The church at Corinth had permitted a very uncomely situation to occur within it. Unjust conduct of one toward another was being addressed in courts of law, instead of before the assembly of the saints. In his rebuke of that situation, Paul alluded to the saint's coming participation in the judgment. "Do you not know that the saints shall JUDGE THE WORLD? and if the world shall be judged by you, are you unworthy to judge in the smallest matters [the matters of this life]?" (I Cor. 6:2).

The implications of this truth are intriguing! We have every reason to believe that those that were themselves judged by the world, will judge their former judges. Thus Cain may be perceived as being judged by Abel (Gen. 4:4-8; John 3:12), Herod by James (Acts 12:1-2), and the Sanhedrin by Stephen (Acts 7:54-60).

The mind of the Lord in such things was demonstrated of old in Mordecai, a man hated by wicked Haman. Because Mordecai would not bow down to him, Haman conceived an ingenious plan to rid the Medio-Persian kingdom of his influence (Esther 3:5-13; 5:5-9). In the end, however, the tables were reversed, and Haman had to publicly acknowledge the acceptance of Mordecai; "Then took Haman the apparel, and the horse, and arrayed Mordecai, and brought him on horseback through the street of the city, and proclaimed before him, Thus shall it be done unto the man whom the king delights to honor" (Esther 6:11). We have every reason to expect that many such reversals shall take place in the judgment of the world!

374

The role of men in the judgment is also alluded to in the teaching of Jesus. He spoke of men rising up in the day of judgment to condemn generations that followed them. "The men of Nineveh shall rise up in judgment with this generation, and shall condemn it: because they repented at the preaching of Jonah; and behold, a greater than Jonah is here" (Matt. 11:41). The message given to them, though marked by extreme brevity and limited content, was sufficient to constrain their repentance. What shall they say to the generations following Christ that have heard truth in such abundance! If their judgment is certain against Jerusalem, who rejected the introductory words of our Lord, what shall be said of those generations that have been subjected to the confirmed testimony of His Apostles!

Again Jesus said, "The queen of the south shall rise up in the judgment with this generation, and shall condemn it: for she came from the uttermost parts of the earth to hear the wisdom of Solomon; and, behold, a greater than Solomon is here" (Matt. 11:42). What is the wisdom of Solomon compared to that of the Lord Jesus Christ? How shall a generation that had eternal truth in abundance available to it, appear before the Queen of Sheba (I Kgs. 10:1)?

The point to be seen in Nineveh and the Queen of the south is not their particular role in the judgment, but that men shall have a part in the judgment of the world. Because the church is the most elevated segment of mankind (Luke 7:28), its role shall be the most significant in this aspect of the judgment. The "saints shall judge the world"!

The Judgment of Angels

The extent of the saints' involvement in the judgment goes beyond men to angels. "Know ye not that we shall judge angels?" (I Cor. 6:2). How out of harmony with that appointment to stumble in confusion at the evaluation of "things that pertain to this life"!

Here is an order of beings that, of themselves, are "greater in power and might" than men (I Pet. 2:11). From among their once larger society, a significant number defected in allegiance to Satan, "the prince of the power of the air" (Eph. 2:2). Speaking of that defection, Peter said, "God spared not the angels that sinned, but cast them down into hell, and delivered them into chains of darkness, to be reserved unto judgment" (II Pet. 2:4) . Jude also mentions them in his epistle. "And the angels which kept not their first estate, but left their own habitation, He

375

hath reserved in everlasting chains under darkness unto the judgment of the great day" (Jude 6). These angels have been consigned to an irremedial state — "chains of darkness." Unlike fallen men, they cannot be extricated from their condition. They have been reserved in their reprobate state in prospect of the day of judgment, when the saints shall judge them!

We ought not to stagger at this revelation. Those that have embraced the Gospel will be capable of exercising the judgment. We already have a number of facts at our disposal which are points of reason. The fallen angels once were in the presence of God. They had a stewardship from Him, and a place with Him ["their first estate"]. There was no reason for them to fall — they "left their own habitation." It was a matter of their will, their choice! The grace of God has taught the saints concerning stewardship and obligation! They know that it is required that stewards be faithful (I Cor. 4:2). Even now they have "the mind of Christ" (I Cor. 2:16) on this matter. Once liberated from the "vile body," their insight shall precisely reflect God's attitude toward those fallen personalities.

There is another aspect to the judgment of angels by the saints. These are the spiritual hosts against which believers now wrestle. They are set to resist the saints' progress to glory by deception and blindness. The Apostle exhorts us to throw ourselves into the battle with intelligence and spiritual insight. Our spirits are to be fortified with truth, righteousness, peace, and faith. An awareness of our standing in Christ, and the apprehension of the good Word of God equips us for the battle (Eph. 6:14-17). This equipment is of little value in physical warfare. It is spiritual in nature, designed to thwart the offensive of Satanic powers.

We "wrestle not against flesh and blood," the Apostle warns. Men are misdirected when they suppose that their primary enemies are fellow men. The resistance which saints confront consists of "principalities . . . powers . . . the rulers of the darkness of this world . . . and spiritual wickedness in high places" (Eph. 6:12). Deception and trickery are in their arsenal. They allure from the truth and into error, and can be successfully resisted only when the mind is armed with spiritual truth.

The day of judgment will bring the saints into confrontation with these spiritual forces. They will face the wicked personalities that have diligently worked to keep them out of the Kingdom of heaven. Not content to have themselves fallen, they zealously attempted to get the saints to fall from their station in grace. Those that, by faith, have successfully resisted their diabolical efforts, shall judge them! The saints shall judge angels!

Sitting with Jesus in His Throne

The resurrection of Christ was necessary for man's justification (Rom. 4:25). It marked the beginning of His reign of righteousness at God's right hand — His exaltation (Acts 2:33; 5:31; Phil. 2:9). His reign is one wherein the covenantal benefits are administered to those that are justified by faith. His earthly mission was consummated by His exaltation.

The "righteous" (I Pet. 4:18; I John 3:7) are identified with Christ in His death and resurrection (Rom. 6:3-5; Col. 2:12). They will also participate in His exaltation and enthronement. This is the promise of Scripture.

The promise of exaltation is a strong incentive for spiritual recovery and growth. In His inscrutable wisdom, Jesus appealed to a church marked by lukewarmness; one that was "wretched, and miserable, and poor, and blind, and naked" Rev. 3:17-18). Not content to let it go, so to speak, He made one of His strongest appeals to it. His words can still be received in hope, for they are truth — in strict conformity with the purpose of God. "To him that overcometh will I grant to sit with Me in My throne, even as I also overcame, and am set down with My Father in His throne" (Rev. 3:21).

Here is a remarkable promise — one worthy of extended consideration. Christ's throne is God's throne — His authority is delegated authority. There are not two thrones, but one, and it is shared by both God and His Son — a Man! Before He could sit upon "His throne" (Rev. 1:4; 12:5), Jesus overcame a corrupted environment. He accomplished His mission amidst handicap and resistance. In fulfillment of the words of the prophet, He did not "fail," nor was He "discouraged" (Isa. 42:4). All who, having received the atonement, overcome the world, shall sit with Jesus in His throne — which is the Father's throne!

Faith, which "is the victory that overcomes the world," addresses several critical areas. It overcomes the environment in which it is being perfected — the world (I John 5:4). It resists the opposition of wicked men — called "evil" — refusing to become identified with their lowly manners (Rom. 12:21). It also endures the malicious attacks of the "wicked one," by maintaining its grasp of reality (I John 2:13,14). There is also the area of false doctrine — "doctrines of demons" perpetrated by "seducing spirits" in an effort to bring men down to perdition (I Tim. 4:1; I John 4:4). Men overcome when they maintain their hold on the truth, their upward progression to glory, and faithfulness in their stewardship.

The time of Divine judgment will follow the resurrection of the dead and the passing of the heavens and the earth. That is when the final evaluation will be made. Those that have overcome will "sit with" Jesus in his throne! It is a promise that cannot fail of fulfillment! The eyes of the church must be set on this lofty prospect. It is unbefitting of the "redeemed of the Lord" (Psa. 107:2) to become enamored of temporal rewards and earthly acclaim — particularly in view of their role in the coming judgment!

Be Thou Over Ten Cities

Christ likened the "Kingdom of God" to a nobleman that "went into a far country to receive for himself a kingdom, and to return." Before leaving, he made distribution of his resources, commanding his servants to "Occupy till I come." During the absence of the owner of the goods, the faithful increased their stewardship, while the unfaithful left it unattended.

Upon returning, the stewards were called into accountability. The "wicked servant" was rebuked, his stewardship taken from him, and given to the diligent. It was, however, quite different with the faithful. Their reliability inducted them into a newer and larger stewardship.

The first faithful steward reported, "Lord, thy pound hath gained ten pounds," The second also reported an increase; "Lord, thy pound hath gained five pounds." The reaction of the nobleman reflected the Divine attitude toward faithfulness, and provided an index to the world to come. "Well, thou good servant: because thou hast been faithful in a very little, have thou authority over ten cities . . . And he said likewise to him [the second], be thou over five cities" (Luke 19:12-25).

The implications are filled with wonder! Our objective here is not to speculate on what the cities are or what they represent. Indeed, that was not the purpose of the parable. There will be something over which the righteous will reign. They will participate in rule and dominion. The

378

extent is of this dominion is unknown, but the nature of it is revealed! The saints do well to set their goals high, and whet their spiritual appetites for the reception of transcendent authority. God, through Christ, is grooming the church for the future — and its prospects are bright!

Power over the Nations

If one will subject his mind to the Word of the Lord, his thought processes will be challenged and his concepts elevated. Those in Christ greatly err by dwelling upon the mundane. There are lofty considerations that are to dominate their minds — considerations that will prepare them for the "ages to come."

In His gracious appeal to the church at Thyatira, Jesus unveiled something of the magnitude of the saints' inheritance. Here was a church that had proved slothful in the responsibility of upholding truth. It had permitted a false prophetess to "seduce" Christ's servants. Rather than permitting spiritual seduction, the church should have forbidden it.

Fastening His attention upon those that had not fallen prey to the seduction of that "Jezebel," Jesus made an unalterable commitment. "And he that overcometh, and keepth my works unto the end, to him will I give power over the nations: and he shall rule them with a rod of iron; as the vessels of a potter shall they be broken to shivers: even as I received of My Father" (Rev. 2:26-27). This marvelous promise is given to the churches, and they have a responsibility to "hear what the Spirit says to the churches" (Rev. 2:29), not staggering at it through unbelief (Rom. 4:20).

This is but another view of the saints judging the world (I Cor. 6:2). It is not meant to connote fleshly or military superiority. The "power" which shall be given to the overcomer is a moral power — a triumph of right. In this present world, believers participate in this type of rule by "casting down imaginations, and every high thing that exalteth itself against the knowledge of God." This is the "pulling down of strongholds," and a rule prefiguring the one to come (II Cor. 10:5).

In the judgment the ultimate confrontation shall take place: "all the nations that forget God" (Psa. 9:17) shall face the saints that remembered Him. All the deceptions that have been embraced by the "nations" shall be exposed as vain. They shall be "broken to shivers" by the exposure of the false gods and philosophies which they embraced. The Egyptians, Babylonians, Medes, and Persians shall have their gods stripped from them by the discerning judgment of the saints. Rome shall be exposed as the temporal city, not the eternal one, and her government cast down as the one that participated in the murder of Jesus and His Apostles. Plato and Socrates shall be judged, and their philosophies proven inadequate as a means to salvation. The wisdom of the world shall be exposed as foolishness in view of God and eternity.

Joint-Heirs with Christ

Jesus is the Divinely appointed "Heir of all things" (Heb. 1:2). Everything of significance will be gathered together in Him (Eph. 1:10), thereby obtaining eternal relevance. Even now "all things" have been "given" to Jesus (John 3:35; 13:3). Whether it is authority in heaven or upon earth, it has "all" been given to Him (Matt. 28:18). This has been done in order to implement God's salvational objective, and with Christ's eternal heirship in mind.

But Jesus cannot be separated from the church — it is His "body," and its members are "of His flesh, and of His bones" (Eph. 5:30). The church is His future "bride," now "espoused" to Him (John 3:29; Rev. 22:17; II Cor. 11:2). His inheritance shall be shared with her — blessed be His Name! Little wonder the Apostle prayed that the church might be able to understand the glory of their inheritance (Eph. 1:18).

The doctrine of Scripture is clear on this point. If we are children (of God), then we are "heirs; heirs of God, and joint heirs with Christ." This heirship is conditioned upon our suffering "with Him" — bearing the effects of the world's rejection (Rom. 8:17). The children of God are "heirs" because there is an inheritance appointed for them. They are "heirs of God" because they are His children — His sons. It is He that "begat" them "with the word of truth" (James 1:18). In a single word, their inheritance consists of God Himself (Josh. 13:33; Ezek. 44:28). That is the summary-view of the saints' inheritance.

But there is another view — a detailed one. Those that are "in Christ" are "joint heirs" with Him! In the ages to come, the saints shall inherit "all things" — they shall be owners. The eternal government of "all things" shall not be by a single person, even though that be Jesus, in dissociation from His brethren. Believers are promised, "If we suffer with Him [Jesus], we shall also reign with Him" (II Tim. 2:12). In John's record of the song of the redeemed, reference is made to their reign; ". . . and [He] has made us unto our God kings and priests: and we shall reign on the earth" (Rev. 5:10). This is not a reference to "this present evil world" (Gal. 1:4), but to the "world to come" (Heb. 2:5) — the "new earth" (II Pet. 3:13; Rev. 21:1).

While "in the body," the Apostles — "first" in rank within the church (I Cor. 12:28) — did not "reign in the earth," but were "despised," "buffeted," "reviled," "persecuted," "defamed," and "made as the filth of the world" and "the offscouring of all things" (I Cor. 4:10-13). They ultimately laid down their lives in a display of seeming inferiority. They were kings in preparation, not in manifestation — much like David during the reign of King Saul (I Sam. 16:13-14). Their rule existed in their handling of the truth, and was only revealed to those that embraced it. The same condition exists for the rest of the "children" — each in his own measure. Here, they "suffer with Him."

But in the "ages to come" it will be quite different. There they "reign with Him." They shall become the "head, and not the tail . . . above only . . . and not beneath," in fulfillment of the ancient promise (Deut. 28:13). It will be a real reign, not a figurative one; apparent, and not hidden!

Current Involvement Determines Extent of Future Participation

The Kingdom of God operates upon the basis of Divine principles. One of those is especially evident in the work of salvation. The degree of one's participation in glory is being determined by the extent of his involvement in the salvation which is in Christ Jesus. Little investment — little reward! Limited effort — limited participation! Were this principle more readily perceived by the church, it would have a remarkable impact on its spiritual activity!

Jesus commented at length upon this principle, because it is crucial. In His elaboration on the requirement of stewards, Jesus distinguished between those that have received much and those that have received little. The particular point of reference is the knowledge of the steward. "And that servant, which knew his lord's will, and prepared not himself, neither did according to his will, shall be beaten with many stripes. But he that knew not, and did commit things worthy of stripes, shall be beaten with few stripes" (Luke 12:47-48).

This earthly parallel reveals the thoughts of the Almighty. "For unto whomsoever much is given, of him shall much be required" (Luke 12:48). Those, for instance, that lived during the time of the Law will not have as much required of them as those that have lived within the fuller light of the Gospel. King Saul, who did things "worthy of stripes," shall be judged with less harshness than Demas, who "loved this present world" after he had walked in the light of the new covenant (II Tim. 4:10).

This situation prevails because of God's eternal objective. The present is the prelude to the future. The responsibilities allocated in this life are indicative of those in the world to come. The parables of the "talents" and the "pounds" establish the relationship of this life to that which is to come. The extent of eternal rule was determined by the stewards' faithfulness in the temporal realm. Thus was it said, "You have been faithful over a few things, I will make you ruler over many things" (Matt. 25:21,23). "You have been faithful over a very little, you shall have authority over ten cities" (Luke 19:17-19).

The church must take its stewardship of the truth very seriously. The extent of its reign with Christ — both collectively and individually — is being determined now, in this world. It is not possible for an abundant reward to be granted for a halting effort. That is not the manner of the kingdom! On the other hand, the faithful and zealous labors of the saints will be rewarded with a significant role in glory. That is the manner of the Kingdom! God is "not unrighteous to forget your work and labor of love . . ." (Heb. 6:10).

Sowing and Reaping

The kingdom of nature faintly mirrors the Kingdom of God! This situation is not coincidental. The purpose of God is "eternal" — a part of His essential Person — and thus may often be perceived in part in His works. Hints and allusions of that eternal purpose" are reflected in what men call the laws of nature.

One such law is that of sowing and reaping. What is sown determines what is reaped, and what is reaped reveals what was sown. In addition, the quantity reaped is significantly greater than what was sown. The Apostle provides the spiritual parallel. "Be not deceived; God is not mocked: for whatsoever a man sows, that shall he also reap. For he that sows to the flesh shall of the flesh reap corruption; but he that sows to the Spirit shall of the Spirit reap life everlasting" (Gal. 6:7-8).

Everlasting life is directly associated with the attention one gives to spiritual things in this life. One "sows" to either the flesh or the Spirit by following their inclinations. The Spirit leads a man to "mortify the deeds of the body" — to subdue the proclivities that anchor one to this "present evil world." Those that follow that leading are sowing "to the Spirit" — they are making investments in eternity!

The flesh leads away from God into self-gratification. It is enamored of things that can be seen and sensed, and has no interest in the "things that are not seen" (II Cor. 4:18). Those that respond to its leading are sowing "to the flesh" — they are living "in pleasure on the earth," and are "wanton;" and are nourishing their "hearts, as in the day of slaughter" (James 5:5).

Men are also determining the degree of reaping that they will experience. Again, God has provided us with a clear statement of this Kingdom principle. "But this I say, he which sows sparingly shall reap also sparingly; and he which sows bountifully shall reap also bountifully" (II Cor. 9:6).

There will be no mansions in glory for those that made small investments in God's Kingdom while "in the body." Those who, like the Apostle, "will very gladly spend and be spent" for God's Kingdom, will reap an abundant entrance "into the everlasting Kingdom of our Lord and Savior Jesus Christ" (II Pet. 1:11). Those, however, that are content to dwell in the tents of mediocrity have every reason to question the reality of their involvement in the heavenly Kingdom.

There is no word of comfort or hope for the indolent, no rewards for the slothful. The Kingdom of heaven is associated with zeal (II Cor. 7:11; 9:2; Col. 4:13; Titus 2:14; Rev. 3:19), working (II Tim. 2:15; Eph. 2:10; Heb. 6:10; I Thess. 1:3), pressing (Phil 3:14), running (I Cor. 9:24-26; Heb. 12:1), and fighting (I Cor. 9:26; I Tim. 6:12). Casualness is a curse, and mediocrity a menace, in the Kingdom of God's dear Son! The position of men in heaven will exactly parallel their lives upon the earth. They will reap what they have sown, and in proportion to the amount they have sown.

Treasures in Heaven

There is an inheritance "reserved in heaven" for the faithful (I Pet. 1:4). It has been promised by God (Heb. 9:15), and is His provision (Eph. 1:18). Men themselves determine whether they will obtain that inheritance, and how great their portion of it will be. They, through their acceptance of God's word, receive an inheritance "among all them

383

which are sanctified" (Acts 20:32). No reception, no inheritance — the determination is theirs!

It is true, as Solomon said, that "the recompense of a man's hand shall be rendered unto him" — even in eternity (Prov. 12:14). In one of His matchless appeals to men, Jesus said, ". . . lay up for yourselves treasures in heaven, where neither moth nor rust doth corrupt, and where thieves do not break through nor steal: for where your treasure is, there will your heart be also" (Matt. 6:19-20).

These are spiritual treasures, and do not consist of tangible riches. Jesus is speaking of man's capacity to participate in heavenly realities — of his appetite for the "things that are above" (Col. 3:13). That appetite is developed in this life, and it shall be fully gratified in the world to come. Every man will have as much of heaven, so to speak, as he wants. He has Divine resources now — "all things that pertain to life and godliness" — which are designed to whet his appetite and prepare him for the transition to the next world. Translated into more pragmatic terms, men's participation in Christ's reign will be in accordance with their aptitude and appetite. Kingdom skills are being cultured now which will enable the proper handling of eternal responsibilities. To develop these skills by grace is to lay "up treasure in heaven."

Jesus yearns for men to have a large inheritance, and an abundant entrance into it. If any man comes short of the inheritance, it is not because of a lack of information or pleading on the part of Deity! Jesus gave "the twelve" (Mark 4:10) an index to their future — and ours as well. "Take heed what ye hear: with what measure ye mete, it shall be measured to you: and unto you that hear shall more be given. For he that has, to him shall be given: and he that has not, from him shall be taken even that which he has" (Mark 4:24-25).

Conclusion

The future is bright for an attentive church; it is fearful for an inattentive one. God has no pleasure in those that "draw back" from involvement in His will and work now. Those that do so are tampering with their eternal inheritance (Heb. 10:38-39; 12:38-39).

Faithfulness will secure an inheritance among them that are sanctified (Acts 20:32) — one that will exactly match the measure of their faithfulness. Given a situation like this, the future is limitless! It is only men's affections that restrict and hinder them (II Cor. 6:12). Let every soul be diligent in the pursuit of heavenly things. Some day all men will face these realities; blessed is the man prepared to inherit them and reign with Christ!

PART SEVEN:
APPREHENSION AND TRIUMPH

22

THE ROLE OF UNDERSTANDING IN GOD'S KINGDOM

It is unfortunate that Christianity has often been identified with mystery and a lack of understanding. Legion is the name of those that have gloried in spiritual ignorance and a religion that cannot be understood. Strange "movings," uninterpretable "leadings," languages that cannot be comprehended, and unconscious states of religious ecstasy, have been credited to God's Spirit. This is not, however, the manner in which God has presented His Kingdom.

The Living God is the supreme Intelligence. When it comes to reasons and reasoning, God is over all. Design and deliberation are woven into everything He does. He does nothing by instinct, impulse, or without intent. Reason and intelligence permeate everything that He does and says.

The first and great commandment is to "love the Lord thy God with all thy . . . understanding . . ." (Mark 12:33). This cannot be accomplished by means of mysterious dogmas and unreasonable doctrines! An intelligent God can be properly served only within the bounds of comprehension. A lack of spiritual understanding withholds Divine benefits and excludes one from participation in the heavenly Kingdom.

Spiritual Ignorance — Man's Chief Handicap

Man's basic part is his spirit — his essential person. This is where the Divine image primarily resides, and where fellowship with God takes place. Man's secondary part is his soul — the seat of sense and emotion. Here is where the intellect, emotion, and will, find expression. His lower nature is the body — his flesh. It has been cursed because of sin, and is destined to return to the dust (Gen. 3:19).

The Apostle refers to these three aspects of man's nature in priority of their importance. "And the very God of peace sanctify you wholly; and I pray God that your whole spirit and soul and body be preserved blameless unto the coming of our Lord Jesus" (I Thess. 5:23). A discerning prayer indeed! The "spirit" is blameless when it is in communion with God, discerning and comprehending the magnitude of His Kingdom in Jesus (John 4:23-24; Rom. 8:15; Phil. 3:3). The soul is blameless when it is not absorbed with the cares of this world — when it is concerned with the contemplation of eternal things (I John 2:15-17; Col. 3:1-3). The body is blameless when it is possessed in "sanctification and honor" (I Thess. 4:4).

Advantages and handicaps are to be judged in accordance with this priority — spirit, soul, and body. The primary advantages are found within man's spirit. The inferior ones are found within the body. The greatest handicaps are spiritual ones, the lesser handicaps are fleshly ones. There are neutral advantages which can become the source of either curse or blessing in the realm of the soul. An extremely intelligent individual can be a smart criminal or a wise steward of God. The determination will be made by the dominant part of his nature — spirit or flesh. An unusually emotional person can be led into sin or worship, violence or goodness, praise or cursing. It all depends on the dominance of his spirit or body.

Given these considerations, spiritual ignorance becomes an enormous handicap. It actually thwarts the purpose of God, which is to have fellowship with man, and to bring him into His eternal purpose. Man cannot, however, participate in what he cannot understand.

The Requirement of Rules

The more ignorance prevails, the more requirement there is for

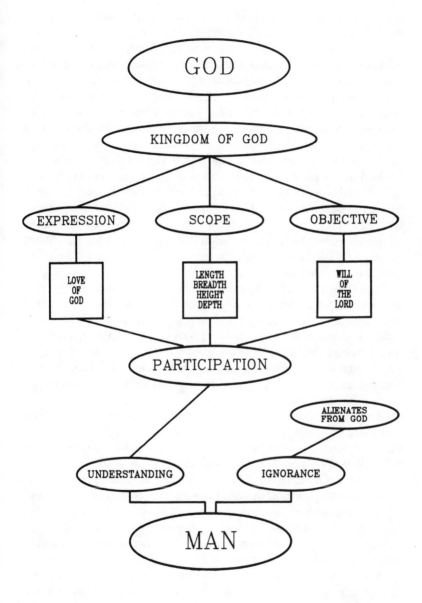

rules and regulations. Rules are for navigating in unknown waters! In the Kingdom of God, they are required to the degree that a person is not dead from the rudiments, or elemental views, of this world. The Apostles' doctrine addresses this situation. "Wherefore if you are dead with Christ from the rudiments of the world, why, as though living in the world, are you subject to ordinances . . . after the commandments and doctrines of men" (Col. 2:20-22). "Living in the world" describes a situation where the individual is basically cognizant of the temporal order, and fundamentally ignorant of the eternal one. Such a person is motivated by the seen, and cannot look beyond it.

In order to produce an appearance of godliness, rules are thus required. The one that lacks spiritual understanding cannot see the issues, and is not persuaded of "things to come" (Heb. 11:20), "things hoped for" (Heb. 11:1), or "heavenly things" (Heb. 8:5). He cannot be drawn by the awareness of "better things" (Heb. 6:9), and so he must be undiscerningly regulated by law. His ignorance has produced a requirement for extended rules.

This is the reason for the many detailed laws of the old covenant. It was a covenant addressed to an alienated and ignorant people. They were unable to decipher right and wrong, and thus were tutored like children. A study of Deuteronomy 21-26 will reveal the marked contrast between the old and new covenants in this respect. It was not Israel's sojourn in Canaan that gave them problems, but their entrance into the arena of morality. There, they simply were not in familiar territory.

The law is, indeed, for the "lawless and disobedient" — for those that dwell on lower levels of understanding. It ought to be noted that this condition is contrasted with righteousness, and has no hope of glory (I Tim. 1:9-10). Those that emphasize rules, focusing upon the "law" in order to the establishment of proper conduct, are said to have "turned aside unto vain janglings; desiring to be teachers of the law; understanding neither what they say, nor whereof they affirm" (I Tim. 1:6-7). They have by their emphasis of moral requirements, acknowledged the spiritual ignorance and alienation of both themselves and them to whom they speak.

The secret to abstinance from sin is not the mere keeping of the law. It is a spiritual matter, involving sensitivity to the rational and perceptible leading of the Holy Spirit. "For if you live after the flesh, you shall die: but if you through the Spirit do put to death the deeds of the body, you shall live. For as many as are led by the Spirit [in putting to death the body's deeds], they are the sons of God" (Rom. 9:13-14). The Spirit leads men through their understanding — through their perception of the nature of both this world and that which is to come.

Foolish Conduct

Throughout pertinent history, spiritual ignorance has occasioned acts of foolishness. Within the greater light of the new covenant, men often marvel at the conduct of those living in ages marked by much less illumination. The blunder of Eve (Gen. 3:1-7), the drunkenness of Noah (Gen. 9:20-23), the lying of Abraham (Gen. 12:13-19; 20:2-12; 26:7-9), the trickery of Jacob (Gen. 27:17-30), the vow of Jephthah (Judges 11:30-40), and the adultery of David (II Sam. 11:1-27) — they all resulted from a degree of spiritual ignorance.

Such aberrations did not occur among the Apostles of Christ, or the great teachers and preachers of the new covenant. The moral short-comings of Peter, Paul, etc. occurred before their conversion, not after it! Uprightness and exemplary conduct are the marks of the new covenant (Titus. 2:11-14).

The times of spiritual ignorance were marked by foolish conduct. "For we ourselves also were sometimes foolish, disobedient, deceived, serving divers lusts and pleasures, living in malice and envy, hateful, and hating one another" (Titus. 3:3). That condition changed, however, "after that the kindness and love of God our Savior toward man appeared" — i.e., was perceived and comprehended. It was then that ignorance was eradicated and care was taken to "maintain good works" (Titus 3:8) — not by legalistic compulsion, but by personal preference.

The world is often confused at the conduct of the righteous, supposing that their separation from the impure is a requirement of an organization. Such is not, however, the case. Saints abstain from sin and the very appearance of evil because it is offensive to them. It is not merely against God's law, it is also against their nature. Spiritual understanding has produced this situation.

The Lack of Wisdom

The "man of God" (II Tim. 3:17) is to be discontent with his lack of wisdom. "Be not unwise," admonishes the Apostle, "but understanding what the will of the Lord is" (Eph. 5:17). An individual content to be "unwise" is out of the will of God! His ignorance constitutes a liability, and he is to be discontent with it.

"If any of you lack wisdom," James writes, "let him ask of God, that gives to all men liberally, and upbraids not, and it shall be given him" (James 1:5). God gives "to all men liberally" because He does not want them lacking wisdom. It is out of harmony with His revealed purpose. The individual in that condition is to set about immediately to find a remedy. God will not rebuke or chide such a one for asking for the removal of ignorance!

Thus is ignorance perceived as a consistent liability, handicap, and restraint. Men are never to boast in it or be content to remain in its grip.

Ignorance Alienates from God

The greatest contradiction of God's will is for His own "offspring" to be alienated from Him — estranged from and at variance with Divine purpose. Alienation from God is evidenced by withdrawal from Him (Heb. 10:38-39), and personal enmity (James 4:4).

The cause of this alienation is spiritual ignorance or blindness. "Having the understanding darkened, being alienated from the life of God through the ignorance that is in them, because of the blindness of their heart" (Eph. 4:18). God cannot be approached or enjoyed by those that are ignorant of Him and His ways. Thus to be unaware of God is to be cut off from Him. "Ignorance," in this case, does not mean that one merely does not know what the Bible says, but that he does not know truth's meaning. He cannot reason to a godly conclusion, and thus is alienated "from the life of God."

It ought to be noted, however, that ignorance of this sort is no longer tolerable — even by a longsuffering God! When the "Word became flesh" the toleration of such ignorance came to an abrupt end! "And the times of this ignorance God winked at; but now commands all men everywhere to repent" (Acts 17:30-31). In times past God overlooked man's ignorance of Himself because of the relative scarcity of revelation. But revelation is no longer scarce! God has abundantly revealed Himself, His purpose, and His love in the Person of His Son, and through the message of the Gospel. All men have a solemn obligation to rid themselves of the ignorance of God by embracing His glorious Gospel!

392

A God of Knowledge

In the twilight age of the Law, a righteous woman — Hannah, by name — prayed with unusual insight and inspiration. "Talk no more exceeding proudly; let not arrogancy come out of your mouth: for the Lord is a God of knowledge, and by Him actions are weighed" (I Sam. 2:3). He is discerning, and His understanding penetrates into the hearts of men, perceiving the reasons for their actions. This is not a display of magic, but of supreme intelligence and perception.

A "God of knowledge" cannot be joined to one in a state of ignorance. He will not abandon His wisdom in order to have fellowship with man. God forbid! One must become a man of knowledge to walk with a God of knowledge! An increase in "the knowledge of God" (Col. 1:10) opens the door for fellowship with Him. As His "thoughts" become so plentiful to man that they "cannot be numbered," heavenly communion is experienced. Even though His "thoughts are very deep," yet they can be entertained by the willing heart (Psa. 92:5). It is to the reader's advantage to eagerly pursue such a fellowship.

Spiritual Blindness

Ignorance is to the heart what blindness is to the eyes. Blind eyes will not permit the entrance of sight, and an ignorant heart will not permit the entrance of truth. One that is spiritually "blind" simply cannot see any significance in the Gospel — it is irrelevant to him. This condition is actually one of the lostness: "But if our Gospel be hid, it is hid to them that are lost: in whom the god of this world has blinded the minds of them that believe not, lest the light of the glorious Gospel of Christ, Who is the Image of God, should shine unto them" (II Cor. 4:3-4).

Observe that failure to perceive the Gospel was not because of deficiency in it, but due to Satanic activity. There are no alternatives here — those that "believe not" the Gospel, are blinded by Satan. Not even the Gospel can break the shackles of unbelief! Where there is unbelief, Satan is invincible! Men will never be able to make sense out of the Gospel if they do not believe it! It is a rule in the Kingdom that men cannot disbelieve God and win over Satan, or believe the truth and lose to him!

The power of unbelief can be seen in an incident that occurred during Christ's earthly ministry. Its presence in the Gospel serves to alert us

393

to the seriousness of the subject. The occurrence was in Christ's "own country" on the sabbath day. People that knew Jesus were "offended at Him," and closed their ears to His wondrous words. The Gospel writer records, "And He could there do no mighty work, save that He laid His hands upon a few sick folk, and healed them. And He marvelled because of their unbelief . . ." (Mark 6:5-6; Matt. 13:58).

Note — He did not marvel because of Satan's work, but because of their unbelief! Through an act of stubborn rebellion, "they" closed their eyes (Matt. 13:15; Acts 28:17). Their willful act was ratified when God finalized their decisions by giving Satan leave to blind them. Men cannot ignore the truth without paying the penalty. God will not be mocked! If they will not "receive the love of the truth, that they might be saved," God will "send them strong delusion, that they should believe a lie: that they all might be damned who believed not the truth, but had pleasure in unrighteousness" (II Thess. 2:10-11).

Men are "alienated from the life of God through the ignorance that is in them through the blindness of their heart" (Eph. 4:18). When the heart does not perceive, the death-shroud of ignorance covers the soul. God then becomes inaccessible to the individual. After all, the one that comes to God "must believe that He is, and that He is a Rewarder of them that diligently seek Him" (Heb. 11:6).

Rulers of Darkness

Ignorance, blindness, darkness — they all speak of the same thing: a failure to comprehend God and His will. Moral darkness exists where the light of truth has not penetrated. That realm is characterized by "works of darkness" (Eph. 5:11), and a "power" from which deliverance is required (Col. 1:13). Those that live in a state of spiritual ignorance walk "in darkness," steadily progressing toward the ultimate night — eternal separation from God (I John 2:9-11; Jude 6,13).

The realm of spiritual night is governed by a Satanic hierarchy. We are told of the "rulers of the darkness of this world" (Eph. 6:12), a confederation of powerful spiritual hosts. They are pledged to maintain a reign of ignorance in this world — employing all of their wretched resources in the work of obscuring God and His Kingdom. They author thoughts (II Cor. 10:5), deeds (Eph. 5:11), and doctrines (I Tim. 4:1), in order to keep man at a distance from his Maker. The only thing that can neutralize their influence is faith — the belief of the truth! That is the victory that overcomes the world, together with its "rulers" (I John 5:4-5).

Vengeance on Them That Know Not God

We must not speak mildly or in a patronizing manner concerning man's ignorance of God. Those that do not know God — that are ignorant of Him and His ways — will be the objects of Divine vengeance. God has spoken clearly on this matter, and men are to take Him seriously! ". . . when the Lord Jesus shall be revealed from heaven with his mighty angels, in flaming fire taking vengeance on them that know not God, and that obey not the Gospel of our Lord Jesus Christ" (II Thess. 1:7-8).

I cannot conceive of a more serious note than that! There is not the slightest ambiguity about it, and anyone with a sound mind can understand what has been declared. This is the word of the Lord — a revelation of His Person and purpose. When Jesus comes again, He will not be tolerant of those that have spurned His love, rejected His Gospel, and devoted themselves to competitive interests! He pleads with the ignorant now, he will condemn them then! Now He offers eternal salvation, then everlasting fire!

Now is the time to know God — to culture a discerning awareness of Him. All of the resources required for such an achievement are at the disposal of the willing. Those that refuse to avail themselves of these provisions will be "punished with everlasting destruction [exclusion] from the presence of the Lord, and from the glory of His power" (II Thess. 1:9). This is not an idle threat — it is a statement of reality. This will come to pass when "He shall come to be glorified in His saints, and to be admired in all them that believe" (II Thess. 1:10). It is the business of all men to see to it that they are excluded from that curse!

Ignorance Requires Rebuke

Ignorance and innocence are not necessarily joined together. Innocence is associated with beginnings. Scripturally, ignorance results from the act of an alienated will. Adam and Eve, for example, were innocent before their disobedience. They were unacquainted with evil experientially, had no legal guilt, and were normally harmless. In all of the history of the world, they are the only individuals of judgment and analysis thus innocent.

Their knowledge of God was introductory — not to be compared with what is experienced in Christ. The Divine fellowship enjoyed by the church was unknown to Adam. Its grandeur "from the beginning of the world" was "hid in God" (Eph. 1:26). The Gospel embodies a "mystery which hath been hid from ages and from generations, but is now made manifest to His saints" (Col. 1:26). God had infinitely more for man than "walking in the garden in the cool of the day" (Gen. 3:8). Think of the transcendent difference between naming all of the animals, for instance, and judging men and angels (Gen. 2:19-20; I Cor. 6:1-2).

Before the fall, man was not rebuked for being ignorant — though even then it proved to be a liability. The "first man" was unaware of God's eternal purpose because it had not yet been revealed, and he was "ignorant" of Satan's "devices" (II Cor. 2:11) because he had not yet confronted Satan. This is no longer the case, however. God has revealed His objectives to men through the Gospel, and a history of Satan's influence has been provided in the Scriptures. There is no longer any acceptable reason for a person "of age" (John 9:21) to be ignorant of either God or devilish ploys.

Ignorance — particularly in the church — is now a cause for shame, and thus of rebuke. "Awake to righteousness, and sin not; for some have not the knowledge of God: I speak this to your shame" (I Cor. 15:34). The inexcusable condition of the alienated Gentile world is described as one "without understanding" (Rom. 1:31). With a note of displeasure, yet with gentleness, Jesus said to His disciples, "Are ye also without understanding? Do ye not understand . . . ?" (Matt. 15:16-17). He was not content for them to remain in an uninformed, undiscerning condition. They had walked with Him long enough to know more than they did. The Pharisees and Sadducees were acutely aware of the text of Scripture, but lacked understanding. They were "Bible scholars," yet unable to identify the Messiah foretold by it. Such ignorance was inexcusable because it was willful.

The early church, having lapsed into an unacceptable state, was soundly rebuked by the writer of Hebrews for its lack of spiritual understanding. "For when for the time ye ought to be teachers, ye have need that one teach you again which be the first principles of the oracles of God; and are become such as have need of milk, and not of strong meat" (Heb. 5:12). The seriousness of spiritual ignorance is underscored in the sixth chapter of Hebrews. A lack of growth in understanding and comprehension produces a spiritual environment which leads to falling away and consequent condemnation (Heb. 6:1-8). Let no one, therefore, treat lightly their lack of spiritual understanding. The comprehension of spiritual realities brings one closer to heaven; the ignorance of them tends to advance one toward hell.

Laboring to Dispel Ignorance

Much of the Apostolic labor was directed toward dispelling spiritual ignorance. They consistently saw the lack of discernment as a liability, and were not content to ignore or excuse it. How often do we read the words, "I would not have you to be ignorant" (I Cor. 10:1; 12:1; I Thess. 4:13). Peter exhorted the church to "be not ignorant" (II Pet. 3:8). There was Divine reason behind these solemn exhortations.

This was not just an apostolic formality — a standard idiom of the times, so to speak. Ignorance hinders growth in God's Kingdom. It opens the door to Satan and closes the door to God. It compels man's attention to be focused upon earth and away from heaven. It makes the Bible dull and boring, and the things of this world tantalizing.

Christian fellowship is achieved by the dissipation of ignorance, or the presence of spiritual understanding. "That which we have seen and heard declare we unto you," wrote John, "that ye also may have fellowship with us: and truly our fellowship is with the Father, and with His Son Jesus Christ" (I John 1:3). The comprehension of God's Son enables fellowship with both the Father and the Son; the discernment of the Gospel brings fellowship among those embracing it. Both forms of fellowship are required, and spiritual ignorance is inhibitive to both.

The Association of Understanding with Faith

Faith has too often been associated with a lack of understanding and a failure to discern. Saving faith is identified with "substance" and "evidence" — both have an undeniable relationship to intelligence. Faith profits man because understanding is integral to it.

The wisdom of this world has long struggled with the fact of the universe and its origin. Numerous theories have been proposed which claim to account for the earth's beginning, and confusion prevails in some circles as to which one is correct. The people of God, however, have no difficulty in this matter. They understand creation, which is a source of confusion to others.

"Through faith," the Word declares, "we understand that the worlds were framed by the word of God, so that things which are seen were not made of things that do appear" (Heb. 11:3). The creation is conducive to reasoning, and faith brings understanding. What God has said about creation, coupled with intelligent observation, will produce sound conclusions. The worlds were "framed" — an objective purpose was the cause of their origin. The precision and order of the natural creation attest to this. "The invisible things of Him from the creation of the world are clearly seen, being understood by the things that are made . . ." (Rom. 1:20).

Faith enables men to comprehend why the worlds were made, why there is order within them, and how the seen results from the unseen. The powers of reason are expanded by faith, because of the union with Deity that is realized by it.

It is the function of faith to "enlighten" the "eyes of the understanding" so that men may have a discerning grasp of their "calling," their "inheritance," and "the exceeding greatness of His power to us who believe . . ." (Eph. 1:18-19). If those benefits are not comprehended to some degree, they cannot be enjoyed. They are administered through man's understanding — and faith is the means through which they are conferred.

The Association of Jesus with Understanding

Those that are adverse to understanding have, by that very attitude, excluded themselves from the ministry of Jesus. The "Son of God is come," proclaims John, "and has given us an understanding." This is not an academic understanding, but a "spiritual" one. He acquaints the believer with God and His ways, in preparation for eternity.

Thus does Jesus fulfill His ministry of "Counsellor" which Isaiah foretold (Isa. 9:6). To the church He offers His gracious invitation — one that will, if received, yield spiritual stability and confidence. "Behold, I stand at the door and knock: if any man hear My voice, and open the door, I will come in to him, and will sup with him, and he with Me" (Rev. 3:20). In this communion men are brought higher — Jesus is not brought lower. He does not come to identify with men's problems, but to identify men with God's solutions. He comes to make things in heaven plain, not the things of the cursed world.

What Does It Mean to Understand?

To understand the truth means that its relevancy is perceived. The unseen body of reality with which God's Kingdom deals is seen as having a direct bearing upon the individual. This perception constrained those on the day of Pentecost to cry out, "Men and brethren, what shall we do" (Acts 2:37)? The Philippian jailor, convinced of eternal issues, said, "Sirs, what must I do to be saved?" (Acts 16:30). The Ethiopian eunuch, also persuaded that he had heard a relevant message, said to Philip, "See, here is water; what doth hinder me to be baptized?" (Acts 8:36). In each instance, they understood the Gospel to the degree that they perceived its relevancy to themselves.

The truth has been understood when its implications are perceived. The mere accumulation of knowledge has never been God's objective, and His Kingdom cannot be served by that means. Proper reasoning upon the truth will produce acceptable conduct in the believer.

"Having therefore these promises, dearly beloved, let us cleanse ourselves from all filthiness of the flesh and spirit, perfecting holiness in the fear of God" (II Cor. 7:1). The commitment of the Almighty to receive men, be a Father unto them, and they His sons and daughters — correctly understood — will provide motivation for uprightness of life (II Cor. 6:17-18).

We have been warned of the certain destruction of the world. God has appointed a day when "the works that are therein shall be burned up" (II Pet. 3:10). Men are to reason upon that revelation and perceive its implications. The conclusion of all thoughtful men will be the same: "Seeing then that all these things shall be dissolved, what manner of persons ought ye to be in all holy conversation and godliness" (II Pet. 3:11). It simply does not make sense to become attached to an order destined for destruction!

Where conclusions of this sort have not been reached, the truth of God has not been understood. No amount of worldly wisdom, further, can produce these conclusions — they proceed from a conviction of things not seen. The heart is involved in spiritual understanding, and thereby man's will is affected. Of itself, information cannot morally motivate. Understanding, however, does accomplish this.

How Can Two Walk Together Except They Be Agreed?

Israel is the only earthly nation with which God has ever identified Himself. In confirmation of this He said through Amos, "You only have I known of all the families of the earth . . ." (Amos 3:2). Almost seven centuries before Amos, Moses proclaimed to Israel, "For you are a holy people unto the Lord your God: the Lord your God hath chosen you to be a special people unto Himself, above all people that are upon the face of the earth" (Deut. 7:6). Never — before nor since — has there been a political entity with which God exclusively identified Himself.

Yet, even that unique association could not be maintained apart from agreement with God. He cannot fellowship with those that are at variance with Himself. Thus did He ask the wandering Israelites; "Can two walk together, except they be agreed?" (Amos 3:3). The point is that unless there is an agreed objective, intelligent personalities cannot be in accord. This is nowhere more evident than in issues that concern man's salvation from sin.

Man's reconciliation to God occurs in his thoughts — when he sees things as God does. The basis for man's reconciliation was achieved by Christ's sacrifice; the experience of it is accomplished by man's recognition and reception of its efficacy (II Cor. 5:18-20).

The condemnation of the wicked is because "God is not in all his thoughts" (Psa. 10:4). The "unrighteous man" is commanded to forsake "his thoughts." Divine pardon will follow man's obedience at that point (Isa. 55:7). The "thoughts" of the unrighteous man are what makes him unrighteous, and he will remain in that unacceptable state until he forsakes his way of thinking.

On the other hand, "the thoughts of the righteous are right" (Prov. 12:5), providing a basis for Divine fellowship. As those that are reconciled to God "think" on things that are above, their lives are brought into conformity to the Divine will and they enjoy the approving presence of the Almighty (Phil. 4:8-9). Men cannot think incorrectly and be well pleasing to God.

Casting Down Imaginations

The most complicated part of man is his thinking process. It is more intricate than in any other part of his being. Here is where the greatest warfare exists. All truth and all delusion is addressed to the mind. The

Gospel, the promises, and the warnings — they are all subjects for thought. Thinking always precedes action; that makes it an area to be disciplined by truth.

The believer's spiritual weaponry is designed to be effective in the arena of thought. "For the weapons of our warfare are not carnal, but mighty through God to the pulling down of strongholds; casting down imaginations . . ." (II Cor. 10:4-5). The people of God, then, are not powerless in the matter of dealing with thoughts — they have been equipped with a Divine arsenal that can deal with wicked intrusions into the mind.

"Imaginations" are thoughts that do not conform to reality. They are distractions which will, if followed, lead to perdition. While they may appear valid and often very sound, they are to be "cast down" — violently overthrown by devotion to the truth. This will occur when the truth is believed, loved, and embraced.

Make It Plain!

The great initiatives of God have been related to His objective of acquainting men with Himself. The choosing of Israel, the giving of the Law, and the confirmation of the Gospel — all were designed to make known God and His will.

Some conclusions are necessary at this point. 1. Any view of Scripture that promotes mystery or obscures God's intentions is wrong, and is to be shunned. The word of God is a revelation, and is conducive to understanding. Things, therefore, that conceal, are contrary to it. 2. Anyone that is content to be without the knowledge of God is on imminently dangerous ground. His soul is in jeopardy, and he treads over the very precipice of hell. 3. Any fervent desire to understand what God has said should be attended with joyful optimism. God desires to be understood — that is why He has provided man with His Word. Those that desire to understand Him, therefore, have every reason to expect the success of their desire!

A Kingdom principle is provided us in the book of Habakkuk. This somewhat obscure prophet was raised up to sound the warning of impending judgment to a lethargic nation. God commanded that a clear message be given by the prophet — one that could not possibly be misunderstood. "Write the vision, and make it plain upon tables, that he may run that reads it" [that he that is passing by may read it on the run]

(Hab. 2:2). The message was to be so obvious that it did not require a delay to comprehend it.

God's revelations are to be communicated; they are not meant to be private. God's purpose involves the whole world, and so does His revelation. The law was written "very plainly" (Deut. 27:8), and Jesus proclaimed He would show men "plainly" of the Father (John 16:25). Obscured messages are ungodly, and incompatible with the Kingdom of God. A message that cannot be understood cannot serve God's objectives. For this reason, the Apostles used "great plainness of speech" (II Cor. 3:12).

This is not a reference to simplistic and juvenile speech. That ought to be apparent from the Apostolic use of such words as "lasciviousness" (Jude 4) and "concupiscence" (I Thess. 4:5). They extended themselves to communicate the truth by teaching it — elaborating upon its implications, and bringing it to bear upon the situations of their day. They "expounded" the truth (Acts 11:4; 18:26; 28:23). This is the significance of "teaching" (Matt. 28:20; Col. 3:16; I Tim. 4:11; 6:2).

Revelation that is not understood cannot profit (Matt. 13:19). Some things, it is true, are "hard to be understood" (II Pet. 3:16), but even they are not beyond understanding. For this reason, preaching that produces questions or confusion is to be avoided (I Tim. 1:4; 6:4; II Tim. 2:23; Titus 3:9). The things of God are to be made "plain"!

Conclusion

The truths of God are never more precious than when they are understood, and never more ordinary than when they are not understood. The Kingdom of God is based on understanding. The truth of the Gospel must be perceived in order to be saved, and the eternal inheritance must be discerned before a quest for it can begin. The enemy of man's soul cannot be successfully resisted if men are ignorant of his devices, and the blessings of God cannot be appropriated apart from the knowledge of Him. In Christ are hidden "all the treasures of wisdom and knowledge" (Col. 2:3). Those who value them can obtain them by faith. They will liberate from delusion, strengthen the inner man, and finally enable the appropriation of glory. Let no man despise spiritual wisdom and understanding. Rather, let every man determine to be "wise unto salvation" (II Tim. 3:15).

23

THE GLORIOUS TRIUMPH OF GOD'S KINGDOM

God's eternal enterprise is being culminated in stages. The creation was the initial stage, the age of law the one of prefigurement, and "the day of salvation" the preparation for the end. No single stage was an end of itself. Once the world and its inhabitants were created, the work was under way. When the Law was given, the purpose began to unfold. The reign of King Jesus has set in motion the final stages of the Divine purpose, leading to the end of all things.

The Distinction Between Divine Purpose and Desire

Division has occurred among professed believers because of failure to distinguish between the purpose of God and His general desires for men. The Kingdom of God is identified with His purpose, and does not center on specific individuals. The only Man that, of Himself, is necessary to the Kingdom is Jesus Christ. Without His sacrifice, resurrection, intercession, and reign, God's Kingdom could not be brought to fruition. He is associated with the total objective and its realization.

Other individuals obtain their value by either identification with a group, or class of men ("prophets," "Apostles," "church," etc.), or with a special work that embraced a phase of the Divine objective (Adam, Abraham, Moses, etc.). The purpose of God is larger than any of these groups or individuals. None of them can be called "truth," "way," or "life," as was Jesus (John 14:6). "The fulness of the Godhead" did not dwell in them, but with the Son of God (Col. 2:9). Only the "law," for instance, was given by Moses, "but grace and truth came by Christ" (John 1:17). Grace and truth are wider in scope than the Law, embracing "all the counsel of God" (Acts 20:27).

The Desire of God

God's desire concerns all men, and is intensely personal. He "will have all men to be saved, and to come unto the knowledge of the truth" (I Tim. 2:4), and "is not willing that any should perish, but that all should come to repentance" (II Pet. 3:9). He longs to "show Himself strong in the behalf of them whose heart is perfect toward Him," and His eyes "run to and fro throughout the whole earth" in search of such ones (II Chron. 16:9; Zech. 4:10). He has "prepared" salvation "before the face of all people" (Luke 2:31) because of His intense longing for them.

Divine desire, however, can be frustrated — not because of weakness in Deity, but because of the manner of the Kingdom! This was illustrated in the ministry of the Lord Jesus. There is no question about His desire for Israel — in particular of Jerusalem. His heart yearned to bring them into harmony with God's eternal purpose. He extended Himself in every respect as He moved among them, "doing good, and healing all that were oppressed of the Devil" (Acts 10:38). He had compassion upon their multitudes (Matt. 9:36; 14:4). He demonstrated His longing for them by healing their sick, feeding their hungry, and raising their dead. To the discerning, there was no question about how Jesus felt about the people of Israel.

One of the most staggering demonstrations of Divine frustration is found in Jesus' words to the hard-hearted leaders of Israel. "O Jerusalem, Jerusalem, you who kill the prophets, and stone them that are sent to you. How often would I have gathered your children together, even as a hen gathers her chickens under her wings, and you would not! Behold, your house is left desolate" (Matt. 23:37-39; Luke 13:34). There is no question about the desire of Jesus. He clearly stated

404

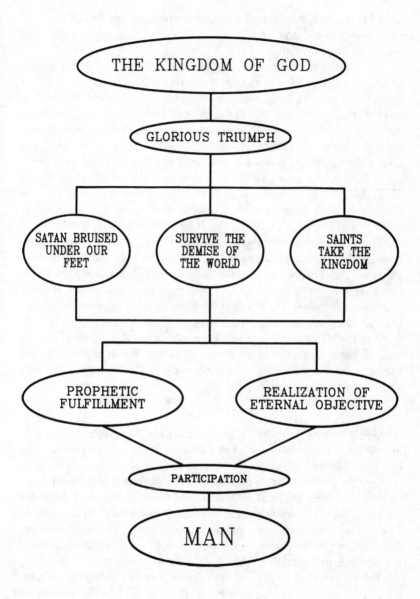

405

what He wanted; but He was inhibited by the stubborn wills of the people — "you would not!" In this case, their will triumphed over His — to their own condemnation!

On another occasion, Jesus came near Jerusalem, and "He beheld the city, and wept over it, saying, If you had known, even you, at least in this your day, the things which belong unto your peace! But now they are hid from your eyes. For the days shall come upon you, that your enemies shall cast a trench about you, and compass you round, and keep you on every side, and shall lay you even with the ground, and your children within you; and they shall not leave in you one stone upon another; because you knew not the time of your visitation" (Luke 19:41-44). Their Deliverer was in their presence, and they did not know it! In their ignorance, they rejected the peace that belonged to them! It was not God's will that this happen — it was their will!

The point in this is not weakness and strength, or wisdom and ignorance, but the moral nature of God's Kingdom. His will for all men is very clear, and cannot be questioned without denying the Gospel. It is that they can be saved. The fact that men can successfully exclude themselves from what God wants for them by no means indicates they are stronger than God. Man possesses a will, which is the primary element of the Divine image which he bears. Were God to bless man in spite of that will, the Divine image would be destroyed, and man would cease to be his "offspring." In such a case, God would also have violated His own nature.

The Purpose of God

God's "eternal purpose" is specific in scope, but general as regards individuals. He has revealed what will occur in the "ages to come," but has not identified all of the individuals that shall participate in it. A "crown of righteousness" is promised to "all them that love His appearing" (II Tim. 4:8). We read of "the heirs of salvation" (Heb. 1:14), "the people of God" (Heb. 4:9), and "him that overcomes" (Rev. 2:7). In Christ, God's commitments are so stated that any individual desiring them may embrace them. Those that, by faith and obedience, receive the Son become identified with God's revealed objectives.

The church shall be presented to Christ "a glorious church, not having spot or wrinkle, or any such thing" (Eph. 5:27). All that overcome will be made a "pillar in the temple of God" (Rev. 3:12). The saints shall judge the world and angels (I Cor. 6:2-3). The world to come shall be placed in subjection to "children of God" (Heb. 2:5-8; Rom. 8:20-21). Those that "endure temptation" shall doubtless "receive the crown of life" (James 1:12). The "meek" shall "inherit the earth, and shall delight themselves in the abundance of peace" (Matt. 5:5; Psa. 37:11).

These are commitments that cannot possibly be frustrated! It is impossible, for instance, for someone to overcome the world only to be denied access to "the tree of life, which is in the midst of the paradise of God" (Rev. 2:7). No personality in heaven or in earth can alter the Divine commitment that "he that does the will of God abides forever" (I John 2:17). God has "prepared" a city for those that "desire a better country, that is an heavenly" (Heb. 11:16); it is not possible for that preparation to be in vain!

God has never altered His purpose — from the creation of the world until now. He has, in Jesus Christ, made full provision for the involvement of every man in His objective. It but remains for the individual to avail himself of that provision. The glorious triumph of the Kingdom of God involves every individual that has received the benefits freely given by God in Christ Jesus. It necessarily excludes everyone that has rejected them.

The Fulfillment of All Spoken by the Prophets

The church — the most extensive revelation of God's Kingdom — is built upon the foundation of the prophets as well as the apostles (Eph. 2:20). God sent the prophets to articulate His mind and purpose to men. As a rule, the world rejected their testimony, even killing them (Jer. 2:30; Matt. 23:37; Mark 12:5; Luke 13:34; I Thess. 2:15). Their words, however, were not destroyed by the taking of their lives. They were God's spokesman, and their words could no more fail of fulfillment than God could cease being God!

Peter made reference to these prophets when he spoke of Jesus: "Whom the heaven must receive until the times of restitution of all things, which God has spoken by the mouth of all His holy prophets since the world began" (Acts 3:21). The correct meaning of the words "receive until" is more clearly represented in several versions of the Scripture: "He must remain in heaven, until . . ." "(Today's English Version and New International Version); "Whom heaven must keep till . . ." (*Jerusalem Bible*).

Jesus will be retained in heaven until there are no further prophecies to be fulfilled — that is the meaning of Peter's words. He, as King, is governing the fulfillment of those prophecies. None of them will be fulfilled independently of Him. The government of the Kingdom — which includes the fulfillment of God's commitments — is "upon His shoulder" (Isa. 9:6).

The earth is ultimately ruled from heaven; all earthly government, theocratic or otherwise, is temporal. It is "the heavens" that "do rule" (Dan. 4:26), and "the Most High that rules in the Kingdom of men" (Dan. 4:17,25,32). The fulfillment of prophetic utterances is the primary manifestation of that rule. The mere manipulation of men is not a satisfactory demonstration of Divine Sovereignty unless it is associated with heavenly objective. The words of the prophets are the means of making that association, and Jesus' reign in "the heaven" is the means of their fulfillment. His rule is incomplete until the prophecies are fulfilled, for that is one of the reasons for which all authority in heaven and earth has been committed to Him.

The Stone that Became a Mountain

Daniel — a prophet ahead of his time — revealed the Kingdom of God in a most unusual way. The obscure revelation was given to Nebuchadnezzar, king of Babylon. In a forgotten dream, he saw a great image of precious metals, which depicted the kingdoms of this world. That image was eventually destroyed by an unassuming "stone" which was "cut out" of a mountain "without hands" (Dan. 2:31-34). That stone, which "smote the image, became a great mountain, and filled the whole earth" (Dan. 2:35).

In his interpretation, Daniel unveiled the Kingdom of God, superior to the kingdoms of men. "And in the days of these kings shall the God of Heaven set up a kingdom, which shall never be destroyed: and the kingdom shall not be left to other people, but it shall break in pieces and consume all these kingdoms, and it shall stand forever" (Dan. 2:44). This heavenly kingdom — set up by the God of heaven — shall have no successor: "it shall not be left to other people." It will stand after all other kingdoms have fallen.

This kingdom was not a political one, and was not to be maintained by military power and overt force. It was, as Jesus later revealed, a kingdom of truth (John 18:37), and was to ultimately triumph over the misplaced objectives of earthly kingdoms. The will of God was to triumph over the will of men. His purpose would be fulfilled, and the purposes of political empires — all of them — would be frustrated. Earthly government has consistently proven to be God's competitor, and as such, every aspect of it shall be cast down to the ground.

Not a single political empire will exist in the ages to come; not a solitary representative of earthly government. All of them shall be swallowed up by Divine purpose! Little wonder that the Apostles proclaimed, "We ought to obey God rather than men" (Acts 5:29). Only God's purpose will have ultimate fulfillment — the will of all unregenerate men shall be frustrated, "though hand join in hand" (Prov. 11:21; 16:5).

The fulfillment of God's eternal purpose is the "mountain" that shall fill the whole earth. As long as one unfulfilled prophecy exists, the mountain has not filled the whole earth. But when all rule and power has been put down, and the purposes of men have been thoroughly frustrated, truth shall stand alone, having vanquished everything contrary to it! Jesus shall remain in heaven until the "times of restitution [restoration or fulfillment] of all things, which God has spoken by the mouth of all His holy prophets since the world began"!

The Glory of the Lord Shall Be Revealed

"God is a Spirit," declared Jesus (John 4:24). As such, He is "the invisible God" (Col. 1:15), inaccessible to the natural senses. He has no form or "shape" that permits carnal observation or analysis (John 5:37; I John 4:12). This has been a stumbling block for men throughout the ages. Gentile nations "changed the glory of the uncorruptible God into an image made like to corruptible man, and to birds, and creeping things." This so incensed the God of heaven that He "gave them up to uncleanness through the lusts of their own hearts . . ." (Rom. 1:23-24).

The reason for this judgment is obvious. While God cannot be perceived with the senses, He may be discerned to a measurable degree by what He has done. On an elementary level, "the invisible things of Him from the creation of the world are clearly seen, being understood by the things that are made, even His eternal power and Godhead" (Rom. 1:20). Before one can become involved in idolatry, he must re-

409

ject those things which can be "clearly seen," and embrace a false and unreasonable view of God. To live in God's world — a world with the stamp of His character upon it — in ignorance of Him is inexcusable!

The revelation of God's Person reaches its apex in Jesus, who is the "Image of the invisible God" (Col. 1:15). That revelation, however, does not consist of mere observation, but of thoughtful analysis. It is Jesus' words and works that reveal the nature of God — the "Image" is one of concept, not one of form. Externally, Jesus appeared no different from other men. It was His character that differed — and that was revealed in His expressions.

A Kingdom principle is perceived here — one that is to be grasped by all men. God is known by what He does and what He speaks. He is glorified when His Person becomes apparent to those before whom He has thus revealed Himself. Thought, not sight, is the means of comprehending the Living God.

The Prophet Isaiah spoke of a time when God would be glorified openly, and without question. "And the glory of the Lord shall be revealed, and all flesh shall see it together: for the mouth of the Lord hath spoken it" (Isa. 40:5). All men, great and small, are appointed to confront God, and to unquestionably behold Him. At that time, none will say that it "thundered" (John 12:29), and no one will fail to comprehend His speech (Acts 9:7).

God's Person shall be revealed by the unveiling of His completed purpose. God has one more appointment for this world — one which He has "promised" will come to pass. "Yet once more I shake not the earth only, but also heaven. And this word, Yet once more, signifies the removing of those things that are shaken, as of things that are made, that those things which cannot be shaken may remain" (Heb. 12:26-27). When all temporality has been removed, and only eternal realities remain, God shall be glorified.

His "eternal purpose" will be openly demonstrated by the presence of a church that is "holy and unblamable and unreprovable in His sight" (Col. 1:22). There will be no contesting of this revelation — Jesus, the express Image of God's Person — will be "glorified in His saints," and "be admired in all them that believe" (II Thess. 1:10). The church, in the aggregate, will reveal the true God. He will be perceived in them. Those "in Christ" are "His workmanship" (Eph. 2:10). His Person shall be clearly perceived by an assembled universe when the finished work is presented "not having spot, or wrinkle, or any such thing . . . holy and without blemish" (Eph. 5:27).

He Who was perceived in the beginning of the work shall be even more clearly comprehended in the completion of it (Phil. 1:6; Rom. 9:28). The consummation of the redemptive undertaking will finish the mystery: ". . . the mystery of God should be finished, as He has declared to His servants the prophets" (Rev. 10:7). What He has been doing now will be fully revealed then.

All Dominions Shall Serve and Obey Him

Even in this world, "there is no power but of God" (Rom. 13:1). Pilate, who overestimated his own authority, was confronted with this truth by the Lord Jesus. "You could have no power at all against Me, except it were given to you from above . . ." (John 19:11). This present age is marked by an ironic distribution of authority — both good and evil men possess it: Nebuchadnezzar as well as David, Ahaz as well as Hezekiah.

There are, and have always been, despotical political powers that aligned themselves against the Lord and His people. The early church, recognizing this, prayed; "For of a truth against Thy Holy Child Jesus, Whom Thou hast anointed, both Herod, and Pontius Pilate, with the Gentiles, and the people of Israel, were gathered together" (Acts 4:27). These powers did not, and could not, overthrow the purpose of the Almighty (Psa. 2:1-4).

Daniel prophesied of a time when "all dominions shall serve and obey" the most High (Dan. 7:27) — a time when all delegated authority will be possessed by His devoted servants. This refers to the "ages to come," when "the kingdom under the whole heaven shall be given to the people of the saints of the most High" (Dan. 7:27a). At that time, no wicked personality will be in a position of authority, visible or invisible. Satan and all of his forces shall be cast into the lake of fire, stripped of their authority. The kingdom in its entirety will be given to those "for whom it has been prepared" (Matt. 20:23; 25:34) — the saints. That is the declared purpose of God from the beginning (Psa. 8:6).

Then shall "all dominions" be occupied by those cultured for righteous reign. Their first assignment, so to speak, will be to judge men and angels — and they shall do it righteously. The positions of authority shall then be held by the righteous, and "all dominions shall serve Him."

411

This is the heritage of the saints!

The Subjugations of the Enemies of Christ

The enemies of Christ are those that have not "received the atonement," and thus conflict with His purpose. There is no neutrality in the Kingdom; "He that is not with Me is against Me; and he that does not gather with Me scatters abroad" (Matt. 12:30). All that have rejected the Gospel, not availing themselves of the reconciliation, are "not with" Him. They are, by that very fact, "against" Him — friends of the world and enemies of God (James 4:4).

Their philosophy of life militates against the truth, inhibits righteousness, and fortifies iniquity. Serving their own "belly," glorying in "their shame," and minding "earthly things," they are "the enemies of the cross of Christ" (Phil. 3:18). They may appear cultured, educated, gifted, and harmless — but they are enemies "of all righteousness" (Acts 13:10). If God ignored their willing rejection of salvation, that would reproach Christ's sacrifice and negate its effect. Those that do not submit to the convicting power of the Spirit (John 16:8-11) are the enemies of Christ, and shall be subdued by Him — openly and completely.

Until His Enemies Be Made His Footstool

Because of the centrality of Jesus, those opposed to God are called "His [Christ's] enemies." All men are viewed in relation to Him; they will either be saved in Him or subdued under Him. He has been exalted "to be a Prince and a Savior, to give repentance to Israel, and remission of sins" (Acts 5:31). Those that spurn His gift are destined to be broken — their purposes frustrated, and themselves cut off from all hope.

David's prophetic eye foresaw the time of the subjugation of Christ's enemies. "The Lord said unto my Lord, Sit Thou at My right hand, until I make Thine enemies Thy footstool" (Psa. 110:1). This passage is quoted at least five times in the New Testament writings (Matt. 22:44; Mark 12:36; Luke 20:43; Acts 2:35; Heb. 1:13), and alluded to at least twice (I Cor. 15:25; Heb. 10:13). It is a pivotal teaching of Scripture, designed to clarify the appointed outcome of Jesus' reign. Like Satan, Jesus' enemies shall be bruised by Him (Gen. 3:15).

During Joshua's takeover of Canaan, five notable kings became a token of the ultimate conquest of the land. Following the battle when

412

the "sun stood still, and the moon stayed" (Josh. 10:13), "those kings" were brought out unto Joshua. In the spirit of triumph, "Joshua called for all the men of Israel, and said unto the captains of the men of war which went with him, Come near, put your feet upon the necks of these kings. And they came near, and put their feet upon the necks of them. And Joshua said unto them, Fear not, nor be dismayed, be strong and of good courage: for thus shall the Lord do to all your enemies against whom ye fight" (Josh. 10:23-25). Thus shall it be with the enemies of Christ. God Himself shall make Christ's enemies His footstool — His foot shall be placed upon their necks in glorious triumph!

Ground to Powder

Jesus is either a cornerstone or a demolishing one; One that will stabilize or destroy. He is "the Stone which the builders rejected" — the foundation upon which all hope is built. The "builders" were the wise among Israel, tutored of God to recognize the Deliverer of mankind. But they did not perceive Him, and thus rejected Him. To them — to the world — He said, "And whosoever shall fall upon this Stone shall be broken: but on whomsoever it shall fall, it will grind him to powder" (Matt. 21:44).

One falls upon this Stone when he abandons his own works of righteousness as a basis of acceptance before God. With a humble and contrite heart, and in faith, the atonement is "received" (Rom. 5:11) and the Gospel "obeyed" (Rom. 10:16). The stout heart is thus broken, and new creatureship experienced "before the great and notable day of the Lord come" (Acts 2:20).

The Stone shall fall upon all that "know not God and that obey not the Gospel" (II Thess. 1:8) in the day of Christ's revelation. Then will come the promised confrontation, when God "shall judge the world in righteousness by that Man Whom He has ordained" (Acts 17:31). The issue will be set before an assembled universe — the ultimate Person, and the ultimate provision, salvation. In flaming fire He shall confront the ungodly. Their words, their works, and their thoughts shall be summoned for consideration. They had opposed Christ and rejected his redemption while in His world. Were they liars or was He? Was their way right, or was His? In that confrontation, the eternal Rock shall "fall upon them," and they shall be "ground to powder." Their cause shall be demonstrated to have been a delusion, their power stripped from them,

413

and they themselves consigned to the lake that burns with fire and brimstone! Thus shall the wicked be "ground to powder."

The Kingdoms of Our Lord and of His Christ

The kingdoms of this world represent a perverted stewardship, an abuse of authority, and competition against God's Son. At the threshold of His earthly ministry, Satan showed Jesus "all the kingdoms of the world, and the glory of them" — and he did it in "a moment of time" (Matt. 4:8; Luke 4:5). They were dazzling kingdoms, characterized by a fading glory that was, nevertheless, attractive. The people of the world could be manipulated, wealth accumulated, and pomp and splendor enjoyed. Satan had infected them all with His rebellion, and now he sought to bring Jesus into his wretched camp.

But instead of surveying those temporal kingdoms from that high mountain, the eyes of Christ focused on the distant future — a time when all of them would be brought crashing to the ground during the passing of the temporal order. He resisted the offer because He had His mind set on "the end." His redemptive work was of a higher order, and the possession of worldly kingdoms could not assist in the implementation of His heavenly commission.

John the beloved, in writing of the consummation of the ages, declared in apocalyptic language the demise of all temporal empires. The time was characterized by the anger "of the nations," as the wrath of the Almighty began to fall upon them. They were being readied for "the time of the dead," when they would be "judged," and God would "destroy them which destroy the earth" (Rev. 11:18). For several millennia it appeared as though heaven was oblivious of their rebellion. But now "the temple of God" is "opened in heaven" as the eyes of the Almighty focus upon the kingdoms of this world. He who "sent redemption" in His Son (Psa. 111:9) now sends "lightnings, and voices, and thunderings, and an earthquake, and great hail" — figures of destruction (Rev. 11:19).

The heavenly hosts perceive the consummation of the ages, the finishing of the mystery (Rev. 10:7), and the completion of the eternal purpose. The cry breaks forth from "great voices in heaven, saying, The kingdoms of this world are become the kingdoms of our Lord and of His Christ; and He shall reign for ever and ever" (Rev. 11:15).

All power in heaven and earth, given to Him in the capacity of a

414

Savior (Matt. 28:18), will have been faithfully employed to accomplish the will of God. The petition which He taught men to pray — "Thy kingdom come" (Matt. 6:10) — will then be brought to fruition. What was started at Pentecost will be brought to its appointed end, and the "kingdoms of this world" will "become the kingdoms of our Lord and of His Christ."

They will become His in two easy ways: 1. He shall overcome them with the sword of His mouth — His triumphant Word (Rev. 19:15,21). He shall frustrate their purpose and put down their rebellion, stripping them of all misused authority. Thus will worldly kingdoms become His. 2. They will become His by way of service. The kingdom shall be given to the saints, as it is written; "And the kingdom and dominion, and the greatness of the kingdom under the whole heaven, shall be given to the saints of the most High . . ." (Dan. 7:27). Then shall be brought to pass the saying, "and the time came that the saints possessed the Kingdom" (Dan. 7:23). Their reign shall be "with Christ," and thus will "the kingdoms of this world become the kingdoms of our Lord and of His Christ."

Every Knee Shall Bow

Christ's enemies will not merely be conquered; they shall recognize before an assembled universe that they have been overcome. All men will confess Jesus is Lord — either to their salvation or condemnation. If they do it in this world, "confession is made unto salvation" (Rom. 10:9-10). If not in this world, confession shall be made at the judgment seat unto condemnation.

The decree has gone forth, and it cannot be recalled: "That at the name of Jesus every knee should bow, of things in heaven, and things in the earth, and things under the earth; and that every tongue should confess that Jesus Christ is Lord, to the glory of God the Father" (Phil. 2:10-11). Those that thought Him an imposter will acknowledge Him to be the Truth! Men supposing that there were multiple ways to God will confess Him as the Way! Those led astray by the engrossing temporalities of this world, will admit that He is the Life! He is "the Way, the Truth, and the Life" (John 14:6), and shall be so confessed! His Gospel will be confessed as true, and all others false. His blood will be acknowledged as the only means of remission, and His sacrifice as the only means to righteousness.

415

Delivering the Kingdom up to God

"The end" is associated with several things in Scripture. The harvest of the world, involving the separation of the godly from the ungodly (Matt. 13:39-40), the termination of suffering and affliction (I Pet. 4:7), and the conclusion of the faith-life (I Cor. 1:8; Heb. 3:6,14; 6:11; 1:13; Rev. 2:26). Believers contemplate "the end" with joy, because of "the grace that shall be brought unto" them "at the revelation of Jesus Christ" (I Pet. 1:13).

Upon completion of this purpose, Jesus will turn the Kingdom back to the Father, Who is the only One not under Christ's authority. "For He [the Father] has put all things under His [Jesus'] feet. But when He [the Father] says all things are put under Him [Jesus], it is manifest that He [the Father] is excepted, which did put all things under Him [Jesus]" (I Cor. 15:27). I fear that many professed believers have been guilty of leaving God out of the church — but Jesus has not! Upon completion of His mission — when His enemies have been made His footstool — He will return the Kingdom to the Father.

This is an extremely sensitive subject, and one where thoughtful deliberation is required. When He came to earth "made of a woman, made under the Law" (Gal. 4:4), an astounding humility was required. Prior to the incarnation, He, "being in the form of God, thought it not robbery to be equal with God." In quest of man, and in fulfillment of God's purpose, He "made Himself of no reputation, and took on Him the form of a servant, and was made in the likeness of men." As a man, He "humbled Himself and became obedient unto death, even the death of the cross" (Phil. 2:6-8). In that capacity He died, was buried, and arose — and as "the Man" He sits at the Father's right hand (I Tim. 2:5).

The results of His humiliation shall extend into eternity. It is a remarkable demonstration of His great love for man, and unity with His Father in eternal objective. Thus is it written, "And when all things shall be subdued unto Him, then shall the Son also Himself be subject unto Him that put all things under Him, that God may be all in all" (I Cor. 15:28). Thus shall the Kingdom be delivered back "to God." This in no way detracts from the Person of Christ, or diminishes His glory. He has been "highly exalted," and shall ever be!

The Last Enemy

Jesus will reign until all of His enemies have been put "under His

416

feet" (I Cor. 15:25). He will not leave the right hand of God until that has been accomplished! He has been directed by God to "sit" there "until" God makes His enemies His "footstool" (Heb. 1:13).

In his elaboration on Jesus' enemies, Paul introduces a very wonderful reality. "The last enemy that shall be destroyed is death" (I Cor. 15:25). Here is an enemy that has reigned from Eden until now, swallowing up the entire race of man with but two exceptions — Enoch (Gen. 5:24; Heb. 11:5) and Elijah (II Kgs. 2:11). Here were two men — each from a different dispensation — that were used to confirm the reality of the world to come.

In "the day of salvation," the Son of God arose from the dead, taking up His life again, as He was commanded to do (John 10:18). His demonstration was superior to that of Enoch and Elijah. They were "taken," He was victorious; theirs was a gift, His was a triumph! He was "the first that should rise from the dead" by His own power (Acts 26:23). He had authority to dismiss His spirit, and to rise again from the dead (John 10:18b). His resurrection, unlike the translation of Enoch and Elijah, was meritorious, being the basis for the conferment of righteousness (Rom. 4:25).

Death has always been an enemy, but never so much as since the Gospel has been preached. It is now perceived as contrary to the purpose of God. Jesus came that men might have "life" (John 10:10) — death contradicts that purpose. He is "the end of the law for righteousness to every one that believeth" (Rom. 10:4) — the "strength of sin is the law" (I Cor. 15:56). He, thus, is the end of death for His people.

The resurrection of the dead shall be the demise of death. Then shall be "brought to pass the saying that is written, Death is swallowed up in victory. O death, where is thy sting? O grave, where is thy victory" (I Cor. 15:54-55). The voice of the Son of man shall summon all men from the grave: "all that are in the graves shall hear His voice" (John 5:28). At that time, death shall lose its sting, and the grave shall be robbed of its victory. Jesus shall continue reigning at the right hand of God until this is accomplished — until the "last enemy" is destroyed.

When Sudden Destruction Comes

God has revealed that the destruction of His enemies shall be abrupt. It will occur in a time of apparent tranquility and safety. "For

417

yourselves know perfectly that the day of the Lord so comes as a thief in the night. For when they [the ungodly] shall say, Peace and safety; then sudden destruction comes upon them, as travail upon a woman with child; and they shall not escape" (I Thess. 5:2-3). Thus will the final curtain be brought down on the stage of mortal life, wherein God's eternal purpose was accomplished.

The suddenness of the destruction will demonstrate the superiority of the heavenly Kingdom. The enemies of the Lord will not see their overthrow coming, and consequently will be unprepared for it. Their wisdom failed them in preparation, and their power shall fail when they confront the "wrath of the Lamb" (Rev. 16:16).

The glorious triumph of the Kingdom of God shall be manifested in the complete overthrow of the enemies of Christ. It shall be total in scope, and eternal in duration. Not one enemy shall rise in rebellion from the ashes of this overthrow — not a single jot or title of authority shall remain among those that chose to oppose the Lord's Christ by not being "with" Him!

The Inheritance of the Saints

The completion of God's purpose not only involves taking from the ungodly what is not theirs, but giving to the godly what is theirs. The "reserved" inheritance shall be dispensed to those for whom it has been prepared. Redemption makes men "meet" [suitable and proper] to be "partakers of the inheritance of the saints in light" (Col. 1:12). It has been "promised" (Heb. 9:15), and in Christ men are "begotten" unto it (I Pet. 1:4). The triumph of truth is irrevocably associated with the people of God obtaining their inheritance.

The Meek Shall Inherit the Earth

Man was made to have "dominion over the works" of God's hands (Psa. 8:6). God has never abandoned that objective, but has rather made provision for its fulfillment in the "salvation which is in Christ Jesus with eternal glory" (II Tim. 2:10).

In one of his psalms, David spoke of a time when the meek would be exalted. "But the meek shall inherit the earth; and shall delight themselves in the abundance of peace" (Psa. 37:11). A refreshing thought, indeed to the just, against whom the wicked plot (Psa. 37:12). As long as war and tumult, opposition and rejection, exist, the earth

418

does not belong to the "meek" — those that with genuine humility accept and rejoice in the will of the Lord.

Jesus, in His enunciation of the principles of the heavenly Kingdom, said, "Blessed are the meek: for they shall inherit the earth" (Matt. 5:5). This promise was alluded to in God's promise to Abraham. "As for Me, behold My covenant is with thee, and thou shalt be a father of many nations" (Gen. 17:4). In his inspired commentary on the Abrahamic covenant, Paul wrote, "For the promise, that he should be the heir of the world, was not to Abraham, or to his seed, through the law, but through the righteousness of faith" (Rom. 4:13). Announced in Eden, confirmed to Abraham, and proclaimed by Christ: the meek "shall inherit the earth"!

This is not the earth as we know it, but refers to the "new earth wherein dwelleth righteousness" (II Pet. 3:13; Rev. 21:1). Once the Lord baptized the earth with water, cleansing it of defilement (II Pet. 3:6). "But the heavens and the earth, which are now, by the same word are kept in store, reserved unto fire against the day of judgment and perdition of ungodly men" (II Pet. 3:7). When the purifying fire has completed its work, "the meek shall inherit the earth, and delight themselves in an abundance of peace." This is "the world to come" which is to be placed in subjection to man (Heb. 2:5-8).

Man shall not rule alone, but shall "reign with Christ," sitting in His throne with Him (II Tim. 2:12; Rev. 5:10). The extent and nature of this reign is not fully known — the Gospel only introduces us to it. Nevertheless, it is a real reign. In keeping with the nature of the Kingdom, truth is never overstated. When the meek do inherit the cleansed earth, their inheritance shall far transcend the introductory revelations of it that they received in this world!

The Kingdom Prepared for Them

In anciticipation of the fulfillment of His purpose, God has "prepared" an inheritance for a "prepared" people (Luke 1:17). Nothing about His Kingdom is characterized by a lack of preparation. He prepared the world for the Law, and He readied it for the Gospel. He is a God of purpose and preparation, objective and provision. In His Kingdom the end does not justify the means, but rather dictates the means. Men are, in Jesus, being readied for the inheritance — it is not being adapted to them.

In the joining of purpose and foreknowledge, hell has been "prepared for the devil and his angels" (Matt. 25:41). Similarly, there are also "things which God hath prepared for them that love Him" (I Cor. 2:9). Those that desire a "better country," and live in accordance with that desire, are told that "God is not ashamed to be called their God: for He hath prepared for them a city" (Heb. 11:16). In His answer to James and John, who requested the chief seats in the Kingdom, Jesus said, "But to sit on My right hand and on My left is not Mine to give; but it shall be given to them for whom it is prepared" (Mark 10:35-40). Matthew adds that "it is prepared of My Father" (Matt. 20:23).

In His depiction of the judgment of "all nations," Jesus revealed the inheritance to the righteous. "Come, ye blessed of My Father, inherit the Kingdom prepared for you from the foundation of the world" (Matt. 25:34). An eternal stewardship, accompanied by discernment and authority — such is the heritage of the saints! When the saints "take the Kingdom, and possess the Kingdom, even for ever and ever" (Dan. 7:18), it shall not be by usurpation. They will inherit what has been prepared for them — and until they do, the purpose of God has not been fully realized!

Let everyone that names the name of Christ set his eye upon the prize and continue patiently in well-doing. In the time of reaping, the saints shall participate in the glorious triumph of God's Kingdom! Not only will Satan and his hosts be dethroned, the righteous shall be enthroned. They shall occupy that which was prepared for them from the foundation of the world, and for which they have been prepared.

Eternal Life

"Eternal life" embodies the summary of all God has for men. This single term gathers all of God's commitments together, and is "the promise which He hath promised" (I John 2:25). It is the totality of what Jesus came to give (John 17:1-2), being the complete fruitage of His ministry (I John 5:20). This is the abundant life of which He spoke in John 10:10, and the life "which is to come" of which Paul wrote (I Tim. 4:8).

The word "eternal" denotes an order, and is an attribute of the Kingdom. Thus we read of the "eternal God" (Deut. 33:27), His "eternal power" (Rom. 1:20), and an "eternal weight in glory" (II Cor.

4:17). God's purpose is "eternal" (Eph. 3:11), His salvation is "with eternal glory" (II Tim. 2:10), and the redemption which Christ accomplished is "eternal" (Heb. 9:12). Think of the "eternal judgment" (Heb. 6:2), the promise of "eternal inheritance" (Heb. 9:15?, and his "eternal glory" to which men have been called" (I Pet. 5:10). This is the manner of the Kingdom.

"Eternal" speaks positively of direct kinship with the Living God, and negatively of the complete absence of corruption and defilement. Even God's vengeance is "eternal," being irreversible and without flaw (Jude 7).

From the standpoint of duration, life in Christ is "everlasting." The emphasis here is not its possession by the individual — like the "Once saved — always saved" heresy states — but its independent quality. Divine life cannot dissipate or wane, but the individual can cease to participate in it. Thus did Jude write of those that were "twice dead" (Jude 12) — once by nature, and once by apostasy.

The possession of "eternal" or "everlasting" life can only be introductory in this world. The righteous will be ultimately secured at the resurrection — they are in jeopardy until then. Therefore, the godly are exhorted to "lay hold on eternal life" (I Tim. 6:12,19) — not because they do not have it, but because they do not have it in its fullness. What they now have of it is held solely by faith, and faith can wane and fail.

Jesus said, "the righteous shall go into life eternal" following the judgment (Matt. 25:46). It is not that they did not participate in it until that time — they shall enter into its fullness then. His Apostles wrote that those in Christ might "know that" they "have eternal life" (I John 5:13) — now, and in this world! "He that believes on Me," affirmed Jesus, "has everlasting life" (John 6:47). It is had, however, in embryo, and in a firstfruit sense — "the firstfruits of the Spirit" (Rom. 8:23). The world to come will not merely be a continuation of what is received in Christ, but an enlargement and elaboration of it.

Jesus — Who always spoke precisely — said those who denied themselves for His sake and the Gospel's would receive eternal life "in the world to come" (Mark 10:30; Luke 18:30). He related reaping with "eternal life" (John 4:36), and spoke of spiritual sustenance which endured "unto everlasting life" (John 6:27). He spoke of the righteous as those that would "inherit everlasting life" (Matt. 19:29).

"Eternal life" will be given to those "who by patient continuance in well-doing seek for glory, and honor, and immortality" (Rom. 2:7). It is something for which we "hope" (Titus. 1:2; 3:7) — it has not yet been fully realized. Those that sow to the Spirit "shall of the Spirit reap life everlasting" (Gal. 6:8). It is their inheritance, but it cannot be possessed in its fullness while they remain in the body!

All Things

One of the final words spoken by God to the church concerns its inheritance. "He that overcomes shall inherit all things; and I will be His God, and he shall be My son" (Rev. 21:7). They will not be excluded from any aspect of the "world to come." This does not speak of equal distribution, but of joint participation with Christ, who has been "appointed Heir of all things" (Heb. 1:3).

To a church struggling with carnality and an inordinate attraction to men, Paul wrote: "Therefore let no man glory in men. For all things are yours; whether Paul, or Apollos, or Cephas, or the world, or life, or death, or things present, or things to come; ALL ARE YOURS" (I Cor. 3:21-23). The church must lift up its eyes, and refuse to be drawn aside by the tangible and seen. God has determined that all who overcome Satan and the world order will "inherit all things." They shall perceive and derive benefit from the whole eternal order. "All things" will be at their disposal, available for use in their "reign with Christ." Here they have them by faith — "all things are yours" — there they shall have them in their immediate fullness.

Then Shall the Righteous Shine Forth

The righteous are concealed in this world — an apparent association is not made between them and their God. Those that live by faith have been "tortured . . . had trial of cruel mockings and scourgings, yea, moreover of bonds and imprisonments: they were stoned, they were sawn asunder, were tempted, were slain with the sword: they wandered about in sheepskins and goatskins; being destitute, afflicted, tormented . . . they wandered in deserts, and in mountains, and in dens and caves of the earth" (Heb. 11:35-38). The princes of the Kingdom — the Apostles — appeared to be "last" in the order of men — "made a spectacle unto the world, and to angels, and to men." They

422

were "despised," experienced "hunger, and thirst," and nakedness. They were "buffeted," and had "no certain dwelling place." They were "reviled," "persecuted," "defamed," and "made as the filth of the world" and the "offscouring of all things" (I Cor. 4:9-13).

But these were heaven's princes — kings in the making. The world to come is to be placed in subjection to them, and they shall judge both men and angels! Faithfully bearing the truth in an alienated world, the righteous are anticipating "a greater weight of glory" which shall offset the "sufferings of this present time" (Rom. 8:18).

A time is appointed when "the Son of man shall send His angels, and they shall gather out of His Kingdom all things that offend, and them which do iniquity" (Matt. 13:41). Their transfer to the "furnace of fire" (Matt. 13:42) shall occasion the revelation of God's great ones. It is "then" that "the righteous shall shine forth as the sun in the Kingdom of their Father" (Matt. 13:43)!

Be patient, faithful pilgrim! It is not important to be recognized now. The day of universal recognition has been appointed for the godly. Its arrival will reveal the glorious triumph of the Kingdom of God.

Mortality Swallowed Up

Mortality is the result of sin and transgression. It is the decay and deterioration that was set in motion when man lost communion with God. The restoration of man to God through Christ is partial now — it will be thorough in the world to come. In this life, our spirits are joined to the Lord, but our bodies are not. They are the "earthen vessel" which must be brought under subjection (I Cor. 9:27). There are also "fleshly lusts" residing in man — anchored in his soulish nature — which must be denied (I Pet. 2:11). All of these handicaps come under the heading of "mortality."

The resurrection of the dead will bring complete victory to the believer. The evidence of the curse, now carried within his earthly frame, will then be completely eradicated. This coming reality is beautifully stated by the Apostle. "For we that are in this tabernacle do groan, being burdened" not for that we would be unclothed [without a body], but clothed upon [with the resurrection body], that mortality might be swallowed up of life" (II Cor. 5:4). In the words of the Apostle, "And there shall be no more curse" (Rev. 22:3).

God Himself Shall Be with Them

Sin separated God and man (Isa. 59:2). For now, Divine fellowship requires a Mediator, and can only be achieved by believing. But it shall not be so in the ages to come. The presence of the Lord will be immediate, not mediate — face to face, not by faith! The surety of this has been confirmed by "a great voice out of heaven." "Behold, the tabernacle of God is with men, and He will dwell with them, and they shall be His people, and God Himself shall be with them, and be their God" (Rev. 21:3). Apparent, unrestricted, and without interruption — thus shall God be with His people. No more spiritual ignorance or lack of awareness. The total removal of obscurity will mean that we will no longer "see through a glass darkly" (I Cor. 13:12). The "children of God" (Rom. 8:16,21) will have an unquestionable discernment of God and His will. The requirement for faith as we know it will be removed.

Thus will the glorious triumph of God's Kingdom be revealed, when He assumes an immediate association with His people.

And They Shall Reign Forever and Ever

All jeopardy will be removed when the purpose of the ages is achieved. The Tempter will be cast into the lake of fire, together with the proponent of false religion and the usurper of delegated power (Rev. 19:20; 20:10). The source of deception and rebellion shall be banished from the society of the saved. In fact, he will be "bruised" under their feet (Rom. 16:20) — they will have a part in his banishment.

In addition to this, the saints shall be delivered from all corruption — the means by which they were lured into sin. They shall be raised "incorruptible," and incapable of being tempted or drawn away by lust (James 1:14). "Weakness" shall be supplanted by "power," and "dishonor" by "honor" (I Cor. 15:42-43). There will be no defections in glory, no falling, and no rebellion. There will be no means through which this could be accomplished. Those that have "received the love of the truth" shall realize their appointed end — to be "conformed to the image of His Son" (Rom. 8:29). They will be as impervious to falling as Jesus Himself — for the shall be "like Him" (I John 3:1-3).

This condition is the reason for the statement, "and they shall reign for ever and ever" (Rev. 22:5). Adam's rule was interrupted — theirs will continue "world without end." Judas fell from his "office" — they

424

will forever occupy theirs! Demas "forsook" the enterprise of God upon earth — none will forsake it in glory. "And they shall reign for ever and ever." This is the heritage of the saints!

Conclusion

I have labored long to show the nature of the glorious Kingdom into which men are being called. I urge the reader to consider no cost too great to pay for the opportunity of participating in it. Christ has purged your sins, and stands ready to mediate the new covenant in His blood. There is no reason why you cannot be part of God's eternal purpose.

"And the Spirit and the bride say, Come. And let him that hears say, Come. And let him that is athirst come. And whosoever will, let him take of the water of life freely" (Rev. 22:17).

Index of Names and Places

A

Aaron, 145, 221, 296, 364
Abednego, 180
Abel, 32, 114, 156, 196, 234, 374
Abimelech, 140
Abraham, 22, 26, 47, 57, 84, 129,
 145, 156, 189, 190, 193, 233,
 256, 269, 276, 298, 300, 302,
 327, 391, 404, 419
Adam, 20, 83, 157, 161, 189, 190,
 191, 196, 211, 233, 234, 239,
 278, 328, 395, 396, 404, 424
Agag, 197
Agrippa, 129, 358
Ahaz, 411
Amalekites, 197
Amos, 100, 145, 270, 400
Ananias, 156, 157
Andrew, 57
Apollos, 242, 362, 363, 422
Apostles, 104, 105, 116, 128, 135,
 165, 179, 216, 217, 230, 257,
 304, 308, 328, 335, 343, 344,
 347, 364, 397, 402, 421, 422
Azariah, 366

B

Babel, 20, 47, 126, 156, 161
Babylon, 192
Babylonians, 379
baker, chief, 140
Balaam, 76, 161
Bartholomew, 104
Bashan, 297

C

Caiaphas, 320
Cain, 156
Caleb, 298
Cephas, 242, 422
Church, See Topical Index
Cornelius, 157, 305
Corinthians, 30, 44, 84, 131, 356,
 362, 374

D

Demas, 424
Daniel, 15, 16, 18, 30, 140, 142,
 143, 144, 145, 191, 202, 230,
 283, 373, 408, 411
David, 44, 46, 55, 76, 78, 106,
 109, 135, 136, 150, 157, 161,
 197, 198, 239, 252, 270, 278,
 309, 359, 391, 411, 412, 418

E

Eden, 88
Egyptians, 379
Elijah, 23, 202, 215, 417
Eliphaz, 178
Elizabeth, 260
Emmaeus, two, 110
Enoch, 196, 211, 353, 354, 417
Ephesians, 330
Ethiopian Eunuch, 399
Eve, 20, 83, 101, 164, 165, 189,
 190, 233, 234, 239, 269, 391,
 395
Ezekiel, 145, 258, 350, 359

F

Felix, 240

G

Galatians, 21, 156, 167, 333
Gideon, 140
God, See Topical Index
Gomorrah, 21, 156, 167, 333
Gospel, 219, 240, 245
Greece, 192

H

Habakkuk, 297, 401
Haggai, 230
Haman, 374
Hannah, 393
Herod, 20, 142, 411
Hezekiah, 411
Horeb, 324

427

Index of Parables

Index of Topics

431

433

Index of Scriptures

(II Corinthians)

7:10 226
7:11 383,399
8:12 73
9:6 383
9:13 360
10:4-5 345,401
10:5 29,107,179,379,394
10:14 362
11:2 380
11:27 241
13:4 173,321
13:14 146,245

Galatians

1:4 59,108,230,237,
312,381
1:8-9 249
1:15 70
1:26 373
2:5 172,360
2:6 263
2:9 263
2:20 282,308
3:1-13 131
3:2 118
3:5 118
3:6 238
3:8 121,193
3:12 237
3:13 173,283
3:16 257,300
3:18 299,357
3:19 187,243,295,300,357
3:20 299,334
3:22 121
3:24 219,358
3:24-25 186
3:27 28,311
3:28 116,123,179
3:29 300
4:4 131,173,321,416
4:4-5 101
4:6 285,302

(Galatians)

4:8 201
4:22-26 218
5:1 138
5:5 331
5:17 81,150,163,309
5:18 308
5:19-21 165
5:22 146
5:23-24 146
6:1 80
6:7-8 382
6:8 422
6:9 53,56,76,78,367
6:14 280
6:15 329

Ephesians

1:1 19
1:3 72,226,265
1:4 200
1:5 70,188
1:7 52,60
1:8 113,160,205,232
1:9 70,102,159,188,200
1:9-10 187
1:10 70,184,320,380
1:11 16,188
1:11-12 187
1:13 149,240,344
1:13-14 188
1:14 331
1:16 362
1:16-17 228
1:17 369
1:17-19 339
1:18 216,243,292,340,
380,383
1:18-19 398
1:19 19
1:20 325
1:21 252
1:22 335
1:23 336

457

461